Studies in Economic Transition

Series Editors
Jens Hölscher
The Business School
Bournemouth University
Bournemouth, UK

Dragana Radicic
Lincoln International Business School
University of Lincoln
Lincoln, UK

This series brings together theoretical and empirical studies on the transformation of economic systems and their economic development. The transition from planned to market economies is one of the main areas of applied theory because in this field the most dramatic examples of change and economic dynamics can be found. It is aimed to contribute to the understanding of specific major economic changes as well as to advance the theory of economic development. The implications of economic policy will be a major point of focus.

István P. Székely • Péter Halmai
Editors

The Future of European Integration

Challenges and Opportunities

palgrave
macmillan

Editors
István P. Székely
European Commission (retired)
Brussels, Belgium

Acta Oeconomica
Budapest, Hungary

Péter Halmai
University of Technology and Economics
Budapest, Hungary

Department of Economics
National University of Public Service,
Budapest, Hungary

ISSN 2662-6675 ISSN 2662-6683 (electronic)
Studies in Economic Transition
ISBN 978-3-032-20185-0 ISBN 978-3-032-20186-7 (eBook)
https://doi.org/10.1007/978-3-032-20186-7

This Palgrave Macmillan imprint is published by the registered company Springer Nature Switzerland AG.
The registered company address is: Gewerbestrasse 11, 6330 Cham, Switzerland

Praise for *The Future of European Integration*

"How to reconcile the EU's enlargement and reform with its cohesion in a turbulent world? This is a dilemma that eminent European experts look at from different vantage points."

Marek Belka, *former Prime Minister of Poland*

"Once a model of regional integration, Europe has been severely tested by the sovereign debt crisis, Covid, the war in Ukraine, and broader geopolitical turmoil. The authors map out a clear path for future European integration, grounded in rigorous economics and political science and a clear-eyed assessment of past successes and failures."

Benoît Cœuré, *former member of the Executive Board of the European Central Bank, President of the French Competition Authority*

"Deepening European integration is now more urgent than ever, given the fraying of Trans-Atlantic relations. The contributors to this volume lay out a much-needed plan."

Barry Eichengreen, *University of California, Berkeley, US*

Contents

List of Figures

List of Tables

CHAPTER 1

What Future for the EU? The Contours of a New Narrative for European Integration

Introduction to the Volume

István P. Székely and Péter Halmai

The formation of the European Union (EU) brought about transformative changes in Europe. The original narrative of European integration, formulated in the early 1950s, focused on securing peace and prosperity in Europe following the devastation of two world wars (Schuman 1950). We have achieved these goals, but with important caveats on both fronts.

The European growth model, which evolved from post-war integration, was primarily characterised by catch-up growth from the 1950s until the mid-1990s. By absorbing the most advanced global technologies and accumulating both physical and knowledge capital, European economies

I. P. Székely (✉)
European Commission (retired), Brussels, Belgium

Acta Oeconomica, Budapest, Hungary

P. Halmai
University of Technology and Economics, Budapest, Hungary

Department of Economics, National University of Public Service, Budapest, Hungary
e-mail: halmai.peter@gtk.bme.hu

I. P. Székely, P. Halmai (eds.), *The Future of European Integration*, Studies in Economic Transition,
https://doi.org/10.1007/978-3-032-20186-7_1

converged towards the US'income level, achieving productivity dynamics higher than those of the world's most developed economy.

The pace of this convergence slowed during the turbulent 1970s but was reinvigorated during the *Great Moderation* of the 1980s, when dynamic growth coincided with an improvement in macroeconomic balance. However, the dynamism of this model gradually lost momentum through a process of erosion (Fig. 1.1). During the *Great Moderation*, the average potential growth rate of 2–3% per annum fell to 1–1.5% after the

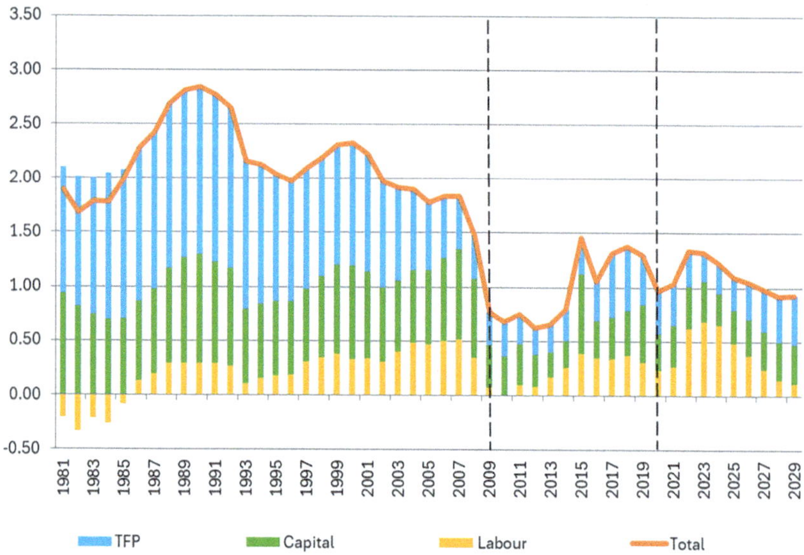

Fig. 1.1 Growth model of the EU14: Development of potential growth and the contribution of its factors (annual percentage). (*Notes*: (1) *EU14*: Member states prior to 2004, excluding the United Kingdom. (2) Growth accounting data are available from 1981 onwards. (3) In the figure, the areas marked in blue and green together indicate the *dynamics of productivity growth*. Between 1981 and 2007, the pace of potential growth was relatively high, but its dynamics declined from the early 2000s onwards. During this period, productivity growth was the decisive factor in growth potential. During and after the major crisis of 2008–2009, the dynamics of productivity growth dropped to a fraction of the levels observed in previous decades. In some years of this period, despite adverse demographic trends, the *contribution of labour* exceeded that of productivity to potential growth. This may illustrate the importance of migration. *Sources:* Authors' own calculations and editing based on data from CIRCA)

Great Crisis. By the middle of the following decade, in the period of *permacrisis*, it declined to below 1%. Except for 1991, the US has consistently recorded a higher annual rate of potential growth than the EU14—and, from the onset of the available data series, also higher than that of the EU27. This persistent growth differential underscores the structural divergence in long-term growth dynamics between the US and the European Union (Fig. 1.2).

Over time, latent structural problems accumulated. The most decisive factor was the *slowdown in total factor productivity (TFP)* growth, and, from the 1990s onwards, the emergence of a negative TFP gap vis-à-vis the US (Halmai and Vásáry 2010a, Fig. 1.3). The underlying causes of this gap were predominantly institutional: the lower intensity of competition within the European economy, and the more advanced development of US capital markets and innovation systems.

The European growth model has run out of steam, and these weaknesses have begun to surface since 2008. The convergence mechanism effectively stalled, particularly in Mediterranean member states hit hardest by the sovereign debt crisis. Consequently, the rise in real incomes

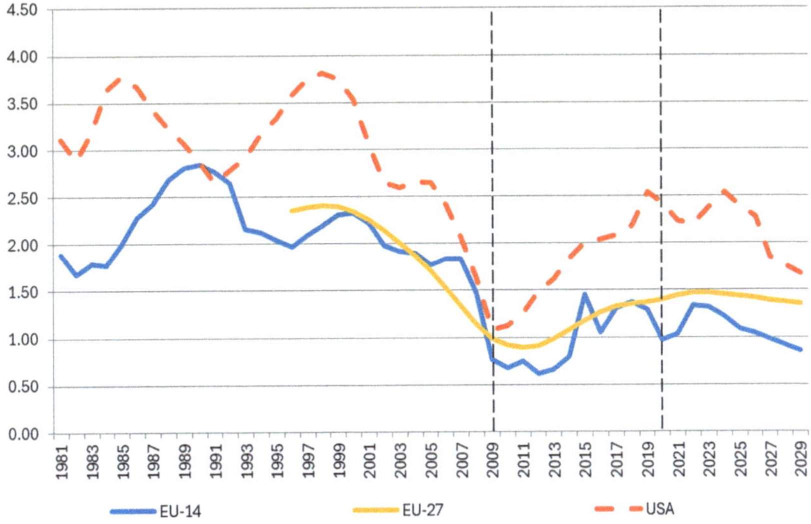

Fig. 1.2 The development of potential growth in the EU14, the EU27, and the US (annual percentage). (*Notes: EU14*: see Fig. 1.1. *EU27*: current EU member states. *Sources:* Authors' own calculations and editing based on data from CIRCA)

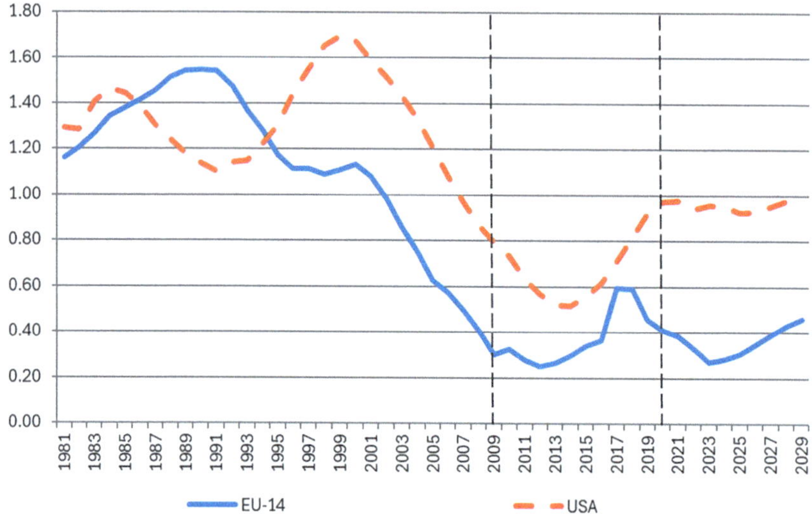

Fig. 1.3 The development of the contribution of Total Factor Productivity (TFP) to potential growth (annual percentage). (*Sources:* Authors' own calculations and editing based on data from CIRCA. *Note: EU14*: see Fig. 1.1)

decelerated, income disparities widened, and the sustainability of the European welfare model became increasingly dependent on substantial public debt accumulation.

Recent developments inside and outside the Union, the permacrisis (the series of crises that started in 2008), and most importantly, the brutal and unjust war Russia waged on Ukraine, brought about new challenges posing potential threats to peace and prosperity in the Union, as well as globally. Moreover, the new US Administration initiated fundamental changes to the global order that evolved following World War II, triggering new geopolitical and geo-economic challenges.

Following the Eastern enlargement, the closing episode of the period of uninterrupted expansion of the EU in prosperous and peaceful Europe, the EU has been hit by a series of large and intensifying shocks: the Great Recession, Brexit, COVID-19, the war in Ukraine that turned Russia into a clear and present military threat for Europe, and the consequent rapid decoupling from Russia. As always, these major shocks created new weaknesses and brought to the surface pre-existing latent structural tensions, further exacerbating the ones that had emerged earlier and remained unaddressed. Despite several efforts in the past, such as the Lisbon Strategy and the Recovery and Resilience Facility (RRF), the EU was losing its technological cutting edge, trailing behind the US and China (Draghi Report 2024).

As a result, the EU became a *shrinking union on a shrinking continent* (Székely 2026), while the two global giants, the US and China, were gearing up for a showdown for world primacy.

However, every major crisis is also an opportunity to escape from previous unfavourable developments and create new dynamics. The US administration's damage to the trust in the US as the guarantor of peace and a reliable ally, the self-inflicted trade war with the rest of the world, and an all-out attack on foreigners residing in the US, including researchers and academics, pose serious threats to the world and to the US itself. However, it also creates a unique opportunity for the EU to become a growing and effective union again on an integrating continent, and thus, regain some of its lost weight in the global economy.

The evolution of European integration has unfolded along two fundamental dimensions: *deepening*, understood as the pursuit of an "ever closer Union," and *widening*, referring to the successive enlargements that have expanded its scope. Yet, given the inherent heterogeneity of member states, the process of integration has also generated a third dimension—*differentiated integration*. This denotes arrangements whereby specific groups of member states are exempt from, or not fully subject to, the common body of Union rules. The benchmark for such differentiation is the prevailing *core integration*. Indeed, the essential content of European integration—embodied in the aspiration for an "ever closer Union"—is reflected in the notion of a *core*, whereas differentiated arrangements represent deviations from this normative ideal. Importantly, not all forms of differentiation carry the same weight in relation to the goal of comprehensive integration. Within the system of integration, core integration - representing at any given time the highest level of the acquis communautaire - serves as the determining benchmark for the various forms of differentiated integration.

From the 1950s until the late 1980s, the European Communities pursued a highly uniform model, despite being institutionally decentralised. Since the 1990s, however, the Union has evolved into a *system of differentiated integration*, characterised by both *vertical* differentiation (variation across policy domains) and *horizontal* differentiation (variation across member states). Notably, progress in deepening and widening has not diminished the salience of differentiation. The euro area, for example, was launched more than 25 years ago with eight founding members; today it encompasses 20, while seven member states with formal "opt-outs" remain outside.[1] Similarly, the internal market and the Schengen zone extend beyond EU membership to include third countries such as the EEA states and Switzerland.

Differentiation has thus become a *permanent—and at times even intensifying—feature of the integration process.* Rather than an anomaly, it should be understood as an enduring structural characteristic of the European Union, shaping both its institutional evolution and its capacity for policy innovation.[2]

Traditionally, the widening (enlargement stricto sensu) and deepening (and institutionally strengthening) of the EU were viewed as two distinct procedures that impacted each other. However, Campos (2026, in this volume) suggests that the interplay between these two processes is so profound that they should be regarded as aspects of the EU's development (enlargement in a broader sense). Mizsei (2026, in this volume) makes a similar point when he emphasises that the EU needs fundamental reforms that deepen core integration in order to be well prepared for the next wave of enlargement. In other words, the Union needs to maintain a proper balance between these two aspects of its development. Without the necessary reforms of the EU, the next wave of enlargement is unlikely to be a success for either group of countries. Instead, without deepening and institutional strengthening, widening is likely to exacerbate the existing problems of the EU and contribute to the wave of euroscepticism in both old and new member states.

In short, the EU needs to pursue a balanced yet effective path of integration. Such a path strikes a balance between deepening and widening, as well as between economic and institutional developments, thereby promoting a fair distribution of the burdens and benefits of economic integration among and within the member states. The creation of "new" European

[1] As of the time of manuscript completion, on 1 January 2026, Bulgaria is scheduled to join the euro area as its 21st member state.

[2] Based on a review of the main policy areas, it can be concluded that the current system of European integration is *not homogeneous*. According to Leuffen et al. (2022a), the system of integration is, in fact, characterised more by strong differentiation across both policies and geographical areas (i.e., countries). Significant variations exist in the patterns *of horizontal and vertical integration and differentiation* across the major policy domains (Leuffen et al. 2022b).

prosperity requires structural reforms at both the Union and member state levels, designed to support productivity growth and coordinated in a mutually reinforcing manner.

The lack of necessary reforms in the newly joining member states is largely responsible for many of the problems that the previous (2004–2013) wave of enlargement brought about. The fundamental problem with the approach applied in the past (based on the fulfilment of the Copenhagen criteria) is that it did not produce lasting institutional improvements in the new member states. Moreover, in some new member states, the institutional structures of a hybrid regime developed precisely during the period of EU membership. Hence, several new member states failed to realise the benefits of EU membership fully and could not ensure a fair distribution of the gains. It not only limited the benefits of EU membership, mainly in terms of social development, but also led to the emergence of populism in the region, with Hungary being the most prominent example.

Despite the transformative changes of recent decades, European integration has not yet delivered fair and sustainable development, primarily because it has failed to foster the creation of better and more effective institutions at both the Union and member state levels. On the one hand, this has harmed the performance and efficiency of the European economy. On the other hand, without adequately strengthened institutions, economic integration and globalisation tend to produce relative—and in some cases even absolute—losers among large segments of the population, even within countries that are otherwise successful overall.

Specific problems of poor macroeconomic management during the 2008–2013 crisis, combined with the low quality of fiscal adjustment in the EU, exacerbated the problems that globalisation had created, leaving public services seriously underinvested in many EU countries. In such an environment, excessively fast immigration combined with poorly designed systems to facilitate the integration of immigrants and a lack of necessary upgrades to public services alienated not only the losers of globalisation but a much broader segment of society.

Hence, Europe could not escape the wave of populism sweeping the world. In Europe, too, it has turned previously fringe parties and politicians into the mainstream and taken over and radicalised previously mainstream parties. These developments test the solidity of Western democracies (Guriev 2026, in this volume). Geopolitical and geo-economic tensions, as well as populism, pose a threat to the unity of the EU and its core policies. The pressure to slow down or even halt the green transition is growing, and not only in the US, where the new administration has made it an official policy.

The evolving trade war waged by the new US administration, combined with growing pressure on Europe to strengthen its military capacity and industry, poses new challenges to macroeconomic management in the EU. With the peace dividend (the savings in defence spending) largely wasted and necessary structural and fiscal reforms repeatedly postponed, fiscal discipline and the Stability and Growth Pact (SGP), the cornerstone of the European Monetary Union (EMU) and the foundation of the euro, are under threat.

EU enlargement is firmly back on the agenda. However, as Mizsei (2026, in this volume) argues, this newly found political stamina for enlargement is not yet coupled with a sufficiently deep understanding of what needs to be done to make this round of enlargement a success. In this area, too, the past neglect of the crucial elements of European integration now haunts the EU. Ironically, the public support for EU membership is the lowest in Serbia, the country which is the most prepared for EU accession. Moreover, Georgia, which was recently granted a candidate country position, is moving rapidly away from respecting European fundamental values.

1.1 The Development of the European Union

Following the devastation of WWII, the Western world quickly realised that a different approach was needed to maintain lasting peace in Europe and avoid repeating the mistakes of the past. Early on, the French Parliament rejected the idea of a European Defence Community to serve this purpose during the ratification process in 1954. Therefore, defence remained firmly a trans-Atlantic matter dealt with in NATO. Soon after the end of the Cold War and the collapse of the Soviet Union in the early 1990s, Europe started to rely increasingly on the US's military umbrella.

Hence, the narrative for European integration hinged on bringing about a quick economic recovery in Europe and integrating Europe economically and (to some extent) politically to increase the cost of breaking up European integration to a level that can hold back politicians.

Peace has been secured in and for the EU. No EU member state has launched a war in Europe or has been attacked by another country since the Union was formed. However, other European countries did launch wars in Europe. The war in Yugoslavia in the last decade of the previous century had a long-lasting impact on the economic development and European integration of the Western Balkans.

The still ongoing war of aggression Russia waged on Ukraine has made it painfully clear that, without further decisive action, the EU cannot secure peace in Europe and that Russia poses a clear and present danger to the EU (and other European countries). Moreover, this war has also revealed that EU member states are ill-prepared for a serious military threat. The security of the EU and Europe continues to depend critically on NATO and, above all, on the US. With the return of the new US administration, Europe is now walking on thin ice in this regard.

EU member states used up the peace dividend, on average, some 1¼% of GDP annually, quickly and fully after the collapse of the Soviet Union, perhaps exceeding what would have been prudent. Russia, on the other hand, restored the level of its military spending after a short and mild decline. Over the past decade, it has spent three times as much as the EU relative to its GDP. Reduced military spending in the EU, combined with the diminishing competitiveness of European arms producers, led to a rapid decline of the military industry in Europe.

With the current US administration, an increasingly assertive China, and the rise of rogue regimes, such as Iran, the pressure is mounting on the EU NATO members to structurally raise military spending and rebuild their military industries. Instead of a peace dividend, the EU will have to invest heavily in restoring its deterrence and defence capacities. It will add to the already existing fiscal pressures, making fiscal policy trade-offs more difficult.

In the early to mid-1950s, European integration primarily involved core Western Europe and Italy, with a focus on cooperation between France and Germany. The UK, the most developed and least devastated economy of the time, chose to stay out of the early wave of European integration. Thus, the Rome Treaty establishing the European Economic Community was signed by six founding member states in 1957.

In the 1960s and 1970s, the member states quickly converged towards the development frontier. During this period, Italy, which had a significantly lower-income level than the rest of the Union in 1957, converged rapidly towards the income level of the other countries. The smooth functioning of the system of European integration presupposes the effective operation of the *convergence machine*. In the presence—or persistence—of lasting divergences, certain regions, and potentially even entire member states, risk falling into a development trap within the framework of the four freedoms (Halmai and Vásáry 2010b). This mechanism operated more or less continuously among the member states up until the financial and economic crisis of 2008–2009. The same holds for the majority of regions within the member states. In other words, from the 1950s until 2008, the system was characterised by strong, albeit temporally varying, *beta- and sigma-convergence.*

The deepening of European integration advanced gradually. The customs union envisioned in the Rome Treaty was completed in 1968 as planned. The European Single Market, perhaps the most monumental achievement of the EU in this regard, was established in 1992, enabling the Union and its member states to fully benefit from the new wave of globalisation. The euro was introduced in 1999, taking forward the implementation of the EMU (Halmai 2020).

The single market for goods and the legal certainty for FDI positioned firms well to create EU-based Global Value Chains (GVCs) and thus remain globally competitive. The timing of the Eastern enlargement was also ideal for EU firms to relocate parts of the GVCs to the new member states, thereby maximising their benefits from globalisation (Piatkowski 2026, in this volume). The EU became a major player in global goods trade and related services, as well as a major innovator in these areas (Székely 2026).

As de Hoyos and Rutkowski (2026, in this volume) argue, Cohesion Policy has played a significant role in supporting convergence across member states, but its effectiveness has been uneven across regions. Empirical evidence shows that funds can boost growth. Yet, their impact is often diluted by weak local administrative capacities and a lack of systematic targeting of regions most at risk of falling into "development traps." Rather than a failure of the policy as such, the challenge lies in ensuring that resources translate into measurable improvements in well-being, especially in lagging regions. This requires simplifying the social policy agenda financed by the European Social Fund+, prioritising interventions most relevant to the poor—such as Guaranteed Minimum Income schemes—while simultaneously strengthening local implementation capacity and promoting innovation and evaluation. In this sense, improving Cohesion Policy is less about replacing it and more about doing fewer things, better, and with a sharper focus on the regions and groups most vulnerable to the pressures of globalisation and economic transformation.

Although more slowly than many had hoped, the EU underwent several waves of enlargement, expanding from its original 6 countries to a union of 28. As Campos (2026, in this volume) points out, each episode of deepening and institutional strengthening preceded one of widening. The aim was to strengthen the EU's internal cohesion through the development of common policies, the strengthening of its governance structures, and the increasing integration of the economies of its member states. Together, these dimensions of EU Enlargement (in the broader sense introduced earlier) have shaped the Union's evolution into a unique supranational entity that tries to balance the challenges of diversity with the pursuit of collective goals. By embracing new members, the EU not only extends its influence but also reinforces its commitment to the values of democracy, rule of law, and regional cooperation.

The geographical enlargement waves brought in highly developed countries, such as the UK, Denmark, Austria, Finland, and Sweden, that were close to the developmental levels of the high-income founding members. Until recently, EU membership has enabled these countries to remain at the forefront of global development and address new challenges.

The enlargement of the EU also admitted countries that were significantly less developed than the high-income members, including Ireland, Greece, Portugal, Spain, the EU11 countries from Central and Eastern Europe, Cyprus, and Malta. The EU's performance regarding the convergence of these countries towards the global frontier of development has been mixed.

Following a prolonged period of non-convergence, Ireland has fully converged to the global frontier and to the income levels of the most developed EU member states. Through an EU-IMF financial assistance programme, the EU has effectively supported Ireland in overcoming its banking crisis and fully restoring its growth potential. Not surprisingly, the country quickly moved on from this episode and maintained strong public support for the European project.

In the EU11 countries, economic convergence has been relatively rapid on average after their accession, although this is not uniform across all countries. However, social convergence has been less impressive, and performance within the group has varied significantly (Chłoń-Domińczak 2026, in this volume). With widespread reform reversals, institutional quality stopped improving or began to deteriorate in some EU11 countries, limiting growth potential and the capacity to convert economic convergence into social convergence, and maintain fair developmental paths

(Landesmann and Székely 2021). In countries where fairness was lacking, populism surged. For many in these countries, the old narrative is no longer appealing.

Following the Eastern Enlargement, the adverse effects of globalisation intensified, particularly in Southern Europe. By now, the EU has resumed including Southern European member states in sizable transfer schemes (RRF) as they failed to converge. Some started to diverge (like Italy and Greece). For some member states, the convergence mechanism temporarily stalled, and in some instances even gave way to divergence. Beyond the Southern member states, the Financial and Economic Crisis (post-2008) also slowed down the convergence processes of several new member states, occasionally resulting in outright divergence. Yet an even more serious concern is the growing divergence among the regions of the EU. Malfunctions in the convergence machine are of cardinal importance for the Union's overall viability.[3] In the absence of institutional quality, political stability, and innovation capacity, persistent divergence may emerge, potentially locking certain regions or even entire member states into development traps. Institutional quality relative to countries with the best institutions has continuously deteriorated in the Southern European member states over the past two decades. The EU failed to sufficiently promote institutional improvements in its member states (Székely 2026).[4] There is now an emerging body of empirical evidence indicating that the impact of EU membership on the economic development of member states significantly depends on how institutional quality evolves within the country concerned (Garoupa and Spruk 2023). Countries that shape up their institutions benefit significantly more than those that do not. The Southern European member states' divergence from the frontier of economic development and the varying performance of the EU11 countries in this respect provide painful examples for this general finding.

Uneven institutional quality among and within countries is not confined to the EU11 and Southern European countries. Hence, the potential benefits of European integration are reaped to varying degrees in many

[3] These phenomena can, in summary, be classified under the notion of a *convergence crisis* (Halmai and Vásáry 2012).

[4] He demonstrates that the EU has failed to improve the functioning of the institutional channel within the EU, as well as the capacity and willingness of member states to enhance their institutions by learning from countries with the best institutions in the world. Many of the EU countries, such as Denmark, Finland, Sweden, and the Netherlands, belong to the latter group.

other member states, most notably in France and Germany. Weak institutions not only hinder economic growth and social development but also fairness. These countries offer painful examples of our finding above: where fairness suffers, populism soars. As populist parties tend to be Eurosceptic or even anti-EU (Guriev 2026, in this volume), the EU's failure to promote institutional improvements eventually threatens the European project.

Following the creation of the European Single Market and the introduction of the euro, the process of deepening integration in Europe has slowed significantly. The lack of a Banking Union (BU), combined with massive cross-border capital flows, facilitated by the single market and global financial liberalisation, and significant macroeconomic imbalances within the EU, led to a double crisis and financial fragmentation in the EU from 2008 to 2013. This crisis lasted much longer and caused much more harm than the Global Financial Crisis did globally. Reforms at the EU level to address the underlying problems came too late, were insufficient, and not always well-designed, and remained incomplete. Despite the beneficial effects of joint banking supervision, banking markets in the EU became more segmented than before, and the European Deposit Insurance Scheme (EDIS) was not fully established.

More importantly, progress in creating a Capital Market Union (CMU) and a single market for (digital) services remained dismal. Unlike in the decade following the creation of the European Single Market, the EU failed to support its firms in becoming major global players in high-value-added (digital) services, where the global frontier was moving rapidly and where most new innovation took place. This development hindered innovation and the growth of new innovative firms in the fastest-growing areas (Draghi Report 2024).

The EU trailed not only the US but also increasingly China, South Korea, Israel, Singapore, and Taiwan. The EU is on the verge of losing its technological cutting edge as innovation remains confined to large incumbent firms locked into slow-developing sectors, such as machinery, traditional cars, and chemistry. While the EU was a leader in green technologies a decade ago, its position has eroded significantly. For example, China has become the technological leader in solar technology. European integration is no longer serving the most developed EU member states as effectively as it once did.

Moreover, the loss of technological cutting edge threatens the European welfare state (Chłoń-Domińczak 2026, in this volume). Without a technological cutting edge, EU companies will lack the necessary pricing power to support prevailing European wages and bear the burden of European levels of taxation.

Fairness has never become a European value. It has remained a national value that was held to varying extents in different EU member states (Székely 2024). The danger is that these new developments will accentuate this characteristic of European integration.

European integration needs a new lease on life and a new narrative that is appealing to the younger generations, who take the achievements as given and are worried about the mounting challenges ahead. European integration needs to serve EU member states well and effectively in different phases of development, as well as different social groups, generations, and regions within its member states. Whether this can be achieved will hinge critically on the capacity of the EU and its member states to learn the lessons from their past developments and address the new challenges they face. This volume aims to identify some of these new challenges, discuss the ways they can be addressed, and contour a new narrative for European integration.

1.2 The Contours of a New Narrative

With the development of the Union stalled and war raging on the Eastern border of the EU, there is an overwhelming need to create a new narrative for European integration and a new approach to institutions and policies that such a narrative should entail.

The EU's updated vision, building on its stated goals and values, should focus on the following three functional elements:

- *Peace through European security.* By relying on its own capabilities and in full alignment with its international alliances, the EU must be able to deter hostile state or non-state actors and ensure effective self-defence. The foundations of this capacity rest on a combination of military strength, comprehensive societal preparedness, instruments suited to the protection of interests, as well as a robust global position and diplomacy. Europe should be the continent of security and prosperity, the cornerstone of lasting peace. By leveraging its economic and commercial strength, as well as its open strategic autonomy, the EU can build and maintain strong relations and partnerships based on common interests with like-minded countries.

- *The values of democracy, human dignity, freedom, equality, fairness, the rule of law, and respect for human rights.* In accordance with *the Treaties (Art. 2* of TEU), the EU should uphold, protect, and enforce these values and its democratic model. It guarantees effective governance through democratic institutions, while enabling the rights and obligations of individuals and enterprises to be fully exercised.
- *The well-being of people, grounded in the "new" European prosperity.* The key drivers of this are the performance of the European economy, intensive economic competition, high levels of innovation and competitiveness, economic resilience, attractive conditions for workers and enterprises, sustainable welfare that respects environmental limits, and inclusive, high-quality, and affordable education, training, and healthcare systems. Europe can be a place of accessible world-class infrastructure, healthcare, and education, as well as flourishing countries, regions, and cities that guarantee the "right to stay" for both present and future generations.

Achieving this vision requires bold transformations. Predictability and stability are core values of the EU, but necessary change is unavoidable. To preserve and reinforce the foundations of the European project, Europe must once again assume a leading role.

How the EU and European integration can serve all member states and the diverse social groups within them should be at the centre of a new narrative. To make this approach operational, we need to recognise that member states are at different levels of development and thus can benefit from the EU in different ways. What is important is to progress with European integration in a way that keeps the right balance between these interests and focuses on helping member states to fully utilise the potential benefits of EU membership.

1.2.1 An EU That Serves All Its Citizens and Businesses Well and Effectively

In Europe, only a fair Union is sustainable, economically, socially, and politically. As we argued earlier, development is a multi-dimensional process. Therefore, fairness is a crucial aspect of development in each dimension (Stiglitz 2012).[5]

The contributions in this volume identify numerous challenges the EU will face in the coming decades. To address these challenges, governments, families, and businesses will often need to undertake significant adjustments, suffer substantial losses, and make substantial new investments. The inevitable burden of adjustment will be high. Efficient companies and governments, along with well-informed and participating families, can mitigate the costs. Others may not be able to do so. Therefore, burdens must be distributed fairly, among and within member states, among generations, social groups, and regions.

Based on a comprehensive assessment and lessons from global experience, de Hoyos and Rutkowski (2026, in this volume) argue that making EU social policy more effective requires prioritising a few critical interventions rather than expanding an already crowded agenda. Their recommendations focus on Cohesion Policy—and particularly the European Social Fund+—as a vehicle for social integration. They highlight the importance of Guaranteed Minimum Income (GMI) schemes, not as a stand-alone policy but as an entry point to connect vulnerable households to broader social services and activation measures. To maximise impact, they stress the need to strengthen implementation capacity at the local government level and to improve the quality of policy design, monitoring, and evaluation.

Their policy advice is also helpful to meet the mounting fiscal challenges the EU faces, offering little extra fiscal room for the numerous competing policy areas. Moreover, they identify the policy areas and levels of government where the quality of institutions and implementation capacity needs to be strengthened. They also point to the need for policy innovation. Making their point more general, strengthening innovation capacity in the Union is equally essential in the public sector. As they are both from the World Bank, they politely avoid promoting their institution. However, we can add that, like the OECD, the World Bank is exceptionally well equipped to help the EU implement such a strategy and promote innovation in the social policy area.

Chłoń-Domińczak (2026, in this volume) analyses the Candidate countries' experience with promoting social fairness and makes a similar point regarding future reforms. It will be essential for the Candidate countries

[5] Székely (2026) calls it a super dimension of development together with sustainability.

to strengthen their policies and implementation capacities in the social area to prepare for EU accession. We will return to this issue below when we discuss the issue of EU enlargement. In a comprehensive sense, what is needed is the elaboration of a new *social contract* that restores trust for the benefit of all European citizens. This should be achieved through renewed welfare policies, with a strong focus on high-quality public services as well as on the regions and populations most affected by inequalities. At the same time, the EU must strengthen its support for social cohesion and community-building through innovative forms of local community engagement and partnership, including participatory territorial development instruments.

1.2.1.1 Sustainability

Traditionally, we think of sustainability as a concept that applies to the environment. However, sustainability applies to all aspects of development, economic, social, and environmental. European integration, as a process, and the EU as an institution, will remain sustainable if it can continue to promote sustainability along all three dimensions.

Economically, the EU will be sustainable if it can serve well and effectively the economic development of all of its members, those that are at, or close to, the global development frontier, those that have embarked, or are about to embark on the transition towards a knowledge-based economy, and those that are in the process of catching up with the high-income countries. The creation of the customs union and then the European Single Market for goods, along with other major achievements regarding the four freedoms, the deepening of the integration acquis was a powerful way to serve all these groups well in the past.

However, as we discussed earlier, the deepening of integration, the progress of core integration, has stalled. Continued delays in completing the single market for services, particularly for digital services, the Banking Union, and the Capital Markets Union, are making it increasingly difficult for the most developed member states to maintain their global positions.

The uneven quality of institutions, both among and within member states, and at the European level, has hindered social development, particularly in terms of fairness, even among the most developed countries. Moreover, it limited the positive economic gains from European integration for the middle group, holding many of them back from completing the perhaps most challenging phase of development, the transition to knowledge-based, highly developed economies. Moreover, it hindered their social development, particularly in terms of fairness. While not yet threatening the sustainability of European integration in this group, these developments pose dangers in this regard. The economic convergence of the third, economically least developed member states—in a differentiated manner from country to country—may continue unchanged. However, ensuring economic and social fairness remains a challenge for these countries, which in turn feeds populist political forces, as demonstrated by the 2025 presidential elections in Romania. As populist parties are inherently Eurosceptic, even in these countries, challenges to European integration may emerge, despite their remarkable economic and overall social convergence. At the same time, the convergence performance of some Central and Eastern European member states is not impressive. In the last decade and a half, there have been signs of the formation of convergence clubs. Regarding environmental sustainability, the central issue is the EU's capacity to promote the green transition of its economies. While the EU and most other developed market economies (DMEs) have made respectable, albeit still inadequate, efforts to meet their own targets on carbon emission reduction, the world as a whole is still far from meeting the generally agreed-upon target of keeping global warming at or below 1.5 °C. Without significant additional efforts in emerging markets and developing economies (EMDEs), the world will not reach its target. The consequences are severe, and EU countries will have to bear a significantly higher share of the costs involved than their current share of CO_2 emissions.

Moreover, the cost of abatement is much lower in EMDEs than in DMEs. Hence, optimal resource allocation at the global level would support a scheme to finance abatement in EMDEs by DMEs. While this is clear theoretically, devising such a scheme and securing the necessary political support for it presents a significant challenge. A strengthened global role for the EU is also needed to rise to this challenge and have the capacity to lead global coordination of efforts and financing.

EU efforts, centred on carbon pricing (ETS) combined with CBAM, will reduce carbon-intensive production and consumption in the EU; however, this will not deter such practices in other parts of the world. It will only reduce the exports of EU companies of carbon-intensive goods and services to non-EU countries. A central issue is that, at the national (or EU) level, the cost of abatement exceeds the SCC (Bolton et al. 2024).

As Borghesi et al. (2026, in this volume) argue, the ETS is an optimal policy tool to ensure allocative efficiency at the European level and for the emission sources it covers. It uses market mechanisms and price signals to allocate private spending on innovation and investment and induce the necessary changes in the structure of production and consumption. It is a mechanism to internalise the externalities of economic activities and impose the social cost on emitters and final users. However, like any other market-based instrument, it is very far from being an optimal instrument to ensure fairness and, thus, political sustainability (policy acceptability).

It is not an argument against relying on market-based policy instruments to achieve a common policy goal at the lowest possible total cost to society. On the contrary, the wider the coverage and the stronger the political commitment to using this instrument stably and predictably, the more it can serve this purpose. However, an unbalanced policy mix which does not entail equally well-designed public policies to ensure a fair distribution of the inevitable total burden will not be economically, socially, and thus, politically sustainable.

Unsustainable policies tend to lead to policy zigzags, diminishing their credibility in the short term, which in turn escalates costs for all but disproportionately affects the most vulnerable groups. The German policy on gas boilers, as mentioned by Borghesi et al. (2026), offers important lessons in this regard.

1.2.1.2 Resilience

Due to the asymmetric nature of European integration, resilience remains a challenging issue for the EU. In the EU, some 80% of idiosyncratic shocks are not smoothed, compared with 50% in the US (Cimadomo et al. 2023). The fact that EU member states are more heterogeneous than US states makes this challenge even more significant (Stempel et al. 2021).

The absence of an adequate central fiscal capacity and the lack of progress with CMU have significant negative implications for resilience and macroeconomic management (Rangvid et al. 2016).

In the absence of collective shock absorption capacity at the European level (risk sharing), individual agents (households and firms) in the EU need to have higher buffers (savings, assets). While the EU as a whole has adequate savings and a comfortable external asset position, this characteristic of the EU is a source of unfairness, as not all member states are in a comfortable position in this regard, and certain types of firms or families are naturally more inhibited in this regard.

A limited degree of resilience leads to excess volatility, which hinders investment and, hence, limits the growth potential of the EU and its member states. It is partly due to this factor that the EU performs worse than the US during major crisis periods, and that major shocks tend to have a stronger and more diverse negative impact on the growth potential of EU member states.

While this factor has been present in the EU since its inception, the current period of repeated major shocks has brought this issue to the forefront. As Fig. 1.4 shows, the 2008–2013 double crisis in Europe slowed the convergence of the EU11 countries for a decade. In the latest period of repeated shocks, starting with the COVID-19 pandemic, the process almost came to a halt, a development not seen since the early 2000s, when the political commitment to EU accession for these countries was made.

As we emphasised before, with institutional weaknesses, slow economic convergence threatens social convergence in these countries. In turn, a combination of slow economic convergence and virtually no social convergence will likely undermine the political sustainability of European

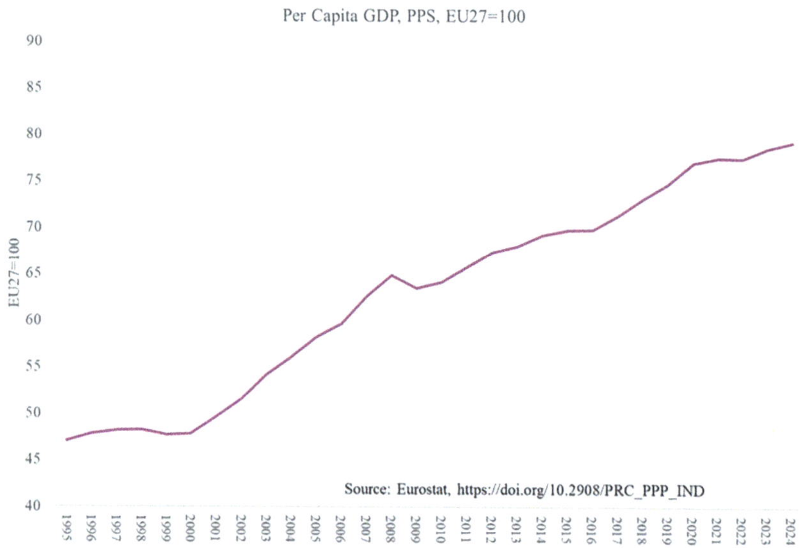

Fig. 1.4 Economic convergence of the EU11 countries, 1995–2024. (Sources: Authors' own calculations and editing based on data from Eurostat (https://doi.org/10.2908/PRC_PPP_IND). Notes: EU11 countries include those Central and Eastern European member states that joined the EU since 2004. The per capita GDP of the EU27 in PPP is 100. Simple arithmetic average of country values)

integration. Similar developments may also take place in other member states. Hence, reforms that can strengthen resilience—above all, the establishment of a Capital Markets Union and some form of central stabilisation capacity—are also important to enhance the sustainability of European integration.

Resilience, however, extends beyond the absorption of crises; it also requires the capacity to withstand systemic shocks and long-term structural trends. Achieving this demands the transformation and advancement of the EU in a sustainable, equitable, and democratic manner. Yet the magnitude, complexity, diversity, and persistence of today's challenges call for a new level of resilience. Beyond a reactive approach, a shift towards proactive and forward-looking strategies is indispensable.

At the same time, strengthening economic competitiveness and strategic autonomy is necessary in parallel. Both priorities are fundamental to resilience. Competitiveness is a central driver of innovation and economic strength, essential for adaptation, leadership, and prosperity in a rapidly changing world. Open strategic autonomy, in turn, can mitigate external shocks and shield the EU from structural dependencies.

Together, these elements define the foundations of a resilient and future-proof European Union.

1.2.2 Balanced Progress with Integration

An unbalanced European integration, combined with the uneven quality of institutions across the Union, which is the current situation, can harm large groups in society across the Union. Thus, it cannot be considered a sustainable system. It is also true for countries that overall converge relatively quickly as part of the EU.

However, this is not, and should not be, an argument against European integration; on the contrary. As several contributions in this volume emphasise, it should prompt us to maintain a balanced approach to European integration, aligning it with progress in improving institutions and reducing existing unevenness in institutional quality, both among and within member states.

Increasing the competitiveness of the EU in the global economy is an essential task. However, it should be combined with reforms and policies that help countries and regions in member states to adjust to a more competitive environment. Deepening European integration *and advancing core integration are* essential to regaining competitiveness. It is perhaps the most important element of a successful strategy at the European level. However, it should equally be matched with improvements in institutional quality, including at the European level.

As many contributions in this volume emphasise, the geographical enlargement of the EU should be back on the political agenda. However, the EU should be reformed to make it fit for this new round of geographical enlargement. Moreover, Candidate countries should make progress in implementing the necessary reforms to make EU accession for them, and for the rest of the EU, a success. Political urgency should not be a cause for leniency in this regard.

1.2.3 *Navigating Europe in the New World Order*

With Brexit and the rapid decoupling from Russia following the brutal and unjustified war Russia waged on Ukraine, the EU got into dangerous dynamics one can describe as "a shrinking Union on a disintegrating continent." It reversed the trend of a fast-growing Union on a fast-integrating continent, which the collapse of the Soviet Union had unleashed. This path endangers the economic and political sustainability of the European project and accelerates Europe's marginalisation in the global economy. Hence, it needs to be reversed urgently.

Brexit and the growing conflict with Russia coincided with a period of geopolitical and geo-economic fragmentation. A new, multipolar geopolitical and geo-economic order is likely to emerge, characterised by the rapid rise of China and the growing potential for conflict between the US and China, among other factors. Therefore, the external challenges the EU faces go well beyond Russia.

The security-related additional burden comes on top of the financing needs for the green and digital transition, as well as restoring the EU's technological cutting edge. According to the latest research, geopolitical instability and conflicts are now viewed by European businesses as the greatest risk they face, more so than in any other part of the world (McKinsey 2025).

The full implementation of the Capital Markets Union is indispensable for the large-scale mobilisation of private capital, in order to channel European savings into strategic investments that enhance economic and climate resilience, competitiveness, and innovation.

The EU is one of the biggest capital exporters in the world. Therefore, it can secure the funds to make the necessary spending, through a combination of reprioritising spending, increasing the efficiency of its spending, and increasing the overall level of spending in the public and private sectors. However, the fiscal space available to EU governments is very uneven. Moreover, the political will and capacity to raise additional revenue, restructure public expenditure, and improve the quality of public finance are also very uneven.

In the three decades since the collapse of the Soviet Union, not only has the peace dividend been fully allocated to other expenditures, but public indebtedness has also increased significantly. The first decade of this period was a golden age for the Union. The creation of the Single Market was one of the Union's most monumental achievements, transforming the EU into a global trade superpower. The creation of the euro is also a challenge to the US dollar.

At the same time, since the mid-1990s, the productivity dynamics of the US have surpassed those of the European Union (see Fig. 1.3). Moreover, Asia has surpassed Europe on the global stage in terms of innovation and the creation of new innovative firms.

1.2.4 *Maintaining Peace in Europe*

Maintaining the EU‘s capacity to defend its citizens and promote peace in Europe (and beyond) will remain fundamentally a transatlantic issue, contingent on EU member states' participation in NATO and the continuation of US military support that characterised the post-WWII era.

The role of the EU in this regard will be primarily to promote the efficient use of public resources in this area and help maintain (or restore) the cutting edge of EU countries in military technologies. Promoting joint procurement of military supplies and equipment is a notable example of how the EU can play this role. Improving the quality of military training is another important dimension. At the same time, in the medium and long term, it is necessary to strengthen Europe's independent defence capacity, given uncertainties surrounding US guarantees.

Building an EU Defence Union (both between the EU and its member states and within EU policies) is an opportunity to implement a coordinated policy that combines competitiveness, security, skills, innovation, and preparedness. The promotion of dual-use technologies and infrastructures requires additional defence investments and research and innovation, particularly by exploiting civil-military synergies along the entire innovation chain, from basic research to capability procurement. Similarly, civilian technologies can also be used to support defence readiness.

1.3 Turning the EU Again into a Growing Union on an Integrating Continent

1.3.1 Reforming the EU's Institutions

The institutional construction of European integration remains unique in the world. Sovereign national states have voluntarily united, based on self-interest and autonomous decisions, and transferred specific, clearly defined elements of sovereignty to a common (supranational) decision-making level. The joint exercise of sovereignty in these domains increases the bargaining power of European states on the global stage. At the same time, compared to global actors, small- and medium-sized member states require guarantees to assert their vital interests and ultimately preserve their sovereignty. The simultaneous enforcement of effective EU-level decisions and member state interests represents a delicate balance that must be periodically renewed as integration both widens and deepens. Taking into account historical legacies and cultural differences, a continuous consensus seemed to be an indispensable condition in the initial period, and it was mostly achieved without major disruptions. However, from the outset, the goal was to establish a system based on majority decision-making. Subsequently, the Luxembourg Compromise prevailed for decades. With far fewer member states than today, and thanks to the integration (and consensus-building) culture that developed among them, the system was able to function within these frameworks for a long time.

Over nearly seven decades, the most profound institutional changes have been enabled by adjustments to the European Treaties. In this way, the system initially designed for six member states has become functional for increasingly broader and deeper integration. However, the most recent major attempt—the adoption of a Constitutional Treaty—failed despite the extensive debates and negotiations that preceded it through the Convention. The Lisbon Treaty was a good and necessary compromise at the time, but new challenges are increasingly pushing its limits.

On the one hand, the number of member states has increased significantly, along with the heterogeneity of their situations and interests. On the other hand, following the major economic and financial crisis, the sovereign debt crisis, and the prolonged European depression, we have entered a period of simultaneous and mutually reinforcing crises—a polycrisis. Geopolitical shocks and the risk of geo-economic fragmentation pose particular challenges. Under these circumstances, it is essential that the EU maintain and improve its capacity to act and that its institutions operate effectively. Simultaneously, further enlargement of the EU is on the agenda. As Mizsei (2026, in this volume) also emphasises, without institutional reform, additional increases in the number of member states would only amplify the outlined problems.[6]

Simplifying decision-making processes at the European level is essential for improving efficiency and agility. An increasing number of member states acknowledge the urgency of institutional reform. In this debate, two fundamental member state approaches can be identified.

In reality, all actors agree that institutional reforms are an inseparable condition for the EU's enlargement and integration ambitions. Addressing existing gaps in competences is a prerequisite for considering the accession of new member states—such as the Balkan countries, Georgia, Moldova, and Ukraine.

Member states advocating for reform argue that re-regulating institutional competences can simultaneously strengthen the EU's mechanisms for protecting democratic values and the rule of law. However, populist governments that define themselves as sovereigntist claim that these mechanisms threaten national sovereignty, excessively expand the powers of the European Parliament and the European Commission, and thereby grant political power to Brussels and Strasbourg. They advocate for simpler EU decision-making, less governed by EU institutions, in which national governments have more leeway and are not "bound by Brussels doctrines." They frequently invoke the principle of subsidiarity while disregarding the foundations of European integration.

The central problem of the decision-making system remains the issues that still require unanimity. Achieving full consensus among the 27 member states, which have vastly different situations, is exceptionally difficult.[7] The requirement of unanimity in the Council of the EU, especially in

[6] This is why it is unsurprising that larger EU member states consider further institutional reform a precondition for enlargement.

[7] The current US administration never misses an opportunity to express its suspicion and contempt for European integration, its institutions, and decision-making system, and seeks to divide the member states whenever possible.

foreign policy matters, clearly weakens the EU's ability to respond quickly to geopolitical changes. In some cases, individual member states use their potential in unanimity-based decisions as a means of blackmail. There are efforts by some populist governments to question the foundations of European integration. The decision-making system must confront the issue of the "destructive EU troll" (DEUT). Within the historically deepening and widening framework of integration, increasingly complex issues have become characteristic, involving a growing number of more heterogeneous participants. Moreover, particularly for some new member states, the original mission of European integration has at times faded. Peace and prosperity came to be seen as natural givens. Free-riding has emerged. In addition, important elements of the acquis extend beyond written law to include European practices - one might say "a European style". A fundamental component of this is the acceptance of the shared value system underpinning European integration, as well as a strategic commitment to an ever-closer union of European nations. At the same time, even amid sharp disputes, this entails understanding among partners and a culture of consensus-seeking. Within this framework, the right of veto, when a vital national interest is at stake, should serve only as an *ultima ratio*. However, today the "club" may include actors who do not adhere to these principles. Member states' behaviours that diverge from the earlier European style, and are destructive in nature, are, to a large extent, unmanageable within the current institutional system of the EU. Over the past decade, a new type of actor has appeared: the destructive EU troll (DEUT), making the continuous threat of veto part of daily routine (embodied by at least one, and sometimes several member states). The blackmail potential of the DEUT endangers the functioning of the EU's decision-making system. Any concession, in turn, risks institutionalising and perpetuating the practice of veto threats. The unanimous decision-making rules of the EU (and NATO), in cases of destructive veto, are reminiscent of the *liberum veto* of the Polish-Lithuanian Commonwealth. (Referring to this historical example: the destructive veto may even serve as an instrument of external subversion. See Wasielewski, 2024. For this, it may suffice to influence and obstruct even a single member state, a "Trojan horse".) Such obstruction by a member state jeopardises the EU's capacity to act, and even its very existence. In cases of a destructive veto, the subject of the decision is not a direct vital interest of the member state concerned, but rather a comprehensive issue affecting the EU as a whole, one of fundamental importance to its effective functioning and/or security. In such instances, this is not a conventional package deal. In reality, it constitutes a form of blackmail, whereby the fulfilment of a specific national demand is set as a condition for adopting a common decision. Such conduct clearly violates the principle of sincere cooperation laid down in Article 4(3) of the TEU., as well as the requirement of solidarity under Article 2.

Some member states' negotiation strategies on unanimity-based issues can currently paralyse EU decision-making. Due to certain national vetoes, there is growing support for reforming the decision-making process to allow most decisions in the Council to be adopted by Qualified Majority Voting (QMV) instead of requiring unanimity. Some member states are effectively using blackmail to obstruct decisions, even in extremely sensitive matters that require a rapid EU response (e.g., sanctions and support due to the Russia-Ukraine war; reactions to China's economic expansion).

Under these circumstances, it seems unlikely that the necessary amendments to the European Treaties—essential to address the growing challenges—can be achieved by consensus. It must be emphasised: this would be the ideal solution.[8] At the same time, under current and foreseeable conditions, the EU should not be held hostage by the lengthy process of treaty amendments. Given the challenges, even a "second-best" option should not be dismissed.

A fundamental question is: what additional options and flexibility do the EU Treaties allow? Special attention must be paid to facilitating decision-making in the Council and the Treaty-based mechanisms that allow certain member states to cooperate more closely in specific areas.

Other high-priority institutional issues include the need to simplify certain EU rules to enhance the EU's competitiveness and the broader concept of EU governance, including reform efforts aimed at improving the methods and functioning of EU institutions.

Parallel to the debate on enlargement, a discussion has emerged regarding the transformation of the European Union. A Franco-German expert group's reform proposal[9]—made public in autumn 2023—aimed at establishing the conditions for better European governance, has several key elements: a simplified institutional system, a smaller European Parliament

[8] In the autumn of 2023, a group of six Members of the European Parliament, led by prominent Belgian federalist Guy Verhofstadt, put forward a provocative proposal for the possible amendment of the EU treaties. The comprehensive draft document outlines proposals that could significantly transform the European Union's functioning.

[9] Report of the franco-german working group on the EU institutional reform, Paris-Berlin, 18 September 2023.

and European Commission, and the abolition of national veto rights. The proposal identifies institutional reform as a prerequisite for EU enlargement. It centres around the concept of a multi-speed EU. In this model, countries willing to cooperate more closely would relinquish their veto rights, while a broader group would continue to function under the current EU rules. A third tier would include candidate countries preparing for accession, potentially with access to the internal market. The outermost circle would consist of countries more loosely associated with the EU.

The proposal's cornerstones:

- *Multi-speed Europe:* If member states cannot agree on the necessary reforms (i.e., cannot amend the Treaties), they could be grouped into four concentric circles based on different statuses. A coalition of willing member states could proceed under a "supplementary reform treaty." The EU would then operate within four concentric circles: the inner core of willing states, the broader current EU, gradually integrating candidate countries, and finally, the European Political Community—a loose association of European leaders.
- *EU Enlargement:* If the proposals are accepted, EU enlargement could become possible by 2030.
- *Conditions for operating a larger EU:* a larger EU budget; stricter linkage of EU payments to the rule of law; majority voting in the Council; and the creation of a new supervisory body to assess the financial integrity of EU institution personnel.

In the category of closely cooperating member states, decisions could be made by qualified majority voting, eliminating the use of vetoes. If a member state persistently uses its veto within these frameworks, it would gradually be excluded from decision-making processes (and likewise not bear the burdens of those decisions).[10] The reform itself cannot be vetoed, as it would be a voluntary agreement among states that wish to cooperate more closely.[11]

[10] In consideration of vital national interests, a form of veto or opt-out (i.e., allowing certain decisions not to apply to specific member states) could be retained on an exceptional basis. would offer a means to gradually and cautiously shift the balance of power and decision-making over the long term.

[11] Through the so-called Passerelle Clause, legislative procedures can be modified without formal treaty amendments.

In reality, today's Europe is already multi-speed. Some member states belong to the Eurozone or the Schengen area, while others do not. What matters for the functionality of the EU is that the door must remain open for all member states—to engage in deeper cooperation (e.g., Eurozone membership)—if they meet the criteria.

The actual situation is well illustrated by the fact that, despite the focused efforts in autumn 2023 for a cardinal EU institutional reform, the proposals stalled in intergovernmental negotiations. Further delays in addressing the most urgent institutional reforms threaten the EU's capacity to act—and ultimately, its very existence.

1.3.2 *The Second Eastern Enlargement*

Besides reducing the growth potential of the EU and hindering public investment, another important adverse effect of the 2008–2013 crisis management was a pause in the enlargement process. The EU became more inward-looking, absorbed by its own problems (BU, EMU design, etc.).

Many view future EU enlargement as a favour to the countries that will be accepted to join the EU. Undoubtedly, EU membership offers significant potential benefits for these countries. However, enlargement is as much in their interest as it is in the interest of the current member states. With strategic autonomy becoming a major goal, relying on candidate countries to host economic activities vital to achieving this goal, but unlikely to relocate to existing members, would be a significant help.

The second wave of Eastern enlargement of the EU is essential to make the EU grow and turn Europe into an integrating continent. It is enshrined in European law and lies at the core of the European project. Nonetheless, it was put on the back burner for far too long, mainly due to political convenience. As Grieveson and Jovanovic (2026, in this volume) and Mizsei (2026, in this volume) explain, an extended delay in the enlargement process had a significant negative impact on the development of the Candidate countries, significantly weakening the anchoring role of the EU in the region, a central role of the EU Campos (2026, in this volume) emphasises.

Potentially, the next wave of EU enlargement could be as transformative as, or perhaps even more transformative than, the first Eastern enlargement of the EU, which began in 2004. It was the collapse of the Soviet bloc, and later that of the USSR, that triggered the Eastern enlargement of the EU. Ironically, it is now the intention to put an end to Russian imperialism, which seems to bring back to the political agenda the next wave of EU enlargement. The Southern enlargement of the EU in the 1980s was equally politically motivated to cement democracy in the south after the collapse of authoritarian regimes.

While political motivation can serve as a powerful engine, it is similar to a car with an overly powerful engine but a poor chassis and brakes. A politically driven enlargement without properly improved institutions and strengthened state capacities is dangerous. As Mizsei (2026, in this volume) argues, it is dangerous to both the incumbent and the newly acceding member states.

There is complete agreement among the authors of this volume that the implementation of the reforms of the EU outlined in the previous section is an essential precondition for a successful enlargement. There is a problematic trade-off between offering the clear prospect of future EU membership, which requires a relatively rapid enlargement process, and the need to ensure that new member states are well-prepared for EU membership. If the process is too fast, the development of new member states may be imbalanced and vulnerable to reversals, as the experience of the EU11 countries demonstrates. On the other hand, if the process is too slow, as argued above, the mobilising power of future EU membership can be dramatically reduced.

An important element of making the political commitment to EU enlargement credible is to provide improved access to the European single market. It has also been a major element of the first Eastern enlargement of the EU. However, in the current situation, the impact of increased trade before enlargement is likely to be more significant than it was before, due to new geopolitical and geo-economic developments (Arjona et al. 2024). If these developments are not accompanied by a sufficiently ambitious reform agenda in the Candidate countries, the negative impacts of European integration may be larger and more pronounced than in the previous enlargement wave.

Candidate countries combined are a larger and more developed (better endowed with production factors) than those regions of China that were integrated into the world economy at the beginning of the recent globalisation wave (the Beijing and Shanghai regions, with a combined population of approximately 40 million). Therefore, there is a similarly significant potential gain for all member states, both old and new, in the next wave of EU enlargement.

However, those regions of China put themselves on a path of rapid human capital accumulation, strengthening of government capacities and gradual improvement of institutions. As they still lack a democratic political system and a free market economy, they cannot serve as a model for European countries. Nonetheless, by now, they are far ahead of the candidate countries in terms of productivity, innovation, and government capacity. This is because institutional reforms in the Candidate countries have slowed, partly due to fading political commitment to EU enlargement.

As Grieveson and Jovanovic (2026, in this volume) point out, in the Western Balkans, it has been the lack of progress in political cooperation (not resolving the numerous constitutional and territorial issues inherited from the past and created by the Yugoslav war) that made the efforts to progress economic cooperation much less effective.

The EU's failure to improve the institutional channel within the EU also manifested itself in the Western Balkans.[12] Following a short period around the Eastern enlargement (2004–2013), when a political commitment to the next wave was perceived as strong, the anchoring role of the EU has dissipated, and reforms slowed (and were reversed). With a lack of institutional improvements, the investment channel worked much less in favour of the receiving countries, bringing in less and lower-quality FDI.

The contributions on enlargement in this volume make it clear that candidate countries will need to undertake major reforms to enable the EU enlargement process to proceed. What we would add is that the reforms they advocate are not only necessary to ensure that EU enlargement does not weaken the EU, but also to increase the benefits of EU membership for new members and ensure that those benefits are lasting and fairly distributed among different social groups.

It is the lack of the latter that is also responsible for the numerous reform reversals observed in countries that joined the EU in the previous wave (Székely and Ward-Warmedinger 2018) and the rise of populist and Eurosceptic parties in several new member states.

As Mizsei (2026, in this volume) warns, the second Eastern enlargement will involve countries with distinctly less established rule-of-law traditions and will require radical reforms from the outset. Hence, the necessary reforms will be more difficult, and backsliding will be more

[12] For a member state, the institutional channel in the EU entails learning from the institutionally most developed member states and fostering the improvement of member state institutions by the EU.

likely and more frequent. The EU needs to find a way to anchor reforms and minimise the risks of reversals.

As Székely (2026) emphasises, the EU should strengthen the functioning of the institutional channel within the Union to promote better institutions and a more even quality of institutions within and among member states. The EU needs to promote fairer economic and social development, meaningful income, and structural convergence in the new member states, and to avoid the catastrophic demographic trends that the free movement of people could create in these states. Increased inward FDI is a powerful force to keep people in their home countries. However, for several reasons, FDI is highly concentrated in less developed parts of the EU. Thus, it does not keep people in underdeveloped regions. Worse, it unleashes powerful agglomeration forces within the new member states, adding to the pressure that cross-border migration puts on these regions.

How to clean up a rotten system, and how to protect the institutions created to clean up the system? External oversight might be a way out, but only if it does not result in a design and approach that are inadequate to the situation. Among other factors, the extent and nature of informality in a society need to be understood and factored in when designing reforms.

Chłoń-Domińczak (2026, in this volume) discusses the challenges that EU accession will pose to the Candidate countries in the area of social policies. Due to their significantly lower income levels and weaker institutions, Candidate countries are less advanced than incumbent EU countries in ensuring social fairness. Joining the EU can undoubtedly accelerate the economic convergence of new member states and promote their social convergence overall, as was the case in the countries that joined the EU during the first Eastern enlargement (Fig. 6.4). However, without adequate strengthening of institutions, a relatively rapid economic convergence and overall social convergence will not alleviate the challenges in this area. On the contrary, unbalanced progress in European integration in this area will likely exacerbate the challenges.

Based on the experiences of the first Eastern Enlargement, unemployment is likely to be significantly reduced as FDI will create new jobs and outward migration will reduce labour supply. However, in the absence of reforms, work-life balance is unlikely to improve in the short run, and gender differences will likely disappear rather slowly, if at all. As Fig. 6.1 in Chłoń-Domińczak (2026, in this volume) illustrates, Candidate countries are particularly prone to a rapid increase in the old-age dependency ratio, putting considerable pressure on their pension and healthcare systems.

Hence, fiscal pressures are likely to mount even more in these countries than in other EU member states. Low unemployment in itself will not help much. What might provide some relief is a significant increase in employment. Hence, polices that create the necessary incentives for and the skills of currently underemployed social groups will also be essential.

Although de Hoyos and Rutkowski (2026, in this volume) primarily propose their policy for incumbent members, it may be most relevant for newly acceding member states, given their limited domestic fiscal resources and weaker capacity compared to incumbent member states. Their point about focusing on the level of government where policies are implemented, which in many cases is at the local government level, is also highly relevant for the Candidate countries. Government capacities are particularly weak at the local government level in these countries, and differences among local governments are even larger than in the countries that joined the EU in the first Eastern Enlargement. Fortunately, these countries have a closer relationship with the World Bank and less political resistance to seeking the Bank's policy advice and technical assistance. As we emphasised above, help is also needed in the area of labour market policies. The EU should advise them to do so and make European funds available as widely as possible for this purpose.

1.3.3 Promoting High-Quality Institutions at All Levels Across the Union

1.3.3.1 Institutional Learning

As we emphasised above, the central role of institutions in promoting (or hindering) development has been getting recognition in the literature, and more recently among policymakers. Analysing the impact of EU membership on development has confirmed this strong relationship and revealed the lack of institutional learning within the EU as a primary factor hindering development and reducing the potentially huge positive effect of joining the EU (Campos 2026, in this volume; Garoupa and Spruk 2023; Landesmann and Székely 2021).

Boschma (2026, in this volume) proposes a line of research on institutional relatedness that could help us understand why institutional learning is so slow within the Union, among countries and regions within and across countries, and what can be done to improve it.

Some member states of the EU, as well as certain regions within the EU, are among the countries and regions with the best institutions in the world. Thus, one of the biggest untapped potentials of the Union is an improvement of what Székely (2026) calls the institutional channel, the promotion of better institutions and institutional learning within the EU. However, Boschma (2026, in this volume) cautions us that there may be natural limits to this learning, as countries and regions should preserve the cohesion of their institutional systems. As we emphasised in many areas, the EU is very heterogeneous, and its future enlargement will make it even more heterogeneous. There are limits to policy learning across countries and regions that have little in common in terms of institutions and policy practices.

As he points out, there is a lack of systematic knowledge regarding what constitutes a good or bad fit of policy mixes, what feasible policy options exist in specific territories given their existing sets of policies, and what the limits to institutional learning across territories are. He expects institutional learning across territories to be more successful when institutional complementarities exist. Therefore, understanding the nature of such complementarities could significantly improve policy design in the EU. With such knowledge, we could abandon the "one-size-fits-all" approach and promote policies that cater to the individual circumstances of member states and regions. A policy change can only become effective when it matches the institutional system and the current policy setting.

The general policy advice of de Hoyos and Rutkowski (2026, in this volume) to do less but better applies to this area. Pursuing the research agenda suggested by Boschma would help us to focus and tailor policies appropriately.

1.3.3.2 Fight Against Corruption

Corruption is one of the biggest enemies of the European project. The control of corruption risk is a vital aspect of institutional quality that significantly determines a member state's capacity to benefit economically from European integration (Garoupa and Spruk 2023). Moreover, it also determines the capacity to turn economic progress into social progress (Székely and Kuenzel 2021).

An important aspect of government efficiency and the quality of public finance is the effectiveness of anti-corruption efforts. Corruption is not a problem exclusive to specific groups of member states; however, its severity varies greatly among member states. Moreover, there are significant differences within member states, across regions and government activities. Corruption is not only a loss of public funds but also a factor that severely deteriorates the business environment. It is particularly harmful to innovative activities and forms, as they are inherently riskier and thus can take less of the additional risks involved in corruption.

As the fiscal pressure will significantly increase in the EU, the size of military spending, an area much more prone to corruption than other spending areas because of less transparency, and the share of innovative firms must increase, the fight against corruption is one of the biggest challenges EU member states face in the coming period. Corruption is a significant factor contributing to inequality in all its forms. It is essential to intensify efforts to combat corruption in all countries and areas. The EU plays a central role in this regard, particularly in promoting the efficiency of the fight against corruption within its member states. As Mizsei (2026, in this volume) emphasises, the fight against corruption is also an essential reform in the Candidate countries.

Toth et al. (2026, in this volume) offer a comprehensive overview of the ways available to member states to increase the efficiency of their fight against corruption, ranging from traditional methods focusing on reducing the financial incentives for corruption to more modern techniques to increase the likelihood of detection raising the moral cost of corruption, and enhancing the moral satisfaction of abstaining from corrupt behaviour. They draw attention to enhancing the perceived likelihood of detection and replacement among economic and political actors. The latter makes the enforcement of core democratic values in the Union essential.

The results presented in this chapter demonstrate a significant decrease in corruption risk in public procurement from 2007 to 2023 in new member states, which is linked to the EU's anti-corruption efforts, particularly those intensified after 2010. Nonetheless, the corruption risk in EU-funded procurements has remained notably higher than in nationally funded procurements consistently throughout the Union. Therefore, the other pressing issue should not divert attention from the fight against corruption, particularly at the European level. In this area, too, there is a need for innovation as traditional efforts have limited impact.

As we emphasise in many areas, an important prerequisite for the political sustainability of European integration is the improvement of the quality of the European institutions. In this respect, too, the fight against corruption in European institutions is central. While the budget of the European Parliament is a tiny fraction of the EU's total budget, the damage caused by the repeated occurrence of high-profile corruption cases and the lacklustre approach to strengthening the rules and their enforcement in this regard should not be underestimated. European institutions should lead by example in this regard,

1.3.3.3 European Institutions

Promoting high-quality, effective institutions and continuously keeping pace with developments in other countries is paramount for the success of this new strategy. The most important role of the EU and European institutions should be to promote this process across the Union and do their best to reduce unevenness in this regard, among and within member states.

An equally important element of a new narrative is to focus on the quality of European institutions and policies. Assigning more functions to the centre without ensuring that it can fulfil those functions well does not help further European integration. On the contrary, it is a sure way to undermine the trust in European integration and prepare a fertile ground for anti-European sentiments. Hence, the focus should be on doing things better and more efficiently at the European level, rather than necessarily doing more. In every area in which the EU plays a significant role, the European institutions involved should undoubtedly be of (and perceived as) the best quality across the Union. It could strengthen the credibility of and the public support for European integration.

As we emphasise throughout, the EU is composed of member states at different levels of development. The lack of central capacities impacts them differently. Thus, it is a source of unfairness. The source of unfairness is more significant in the EU than in the US, primarily because the EU is more heterogeneous and has a smaller federal level. While expanding the EU level is optimal in some areas, the political support for such reforms is dubious in the case of high autonomy costs. However, improving the quality of European institutions and strengthening their implementation capacity is an approach that can gather strong political support throughout the EU.

1.3.3.4 Promoting High-Quality Public Finances

Overall, public debts and government budgets in the EU are among the largest in the world. However, the quality of public finances varies significantly in the EU. Hence, the outcomes in many key policy areas, such as education, health, and social support, fall short of what European citizens expect from their governments. In some countries and certain areas, increasing public spending may be a viable option. However, overall, the only promising avenue moving forward is to focus on the quality of public spending. Hence, the importance of getting more value for taxpayers' money.

As mentioned, fairness and sustainability are central elements of any new narrative for the EU, where these concepts apply to the economic, social, institutional, and environmental dimensions of development. The public sector and government budgets play a central role in ensuring fairness and sustainability. The effectiveness and efficiency of many budget programmes, particularly in education, significantly impact market outcomes. As Schucknecht (2023) demonstrates, ensuring the efficiency of public spending remains a challenge in the EU. The more unequal and unfair the market outcomes, the greater the pressure on governments to intervene. Some of the fairest societies in the EU have relatively low spending on social programmes and rely more on better market outcomes. In short, improving the quality of public spending is essential to making the EU a fairer and more sustainable union, and the only way to cope with the mounting fiscal challenges in the EU. International experience (Schwartz et al. 2020) demonstrates that sustained reforms can lead to significant improvements in this regard. The EU should find ways to strengthen its capacity to promote the proven reforms that can help member states in this regard.

1.3.3.5 Re-Regulation Instead of Deregulation

The Draghi Report (2024) advocates for a comprehensive deregulation to enhance Europe's competitiveness. Landesmann (2026, in this volume) argues that the problem is "not the extent of regulation but the need for a careful screening and the design of a regulatory framework that can combine different targets, such as consumer protection, health and safety, environmental concerns, together with achieving or even contributing to competitiveness."

Improving regulation in Europe is an evergreen idea. The European Commission established its Impact Assessment Board in 2006 (later renamed as Regulatory Scrutiny Board). Following the 2009–2010 Great Recession, the European institutions invented the concept of *smart regulation* as a step forward from *better regulation* (European Council 2011). The fact that this aspect is so much emphasised today indicates that a fundamental rethinking of this area is well warranted.

The EU's regulatory advantage—the early introduction of strict standards—has begun to turn into a disadvantage today. Overly complex EU rules are reducing both the continent's global influence and the competitiveness of its own companies. The European Commission has recognised the problem and has made "better regulation" and simplification a top priority of the current cycle. In 2023, a comprehensive simplification package (Omnibus) was announced. Financial supervisory authorities have begun reviewing overregulation. The dialogue on reducing bureaucracy has also gained new momentum. According to research by CEPS and ECRI, these initiatives can improve business opportunities and the EU's global competitive position only if the governance failures of rule-making (political bargaining, national-level fragmentation, lack of review mechanisms, etc.) are also addressed. The success of simplification requires better governance: a shared vision of the objective, fewer political "free riders" in legislation, more uniform implementation, regular monitoring, and the conscious consideration of competitiveness in the creation of every new rule (Arnal 2025).

Regulation should promote competition and innovation in a way that enhances the well-being of people, rather than stifling competition and thereby hindering innovation. What Europe needs is a comprehensive and well-designed re-regulation, weeding out elements that hurt and strengthening those that help. As the world is changing rapidly, re-regulation should be a systematic part of structural policies, not an ad hoc, politically driven initiative. It should be a fundamental principle in European policy formulation. As Landesmann (2026, in this volume) argues, the EU should also consider its diminishing geo-economic weight and adapt to the new realities of the fading of multilateralism when re-regulating its economy.

1.3.3.6 Periodic Review of Previous Reforms

The basic attitude of continuous adaptation to the changing realities should also extend to institutional reforms in the EU. Every crisis episode triggers a significant wave of institutional and policy reforms. However, not all these reforms turn out to be helpful. Therefore, it is essential that the EU periodically pause to review previous reforms and eliminate those that have not served the interests of European citizens well. The recent reform of the SGP is a good example of taking the courage to reflect and change direction in a major policy area.

The EU's decision-making process does not facilitate rapid institutional adjustment. Moreover, with 27 sovereign states, political cycles in the EU have not been synchronised to the extent that could create the dramatic shift we have seen in the US recently. The stability and predictability this built-in inertia produces may be advantageous, but only if it comes in a healthy dose. Locking in premature and overambitious reforms and regulations is likely to backfire eventually. As Landesmann (2026, in this volume) points out, the world is heading towards a multiplicity of competing and less coordinated regulatory frameworks. In a European way, but we need to adapt to the new geopolitical and geo-economic realities of the world, also to avoid losing our chances to do things in Europe in a European way.

1.3.4 *Maintaining the Cutting Edge of the EU*

The EU has been falling behind in the global technological race in many critical areas (Dietrich et al. 2024; Draghi Report 2024). This trend must be reversed because the consequences of losing its technological cutting edge and competitiveness would be severe for the EU.

Doing so would benefit the group of the most developed member states most directly, as well as some regions in countries transitioning towards a knowledge-based and innovation-driven economy and society.

EU member states are increasingly turning towards industrial policy to boost growth and productivity, while accelerating the green transition within the constraints of limited fiscal space (Hodge et al. 2024). Europe is facing a so-called "size gap" (Letta 2024; Draghi Report 2024). Transforming Europe into a fully integrated single market—while remaining fully compliant with EU competition rules—would create opportunities for market-driven consolidation and scalable growth. For example, a strong and effective digital industrial policy is needed within the framework of EU regulatory and innovation policies. Efforts at both national and EU levels must be coordinated to develop autonomous infrastructures and reduce dependence on large technology companies (Caffarra and Lane 2024). These investments benefit all member states, yet no single country can undertake them alone. In fact, integrating industrial policy at the EU level would generate European public goods: it is essential for breakthrough technological development, efficient resource allocation, avoiding distortions of competition within the single market, and addressing rising geopolitical tensions outside the EU.

The green transition is at the centre of European policymaking, with carbon pricing as its central element. Carbon pricing with CBAM and a weak global policy coordination will inevitably shrink high-carbon (and energy) intensive economic activities in Europe, particularly the exports of such sectors outside the EU.

Such a policy-induced structural change can be an integral part of a successful development policy for the EU, but only if the EU economy has the capacity to quickly expand activities in other, mostly newly emerging, high-value-added sectors. High-value-added activities are typically knowledge-based and innovation-driven. Moreover, the fast-expanding sectors are driven by newly emerging, rapidly growing, and innovative firms.

However, the EU faces major challenges regarding almost all factors that can support such a development path (Draghi Report 2024). It has been losing its technological cutting edge, it has an old firm population with little churning, and it lacks a vibrant growth-capital financial services industry.

Moreover, the inevitable shrinking of old, carbon-intensive sectors will impact member states and regions within member states unequally.

The EU must assume a leading role in shaping the global governance and safeguards of high-impact technologies, particularly innovative and clean technologies. At the same time, it is essential to ensure that there is a choice among the EU's critical technologies.

Harnessing the transformative potential of artificial intelligence is of fundamental importance for the EU and its member states. It is crucial that frontier AI can be developed safely in Europe. Equally important, however, is that the adoption and diffusion of AI align with Europe's values of dignity, fairness, and solidarity. At the same time, systematic preparation is needed for the profound changes induced by AI, for example, in the labour market and in the security environment. The revolutionary power of AI can become a driver of prosperity, inclusiveness, security, defence, and democratic trust. The EU should position itself as a global leader in the development of ethical and safe AI—promoting transparent, accountable, and human-centred artificial intelligence.

The EU must also strengthen its technological sovereignty in key areas. It should assume future-oriented, ethical, and scientifically grounded leadership in adopting a responsible and precautionary approach to controversial emerging technologies, such as superintelligence or human augmentation, advanced ocean exploration, or solar radiation modification. This includes, among others, advancing governance structures based on global cooperation to address potential risks, benefits, and distributional effects. A fundamental requirement is the proactive identification and management of possible trade-offs (e.g., between supply chain efficiency and strategic autonomy, or between new digital technologies and energy consumption), the strengthening of synergies across different policy fields (e.g., industrial policy and security), and the promotion of enhanced international cooperation and standard setting with willing partners.

A fundamental renewal of the education system is also imperative. Lifelong learning must be established as a societal norm. Adaptability and creativity should be fostered, preparing citizens not only for specific jobs but also for multiple career transitions throughout their lives. By linking educational reform to forward-looking labour market and social policies, the EU can transform revolutionary change into an opportunity for greater fairness and intergenerational solidarity.

1.3.4.1 Making European Universities Great Again

Due to Brexit, the number of world-class universities in the EU member states has decreased significantly. Asian countries put strong emphasis on accelerating human capital accumulation and making their universities globally competitive. As a result, many of them are overtaking leading European universities in global rankings. This is inconsistent with the EU's ambition to remain a leading economic power globally. Therefore, this trend needs to be changed. The EU needs to focus on policies that can help make European universities globally competitive. Supporting higher education and addressing structural labour shortages are of fundamental importance for a productivity turnaround and for fostering innovation. Achieving a breakthrough would require innovation-oriented reforms of higher education systems (Adilbish et al. 2024).

1.3.5 Managing Migration and Educating Migrants

Poor management of migration, particularly during the 2015–2016 wave, has fuelled populism in Europe (Guriev 2026, in this volume). Moreover, sizable migration from less developed countries outside Europe, combined with a lack of capacity to help migrants acquire the skills necessary for meaningful employment, significantly reduced the potential economic gains for the receiving countries. As Fig. 1.5 shows, with very few

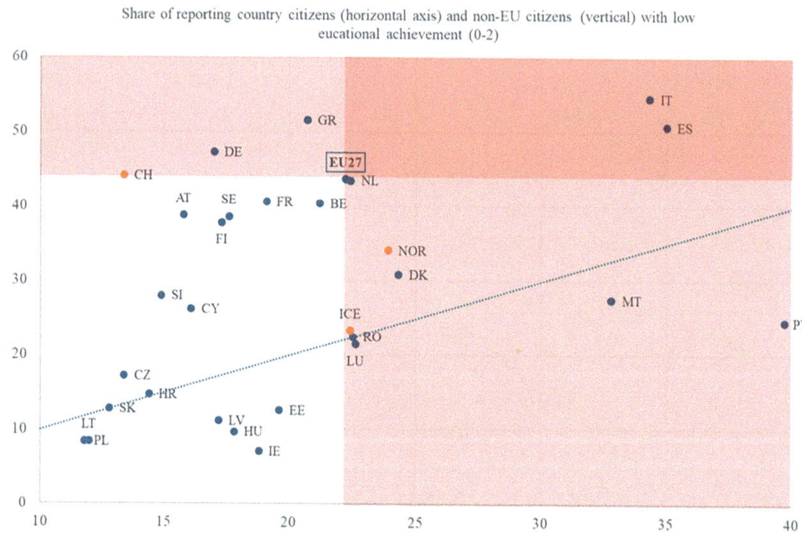

Fig. 1.5 The share of reporting country citizens with low educational achievement (Educational achievement (0–2) and the difference with non-EU27 citizens. (Sources: Székely (2026) based on Eurostat data (https://doi.org/10.2908/EDAT_LFS_9911). Notes: The share of reporting country citizens with low educational achievement (0–2) is shown on the horizontal axis, and the same share for non-EU27 citizens is on the vertical axis. In countries above the dotted line, this share is higher among non-EU citizens than among the reporting country citizens. Countries in the shaded areas are above the EU average)

exceptions, the share of people with low educational achievement among immigrants from outside the EU is significantly higher than among EU citizens, on average, by more than 20 percentage points. This gap tends to be small (or even negative) in countries where the share of non-EU immigrants is tiny.

Accepting migrants with low educational achievement without creating the necessary capacity to help them improve their skills is not only questionable ethically, but it also creates major problems in the future, economically, fiscally, and socially.

Primarily due to a massive inward migration, the EU experienced moderate population growth. Within the EU, the countries that were members before the 2004–2013 Eastern enlargement experienced healthy population growth, while the countries that joined afterwards saw a significant decline (of around 3.5% in a decade). Besides poor demographics, migration to Western European member states is a contributing factor to this trend. The COVID-19 pandemic also affected the latter group more severely.

Looking ahead, there is little potential left for the East-West migration within the EU. If anything, a moderate reversal may happen in Poland. With limited migration from the EU11 countries, the importance of utilising the potential gains from migration from outside the EU is becoming even higher.[13]

As Fig. 1.6 shows, the population trends in the Candidate Countries were disastrous over the past decade, and outward migration played a significant role in this story. Therefore, the second Eastern enlargement will not offer a significant source of inward migration. On the contrary, the EU should support these countries in finding policies that can slow population decline and mitigate the devastating economic, fiscal, and social impacts of their demographic trends.

1.3.6 Core Integration Versus Differentiated Integration

The development of European integration is characterised by deepening, widening, and differentiation. A key component of the system is the integration core (core integration), meaning close and ever-deeper integration. The European Union represents a consolidated system of core integration, supplemented by differentiated integration.

Mutual interdependence and politicisation[14] are the main driving forces of differentiated integration. Growing interdependence generates demand for deeper integration. As long as integration is limited to core state competences and to countries with a strong need for integration, it is likely to

[13] The key structural factors determining growth potential are labour supply, capital accumulation, and the dynamics of *total factor productivity* (TFP). Due to demographic developments and ageing, migration has become an indispensable channel for sustaining Europe's growth potential at the EU level.

[14] Politicisation is an obstacle to integration. The politicisation of European integration refers to the growing polarisation of opinions, interests, or values, and the extent to which these are publicly expressed within the EU's political agenda-setting process (De Wilde 2011). The main indicators of politicisation in the European Union include: questioning European integration itself; the mobilisation of Eurosceptic public opinion by parties sharing similar platforms; and the expression of Eurosceptic views during national referendums, elections, or European Parliament elections.

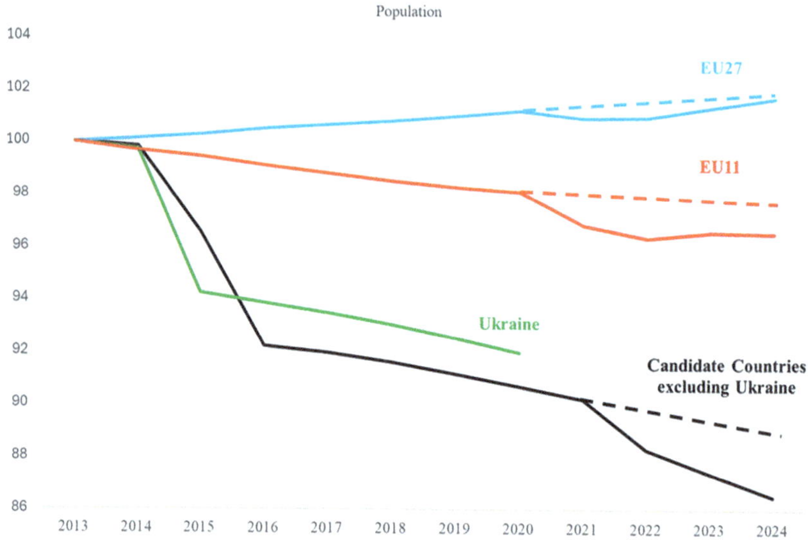

Fig. 1.6 Population trends in EU member states and Candidate countries in the past decade. (Sources: Eurostat (https://doi.org/10.2908/TPS00001). Notes: EU11 countries include the Central and Eastern European countries that joined the EU between 2004 and 2013. Dotted lines show the population trends that prevailed before the COVID-19 pandemic. The level of population in 2013 = 100)

avoid politicisation and remain unified (unitary). This was the general direction of European integration until the late 1980s. Politicisation emerges in parallel with the growing pressure of interdependence. This can exert a powerful impact on key areas of core state competencies and on less integration-friendly countries. Such a situation has been characteristic since 1990. Member states with partly Eurosceptic public opinion may challenge the supranational integration promoted by the core states of European integration. This leads to internal differentiation. Where deeply entrenched Euroscepticism blocks accession, selective integration into the internal market—based on high interdependence in non-politicised areas—becomes the response. This process results in external differentiation (Leuffen et al. 2022b).

Depending on preference convergence and low politicisation, interdependence facilitates integration. Once integration reaches a critical level of centralisation, its path diverges. If politicisation remains low—i.e., in areas of weak autonomy and identity relevance—integration stabilises through supranational constraints on intergovernmental bargaining and supranational implementation capacities. In addition, various spillover processes foster endogenous interdependence and preference convergence, thereby promoting further integration. In contrast, in policy areas or countries particularly sensitive to autonomy and identity concerns, integration heightens sensitivity, generates resistance to (further) integration, and leads to diverging governmental preferences. Under such circumstances, integration either stagnates or further differentiation accompanies deeper integration.

Interdependence generates demand for integration, particularly when governmental preferences are compatible, and politicisation remains weak. The initial integration outcome produces spillover and institutionalising effects, reinforcing interdependence and requiring greater integration at the next stage. Depending on the autonomy and identity costs perceived by governments and citizens as a result of spillover effects, integration paths then diverge. If further integration steps affect autonomy and identity only marginally, preferences remain compatible or converge, and politicisation is weak or even decreasing, further integration is likely to manage spillover and institutionalisation effects. However, if autonomy and identity costs are high, preferences are likely to diverge, politicisation rises, and integration either stagnates at the status quo level or becomes more differentiated.

The basis for differentiation lies in the further increase of exogenous and endogenous interdependence. Experience from recent financial and economic crises, including the sovereign debt crisis, shows that both the pressure of interdependence and the politicisation of integration remain persistent features. These factors may deepen the divide between the euro area and the rest of the European Union. They may also extend to newly integrated policy areas.[15] EU policies continue to create externalities even for outsider states (those unwilling or unable to join). Such externalities generate a permanent demand for external differentiation (Gstöhl 2015).

The combination of vertical and horizontal differentiation has become a fundamental characteristic of the EU and will likely persist in the future. Brexit indicates that integration is under constant threat. With 27 member states at present, and more countries set to join in the future, heterogeneity is likely to increase—alongside pressures for further deepening. In this

[15] For example, in banking regulation. See: Schimmelfennig (2014).

light, differentiation may be one possible way to reconcile the tensions between deepening and widening.

At present, the prospects for European integration remain uncertain. On the one hand, the EU has achieved an unprecedented level of regional integration; yet, some of its policies rest on a fragile intergovernmental consensus. EU crises have exposed shortcomings in effective decision-making, operational capacity, and solidarity, creating functional incentives for deeper integration. At the same time, European public opinion has grown increasingly sensitive towards integration, with heightened reservations.

The COVID-19 pandemic highlighted the unavoidable interdependence among member states and the functional necessity of cooperation. However, citizens are reluctant to pay the price of integration. Solidarity among EU citizens is much weaker than in national contexts. Regional divisions are also reflected in evaluations of differentiated integration, with Southern citizens opposing horizontal differentiated integration far more strongly than those in the north and east. One possible reason is fear of growing discrimination within the EU (cf. Leuffen et al. 2022a).

The trend of growing politicisation in Europe is linked to the strengthening of populist political forces. Populism, along with its strong economic and political nationalism, is deadly poison for European integration. For smaller member states outside core integration, free-riding behaviour and the emergence of the "destructive EU troll" (DEUT) phenomenon may be direct consequences. This can lead to stronger differentiated integration, weaker determination within core integration, and ultimately a weakening of the integration system itself. Within core integration states, the advancement of populism may increasingly lead to paralysis in integration policy. The halt of progress in core integration—deepening—is a mortal danger to European integration. Recent developments, both in the world and within key EU member states, are increasingly pointing to this risk.

Despite generally successful crisis management, systematic reforms have been disappointing for more than a decade and a half. Comprehensive EMU reform stalled and entered a "hibernation state" in 2018. Within it, the banking union remains incomplete due to the absence of EDIS. No breakthrough has occurred in building the capital markets union, despite its crucial importance for EU competitiveness and prosperity. Since the signing of the Lisbon Treaty, the European Treaties have remained essentially unchanged—apart from Croatia's accession and the forced consequences of Brexit. Initiatives for reforming the EU's institutional and decision-making system repeatedly collapse, despite pressing problems. The main factors behind global and competitiveness-related challenges, as well as the key elements of required action, have been identified, but comprehensive reforms have so far failed to materialise. In fact, real debate among member states on them has not even begun. In the emerging debate over the next multiannual budget, narrow lobbying interests dominate, with no comprehensive reform approach in sight.

European integration has reached a crossroads—indeed, a turning point. In addition to long-unanswered internal structural challenges, it now requires comprehensive responses to drastic geopolitical and geoeconomic challenges. What is needed is a comprehensive, mobilising narrative and action programme. Unanimous adoption by all 27 member states is unlikely. Therefore, the most urgent task is for the most committed core integration states (the "willing and able") to develop a comprehensive reform concept and related roadmap, at least for the euro area. Such adoption could provide a clear orientation for core integration. The states involved in differentiated integration could then choose what they can and wish to implement in the shorter term. Within core integration, reforms in the institutional-decision-making system could also begin, aimed at effectively curbing free riding and the DEUT phenomenon. It must be underlined: in the absence of a new, determined integration impulse, the danger may grow—already warned of by President Macron—that Europe could be lost.

Differentiated integration based on member state consensus—while underlining the primacy of core integration—can be a pragmatic, second-best solution.[16] The method of differentiation can be applied in certain policy areas as a transitional construction on the way to more effective and unified decision-making. However, it cannot replace the process of building an ever-closer Union (core integration). It must not lead to first- and second-class EU membership. Its ultimate goal should be to promote inclusion, not exclusion of member states. Other dangers to avoid include political and institutional fragmentation, as well as further complications to the decision-making process.

[16] According to the European Parliament's resolution of 17 January 2019: "any accepted form of differentiated integration can only be a second-best solution, not a strategic priority" (2018/2093(INI)).

The EU is a dynamic (to some extent unstable) state-like entity, with a changing membership base, sometimes partly dysfunctional policies, and constitutional conflicts both among and within member states and EU-level actors. However, in a time of geo-economic fragmentation, EU unity and effective action are of fundamental importance—indeed, unavoidable. The effective renewal of the EU cannot be postponed any longer.

References

Adilbish, O., Cerdeiro, D., Duval, R., Hong, G. H., Mazzone, L., Rotunno, L., Toprak, H., & Vaziri, M. (2024). Europe's Productivity Weakness: Firm-Level Roots and Remedies, IMF Working Paper, 2025/40, Washington DC.

Arnal, J. (2025). EU simplification will fail without better governance: Three necessary reforms to make sure it doesn't fail. Policy Brief, ECRI – CEPS. https://cdn.ceps.eu/2025/09/Simplification-and-governance-policy-brief-formatted.pdf

Arjona, R, Connell, W., & Herghelegiu, C. (2024). Supply Chain Tectonics: Empirics on how the EU is plotting its path through global trade fragmentation, Single Market Economy Papers WP2024/28, Publications Office of the European Union.

Bolton, P., Kleinnijenhuis, A. M., & Zettelmeyer, J. (2024). The economic case for climate finance at scale, Policy Brief 09/2024, Bruegel.

Borghesi, S., Ferrari, A., & Heinrich, L. (2026). Domestic acceptability as a condition for ambitious climate policies. In I. P. Székely & P. Halmai (Eds.), *The Future of European Integration*. Palgrave-Macmillan, *forthcoming*.

Boschma, R. (2026). The role of institutional relatedness to promote regional innovation in the EU. In I. P. Székely & P. Halmai (Eds.), *The Future of European Integration*. Palgrave-Macmillan, *forthcoming*.

Caffarra, C. & Lane, N. (2024). Not a 'side dish': New industrial policy and competition, VoxEU.org, 24 April. https://cepr.org/voxeu/columns/industrial-policy-eu-working-together-get-it-right

Campos, N. (2026). The Economics of EU Enlargements. In I. P. Székely & P. Halmai (Eds.), *The Future of European Integration*. Palgrave-Macmillan, *forthcoming*.

Chłoń-Domińczak, A. (2026). The future of the welfare state in the European Union and the foreseen EU enlargement. In I. P. Székely & P. Halmai (Eds.), *The Future of European Integration*. Palgrave-Macmillan, *forthcoming*.

Cimadomo, J., Giuliodori, M., Lengyel, A., & Mumtaz, H. (2023). Changing Patterns of Risk-Sharing Channels in the United States and the Euro Area. ECB Working Paper Series No 2849. https://doi.org/10.2139/ssrn.4592980

de Hoyos, R. & Rutkowski, M. (2026). Effective Cohesion Policies to Strengthen Social Integration in the EU. In I. P. Székely & P. Halmai (Eds.), *The Future of European Integration*. Palgrave-Macmillan, *forthcoming*.

De Wilde, P. (2011). No Polity for Old Politics? A Framework for Analysing the Politicisation of European Integration. *Journal of European Integration*, *33*(5), 559–575. https://doi.org/10.1080/07036337.2010.546849

Dietrich, A., Dorn, F., Fuest, C., Gros, D., Presidente, G., Mengel, P., & Tirole, J. (2024). Europe's Middle-Technology Trap. *EconPol Forum* 25(4), CESifo, Munich.

Draghi Report (2024). The future of European competitiveness. European Commission, Brussels.

European Council (2011). Conclusions on Smart Regulation, 3094th COMPETITIVENESS (Internal Market, Industry, Research and Space) Council meeting, Brussels, 30 May 2011. https://www.consilium.europa.eu/uedocs/cms_data/docs/pressdata/en/intm/122321.pdf

Garoupa, N., & Spruk, R. (2023). Does European Union Really Matter for Long-Run Growth and Development? In Search of the Missing Counterfactual/ Paper presented at the 2023 Annual Research Conference of the European Commission, Brussels, 13–15 November 2023.

Grieveson, R., & Jovanovic, B. (2026). Growing challenges and ways forward in light of the war in Ukraine and regional tensions in the Western Balkans. In I. P. Székely & P. Halmai (Eds.), *The Future of European Integration*. Palgrave-Macmillan, *forthcoming*.

Gstöhl, S. (2015). The European Union's Different Neighbourhood Models. In: Erik Oddvar Eriksen, E. O. and John Erik Fossum, J. E. (eds) The European Union's Non-Members, Routledge, 2015. https://doi.org/10.4324/9781315751030

Guriev, S. (2026). The recent rise of populism and European integration. In I. P. Székely & P. Halmai (Eds.), *The Future of European Integration*. Palgrave-Macmillan, *forthcoming*.

Halmai, P., & Vásáry, V. (2010a). Growth Crisis in the EU: Challenges and Prospects. *Intereconomics: Review of European Economic Policy*, 45(5), 329–336. https://doi.org/10.1007/s10272-010-0353-4

Halmai, P., & Vásáry, V. (2010b). Real convergence in the new member states of the European Union (Shorter and longer term prospects). *European Journal of Comparative Economics*, 7(1), 229–253.

Halmai, P., & Vásáry, V. (2012). Convergence crisis: economic crisis and convergence in the European Union. *International Economics and Economic Policy*, 9(3), 297–322.

Halmai, P. (2020). *Mélyintegráció. A Gazdasági és Monetáris Unió ökonómiája*. (Deep Integration: The Economics of the Economic and Monetary Union.) Akadémiai Kiadó, BudapestAkadémiai Kiadó, Budapest.

Hodge, A, Piazza, R., Hasanov, F., Li, X., Vaziri, M., Weller, A., & Wong, Y. C. (2024). Industrial Policy in Europe: A Single Market Perspective. IMF Working Paper No. 2024/249.

Landesmann, M. (2026). A new industrial policy for the EU to meet future challenges. In I. P. Székely & P. Halmai (Eds.), *The Future of European Integration*. Palgrave-Macmillan, *forthcoming*.

Landesmann, M., & Székely, I. P. (Eds.). (2021). *Does EU membership facilitate convergence? The experience of the EU's eastern enlargement. Volumes I and II.* Palgrave-Macmillan. https://doi.org/10.1007/978-3-030-57686-8, https://doi.org/10.1007/978-3-030-57702-5.

Letta, E. (2024). Much More Than a Market-Speed, Security, Solidarity: Empowering the Single Market to Deliver a Sustainable Future and Prosperity for all EU Citizens, Jacques Delors Institut, April 2024.

Leuffen, D., Schuessler, J., & Gómez Díaz, J. (2022a). Public support for differentiated integration: individual liberal values and concerns about member state discrimination. *Journal of European Public Policy*, 29(2), 218–237. https://doi.org/10.1080/13501763.2020.1829005

Leuffen, D., Rittberger, B., & Schimmelfennig, F. (2022b). *Integration and Differentiation in the European Union. Theory and Policies.* Palgrave – Macmillan.

McKinsey & Company (2025). M&A Annual Report. Is the wave finally arriving? February 2025. https://www.mckinsey.com/~/media/mckinsey/business%20functions/m%20and%20a/our%20insights/top%20m%20and%20a%20trends%20report/manda-annual-report-2025-final-v11-cs.pdf?shouldIndex=false

Mizsei, K. (2026). EU Enlargement – How to do it to strengthen internal cohesion? In I. P. Székely & P. Halmai (Eds.), *The Future of European Integration*. Palgrave-Macmillan, *forthcoming*.

Piatkowski, M. (2026). The Golden Age of Central and Eastern Europe: How to Keep it Going? In I. P. Székely & P. Halmai (Eds.), *The Future of European Integration*. Palgrave-Macmillan, *forthcoming*.

Franco-German Working Group (2023). Report of the Franco-German Working Group on the EU institutional reform Sailing on High Seas: Reforming and Enlarging the EU for the 21st Century, Paris – Berlin, 18 September 2023. https://institutdelors.eu/content/uploads/2025/04/20230919-Group-of-Twelve-REPORT.pdf

Stempel, D. et al. (2021). Risk Sharing Heterogeneity in the United States, *Economics Bulletin*, 41, 1223–1240.

Rangvid, J., Santa-Clara, P., & Schmeling, M. (2016). Capital Market Integration and Consumption Risk Sharing Over the Long Run. *Journal of International Economics*, 103, 27–43.

Schimmelfennig, F. (2014). European Integration in the Euro Crisis: the Limits of Postfunctionalism. *Journal of European Integration* 36 (3): 321– 337.

Schucknecht, L. (2023). Public Spending and Government Performance in Europe and Asia: Tigers Today and in the Future. In M. Ratto & I.P. Székely (Eds.), *A New Era for Europe. Volume II: Emerging Challenges.* Luxembourg: Publications Office of the European Union.

Schuman, R. (1950). Schuman declaration, 9 May 1950.

Schwartz, G., Fouad, M., Hansen, T. S., & Verdier, G. (Eds.). (2020). Well Spent: How Strong Infrastructure Governance Can End Waste in Public Investment, IMF, Washington. https://doi.org/10.5089/9781513511818.071

Stiglitz, J. (2012). *The price of inequality: How today's divided society endangers our future.* WW Norton & Company

Székely, I. P. (2024). Is social solidarity and fairness a European value? (Európai érték-e a társadalmi szolidaritás és méltányosság?) In I. Benczes, D. Győrffy, & M. Rosta (Eds.), *Ünnepi kötet a 70 éves Csaba László tiszteletére.* Akadémiai Kiadó. https://doi.org/10.1556/9789634549888. Published in Hungarian. An English version is available at https://www.researchgate.net/publication/374740418_Is_social_solidarity_and_fairness_a_European_value

Székely, I. P. (2026). *The Impact of the European Union on the Economic, Social, and Institutional Development of its Member States.* Palgrave-Macmillan, *forthcoming.*

Székely, I. P., & Kuenzel, R. (2021). Convergence of the EU member states in Central-Eastern and South Eastern Europe: a framework for convergence inside a close regional cooperation. In M. Landesmann and I. P. Székely (Eds.), *Does EU membership facilitate convergence? The experience of the EU's eastern enlargement. Volume I: Overall Trends and Country Experiences* (pp. 27–87). Palgrave-Macmillan. https://doi.org/10.1007/978-3-030-57686-8

Székely, I. P., & Ward-Warmedinger, M. (2018). Reform Reversals: Areas, Circumstances and Motivations. *Comparative Economic Studies,* 60(4), 559–582.

Tóth. I. J., Hajdu, M., & Vida, M. (2026). EU Anti-Corruption Policies: Methods, Results and Challenges. In I. P. Székely & P. Halmai (Eds.), *The Future of European Integration.* Palgrave-Macmillan, *forthcoming.*

Wasielewski, P. (2024). The Liberum Veto: A History and a Warning. https://tdhj.org/blog/post/liberum-veto-history/

CHAPTER 2

The Recent Rise of Populism and European Integration

Sergei Guriev

2.1 Introduction

As shown in Guriev and Papaioannou (2022) and Funke et al. (2023), we live in the era of unprecedented rise of populism, around the world and especially in Europe. Populists are not just an increasingly important political force; in many countries, they are coming to power, winning elections and becoming members of ruling coalitions.

This has important implications for the future of European integration. Many populists are Eurosceptics, portraying the European project as the creation of corrupt cosmopolitan elites detached from ordinary people. If Europe is to advance in meeting its key challenges, such as the green and digital transitions, immigration, enlargement, and security, its leaders need

This chapter is based on Algan et al. (2017), Guriev et al. (2021), Guriev and Papaioannou (2022).

S. Guriev (✉)
London Business School, London, UK
e-mail: sguriev@london.edu

I. P. Székely, P. Halmai (eds.), *The Future of European Integration*, Studies in Economic Transition,
https://doi.org/10.1007/978-3-032-20186-7_2

to understand how to tackle the rise of populism and how to regain the trust of voters who have been attracted by populist narratives.

This chapter first documents the recent rise of populism, presents a summary of evidence on its causes and consequences, and, based on this analysis, proposes policies that can reduce the risks to the European project.

2.2 The Recent Rise of Populism

In order to understand whether we live during the unprecedented rise of populism, we need to define what populism is. As noted by Müller (2016), there is a tendency among the liberal elites to label any politicians they do not like as "populists". Fortunately, in recent academic literature, there is an emerging consensus on the definition of populism. Mudde (2004) and Mudde and Rovira Kaltwasser (2017) define populism as an anti-elitist and anti-pluralist "thin-centered" ideology. Populism is a view of the world where the society is divided into two antagonistic and homogenous groups: "corrupt elites" and "pure people". The main goal of populists is to transfer power from the "elites" to the "people".

The homogeneity assumption is exactly what makes populists anti-pluralist. If all pure people are similar to each other, why need checks and balances? Also, if all elites are equally corrupt, how can we entrust power to even some members of the elites (such as central bankers, regulators, or mainstream media) that may enforce checks and balances?

This minimal definition, consisting of anti-elitism and anti-pluralism, is sufficiently broad to cover more than 50 parties in Europe in 2013 (van Kessel 2015) and about 165 parties that have either won at least one seat or 2 per cent of the vote in national parliamentary elections since 1989 overall (Rooduijn et al. 2024). While populism scholars occasionally disagree on labelling individual parties or politicians as populist, these differences usually involve smaller parties and do not change the big picture. As Guriev and Papaioannou (2022) show, whatever classification of European populists we use, the result is the same: there was a substantial growth in the populist vote share in Europe during the first decade of the twenty-first century and an even faster growth in the second decade. Overall, the average vote populist share (weighted by population) in European countries has increased from 10–15 per cent to 25–30 per cent.

In many European electoral systems, such vote shares are sufficient to form a government or at least become a member of the governing coalition. This is exactly what has happened. Funke et al. (2023) have collected data on populists in power in 1900–2020 in 60 large countries (representing 95 per cent of global GDP), including all EU members and all OECD countries. According to these data, the second decade of the twenty-first century was an unprecedented period of populist success. In terms of the proportion of countries with populists in power, each of the years 2010–2020 was above previous historical maximums. In the peak year of 2018, populists were in power in 16 out of the 60 countries in the global sample, including 6 EU members.

2.3 Why the Rise of Populism and Why Now

For an economist, the recent rise of populism represents a puzzle. Economic studies of populism have traditionally focused on Latin American populists in the second half of the twentieth century. These were left-wing politicians who ignored basic economic laws; their policies have always resulted in macroeconomic meltdowns. The lessons have been learned; today, in Latin America or elsewhere, it is hard to find a populist who does not believe in macroeconomic orthodoxy; hyperinflation, price controls and macroeconomic crises are very rare.

Yet, populism is on the rise: the narrative that the corrupt elites neglect the interests of the left-behind ordinary people and, therefore, should be removed from power is increasingly popular. As shown in Guriev and Papaioannou (2022), there are several factors that explain this.

First, there are long-term trends of globalisation and technological progress. Both contribute to global economic growth and the elimination of global poverty. But both create winners and losers, especially in the developed countries. The benefits of technological growth are accrued to high-skilled "knowledge workers" while the jobs of middle-skilled blue-collar workers and routine white-collar workers are automated. Similarly, globalisation benefits high-skilled, knowledge-intensive service producers who sell their services to a larger, now global market. At the same time, the middle-skilled jobs are offshored and outsourced. Low-skilled manual workers are less vulnerable—their salaries are too low to be replaced by robots, and manual jobs are hard to offshore and outsource. The fact that the most vulnerable jobs are situated in the middle of the skill distribution implies that globalisation and technological progress result in higher inequality.

While there is evidence of the importance of either of these two forces—globalisation and technological progress—for creating middle-skilled "left-behind" who are likely to vote for populists, it is hard to distinguish their individual contributions. Indeed, these two trends reinforce each other. Technological progress reduces transportation and communication costs, thus accelerating globalisation. In turn, globalisation accelerates technological progress: access to larger markets strengthens incentives to invest in research and development. (The costs of investment in developing new technologies are fixed, while the returns are proportional to the market size.)

Both globalisation and technological progress are long-term trends. While they may explain the rise of populism in the first decade of the twenty-first century, it is hard to understand why the growth of populism significantly accelerated in the second decade. If anything, during that period, globalisation began to stagnate, and there was no sign of an acceleration in technological change. As shown in Guriev and Papaioannou (2022), Algan et al. (2017) and Guriev et al. (2021), two important explanations of the rise of populism in the second decade of the century were the Global Financial Crisis (and the subsequent austerity) and the rise of mobile broadband internet (and the social media).

The Global Financial Crisis (GFC) was the first major macroeconomic crisis in developed countries since the Great Depression. The populists blamed the GFC on the global elites, who have allegedly shown an inability to regulate financial markets and an unwillingness to protect ordinary citizens who have suffered from the crisis. In many European countries, governments have even gone in the opposite direction, reducing public expenditures, thus aggravating the original impact of the crisis.

The rise of mobile broadband internet and social media also took place in the 2010s, but its impact was of a different nature. Social media did not undermine the economic well-being of the "left-behind", but they provided an ideal platform for propagating the populist message.

Populists have always used the new communication technology (e.g. telegraph and railroad by William Jennings Bryan or radio by Goebbels or Father Coughlin). Indeed, since the populists blame the corrupt elites, they need to circumvent the existing communication channels controlled by the very same elites. So, it is not surprising that today's populists prefer social media to mainstream newspapers and TV channels. Furthermore, social media is not just a new communication technology; they have additional properties that make them even better suited for populist narratives

(Zhuravskaya et al. 2020, Guriev et al. 2021). First, the new social media have almost trivial barriers to entry. Populist politicians do not have to rely on large donors—which is especially important for the authenticity of the anti-elite narrative. Second, social media provide a technology for two-way interaction—which helps to create a perception of populist politicians "listening to the ordinary people". Finally, the advertising-based business model of platform companies maximises attention and thus disproportionally propagates attention-grabbing content—which is more likely to be the one coming from populist politicians rather than from the "boring" mainstream incumbents.

2.4 The Role of Immigration

While the evidence on the contribution of economic and technological factors to the rise of populism is strong, the role of the rise of immigration is not as straightforward. Yes, the recent decades have witnessed a substantial increase in immigration into Europe (as well as other developed countries). While the average share of the foreign-born population around the world remained stable at 3 per cent, in Europe, this share has grown from 6.8 per cent in 1990 to 11.6 per cent in 2020. (The increase in North America was from 9.9 to 16.3 per cent, and in high-income countries, from 7.1 to 13.9 per cent, respectively.)[1] Like globalisation and technological progress, this growth in immigration to developed countries represents a secular trend. Despite all the progress in reducing global poverty, the income gaps between rich and poor countries remain large—thus providing strong incentives to emigrate. If anything, the successes in alleviating global poverty may increase rather than decrease immigration. While *incentives* to move remain very strong, the wealthier residents of poor countries have a higher *capacity* to move to the rich countries. Therefore, as poor countries are likely to continue catching up with middle-income and rich countries, cross-border immigration will grow rather than fall.

Similarly to the economic drivers of populism that can be classified into secular trends (like globalisation and technological progress) and one-off events (the Global Financial Crisis), the effects of immigration are also due to both slowly growing immigration into rich countries and one-off shocks like the Syrian and Iraqi refugee crisis in 2015–2016 when the number of asylum seekers in Europe more than doubled.

[1] Source: UN Population Division.

How do both secular growth in immigration and one-off refugee crises affect populist voting? The evidence shows that the answer to this question depends on the composition of the immigration flows (in terms of immigrants' cultural characteristics and skills), the intensity of these flows and the host countries' success in integrating them. If the flows are relatively limited (e.g. about 1 refugee per 100 native residents), an increase in immigration arrival actually reduces voting for anti-immigrant populists. Native residents do not see them as a threat and instead exercise empathy and willingness to help and cooperate with the refugees. Vice versa, if the natives see the uncontrolled flow of newly arriving refugees and the failure of integration policies, they lose trust in incumbent politicians and prefer to vote for the populists.

2.5 The Dangers of Populism

If the rise of populism is a response to the real failures of mainstream elites, should it be considered a problem? If populists proposed and implemented realistic solutions, the answer to this question would be negative. Unfortunately, as shown in Funke et al. (2023), once in power, populists are likely to underperform. Relative to their non-populist peers, the populist governments deliver significantly slower economic growth (by about 1 percentage point of GDP growth per year). Furthermore, understanding that they cannot fulfil their electoral promises, populists work hard to avoid being voted out of office. In order to do this, they undermine political checks and balances and suppress free media and independent judiciary. Populists in power are bad news not just for economics but also for politics.

The other danger of populism is the normalisation of illiberal and extreme views. As populist vote share increases, their anti-minority statements become more widespread and generally accepted. This leads to the spread of hate speech and even to the rise of hate crime.

2.6 The European Dimension

Most European populists are anti-EU. This is not surprising: the populist narrative is that the European Union represents the detached elites par excellence. European Commission is not elected and is not accountable to citizens. European bureaucrats promote an agenda that is orthogonal or even contradicting the European citizens' interests: green transition—even if it is too costly for European drivers and European farmers; liberal immigration policies—in order to deprive "ordinary Europeans" of their welfare benefits and their voting shares; sanctions against dictators like Putin—even if this results in higher prices; enlargement—at the expense of existing members that will have to pay subsidies to the new members.

The Euroscepticism of the European populists (even those participating in the European parliamentary elections!) represents a real threat to the European project. Europe needs a faster green transition. Europe must reinvest in its security. Europe should stick to its values regarding enlargement and political refugees. European values are the foundation of the European project. This makes the European Union unique; this makes it successful; this is why people from all over the world want to move to Europe rather than to non-free countries. Europe cannot, therefore, close its doors to foreigners escaping persecution and genocide. Europe should welcome countries that share its values and deliver on EU accession conditionalities.

We should also emphasise the about-face of many populists who used to support Putin (for his own anti-liberal and anti-EU views). After 2022, no European politician can speak in Putin's favour. But many of his former friends (all of them are populists!) have reinvented themselves into supporting Putin's agenda while criticising him. Their narrative has become as follows: (1) yes, Putin is a criminal; (2) but let's not introduce sanctions because they do not hurt Putin and they hurt Europe; (3) let's not help Ukraine as this would provoke Putin further thus leading to a World War III.

It is worth noting, however, that many European populists (most importantly in Italy and Poland) have decided to part ways with Putin. This shows that they understand that Putin's aggression is very unpopular among European voters.

2.7 What Is to Be Done?

While the analysis above is bleak, it also suggests potential solutions. Furthermore, the EU has demonstrated that these solutions are feasible and can deliver. For example, in the aftermath of the Global Financial Crisis, many EU countries implemented austerity policies, creating a fertile ground for the rise of populism. This lesson has been learned, and a decade later, European governments have rolled out generous support programmes during the Covid pandemic to avoid leaving more people behind. They have also created unprecedented mechanisms, such as the Next Generation EU, providing struggling countries with resources to address the twin challenges of environmental and digital transitions.

Europe has also managed the large influx of Ukrainian refugees after the 2022 Russian invasion much better than the 2015–2016 Syrian refugee shock. The EU has extended a candidate status to Ukraine, Moldova and George—but also suspended Georgia's candidate status once its government turned away from liberal values. This conditionality shows that the EU has learned the lessons from the accession of countries with unaligned values.

2.8 Unfinished Work

While the European Union has made substantial progress, there is more work to be done. First, given that social media provides unlimited transparency of economic and social problems, it is important to address the issue of inequality. Even if the after-tax inequality has not increased as much as in the US, the perceptions are very negative, so the problem of inequality has to be urgently addressed. Europe is built on the idea of equal opportunity. Redistribution towards the most vulnerable families and providing them with access to health and skills are crucial for Europe's success.

Second, Europe has to face the criticism of its "democratic deficits" both at the European and national levels. The most powerful EU entities—the Commission and the Council—are not elected. The elected one—the European Parliament—plays a very limited role.

The representation gaps are also large at the national level. The French electoral system is such that the 2024 general election delivered Marine Le Pen's party 33 per cent of the votes in the first round and 37 per cent in the second round but only 25 per cent of the seats. The 2024 British election brought the winner, the Labour Party, 34 per cent of the votes and 53 per cent of the seats. The populist Reform Party received 14 per cent of the votes but less than 1 per cent of the seats. The populist voters are, therefore, strongly underrepresented in both countries. This adds credibility to the claims of the populist politicians that their voters are not heard by the mainstream politicians.

The populist claim about the gap between the "elites" and the "ordinary citizens" can be potentially addressed by deliberative democracy. The use of citizens' assemblies and other forms of deliberative democracy has grown dramatically around the world in recent years at the local, national, and even European levels (the Conference on the Future of Europe and the follow-up European Citizens' Panels); see OECD (2020, 2023). Certainly, it is still too early to judge the deliberative democracy's effectiveness. As shown in other papers in this volume, elected politicians often ignore the citizens' assemblies' recommendations, which undermines citizens' trust in deliberative democracy and their incentives to participate in the assemblies. However, they have also been important successes, in particular, Ireland's removal of the constitutional ban on abortions and legalisation of same-sex marriage.

In order to prevent political polarisation, Europe and its member states may also expand the use of ranked-choice voting—the system that promotes the election of the "least-hated" candidates, which is likely to benefit centrist rather than extreme candidates. Some populists would claim that electoral rules raising the likelihood of electing centrist politicians are further increasing the representation gap. But the advocates of ranked-choice voting should be able to respond that this system provides a compromise acceptable to more voters than the current "winner takes all" system in a polarised society (when the elected extreme candidate does not represent neither the centrist voters nor—to a much greater extent—the voters from the other extreme).

Finally, given the importance of social media in the rise of populism in Europe, the EU has correctly chosen to take bold steps in regulating platform companies. Digital Markets Act and Digital Services Act have finally come into effect, and the whole world is watching if their implementation will reduce the spread of misinformation and hate speech online.

2.9 Concluding Remarks

Many European populists focus on the anti-EU sentiment. This is natural: Brussels-based civil servants are unelected—and therefore "unaccountable" rulers of the EU-27 community of some 450 million people. Whenever the European Commission makes mistakes, the populists rejoice in pointing out that the EU is detached and elitist.

The European Union has been uniquely successful in assuring peace and prosperity on the continent. Does this imply that it is easy to defeat the Eurosceptic populists? Certainly not. In the twenty-first century, political narratives are shaped on social media where evidence is "downgraded" and where the anti-elite content goes viral (Gurri 2018). European voters blamed European institutions for the Great Recession (Algan et al. 2017), but the EU elites have learned and done better in 2020–2021. Facing the Covid-19 pandemic, the EU understood that it was a "Hamiltonian moment" and did the opposite of the post-Great-Recession austerity. The EU rolled out the "Next Generation EU" (NGEU) spending plan, which supported growth in the most vulnerable communities. The NGEU helped avoid the crisis-cum-austerity backlash in the Covid-affected areas and thus limited the rise of populism. With its reform- and rule-of-law-conditionality, the NGEU remains the gold standard of the anti-populism policymaking in Europe that combines the commitment to European values and to supporting those left behind. This combination is critical for standing up to the challenge of the rise of populism in Europe.

References

Algan, Yann, Sergei Guriev, Elias Papaioannou, and Evgenia Passari. 2017. "The European Trust Crisis and the Rise of Populism." Brookings Papers on Economic Activity 48 (2): 309–82.

Funke, Manuel, Moritz Schularick, and Christoph Trebesch. 2023. "Populist Leaders and the Economy." American Economic Review, 113 (12): 3249–88.

Guriev, Sergei, Nikita Melnikov, and Ekaterina Zhuravskaya. 2021. "3G Internet and Confidence in Government." Quarterly Journal of Economics 136 (4): 2533–2613.

Guriev, Sergei, and Elias Papaioannou. 2022. "Political Economy of Populism." Journal of Economic Literature 60(3): 753-832.

Gurri, Martin. 2018. The Revolt of the Public and the Crisis of Authority in the New Millennium. San Francisco: Stripe Press.

Mudde, Cas. 2004. "The Populist Zeitgeist." Government and Opposition 39 (4): 541–63.

Mudde, Cas, and Cristóbal Rovira Kaltwasser. 2017. Populism: A Very Short Introduction. New York: Oxford University Press.

Müller, Jan-Werner. 2016. What Is Populism? Philadelphia: University of Pennsylvania Press.

OECD (2020), Innovative Citizen Participation and New Democratic Institutions: Catching the Deliberative Wave, OECD Publishing, Paris, https://doi.org/10.1787/339306da-en.

OECD (2023) Deliberative Democracy Database.

Rooduijn, Matthijs, Andrea Pirro, Daphne Halikiopoulou, Caterina Froio, Stijn Van Kessel Sarah L. De Lange, Cas Mudde and Paul Taggart. 2024. "The PopuList: A Database of Populist, Far-Left, and Far-Right Parties Using

Expert-Informed Qualitative Comparative Classification (EiQCC)." British Journal of Political Science. 54(3):969–978.
van Kessel, Stijn. 2015. Populist Parties in Europe: Agents of Discontent? Hampshire, UK: Palgrave Macmillan.
Zhuravskaya, Ekaterina, Maria Petrova, and Ruben Enikolopov. 2020. "Political Effects of the Internet and Social Media." Annual Review of Economics 12: 415–38.

CHAPTER 3

The Economic Dynamics of European Union Enlargements: A Call to Arms

Nauro F. Campos

3.1 Introduction

The concept of an Enlargement of the European Union (EU) can be understood both in its strict and in its broad senses.

Strictu sensu, EU Enlargement refers specifically to the process by which the EU formally accepts new member states . This process currently involves meeting the Copenhagen criteria, which include stable democratic institutions, a functioning market economy, and the adoption of EU laws and regulations.

In a broader sense, however, the concept encompasses a more wide-ranging perspective. The distinction between the strict and broad senses of EU Enlargement reflects the multifaceted nature of the EU's growth, which goes beyond mere territorial expansion to include profound economic, political, and cultural transformations within both the EU, its member states, and its candidate countries (Campos et al. 2019).

In this light, EU Enlargement has been a central mechanism through which the European integration project has developed, intertwining the

N. F. Campos (✉)
University College London, London, UK
e-mail: n.campos@ucl.ac.uk

I. P. Székely, P. Halmai (eds.), *The Future of European Integration*, Studies in Economic Transition,
https://doi.org/10.1007/978-3-032-20186-7_3

dimensions of widening and deepening. Four key episodes of wider integration are the 1973 Northern Enlargement, the Southern Enlargement in the 1980s, the 1995 Scandinavian Enlargement, and the Eastern Enlargement in the 2000s. Four main episodes of deeper integration are the Treaty of Rome in 1957, the completion of the customs union in 1968, the 1986 launch of the Single Market, and the creation of the single currency in 1999. Widening refers to the inclusion of new member states, which has expanded the EU from its initial six founding members to the current 27. Each episode of deepening preceded one of widening, although it is unclear whether this was by design (in the sense that there was sufficient clarity about the expected economic and political consequences of this sequencing). The Treaty of Rome launched the customs union, but its successful, ahead-of-schedule completion has perhaps less to do with the 1973 Enlargement than the 1970 Budgetary Treaty. The launch of the Single Market had, in all likelihood, much less to do with the Scandinavian Enlargement than the collapse of the socialist bloc. Likewise, it may be rather difficult to see what direct role the creation of the European single currency played in the Eastern Enlargement.

This geographical and institutional growth has been accompanied by deepening, a process that enhances the EU's internal cohesion through the development of common policies, the strengthening of its governance structures, and the increasing integration of member states' economies (Tatham 2009).

Together, these dimensions of EU Enlargement have shaped the Union's evolution into a unique supranational entity that tries to balance the challenges of diversity with the pursuit of collective goals. By embracing new members, the EU not only extends its influence but also reinforces its commitment to the values of democracy, rule of law, and regional cooperation. It needs to be added that, although the focus here is on the interaction between deepening and widening, one should recognize that there are other factors that shaped both processes, including the internal development of the EU (the role of incumbent member states) and global developments (e.g., trade liberalization and capital market liberalization).

EU enlargement presents a unique opportunity for economic analysis, as it involves significant shifts in market dynamics, resource allocation, and regional integration. Here we argue, like "big bills lying on the sidewalk," the process of expanding the European Union offers immense potential for furthering our understanding of growth and development that economists should not overlook. The inclusion of new member states transforms the EU's single market, creating larger economic zones, enhancing trade flows, and fostering cross-border investments. Furthermore, the economic reforms undertaken by candidate countries to align with EU standards generate improvements in governance, infrastructure, and institutional stability, which ultimately benefit the broader Union.

The December 15, 2023 decision by the European Council to open accession negotiations with Ukraine and Moldova highlights the relevance of this process. This milestone reflects the EU's vision to integrate nations with significant economic and geopolitical importance (Alesina et al. 2017). For Ukraine and Moldova, the prospect of accession provides incentives to pursue ambitious reforms, attract foreign direct investment, and deepen economic ties with EU member states. For the EU, integrating these nations offers access to new markets and resources while promoting stability and security in a region of strategic importance. Economists have much to gain from analysing these dynamics, including the costs and benefits of integration, the substantial political economy aspects, the redistribution of economic activities, and the effects on global markets. Understanding the motivations, processes, and outcomes of EU enlargement not only enriches the study of regional integration but also sheds light on the broader economic implications of fostering cooperation and interdependence in an increasingly challenging and complex geopolitical environment.

The objective of this chapter is to briefly re-examine the theoretical, historical, and econometric literatures on European Enlargements. It intends to provide a call to arms for academic economists to be more involved in the next future (expected to be Ukraine-led) EU enlargement.

This essay is organized as follows. The next section discusses the main features of an economist's conceptual framework (stressing the economic theories of integration, clubs, and convergence) and identifies areas that may need further research. The third section focuses on context and implementation: it provides a brief historical overview of the four enlargements so far (i.e., Northern, Southern, Scandinavian, and Eastern) and also distils three main lessons. The next Section 3.4 focuses on the evidence, the attempts so far to estimate the net economic benefits from previous enlargements. It documents the huge heterogeneity at both enlargement and country levels. For example, productivity gains for the Scandinavian enlargement were substantially lower than that for all others and, for an example on cross-country heterogeneity, Latvia benefitted the most from membership while Greece benefitted the least, with the productivity gains enjoyed by the former being at least three times larger than those by the latter. The chapter concludes with suggestions for an ambitious 9-point future policy-oriented research agenda.

3.2 Towards a Conceptual Framework

The objective of this section is to put forward a set of elements that can form a useful conceptual framework to understand the phenomena of EU Enlargements. It builds upon three main bodies of theoretical work: clubs, integration, and convergence. The first refers to the economic theory of clubs originally formulated by Buchanan (1965) which has seen significant developments recently, especially regarding networks. The second is the economic theory of integration which goes from Viner to Tinbergen to Balassa and more recently extends into the discussion about the optimal number and size of nations, as well as about institutional integration. The third is the economic literature on growth convergence that goes from Romer in the 1990s to Kremer more recently. The main point this section tries to make is that there is a sizable body of knowledge from mainstream economics ready and able to inform the upcoming discussion about the next EU Enlargement. This is without even adding the highly relevant recent work on institutions (Acemoglu et al. 2017). The fact that more than half of the names in this paragraph won the Nobel Prize in Economics helps corroborate the view that this framework is ripe to be properly assembled and put into use. In what follows, I discuss each of these three strands in more detail.

The theory of clubs, first conceptualized by James Buchanan in the 1960s, provides a foundational framework for understanding the European Union. Buchanan, who was later awarded the Nobel Prize in Economics in 1986, challenged the then-prevailing binary categorization of goods as either private or public (Marciano 2021). Buchanan introduced the concept of club goods, that is, goods which share characteristics of both private and public goods. Club goods are excludable, meaning access can be restricted to members of the club, but they are also non-rivalrous, implying that one individual's consumption does not diminish availability for others. Typical examples of club goods include private parking structures or cinemas. This offered a novel lens through which economists could analyse collective decision-making and shared resources.

In this context, the European Union can be viewed as a club that provides its members with a series of ever more diverse and sophisticated club goods. These goods include access to a single market, shared regulatory frameworks, and collective security arrangements.

One name that can be cited as having made various important contributions linking the theory of clubs and European integration is Erik Berglof. He has extended Buchanan's insights to analyse the dynamics of EU membership. Berglof and Roland (1997) is a seminal and insightful piece that posited that even the expectation of EU membership itself generates significant economic and institutional benefits. They emphasize the role of accession processes in incentivizing institutional reforms and market deepening in candidate countries. The prospect of membership, rather than membership itself, thus emerges as a powerful driver of economic and political change. It is unclear, to say the least, how much this is true for all Enlargements before 2004.

In another important contribution, Berglof et al. (2008) develop a theoretical model to explore the interplay between deepening and widening within the EU. Deepening refers to the process by which the EU enhances its integration by expanding the range and quality of shared goods and policies. Widening, on the other hand, involves increasing the number of member states. Their model highlights how highly committed member states, such as France and Germany, often advocate for deeper integration, whereas more reluctant members, such as for instance the United Kingdom, may prioritize widening to include additional states. Historical examples, such as Greece's accession to the EU, can underscore these dynamics. Greece's entry, despite well-documented reservations from the European Commission (1976) regarding its readiness, illustrates how political considerations and strategic interests played an important role in influencing the widening process. Although one should note that while earlier enlargements were heavily determined by individual member states, their influence has steadily declined, with the Commission playing an increasingly more determinant and powerful role (Campos 2021).

The second strand of literature rests on the concept of convergence. This concept offers another crucial lens for understanding European integration. Rooted in the Solow growth model, convergence theory examines how economies grow and whether poorer economies catch up with wealthier ones over time. Robert Solow's pioneering growth work, which earned him the Nobel Prize in 1987, introduced the notion of unconditional convergence. This theory posits that economies with similar structural characteristics and access to capital will eventually converge in their income levels.

However, subsequent research challenged the universality of unconditional convergence. Paul Romer's work on endogenous growth, which earned him the Nobel Prize in 2018, emphasized the role of human capital, innovation, and institutions in driving economic growth. Romer argued that convergence is conditional upon the presence of conducive factors such as education, governance, and investment in research and development.

More recently, a third Nobel laureate has made important contributions concerning the issue of convergence. Kremer et al. (2022) further refine our understanding of convergence by providing novel evidence of conditional convergence driven by institutional and policy frameworks.

Within the European context, convergence has been a key objective of integration. By fostering economic cohesion, the EU aims to reduce disparities between member states and promote balanced development. The introduction of structural and cohesion funds reflects this commitment. These funds are designed to support less-developed regions, enhance infrastructure, and improve competitiveness.

Empirical evidence suggests that EU membership has accelerated convergence in many countries, particularly in Central and Eastern Europe. Investments in education, infrastructure and, fundamentally, institutional reforms have contributed to sustained economic growth and improved living standards in these regions (Bruszt and Campos 2019).

Nevertheless, the convergence process has not been uniform across the EU. Persistent disparities in income levels, productivity, and innovation capacity remain significant challenges. Many countries, despite benefitting from EU membership, have struggled to achieve sustained convergence with wealthier member states (Demertzis et al. 2019).

Such persisting disparities highlight the importance of addressing structural weaknesses and ensuring that integration mechanisms are inclusive and equitable.

Integration itself constitutes the third foundational concept underpinning European integration. Theories of economic integration have evolved significantly since the mid-twentieth century, reflecting the changing nature of global trade and economic interdependence. The concept of economic integration, despite sometimes being viewed as unexciting, is far from trivial. This area of study is deeply rooted in substantial academic research, often of the highest calibre, that has helped shape our understanding of international economic relations. Its significance lies not just in its theoretical foundations but also in the real-world impacts of integration processes that have shaped global and regional economic landscapes.

Viner (1950) laid the groundwork for modern integration theories. His insights into customs unions and trade liberalization introduced the concepts of trade creation and trade diversion. The concept of positive and negative integration, introduced by Jan Tinbergen, another recipient of the Nobel Prize in Economics, further enriches our understanding of the EU's development. Tinbergen (1957) argues that positive integration involves the creation of new institutions and policies to support cooperation, such as the establishment of a common external tariff or the harmonization of regulations. Negative integration, by contrast, entails the removal of barriers to trade and investment, such as tariffs and quotas.

Building on Tinbergen's work, subsequent economists have explored the institutional dimensions of integration. Bela Balassa's influential framework (Balassa 1961) outlined six stages of economic integration: free trade areas, customs unions, common markets, economic unions, monetary unions, and complete economic integration. This staged approach has provided a roadmap for the EU's evolution, from the establishment of the European Economic Community in 1957 to the creation of the eurozone and the deepening of political and fiscal cooperation.

In recent decades, the nature of integration has undergone significant changes, reflecting broader shifts in global economic dynamics. Robert Lawrence's distinction between shallow and deep integration highlights this evolution (Lawrence 2000). Shallow integration focuses on reducing barriers to trade in goods, such as tariffs and quotas. Deep integration, however, encompasses a broader range of issues, including labour standards, environmental protections, intellectual property rights, and regulatory harmonization. This deepening of integration reflects the growing complexity of global trade and the increasing importance of non-tariff barriers in shaping economic relations.

Some authors believe that in the twenty-first century, we have now gone beyond deep versus shallow integration, and we can start to witness the emergence of something that can be better described as "Institutional Integration" (Campos et al. 2019). As global trade has shifted from goods to services, intellectual property, and digital platforms, the role of institutions in facilitating and regulating these activities has become increasingly important. The EU's efforts to establish common standards for data protection, financial regulation, and competition policy exemplify this trend.

These initiatives not only enhance the efficiency of the single market but also reinforce the EU's position as a global regulatory leader (Gutierrez and Philippon 2023).

The interplay between deepening and widening has been a recurring theme in the EU's integration history. It might be helpful to clarify how the concepts of strict and broad senses of enlargement introduced at the beginning relate to the concepts of deepening and widening used here: deepening and widening refer to the broader concept, while widening corresponds to the narrower. The deepening of integration, through initiatives such as the Maastricht Treaty and the Lisbon Treaty, has strengthened the EU's institutional framework and expanded the scope of its competencies. At the same time, the widening of membership, particularly following the accession of Central and Eastern European countries in 2004 and 2007, has brought new challenges and opportunities. Balancing these two dimensions remains a central challenge for the EU as it seeks to enhance its global influence while preserving its internal cohesion.

In conclusion, the economics of European integration is a rich field, underpinned by various economics Nobel Prize-winning concepts: the theory of clubs, convergence, and integration. Each of these theoretical frameworks provides valuable insights into the processes and outcomes of European cooperation, from the provision of club goods to the dynamics of economic convergence and the evolution of integration mechanisms. While significant progress has been made, considerable more effort could be directed at more closely and tightly linking these three strands of theoretical work with a focus on helping improve the design and effectiveness of any future EU enlargement.

3.3 Lessons from History

What are the main lessons from history that can help improve our understanding of EU Enlargements? The devastation wrought by World War II left much of Europe in ruins. Images seen in the media today, such as those depicting the conflict in Ukraine or Gaza, bear a striking resemblance to the scenes Europe faced in the aftermath of World War II. In response, the United States, motivated by strategic, economic, and ideological considerations, launched the Marshall Plan, offering unprecedented foreign aid to help European countries rebuild. However, this aid came with the condition that European countries coordinate and integrate their economic activities. This period marked the beginning of the post-war institutional framework, which was designed to prevent further conflict and promote economic recovery and integration.

In 1948, the Organization for European Economic Cooperation (OEEC) was established to manage the distribution of Marshall Plan aid. The OEEC would later evolve into the Organization for Economic Cooperation and Development (OECD), headquartered in Paris. This organization played a pivotal role in the reconstruction of Western Europe and laid the groundwork for future forms of economic integration (Eichengreen 2006). A key feature of this early phase was the recognition that integration was necessary not only for economic recovery but also to prevent the recurrence of war, a concern that had been central to European political thought since World War I.

In the same period, the Eastern Bloc, under the influence of the Soviet Union, established the Council for Mutual Economic Assistance (COMECON) in 1949. This organization was intended to facilitate economic cooperation and integration among the centrally planned socialist countries of Central and Eastern Europe. Although COMECON was an alternative to the OEEC and later the OECD, it was less effective in achieving the same levels of economic cooperation and integration.

By the 1950s, Europe was immersed in a battle of ideas regarding the best model of economic cooperation. On one side were proponents of a customs union, which would establish a common external tariff among members while allowing for the free movement of goods within the union. The customs union concept had strong support in countries like France and Germany. On the other side were those who favored a free trade area (FTA), which would remove barriers to trade between countries but without imposing a common external tariff (and the institutions required for its enforcement). The UK, for example, was a prominent advocate of the FTA model. These debates on the type of integration structure to adopt were critical in shaping the direction of European economic policy.

The Treaty of Rome, signed in 1957, was the result of this debate, establishing the European Economic Community (EEC) and committing its members to the formation of a customs union. At around the exact same time, a competing organization, the European Free Trade Association (EFTA), was founded in 1960 by a group of countries that were not part of the EEC. The EFTA's founding members included the United Kingdom, Portugal, Sweden, Switzerland, Denmark, Austria, and Norway. While the EEC focused on deeper economic integration through a customs union, the EFTA prioritized the removal of tariffs but without the coordination of common external policies.

In the 1960s, the EEC successfully completed the creation of its customs union, marking a significant achievement in the history of European integration. By 1968, the basis for EEC's internal market had been established, allowing for the free movement of goods, services, and capital among its six founding members—France, Germany, Italy, Belgium, the Netherlands, and Luxembourg. Meanwhile, the EFTA struggled to gain the same level of integration and influence.

As the 1970s progressed, the differences between the two organizations became increasingly apparent, and in 1973, the United Kingdom, Denmark, and Ireland decided to leave the EFTA and join the EEC, signaling a clear victory for the customs union model (Aitken 1973).

This shift in membership represented the first significant enlargement of the EEC, which was followed by another round of expansion in 1981 with the inclusion of Greece, and in 1986, Spain and Portugal joined the Union. Alongside these enlargements, the EEC also began to deepen its integration through the creation of the Single Market, a project largely spearheaded by British Prime Minister Margaret Thatcher. The Single Market aimed to eliminate non-tariff barriers to trade and establish a more unified economic space, which was officially implemented in 1992. These deepening processes culminated in the Maastricht Treaty of 1992, which laid the groundwork for the creation of the Economic and Monetary Union (EMU) and the introduction of the euro as a single currency in 1999 (Campos and Macchiarelli 2021).

By the mid-1990s, the European Union had begun to look beyond its core members and towards Northern and Eastern Europe. The Scandinavian enlargement of 1995 saw the accession of Austria, Sweden, and Finland, countries that had previously been outside the EEC. The reasons for this enlargement were intertwined with the geopolitical changes brought about by the end of the Cold War. Austria, for instance, had been neutral during the Cold War and required Soviet consent to join the EEC. The 1990s also saw the introduction of the single European currency, the euro, which further integrated the economies of the EU member states, as well as the Treaty of Amsterdam, which consolidated the legal and institutional framework of the European Community.

The next major enlargement took place in 2004, with the accession of ten new countries, including Poland, the Czech Republic, Slovakia, Hungary, Slovenia, the Baltic States (Estonia, Lithuania and Latvia),

Malta, and Cyprus. This enlargement was a significant milestone, as it marked the first time former communist countries had joined the EU (Campos and Coricelli 2002). It was followed by Bulgaria and Romania in 2007, and Croatia's accession in 2013.

The Eastern Enlargement, the fourth major expansion of the European Union, stood out in at least three fundamental ways. Firstly, it involved a significantly higher number of candidate countries than any of the previous Enlargements. Even when accounting for earlier candidates such as Norway, which pursued membership for 1973 and 1995, and Switzerland for 1995, the scale of this Enlargement has been unmatched. Despite the large number of applicants, there was a strong consensus that the benefits of the Eastern Enlargement would far outweigh its costs, with advantages expected to be shared between both Eastern and Western Europe (Baldwin et al. 1997).

Secondly, the 2004 Enlargement was distinct due to the extensive range of policy areas that the transitioning economies were required to address during negotiations. Unlike earlier rounds of enlargement, which involved relatively narrower frameworks, this wave required conformity to a much more comprehensive and detailed set of rules. For instance, the 1973 Enlargement followed the formation of the Customs Union, while the 1995 Enlargement occurred after the establishment of the Single Market. However, by the time the transition economies began their accession process, the acquis communautaire had grown to encompass approximately 30 chapters, each focusing on a specific policy area. These were in addition to the customs union, the Single Market, and the euro framework. This made the negotiation process substantially more intricate and demanding compared to previous rounds.

The third and final distinctive feature of the Eastern Enlargement was the heightened level of formalization and direct management by European institutions. This shift was largely a consequence of the higher number of candidate countries involved. The accession process became more systematically structured and explicitly overseen by European institutions, as highlighted in the European Council's 1994 report (p. 12). In this more formalized framework, the role of individual member states was notably reduced compared to earlier Enlargements, signifying a move towards a more institutionally driven approach to EU expansion.

The 2004 EU enlargement profoundly impacted the new member states and the Union itself. For the new members, accession drove institutional improvements, greater labour mobility, increased trade, integration into global value chains, and advancements in technological development. Negotiations for EU membership not only anchored but also refined institutional reforms (Campos 2021), while financial integration facilitated flows of capital and people, enhancing economic dynamism. On the other hand, the EU underwent significant changes due to the enlargement. Diversity among member states increased substantially, with the lowest GDP per capita dropping from 67% to 48% of the EU average. Labour mobility surged, and cross-border banking acquisitions in new member states rose sharply, reflecting deeper integration of both capital and labour markets. These changes, alongside efforts to strengthen democracy and institutional efficiency, created substantial opportunities for the EU.

However, the positive effects of enlargement have been tempered by the aftermath of the Great Recession and the EU's challenges in formulating a cohesive policy response (Guiso et al. 2019). These difficulties have fuelled populist movements in both old and new member states, undermining political stability and unity. Without a robust and unified response, the long-term benefits of the enlargement risk being overshadowed by these emerging challenges, highlighting the need for a renewed commitment to addressing economic disparities and political divisions across the Union.

Despite these successes, the process of enlargement has not been without its challenges. The 2016 Brexit referendum, in which the United Kingdom voted to leave the EU, was a dramatic event that underscored the complexities and tensions involved in the integration process. Brexit raised important questions about the future of the EU and its capacity to manage its internal challenges, particularly in terms of economic integration and political cohesion.

Additionally, in 2023, the EU signalled its openness to potential future expansions, with Ukraine and Moldova (and Georgia) being considered for membership. This expansion was part of the EU's response to the geopolitical shifts following Russia's invasion of Ukraine.

In summary, the history of European integration is marked by a series of widening and deepening processes that have transformed the economic and political landscape of the continent. From the post-war efforts to rebuild Europe to the creation of the European Economic Community, the EU's trajectory has been shaped by both internal debates and external challenges. The ongoing process of enlargement, deepening, and the potential for future expansion reflect the dynamic nature of the EU. As the

EU continues to navigate complex political, economic, and geopolitical issues, the lessons of its past will likely inform its future directions.

The process of European integration has provided economists with valuable insights into the complexities of regional economic cooperation. While the story of integration is often depicted as a neat and linear progression, this portrayal oversimplifies the sometimes contradictory nature of the process. The lessons drawn from this experience reveal the complexity, variability, and difficulty of measuring the economic impacts of such integration.

Here I put forward three key potential lessons from this historical reading of the European integration experience, which will help to illuminate not only the intricacies of the process itself but also the challenges involved in assessing its overall success, provided they receive further attention in future research.

The first lesson from European integration is that while the process may appear linear and easy to follow on the surface, it is far from straightforward. The common narrative of European integration may suggest a neat, chronological evolution of the European Union, with successive enlargements and deepening of integration. However, such an understanding of this history is flawed and incomplete, as it overlooks many of the awkward moments and unanticipated developments that have occurred along the way. For instance, such an account of European integration often omits the countries that sought membership but were ultimately excluded from the process. In the 1960s, for example, the United Kingdom was initially rejected by a founding member of the European Economic Community (EEC), a decision that would later be reversed when the UK joined the EEC in 1973. Similarly, Morocco and Spain, both of which expressed interest in joining the EEC, were informed that their membership was not forthcoming. These times in the 1960s, in which countries were effectively excluded from the integration process, are rarely highlighted in mainstream narratives but are important to understanding the full scope of European integration.

Another noteworthy example of the non-linearity of European integration is the case of Norway (Campos et al. 2022). Norway had met all the necessary requirements for membership and was poised to join, only to vote against membership in two referenda, in 1972 and in 1994. Despite having fulfilled all the procedural prerequisites for joining the European Union, Norway made the conscious decision to remain outside. This decision underscores the fact that, while the formal integration process may appear smooth, political decisions and public sentiment often intervene, complicating the linear narrative of integration. Norway's reluctance to join the EU reflects the broader challenge of balancing national sovereignty with the benefits of economic cooperation, a theme that recurs throughout the history of European integration.

Additionally, the integration process has not been entirely uniform across all countries. Some nations joined the European Union quietly and almost unnoticed, such as East Germany following reunification. After the fall of the Berlin Wall and the subsequent reunification of Germany in 1990, East Germany effectively became part of the European Union without the extensive political and public debate across European capitals that has typically accompanied enlargement. On the other hand, Greenland left the European Union in an unconventional manner. Greenland voted to exit the European Economic Community (EEC) in 1985 despite remaining as an Overseas Countries and Territories of the EU with special privileges (such as duty-free and quota-free access to the EU market). The departure of Greenland represents another example of how the integration process is not only about enlarging membership but also about countries choosing to disengage from the Union for a variety of political and economic reasons.

Switzerland provides yet another important example of the complexities and non-linear nature of integration. Unlike other European countries that pursued full membership in the European Union, Switzerland has followed a more piecemeal approach to integration. Switzerland is not a full member of the EU but has negotiated a series of bilateral agreements that allow it to participate in various aspects of European cooperation. This gradual, selective integration highlights the fact that there is no one-size-fits-all approach to economic integration, and countries choose to engage with the EU at different levels and through different mechanisms, based on their unique political, economic, and social contexts.

Finally, the United Kingdom's experience serves as another example of the non-linearity of the integration process. The UK initially joined the European Economic Community in 1973, only to later vote to leave the European Union in the 2016 Brexit referendum. The UK's decision to leave the EU marked a dramatic reversal of its previous stance and underscored the fluctuating nature of political and economic priorities within individual countries. The case of Brexit highlights the fact that even once countries have integrated into the EU, the possibility of departure remains a real yet costly option.

The second key lesson I think we should draw from the process of European integration is that the experiences of individual countries are highly heterogeneous. The experiences of member states vary considerably, not only in terms of their accession to the EU but also in their involvement in the deepening of integration. Each enlargement event, by definition, is unique, and the experience of joining the EU is shaped by the specific historical, political, and economic context of each country. The process of enlargement, for example, changes each time a new group of countries enters the Union. As new countries join, the overall membership of the EU becomes more diverse. The process of enlargement also introduces significant changes in the distribution of power within the Union. Countries that join the EU at different times have different levels of influence and access to resources, depending on the stage of integration at the time of their accession.

The heterogeneity of the European integration process is further complicated by the fact that the EU itself has evolved over time. Each enlargement involves not only the addition of new members but also the deepening of integration, as the EU expands its policies, competencies, and areas of cooperation. The single market and the creation of the euro are just a few examples of how the nature of the Union has changed over time. As new countries join the EU, they must adapt to these changes and integrate into a system that has already undergone significant evolution. This makes the experience of integration fundamentally different for each new member, depending on the timing of their accession and the specific reforms and policies in place at the time.

For example, the countries that joined the EU in the 1970s, such as the United Kingdom, Denmark, and Ireland, had a different experience from the countries that joined in the 2000s, such as Poland, Slovakia, and the Baltic States. These later entrants, which had formerly been part of the Eastern Bloc, faced distinct challenges and opportunities as they sought to align their economies with the more advanced economies of Western Europe. The process of integration was not only about joining a common market but also about adapting to democratic norms, establishing the rule of law, and implementing economic reforms that would allow them to compete within the EU framework.

The third and final lesson we would like to draw is that the benefits and costs of European integration are incredibly difficult to measure. This lesson is closely related to the earlier discussion of the non-linearity and heterogeneity of the integration process. Measuring the net benefits of integration is challenging due to the differing experiences of member states and the complexities of the integration process itself (Campos et al. 2020). As new countries join the EU, they must adapt, and their benefits from integration are shaped by their ability to navigate this complex landscape.

The situation is further complicated by the fact that integration involves different speeds and levels of engagement, with some countries adopting policies and commitments faster than others, Sweden and the euro being one clear example.

Economic benefits, such as the removal of trade barriers, access to structural funds, and the ability to influence EU policy, are often relatively straightforward to quantify. However, non-economic factors, such as the political stability provided by integration, the ability to influence regional policies, and the broader social benefits of membership, are more difficult to measure. The lack of clear and consistent metrics for these benefits makes it hard to assess the overall success of integration for any given country. Moreover, the uneven distribution of benefits across countries complicates the task of measuring net gains and losses. For instance, countries that joined the EU later may have faced greater challenges in adapting to EU norms and regulations, which could offset some of the economic benefits of membership.

In summary, the process of European integration offers several important lessons for economists and policymakers. The first lesson highlights the non-linearity and complexity of the integration process, which is shaped by political decisions, public sentiment, and the evolving nature of the European Union itself. The second lesson emphasizes the heterogeneous experiences of individual countries, which means that each accession event is unique, and the benefits of integration are distributed unevenly. The third lesson underscores the difficulty of measuring the costs and benefits of integration, as the process involves both economic and non-economic factors that are challenging to quantify. Together, these lessons provide a more nuanced understanding of the European integration process and its broader implications for regional economic cooperation.

3.4 Assessing the Empirical Evidence

The empirical evidence on the net benefits of EU Enlargements remains much less voluminous than what one would normally expect, given the importance of the topic. Indeed, Sapir (2011) notes that while the static benefits of integration have been extensively documented, the dynamic benefits remain underexplored. The objective of this section is to look into three main strands of literature. The first asks whether EU integration deepening is occurring; the second is the literature asking whether integration pays off economically; and the third and last focuses on the mechanisms through which these benefits take root. Anticipating the main findings from this section, the existing evidence shows that the level of integration in the EU has increased over time (i.e., deepening has indeed occurred), that there seem to be significant and substantial benefits from EU membership, and that these benefits seem to take root essentially through the improvement and building of key economic and political institutions.

The first question is to examine whether there is any evidence available that EU disintegration is underway. Head and Mayer (2021) provide a recent and insightful analysis of these issues using the standard gravity model of trade. The gravity model, inspired by Newtonian principles of mass and distance, explains trade flows between two countries based on their gross domestic product (GDP) and the physical or logistical distance between them. In its application, this model can consider "distance" in a broad sense, including variables such as bureaucratic delays, geographic proximity, and economic scale.

Head and Mayer (2021) use the gravity model to benchmark EU trade openness and overall economic integration against the US, as the latter is often considered a high standard of economic and political integration. Their comprehensive investigation into EU integration uses this model to assess the extent of integration since the 1960s in terms of four fundamental freedoms—goods, services, capital, and migration—alongside political alignment, which is captured by voting patterns in the United Nations (UN). The results throw new light on the EU integration process and its outcomes, providing a basis for examining whether integration in the EU is comparable to that of the US.

Their econometric evidence demonstrates that EU integration has followed a dynamic trajectory. Trade in goods, for instance, has shown marked periods of acceleration and consolidation. The completion of the

EU customs union in 1968 marked a significant leap forward, eliminating tariffs and fostering greater trade openness. Subsequent phases, such as the creation of the single market, reinvigorated integration by reducing non-tariff barriers. This progression is evident in studies that graphically illustrate the increasing intensity of trade flows over time, as measured by gravity model estimates. While the rate of growth in trade may decelerate in some phases (e.g., the 1970s), the data reveals no evidence of disintegration (in the sense of a reversal or even a marked stagnation in the estimated levels of integration). Instead, the EU continues to exhibit increasing levels of integration, albeit at varying speeds and capacities across member states.

Perhaps the most attention-grabbing finding in this research is that EU integration, measured across the four freedoms and UN voting patterns, often surpasses that of the US: "European states have matched or surpassed the levels of openness prevailing amongst the 50 American states"(Head and Mayer 2021, p. 24). This conclusion challenges assumptions about the comparative strength of US integration and underscores the complexity of evaluating political and economic cohesion. This is an area in which further research will be much welcome.

Turning to the second question—whether integration pays off economically—the focus shifts naturally to the economic impact of EU membership. Existing studies often find positive net benefits from EU integration while at the same time acknowledging the statistical fragility of these findings. For instance, Henrekson et al. (1997) estimated that EU membership could increase growth rates by 0.6% to 0.8% per year but openly admitted that these estimates were not entirely robust. Crespo et al. (2008) also identified significant growth effects from EU membership but highlighted the issue of country heterogeneity as a critical challenge to robustness. This heterogeneity, frequently cited as a limitation, underscores the difficulty of drawing generalized conclusions about the benefits of EU membership across a diverse range of country contexts and experiences.

This heterogeneity is important and should not be ignored. Instead, it needs to be fully explored and accounted for. This heterogeneity naturally leads to counterfactual analysis, namely studies that can address what would have been the economic trajectory of a specific individual country if it had not joined the EU at the date it actually did. The synthetic control method (SCM) offers a robust framework for answering such questions. Unlike simple comparisons between countries, SCM constructs a synthetic counterpart for a given country by assigning weights to potential comparators based on their relevance in terms of a set of comparative dimensions. For instance, in analysing the impact of EU membership on financial markets, the model might assign greater weight to France than to Italy for the UK, given the closer alignment of financial market characteristics between the UK and France.

The synthetic control method allows researchers to estimate the hypothetical economic performance of a country in the presumed absence of EU membership. For example, what would Poland's per capita income have been in 2020 if it had not joined the EU in 2004? The model generates a set of counterfactual scenarios, enabling comparisons between observed outcomes and the estimated alternatives.

In this context, the synthetic control method (SCM) provides a framework to compare the aggregate outcomes of countries that joined the EU with those of an artificial control group composed of weighted combinations of other countries. This approach is particularly flexible for evaluating the effects of joining the EU in 2004. Because EU accession involves lengthy negotiations, anticipation effects can influence outcomes even before the official accession date. For this reason, Campos et al. (2019) analysed data from both the actual date of enlargement (2004) and the start of the officially monitored accession period (post-1998). Their analysis assessed the net economic benefits of EU membership for eight former transition economies that joined in 2004. By comparing the difference between actual and synthetic counterfactual per capita GDP over five- and ten-year periods post-accession, they provided a detailed evaluation of the 2004 enlargement and compared its effects to those of previous enlargements (for which, they argue, anticipation effects were not as important).

The findings revealed substantial heterogeneity in the benefits of EU membership across countries. For instance, Lithuania and Latvia experienced much larger net benefits than Slovakia and Slovenia, although all eight countries that joined in 2004 and for which the necessary data exists saw positive gains. Over the first ten years following accession, the estimates suggested that, on average, per capita incomes in these countries would have been approximately 15% lower without EU membership. These gains ranged from 31% for Latvia to just 0.3% for Slovakia, with the Baltic States and Hungary showing particularly significant benefits. One may conjecture that although Slovakia is a small and open economy, it has experienced a trajectory for the consolidation of inclusive political institutions in the first decade or so of the transition that is quite different from that of the other candidate countries.

Campos et al. (2019) also addressed the question of whether the benefits from the 2004 enlargement differed from those of earlier enlargements. Their analysis considered the varying contexts, criteria, and sets of incumbent EU countries over time. They estimated smaller net benefits (over the first ten years after accession) for the Scandinavian enlargement (around 4%) and for the 1973 Northern Enlargement (around 12%), but slightly larger benefits in the 1986 experience of Spain and Portugal (around 17%) as Greece was the only country found to have experienced negative returns from EU membership.

Applying this method to EU membership, Campos et al. (2019) find that integration generates substantial economic benefits. For instance, countries that joined the EU experienced higher levels of per capita income and productivity growth than their estimated synthetic counterparts. These results highlight the transformative role of EU membership in fostering economic convergence among member states. These findings strongly suggest the importance of institutional integration.

In summary, these two questions of integration deepening and economic payoffs are intricately linked to the broader dynamics of integration. Empirical evidence, supported by robust methodologies such as the gravity model and synthetic control methods, provides a fruitful way to start understanding these issues. The findings challenge simplistic narratives of disintegration and underscore the enduring value of integration, both economically and politically. As debates about the future of the EU continue, it is crucial to ground discussions in evidence-based analysis, recognizing that integration is a complex but ultimately beneficial process.

The third important question is about the mechanisms. For instance, whether the prospect of EU membership has generated economic payoff thanks to fostering institutional development. The assumption here is that this is a key channel or mechanism.

Bruszt and Campos (2019) investigate the hypothesis that the institutional channel is crucially important. They focus on the following key institutional dimensions: the capacity and independence of the public administration (bureaucracy), the capacity and independence of competition policy, and the capacity and independence of the judiciary (rule of law.) For example, judiciary capacity refers to access to the necessary resources and expertise, while judiciary independence is defined in terms of appointment and promotion of judges as EU norms establish basic parameters for the functioning of the judiciary, emphasizing workload and bottlenecks of the judicial system.

The EU Anchor thesis, introduced by Berglof and Roland in 1997, suggests that the prospect of European Union membership played a pivotal role in addressing the institutional void left by the collapse of socialism (Campos and Coricelli 2002). This hypothesis highlights the potentially transformative impact of EU membership aspirations on institutional development across Central and Eastern Europe and some parts of the former Soviet Union. The promise of EU accession served as a catalyst for institutional change, driving countries towards compliance with EU norms and standards. To assess these effects, the European Union implemented a standardized monitoring system starting in 1997. This monitoring system assessed institutional performance across various areas corresponding to the chapters of the acquis communautaire. The annual Progress Towards Accession reports, published by the European Commission, offer a unique lens through which the institutional trajectories of candidate countries can be analysed. By quantifying these reports, Bruszt and Campos (2019) have been able to create a longitudinal dataset that traces the evolution of institutional development, capturing the speed, direction, and nature of reforms in these specific areas. These reports were prepared by teams of independent experts on each of the various areas or chapters and provide an invaluable resource for understanding how nations navigated the process of aligning with EU requirements, from the adoption of new laws to the establishment of regulatory bodies equipped with adequate resources and personnel.

Building on this framework, Bruszt and Campos (2019) quantified the progress towards EU accession, constructing a panel of institutional measures for 17 candidate countries from 1997 onwards, covering most of the accession process. These measures captured both de jure (independence) and de facto (capacity) aspects of institutional development. The 17 countries were categorized into New Member States (NMS) and Candidate Countries. The NMS group included Bulgaria, Croatia, Czech Republic, Estonia, Hungary, Latvia, Lithuania, Poland, Romania, Slovakia, and Slovenia. The Candidate Countries group consisted of Albania, Bosnia, Kosovo, Macedonia, Montenegro, Serbia, and Turkey. The analysis focused on three key institutional areas: the judiciary, bureaucracy, and competition policy. The resulting dataset utilized categorical variables ranging from 1 to 4, with 4 signifying institutional development levels comparable to established EU members and 1 indicating significant deficiencies. For the NMS group, data were available annually from 1997 to 2005, while for the Candidate Countries group, data spanned from 2005 to 2013. By overlapping these nine-year windows, Bruszt and Campos (2019) were able to draw comparisons across different periods and groups.

Three additional results from this analysis and data merit attention, as they raise important questions for future research. First, the analysis revealed that levels of institutional development at the end of the time period were generally higher for de jure (independence) dimensions compared to de facto (capacity) dimensions. This discrepancy underscores the need for further research to understand the challenges of translating formal institutional frameworks into effective practical capacities. Moreover, having comparable institutional data for earlier EU member states would enable researchers to benchmark the progress of newer entrants against historical standards within the EU. Second, neither the New Member States nor the Candidate Countries achieved an average score of 4 in any of the six institutional dimensions by the end of the analysis period. This finding underscores the independence of the team of experts that the EU put together to evaluate accession progress and the value of their judgements. Third, the analysis identified a slower rate of convergence among Candidate Countries compared to New Member States. Although initial institutional levels were similar, the slower pace of reform in Candidate Countries suggests variations in the credibility of EU membership as an anchoring mechanism over time, a phenomenon that warrants further exploration.

The evidence shows that this anchoring effect was particularly pronounced in areas such as competition policy independence and judiciary capacity, both of which saw significant improvements in a relatively short timeframe. The analysis also highlighted the positive impact of EU membership prospects on the capacity and independence of civil service institutions (bureaucracy) and the implementation of competition policy measures. However, one notable exception was judiciary independence, where evidence of institutional development was relatively weaker. This could be attributed to two potential factors: either significant reform occurred prior to 1997, which is beyond the scope of the dataset, or this area lagged behind during the transition period.

Institutions seem to be a crucial channel through which EU membership generates superior economic performance. The data analysis offers evidence of the EU's transformative influence on institutional development in candidate countries in the run up to their actual accession. The prospect of EU membership emerges as a powerful driver of reforms, facilitating the narrowing of institutional development gaps between candidate countries and existing EU members.

In conclusion, the EU Anchor thesis provides a compelling explanation for the transformative effects of EU membership aspirations on institutional development in post-socialist countries that joined in 2004 and 2007. The monitoring and assessment mechanisms implemented by the EU have provided invaluable data, enabling researchers to trace the trajectories of different institutional reforms across different countries and time periods. The findings highlight the pivotal role of EU membership prospects in driving institutional change, particularly in areas such as competition policy and civil service reform. However, the analysis also underscores the challenges of achieving full convergence with EU standards and the variations in reform trajectories across different groups of countries. These insights not only enhance our understanding of the EU's role as a driver of institutional change but also point to the need for continued research into the long-term effects of EU enlargement and the factors that influence the credibility and effectiveness of the EU's anchoring mechanism. The extraordinary pace of institutional transformation achieved within a relatively short timeframe serves as a testament to the EU's ability to foster institutional change, even in the absence of prolonged conflict or external shocks. However, as the data suggest, institutional convergence remains a complex and ongoing process where setbacks and reversals can and do occur.

3.5 Conclusions and Suggestions for Future Research

The enlargement of the European Union is normally thought of as the pivotal process through which the EU incorporates new member states. Yet it can also be conceived in much broader terms, for instance, as going beyond widening and further encompassing new capacities and competencies. This chapter explored three key dimensions of EU enlargement: the theoretical foundations, the historical trajectory, and the estimation of net benefits. Regarding theory, economists have examined the mechanisms underlying the integration of member states, such as the balance between deepening (increased integration among current members) and widening (accepting new members). Historically, economists have sought to understand the unique characteristics of each enlargement wave and the factors influencing their outcomes. Furthermore, empirical studies have aimed to quantify the net benefits of enlargement, evaluating its impact on economic growth, institutional development, and broader societal outcomes. Building on these findings, we propose a comprehensive nine-point research agenda to address critical unanswered questions and guide future inquiry.

The first set of research suggestions stems from theoretical considerations. One key question relates to the interplay between deepening and widening: does deeper integration among existing members enhance or hinder the capacity to expand the Union to new members? Similarly, from the perspective of convergence theory, it is essential to investigate whether the significance of economic and political institutions in driving convergence is diminishing over time, potentially exhibiting non-linear patterns or varying across different stages of integration. Thirdly, further research could explore the future trajectory of institutional integration: to what extent will the EU pursue deeper harmonization of institutions, and what are the implications for prospective and current members? These theoretical inquiries hold the potential to enrich our understanding of the dynamics underpinning the enlargement process and its broader implications.

The second set of research questions draws inspiration from the history of EU enlargement. Reflecting on historical counterfactuals, such as the potential impact of the UK joining the EU in 1960 or Norway becoming a member, may offer valuable insights into the interplay of political and economic forces in shaping enlargement outcomes. Additionally, the heterogeneity of enlargement waves suggests that the next round of expansion will likely be distinct in its challenges and opportunities. Understanding how future enlargements might differ from previous ones is crucial for both policymakers and scholars. Finally, the historical analysis of net benefits raises important questions about the role of interactions between political, economic, and institutional factors in shaping the success of enlargement. By delving into these historical dimensions, researchers can uncover lessons that inform the design and implementation of future enlargement strategies.

The third and final set of research suggestions is motivated by the existing body of relevant empirical evidence. One pressing question concerns the possibility of staggered treatment in deepening integration: can the process of integrating new members be sequenced in ways that optimize outcomes for both the EU and the candidate countries? Additionally, a more comprehensive evaluation of the EU's role as an institutional anchor is needed to fully understand how the promise of membership influences institutional reforms and capacity building in candidate countries. Third and finally, further empirical investigation is required to assess how interactions between deepening and widening, as well as between theory, history, and data, influence the net benefits of enlargement. These evidence-based research avenues offer a pathway to refine our understanding of the enlargement process and enhance its effectiveness as a tool for fostering economic and political convergence.

In conclusion, EU enlargement represents a transformative process with profound implications for member states and candidates alike. By combining insights from theory, history, and evidence, this essay highlighted the complexities and opportunities associated with enlargement and the many questions that have not yet received full attention by academic economists. The proposed research agenda underscores the importance of addressing unanswered questions about the dynamics of deepening and widening, the unique characteristics of future enlargement waves, and the interactions that shape key political economy outcomes. By pursuing these avenues of inquiry, scholars and policymakers can ensure that enlargement continues to serve as a catalyst for economic growth, institutional development, and European integration.

Acknowledgements I am grateful for the various insightful comments from seminar participants at ECFIN in June 2024 and, especially, to István P. Székely for the valuable suggestions and encouragement. The usual disclaimer applies.

References

Acemoglu, D., J. Robinson and T. Verdier (2017), "Asymmetric Growth and Institutions in an Interdependent World," Journal of Political Economy, 125(5), 1245–1305.

Aitken N. 1973: The effect of the EEC and EFTA on European trade: A temporal cross-section analysis. American Economic Review 63(5): 881–892.

Alesina, A., G. Tabellini and F. Trebbi (2017), "Is Europe an Optimal Political Area?" Brookings Papers on Economic Activity, Spring, pp.169–213.

Balassa, B. (1961). The theory of economic integration. Homewood: Richard D. Irwin.

Baldwin, R, J François and R Portes (1997), "The Costs and Benefits of the Eastern Enlargement: The Impact on the EU and Central Europe," Economic Policy 12:125–176.

Berglof, E., Burkart, M., Friebel, G., and E. Paltseva (2008), "Widening and Deepening: Reforming the European Union," American Economic Review, 98(2), 133–137.

Berglof, E. and G. Roland (1997), The EU as an 'Outside Anchor' for Transition Reforms, Stockholm, Östekonomiska Institutet.

Buchanan, J. M. (1965). An economic theory of clubs. *Economica, 32*, 1–14.

Bruszt, László, and Nauro F. Campos (2019), "Economic Integration and State Capacity," Journal of Institutional Economics 15 (3): 449–468.

Campos, N, (2021), "The EU Anchor Thesis: Transition from Socialism, The Institutional Vacuum and Membership in the European Union," in E. Douarin and O. Havrylyshyn (eds.), Handbook of Comparative Economics, Palgrave.

Campos, Nauro F. and Fabrizio Coricelli (2002), "Growth in Transition: What We Know, What We Don't, and What We Should," Journal of Economic Literature 40(3): 793–836.

Campos, N, F. Coricelli and Franceschi, E., (2022), "Institutional Integration and Productivity Growth in Europe: Synthetic Differences-in-Differences Evidence from the 1995 Enlargement of the European Union," *European Economic Review*, Volume 142, 104014, February.

Campos, N., F. Coricelli and L. Moretti (2019), "Institutional Integration and Economic Growth in Europe," *Journal of Monetary Economics*, 103 (1), 88–104.

Campos, N, V. Eichenauer and J.-E. Sturm (2020), "Close Encounters of the European Kind: Structural Reforms, Economic Integration and Sectoral Heterogeneity," *European Economic Review*, Volume 129, 103511, October.

Campos, N and C. Macchiarelli (2021), "The Dynamics of Core and Periphery in the European Monetary Union: A New Approach," *Journal of International Money and Finance*, Volume 112, 102325.

Crespo Cuaresma, Jesus, Doris Ritzberger-Grünwald, and Maria Antoinette Silgoner (2008), "Growth, Convergence and EU Membership," Applied Economics, 40: 643–656.

Demertzis, M., Sapir, A., & Wolff, G. B. (2019). "Promoting sustainable and inclusive growth and convergence in the European Union" (No. 2019/7). Bruegel Policy Contribution.

Eichengreen, B. (2006). The European Economy since 1945: Coordinated Capitalism and Beyond, Princeton University Press.

European Commission (1976), Opinion on Greek application for membership (transmitted to the Council by the Commission on 29 January 1976). Bulletin of the European Communities. February 1976, n° Supplement 2/1976. Luxembourg: Office for Official Publications of the European Communities.

European Council (1994), Essen European Council: Conclusions of the Presidency, Reproduced from the Bulletin of the European Communities 12/1994.

Guiso, Luigi, Helios Herrera, Massimo Morelli, and Tommaso Sonno (2019), "Global Crises and Populism: The role of Eurozone Institutions," Economic Policy 34: 95–139.

Gutierrez, G., & Philippon, T. (2023). How European markets became free: A study of institutional drift. *Journal of the European Economic Association*, *21*(1), 251–292.

Head, K. and Mayer, T. (2021), "The United States of Europe: A Gravity Model Evaluation of the Four Freedoms," Journal of Economic Perspectives, 35(2), 23–48.

Henrekson, Magnus, Johan Torstensson, and Rasha Torstensson (1997), "Growth Effects of European Integration," European Economic Review, 41: 1537–1557.

Kremer, M., J. Willis and Y. You (2022), "Converging to Convergence," NBER Macroeconomics Annual, 36(1), 337–412.

Lawrence, R.Z., 2000. Regionalism, multilateralism, and deeper integration. Brookings Institution Press.

Marciano, A. (2021), "James Buchanan: Clubs and Alternative Welfare Economics," Journal of Economic Perspectives, 35(3), 243–256.

Sapir, André (2011), "European Integration at the Crossroads: A Review Essay on the 50th Anniversary of Bela Balassa's Theory of Economic Integration," Journal of Economic Literature 49 (4): 1200–1229.

Tatham, Allan F. (2009), Enlargement of the European Union. Kluwer Law.

Tinbergen, J. 1957. Customs unions: Influence of their size on their effect. Zeitschrift der gesamten Staatswissenschaft 113: 404–414.

Viner, J. 1950. The customs union issue. New York: Carnegie Endowment for International Peace.

CHAPTER 4

Enlargement: How to Do It Without Undermining the EU's Internal Cohesion?

Kálmán Mizsei

"*Europe is mortal, it can die. It only depends on our choices*", said the President of France, Emmanuel Macron, on 24 April 2024, in a major programmatic speech at Sorbonne (Macron 2024). Regardless of one's attitude to the recipe, it is easy to agree that Europe faces many formidable existential challenges simultaneously. From a long-term perspective, it is rather unexpected that some three decades after what seemed to be a historical and lasting victory of freedom and democracy over tyranny on our continent, we have arrived at this situation.

The ultimate trigger of the sense of crisis and call for awakening was Russia's terrible war against Ukraine. However, many crisis phenomena had already boiled for quite a while. Europe faces an institutional challenge, as it has not yet fully adapted to the expansion from 6 to 27 members, and to more than 31 if current integration efforts prove successful. Not only are its institutional mechanisms not suitable for the sharply increased number of participants, but some of the countries show a kind of rule of law (RoL) deficit, even regression, and sometimes rogue behaviour (understood as a lack of basic solidarity with the rest and

K. Mizsei (✉)
Budapest, Hungary

I. P. Székely, P. Halmai (eds.), *The Future of European Integration*, Studies in Economic Transition,
https://doi.org/10.1007/978-3-032-20186-7_4

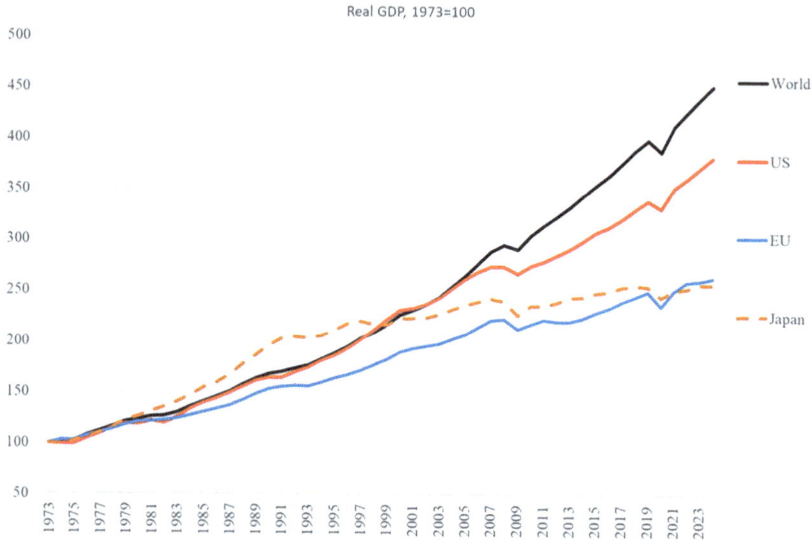

Fig. 4.1 Economic growth in the US, EU, Japan, and the global economy, 1973–2023. (Source: World Bank, World Economic Indicators, NY.GDP.MKTP.KD. Accessed on 4 January 2026. Note: GDP in constant 2015 USD. 1973=100)

disregard for the community rules) that threatens to derail the train of European integration.

Moreover, Europe is lagging behind the United States and, increasingly, China in terms of economic growth and innovation (see Fig. 4.1), the latter being the long-term foundation of competitiveness. Since handling the aftermath of the 2008 crisis, the growth and innovation gap has become even more yawning. The United States has a competitive advantage because it operates a much more unified market, particularly regarding its capital markets, than the European Union. Moreover, it is also one country with one legislation and fundamentally with one language. On the other hand, Europe's catch-up is hindered by an ideological setup that is much less attuned to market competition than the United States and what it used to be.

Against these odds, it is worthwhile to stress that the European Union is worth saving. The author has criticised the EU for many of its problems. However, the EU's fundamental design—a genuinely voluntary cooperation based on liberal democratic, rule of law and free enterprise principles, where its members give up some elements of their sovereignty if they are convinced the collective good must be protected—is at the core of maintaining peace on our continent for almost eight decades, and by this example also represents an incredible global public good, is very much worth to continue to fight for. The leitmotiv of this essay is: never miss a good crisis. We have that crisis now at hand that we need to face head-on.

This chapter will not try to give a thoroughly documented answer to how we have gotten here; moreover, it only seeks solutions to one aspect of the puzzle: enlargement. Why is enlargement at all part of the puzzle? The primary reason is security-related: the European Union cannot develop in peace in the face of a revisionist, militarised Russia unless it can integrate those countries that have remained outside the Union so far but are now in direct danger. Even the countries of the Western Balkans are facing hostile, uncooperative competition from Russia and, increasingly, China. However, this is not the only reason the Western Balkans and Eastern Europe should be part of the European Union. They also potentially represent a source of "frontier-dynamism" of the EU, similar to how the new EU members have inserted positive economic dynamism into the EU.

Enlargement is a necessary, indispensable element of meeting Europe's existential challenges. At the same time, it is a formidable challenge, sometimes underestimated in the geopolitical fervour of the day. While concentrating on the EU's further enlargement, the author is driven by the desire to help continue making the European project successful, to protect it from powerful global and home-made challenges, and to reinvigorate its ambitions as a successful integration model for the world.

This pursuit triggers two sub-themes that are not easy to reconcile. On the one hand, the author is keenly aware of the necessity of successfully integrating the countries that are not yet inside the dominant integration institution of the continent, the European Union; otherwise, a new colonialism under Russia is waiting, at least for some of them (Gobble 2024), and malign interference for the rest from Russia and, increasingly, China, as well as prolonged uncertainty and outside challenges for the whole continent. The barbarians will indeed be, and to some extent already are, not at, but inside, the gates. Failure to integrate countries currently outside the EU would also pose a dangerous impact, a mortal threat to the whole of the eight-decade-old European project.

On the other hand, the author is also aware of the enormity of the task of integrating the remaining countries—without jeopardising the European project itself. Throughout this section, we will point out those difficulties and try to reconcile them. Hopefully, it will not create the impression that the author is a naysayer or pessimist. The desire for lasting success motivates the effort to promote a realistic but ambitious, determined and well-informed process. If candidate countries are not sufficiently well-prepared (by deep and radical long-term reforms) for membership, the next wave of enlargement will likely harm the Union's future development. In the current setup, the conditions required of candidate countries cannot be effectively imposed on member states once they have joined (the so-called Copenhagen dilemma) (Thisell 2022).

Also, the warning throughout this chapter about the complexities of the task serves the purpose of saving us from the bureaucratic disillusionment that we experienced while dealing with the Western Balkan countries' accession stories; only if we are aware of the size of the challenge can we soberly face up to it (Grieveson et al. 2018). We are also addressing the frequently raised objection that the geopolitical challenge posed by Russia (and China) does not allow a lengthy accession process. Yes, we cannot wait. However, we cannot rush either if the price is to give up the core preconditions of a successful integration of nations.

At the same time, as argued throughout this chapter, a successful integration of the new member states may, and should, become a significant factor invigorating the entire European project. However, for the time being, neither the European Union nor the candidate countries are aware of how much better they need to perform in reforming the candidate countries. The primary area of improvement is the rule of law. However, reforms are also needed in economic policy areas to enable rapid economic growth and successful convergence of the new members. These goals are achievable, but only with an intelligent drive towards deep, comprehensive reforms of the candidate countries, and if this reformist approach is maintained *once inside* the EU.

When thinking of the integration, the focus should be broader than "just" the European Union. When thinking about European integration, the ultimate goal should be to create a united Europe based on the values of democracy, the rule of law, free enterprise, an extensive system of human rights, and the principle of social solidarity. In this general framework, however, one should not limit the thinking to EU membership. To mention the most significant ones, we have NATO and EFTA, all of whose members are deeply integrated economically with the EU and vitally important institutions like Schengen that have members also from outside the European Union, and within the EU, we have the euro with the European Central Bank and even some European countries outside the EU using the euro as their currency. It is not to deny that the European Union remains the most important and core integrative institution, but to invite flexible and yet realistic thinking, as it is colloquially said, out-of-the-box.

One of the core reasons why the European project as an integration model became very successful and also attractive to outsiders has been the "widely enough" shared principles of statecraft among its founding fathers, among which the most crucial were the sanctity of the rule of law, democracy, and the market economy. Subsequent waves of expansions did not challenge this until 2004, as most additional members shared those characteristics no less than the original 6.

Things became more complex with the 2004 and 2007 enlargements towards former socialist countries and Cyprus and Malta. While all the applicant countries adhered to those principles, crucially, by history and tradition, the level of informality, as contrasted to the rule of law, was higher in the new member states than in the case of most old members. Nonetheless, the picture is not entirely black and white. As Fig. 4.2 illustrates, while seven of the worst eight RoL performers are new member states, and only Greece is there from former accessions, there is also a marked difference between the North-Western cluster of EU members and the Southern tier. The latter's RoL quality is only slightly better than that of the new members. As Pech (2022) and the data of the World Justice programme show, there has been a clear deterioration in the quality of democracy and that of the RoL continent-wide over a longer period; this cluster of issues has become a major challenge to the whole European Union. There are too many countries whose RoL record is a source of concern, but the ones that challenge the whole architecture so far are from among the new member states. The latest problem country is Slovakia, which has amended its legal acts to serve particular, often criminal, interests and is facing potential EU sanctions over these changes (Silenská 2024).

Deterioration of the level of the rule of law in some member states, together with reform reversals in some new members that we discuss in more detail later, as well as deterioration of democracy also in some (obviously overlapping) new member states, became a cluster of crucial problems for the European Union at the time when urgent challenges burdened

a

Regional Rank	Country/Jurisdiction	Overall Score*	Annual % Change in Overall Score*	5-Year % Change in Overall Score*	Global Rank	Change in Global Rank†
1/15	Georgia	0.60	0.3%	-1.2%	48	1 ▲
2/15	Montenegro	0.56	-	-	57	-
3/15	Kosovo	0.56	0.4%	-	58	1 ▲
4/15	Kazakhstan	0.53	1.0%	3.1%	65	2 ▲
5/15	North Macedonia	0.53	-0.9%	-0.4%	67	2 ▼
6/15	Moldova	0.53	1.3%	7.7%	68	2 ▲
7/15	Bosnia and Herzegovina	0.51	-1.2%	-3.5%	75	3 ▼
8/15	Uzbekistan	0.50	0.1%	7.7%	78	2 ▲
9/15	Ukraine	0.49	-2.9%	-2.7%	89	11 ▼
10/15	Albania	0.48	-0.7%	-5.2%	91	2 ▼
11/15	Serbia	0.48	-1.6%	-4.0%	93	8 ▼
12/15	Kyrgyz Republic	0.45	-1.4%	-4.5%	103	1 ▼
13/15	Belarus	0.45	-1.9%	-12.0%	104	3 ▼
14/15	Russian Federation	0.44	-2.2%	-7.0%	113	4 ▼
15/15	Türkiye	0.41	-0.7%	-1.3%	117	1 ▲

b

EU, EFTA, and North America *(European Union, European Free Trade Association, and North America)*

Regional Rank	Country/Jurisdiction	Overall Score*	Annual % Change in Overall Score*	5-Year % Change in Overall Score*	Global Rank	Change in Global Rank†
1/31	Denmark	0.90	-0.3%	0.7%	1	0
2/31	Norway	0.89	0.3%	0.3%	2	0
3/31	Finland	0.87	0.4%	0.3%	3	0
4/31	Sweden	0.85	-0.4%	-1.1%	4	0
5/31	Germany	0.83	0.0%	-0.2%	5	1 ▲
6/31	Luxembourg	0.83	0.8%	-	6	2 ▲
7/31	Netherlands	0.83	-0.3%	-2.5%	7	2 ▼
8/31	Estonia	0.82	0.0%	2.3%	9	0
9/31	Ireland	0.81	0.3%	-	10	0
10/31	Austria	0.80	-0.3%	-2.0%	11	0
11/31	Canada	0.80	0.0%	-1.6%	12	0
12/31	United Kingdom	0.78	-0.4%	-3.1%	15	0
13/31	Belgium	0.78	-1.0%	1.2%	16	2 ▼
14/31	Lithuania	0.77	0.4%	-	18	0
15/31	Czechia	0.73	0.1%	-1.3%	20	0
16/31	France	0.73	-0.4%	-1.4%	21	0
17/31	Latvia	0.73	0.7%	-	22	2 ▲
18/31	Spain	0.72	-0.8%	2.4%	24	1 ▼
19/31	United States	0.70	-0.6%	-4.0%	26	0
20/31	Slovenia	0.69	1.6%	2.3%	27	4 ▲
21/31	Portugal	0.68	-0.9%	-5.2%	28	1 ▼
22/31	Malta	0.68	0.1%	-	30	0
23/31	Cyprus	0.68	-0.9%	-	31	3 ▼
24/31	Italy	0.67	0.0%	2.0%	32	0
25/31	Slovak Republic	0.66	0.3%	-	34	1 ▲
26/31	Poland	0.64	-0.6%	-5.3%	36	0
27/31	Romania	0.63	-0.4%	-4.1%	40	2 ▼
28/31	Croatia	0.61	0.3%	0.2%	45	2 ▲
29/31	Greece	0.61	-1.4%	-0.3%	47	3 ▼
30/31	Bulgaria	0.56	1.7%	3.9%	59	3 ▲
31/31	Hungary	0.51	-0.2%	-6.0%	73	2 ▲

Fig. 4.2 (**a**, **b**) Rule of Law in Europe and North America, various countries, 2022. (Source: World Bank Database 2024, https://databank.worldbank.org/databases/rule-of-law, own calculation)

its agenda, like the 2008 crisis and the debt crisis in Europe right thereafter, COVID and in general lacklustre economic performance compared to the United States and China and now the frontal Russian attack on the European security status quo.

Thus, the challenges are formidable. At the same time, the result of the elections for the European Parliament is a glimmer of hope. The traditional parties have kept a working majority, which also means continuity in the European Commission. Admittedly, this is a double-edged sword: it can signal politics as usual for another five years, but in case there is a recognition that the survival of the European project requires bold action, this mainstream victory may result in meaningful reform initiatives. This chapter offers some ideas for the latter scenario.

4.1 No Enlargement Before EU Internal Reform

Politicians are not often straightforward about this, but we need to state as clearly as possible: the mechanisms and rules of the European Union are simply inadequate for 30+ members; they were designed for a smaller, loser, and more homogeneous integration space. There have been several attempts to adjust the fundamental rules of the European Union to its much-enlarged format. However, the efforts to adopt the European Constitution have only partially succeeded. The Lisbon Treaty bridged the gap after the failure to adopt the constitution. Nonetheless, these rules are still inadequate and, thus, cannot serve an enlarged and more diverse Union of more than 30 participants, many with no or thin rule of law traditions and low income relative to the core members.

Again, one needs to emphasise the enormity of the task. Historically, governance of states and empires emerged as a result of fights, including wars, for dominance. The European Union has emerged as a historically completely new model of integration, a genuinely voluntary one among national states. Its rules have also fortified the inviolability of national sovereignty in order to protect the constituent nations, particularly the smaller ones. Now, geopolitical events and the slow but accelerating erosion of the European Union's overall competitiveness have dictated the need for reform *and* further enlargement. However, part of the challenge is at least to partially return to the liberal roots of the Union from a much more bureaucratic and ideologically more redistributive worldview where social and now also environmental concerns often take so much precedence over the principles of a free (and unified) market that would be at the core of any regaining of competitiveness.[1]

The debate within the Union about widening and deepening is not new; however, reform of the functioning of the Union has never been deep and radical enough. It usually just enabled muddling through. Thus, right after the European Parliament elections, it is worth stating that the most important mission of the new European Parliament and European institutions should be to rise to the existential challenge of the time for the Union and to launch and accomplish the reforms of the European Union as well as to pave the way to "near accession" for at least a few candidate states by 2030. In this subsection, we have laid out what we consider to be

[1] Even Mario Draghi's competitiveness report envisions 500 billion euros of investment in decarbonisation alone over the next 15 years (Donnachie 2024).

the *minimum* internal reform conditions of the European Union to enable it to accept new members, while in the next one, we have addressed the reform challenges of the candidate states. Thus, we do not aim to discuss an ideal EU reform; we confine the discussion to what is indispensable not to expose the EU to unbearably high risks.

Three official and highly publicised efforts have been commissioned and prepared in the last two years to articulate structural reforms of the European Union. One of them explicitly conditioned enlargement on the accomplishments of the critical mass of these reforms (Franco-German Working Group 2023). At the centre of the Franko-German proposal is a fundamental strengthening, one could even say guaranteeing, of the rule of law in the existing Union. Another proposal is primarily about strengthening "participatory democracy" in the Union.[2] As Gunther (2025, Chapter 10) also emphasises, there is a "democracy deficit" in the European Union that needs to be addressed. However, concentrating predominantly on this, as the Conference on the Future of Europe did,[3] has helped avoid, but at least missed addressing, some of the main problems of the European Union. At the European Commission's request, Mario Draghi published an important report about the European Union regaining its competitive edge.[4] His report also draws attention to an "existential challenge" for the EU.

From the perspective of the task this chapter sets for itself, the German and French experts' work is the most directly relevant, albeit finding the solution to the rapid loss of competitive edge is also vital for the success of enlargement. They have focused on most, if not all, of the main issues. Thus, it is worth recapping those recommendations that are particularly relevant to the prosperity of the European Union and its capacity to integrate the rest of the continent.[5] We will not give a detailed synopsis of this

[2] Pingen (2022). The European Commission's assessment of, and reactions to, the proposal are available at: https://commission.europa.eu/strategy-and-policy/priorities-2019-2024/new-push-european-democracy/conference-future-europe_en

[3] See the final document of the European Parliament organised process: The Report on the Final Outcome. May 2022. Conference on the Future of Europe. https://www.europarl.europa.eu/resources/library/media/20220509RES29121/20220509RES29121.pdf

[4] The future of European competitiveness Part A. A competitiveness strategy for Europe. September 2024. https://commission.europa.eu/document/download/97e481fd-2dc3-412d-be4c-f152a8232961_en?filename=The%20future%20of%20European%20competitiveness%20_%20A%20competitiveness%20strategy%20for%20Europe.pdf

[5] "the EU's institutions, policies, and budget must be reformed before any further enlargement, or at the very moment of the next one. If this does not happen, the EU's ability to

very thoughtful, heavyweight proposal that deserves[6] much more serious attention and a Europe-wide debate (and action).

However, we will highlight the important elements of the reform package that are most useful for the ensuing discussion of handling the accession challenge. We want to stress again that what we highlight is not exhaustive, but perhaps the minimum sufficient reform needed for a successful institutional EU support to accession. The internal reform challenge is indeed complex and formidable.

The proposal addresses head-on the most fundamental issue, the rule of law (RoL), from two angles: strengthening budgetary conditionality as well as simplifying the Article 7 procedure of the Treaty on European Union (TEU) up to the point that "at a certain level of persistency and gravity of violations, countries can no longer remain an EU Member State". These are vital, indispensable tools for the use of which the road should be paved by the newly elected and installed EU institutions. The emphasis is on both tools. On the one hand, budgetary incentives are an important tool in trying to make sure that countries do not deform their rule of law legislation and practice. On the other hand, the European Union, its member collective, should possess the tools for sanctioning behaviour that risks eroding the vital principles of its functioning.

Tightening the retaliatory mechanisms in case a country breaches the EU's fundamental norms also requires significantly narrowing the veto powers. Again, the current experience with Hungary teaches us that even one country acting contrary to the EU's principles can paralyse the EU's decision-making mechanisms. In case of enlargement, the already existing risk of more countries joining the rogue state significantly increases because of the weak RoL traditions in these countries. So, besides the budgetary and sanctioning measures, the EU needs to increase the qualified majority decision-making areas radically.

The Franko-German team has also given several meaningful suggestions on extending the scope of qualified majority voting in the Council. As the authors write, many vetoes are, in fact, related to other negotiations

function well will be at risk. Reforms after enlargement will be more difficult and very unlikely". In: https://www.auswaertiges-amt.de/blob/2617206/4d0e0010ffcd8c0079e21329bbbb3332/230919-rfaa-deu-fra-bericht-data.pdf. See also https://www.politico.eu/wp-content/uploads/2023/09/19/Paper-EU-reform.pdf

[6] The President of the Commission visibly and understandably focused on following up on the Draghi report. However, the Franco-German proposal seems to have fallen off the radar screens in Brussels.

and not the subject matter.[7] They are too polite to say that we need to radically reduce the potential scope for rogue behaviour and blackmailing in the Council.

The Franko-German paper does not discuss the rules regulating EU fund spending. However, this aspect is highly relevant for the economic convergence and systemic evolution of new and future EU members. These countries are much poorer than the old EU members. Therefore, the EU funds represent a much higher proportion of their GDP.

Thus, we should ask how to guarantee that EU structural funds are spent in a maximum pro-growth manner and are not catalysing the kind of political distortions, the evolution towards oligarchic rule, the way they have arguably done in Hungary and to a lesser extent also in some other new member states.

The question is not straightforward since one can argue that there has been a direct and obvious link between the emergence of the kleptocratic, oligarchic state and the EU funds in only one country. Nonetheless, it is vital to ask the question as the example of Hungary shows a very tangible risk: for the reason we have just mentioned, in the poorer new member states (and even poorer candidate countries), the temptation is very high to use EU funds to enroot practices and oligarchic systemic characteristics that are contrary to the EU principles and the interests of long-term economic development of the East.

While Hungary has violated the EU rules on the most massive scale, all the constituent phenomena are also known in other countries. When the structural funds were designed, nobody thought of mafia states emerging inside the EU. Hungary's example shows that this is not only a very real risk, but the funding mechanisms themselves may trigger such systemic deformations. Some of the candidate countries themselves demonstrated a strong patronal state[8] tradition in the last three decades. Thus, the risk of the (relative to GDP) sizable EU funds to generate adverse systemic effects is significant.

[7] Franco-German Working Group (2023), pp. 21–22.

[8] Hale (2014). We use the patronal state, mafia state, and kleptocratic state terms to a large extent interchangeably and mark a political system in which political overpower has emptied the democratic institutions, has grown legally and illegally together with the largest oligarchic interests in the country, and non-legal means of concentrating economic and political power is essential. It has also subordinated essentially the legal system to its arbitrary functioning, serving predominantly the interests of the ruling group. A detailed analysis of this type of regime is given in Magyar and Madlovics (2020).

Therefore, the European Union should improve the efficiency of the use of the funds and guarantee that they do not feed the emergence of oligarchic states, principally in four ways:

1. The European Union should significantly increase the role of the European Commission in the process in several ways. They should be more involved in formulating the programmes for the various structural funds, and, crucially, they should use the wisdom of the science of international development.[9] Moreover, taking stock of the experiences, good and less good, with the Recovery and Resilience Facility (RFF) would be particularly useful in designing the cohesion funds of the EU in the future.[10] The old rules were feasible when the EU was smaller and more homogenous. Even then, sometimes, it did not work as in the case of the Mezzogiorno, but the community could live with this burden. It does not and will not work with some of the new members and candidate countries. However, contrary to the past, quantity will inevitably transform into quality, and paralysis will set in if we do not change the rules.
2. Cohesion, an important goal emphasised in the name of these funds, should be reinvigorated as a concern. Concretely, infrastructure, connectivity and the density of interaction among European citizens, international competitiveness, reversing the trend of massive depopulation of the Eastern part of the current and even more the future EU, and the integration of disenfranchised people, such as Roma, should be the overarching concerns of the developmental support of the cohesion funds. Current practice is too diffuse. Leaving priorities to the member states, even if iterative consultations between the member state and the EC occur, results in a lack of focus because on the national level, usually, not developmental priorities but particular interests take the driver's seat.

[9] The Commission president's efforts go in this direction. However, the devil is in the details. Particularly regarding the purpose for which this intended centralisation of the distribution of cohesion funds will be used. Moreover, all this will matter only if the member states endorse this effort. European Commission maps out "power grab" over €1.2 trillion money pot (Politico (2024)).

[10] There is no justification for such a potent, well-resourced and paid apparatus as the European Commission not to rely on the state-of-the-art and practically employable knowledge of what works and what does not work in international aid in any given country.

3. The European Commission should develop a monitoring mechanism that is much more in-depth than the current one in assessing the national uses of structural funds. Currently, the Commission's role in practice is largely limited to fiduciary analysis at best, sometimes reducing it to the routine of ticking the boxes.[11]
4. If a country has a contested record in RoL or a demonstrated deficit in prudence in the way they spend European funds, the possibility of a radically increased share of direct allocation to beneficiaries/implementers should be triggered. There is no justification for allowing the EU funds to serve as the main financial catalysts for creating mafia states.

In sum, the most important finding is that there should be no further enlargement before a thorough reform of the EU. The Franko-German think-tank concentrated on the system's mechanics and formulated important and necessary reform proposals. We want to highlight one area missing from most of the contemplations on EU enlargement: any integrated community of nations can only remain successful in the long haul if it is self-confident and dynamic. The European Union, while still one of the largest economic areas of the world, is lagging behind others in terms of economic growth, innovation, and provision of security services. It is definitely behind the United States but, by many indicators, also behind China.

As discussed earlier, it is not the task of this chapter to formulate recommendations in this respect; other authors in the volume are eminently more qualified to do it. However, our task is to highlight here that while procedural reforms of the EU's functioning are indispensable, two additional issues have a crucial bearing on the long-term sustainability of the European experiment: economic dynamism and security provision for the whole community. In the latter respect, the perspectives of the relationship with the United States after the US presidential elections are an important reminder that past complacency is not an option for the future in this regard either.

[11] On the rule of law monitoring, see Kochenov and Pech (2015). A lighter critique of the lack of policy coherence is in Schoenefeld et al. (2019). However, the principal *reason* for this lack of policy coherence is what we are stating here.

4.2 Hard Reforms: How to Help and What Not to Do?

The European Commission and some candidate countries have been targeting 2030 as a quasi-deadline for finishing the pre-accession negotiations and adjustments. There is nothing wrong with establishing ambitious anchoring agendas. First, reflecting on the previous subsection, it must be stated that the European Union should be ready with its internal reforms by then. We identified this previously as an indispensable prerequisite of being able to accept new members without taking on board unacceptable levels of existential risk. It is a very demanding and challenging task. It presupposes that the European Commission and the European Parliament work hard to launch and conclude those complex reforms and touch on vital member states' interests, which, in turn, will need some adjustment and compensatory mechanisms so that members accept those reforms.

However, it is even more challenging to successfully orchestrate deep, breakthrough *systemic reforms* in the candidate countries, in any of them, let alone in a critical mass of the candidate countries to really matter. The inherent tension is the following: the brutal Russian aggression against Ukraine made our political leaders understand that there is no such thing as a "sanitary zone". If we do not integrate those outside the EU, Russia will sooner or later (but rather sooner) grab them.

Our political elites do not communicate this well towards the European citizens, but they at least understand it. However, the fact that geopolitically it is compelling to bring those countries in the Western Balkans and Eastern Europe under the Western umbrella does not mean that their politico-economic systems become compatible enough with the European norms, thus ready for accession to the club of liberal democracies with a strong rule of law—an indispensable prerequisite of deep integration.

Simply letting them in without *comprehensive and irreversible reform* would mean the end of the Union as we know it. Many more Brexits may follow even by old or founding member countries that are in because the EU is based on the principle of rule of law and liberal markets and it is sophisticated and, well, rich. Moreover, putting an overambitious goal post as 2030 may even be detrimental to the project's success because it enhances looking more at formalistic indicators and not substantive ones. Also, it may enhance "looking the other way" when countries do not fulfil essential reform criteria, which in the given moment may seem politically expedient but, in the long run, may hurt the whole community.

While we must integrate these countries into the EU, we do not know how to create fast-track *convergence based on economic as well as institutional development.* As international development is not a particularly exact science, it does not offer ready recipes for reform. Even less is known about how to prepare decisions related to the accession process, let alone this fast.

This aspect is particularly relevant since some of the motives for EU accession in the candidate countries are less related to the fundamental values discussed earlier and more to other perfectly understandable motives, such as financial benefits and presumed security provisions by the EU. This makes gathering the resolve for the necessary reforms even more challenging.

In the former Soviet states, perhaps, the most important, and certainly by now finally evident to everybody, motive is the fear of renewed suppression and contemporary-day colonisation by Russia. People and thus countries seek safe haven from this. While it is a fully understandable motive, it is worth still contemplating how much the European Union is the right integration forum for this. One could have said, as I also argued, that NATO exists for that purpose (Mizsei 2024). However, in the fast-changing security environment, it is likely that over time, the European Union's direct and indirect, de facto, security role is going to increase, or a related European defence structure will emerge. Still, NATO membership for countries on the continent is important to ease the burden of rushed full EU membership. However, in the former Soviet states, NATO membership is a dilemma: Russia is threatening Europe in a way that makes some NATO members reluctant to take that risk. Significant parts of the population in some countries would also like to avoid the risk. In Moldova, neutrality is even codified in the country's constitution. The situation is complex. However, on balance, it still seems wise not to put the entire burden of security "guarantees" on the European Union, whose security function is still in a very early stage and whose security so critically hinges on an outside power, the United States.[12]

[12] There is intensive thinking about how to take Ukraine on board in NATO without triggering an escalation of the conflict with Russia. Recently, The Economist has also advocated NATO membership to Ukraine: https://www.economist.com/leaders/2024/09/26/the-war-is-going-badly-ukraine-and-its-allies-must-change-course. Also, Stoltenberg suggested that Ukraine could be granted NATO membership even with territories occupied by Russia. In *Kyiv Independent* 6 October, 2024. https://kyivindependent.com/stoltenberg-says-

The other main motive is money. Even for the new member states, transfers via the structural and agricultural funds are of a completely different proportion relative to the countries' wealth than for most of the old members. Thus, how these funds are spent is critical for their systemic development and, via this, for the European Union's internal cohesion. We have at least one example, that of Hungary, where the funds were instrumental in fuelling the emergence of a hugely corrupt autocratic state. This development does not negate the view that the EU structural funds are, overall, probably the most successful de facto "developmental aid" mechanism in history. However, besides other examples, such as the case of the Mezzogiorno in Italy, it still points to the need to improve the principles of its use as circumstances have changed over time. In the previous subsection, we tried to define how to improve structural funds' use. Here, we highlight that access to those funds is a critical motive for the accession of applicant countries, and the EU funding mechanisms have not yet adapted satisfactorily to the challenges of cohesion funds' use by poorer former socialist countries generally with weaker rule-of-law traditions.

European values, such as freedom, democracy, decency and the rule of law, became important mainly for the young and creative members of the middle classes in large urban areas in the region. This development is very important: in electoral terms, they do not represent an overwhelming force, but their voices still often magnify, including in times of social conflicts.[13] This set of values is particularly in sync with those of Europe in its more classically liberal period, and therefore, it is vital to have these values based on the experiences of the younger creative strata of the applicant countries *within* the Union.

Given the knowledge gap mentioned above regarding the efficient developmental approach to the necessary systemic changes in the aspiring countries of the East and South East of the continent, as well as bureaucratic inertia, our default mode is still "adopting the acquis communautaire". The point is not to challenge the acquis communautaire per se (a different debate outside of the scope of this essay) as an ultimate goal of

ukraine-can-be-granted-nato-membership-even-with-occupied-territories/ . This idea and Ukraine's NATO membership are, however, adamantly opposed by President Trump.

[13] Hence the eagerness of anti-liberal governing circles in the region, such as Georgia, or in a bit more camouflaged way, Hungary, to codify, perversely, the Russian "innovative" practice of stigmatisation of these people and their organisations as "agents of foreign influence".

the body of legislation to adopt and use. However, their premature mechanical adaptation in countries that (a) are not at the level of development where it would be instrumental and (b) do not have the bureaucratic capacity to implement it could be outright harmful.

There are signs that the EC bureaucracy is learning that priorities need to be defined and established among the reforms, but this learning so far has been limited: fundamentally, the whole process still entails negotiating 35 chapters. Ultimately, of course, it needs to happen. But this should be preceded by a hard-nosed, scientific definition of reform *priorities* that then would likely trigger a wide base of reforms that enable countries to join the club. Put differently, we need to concentrate first and foremost on the systemic character of these countries: they should become liberal market economies and democracies based on the rule of law. That should be our primary and immediate focus, and only *as a next step*, as important as it is, should come the alignment with the acquis communautaire. The current thinking, practice and bureaucratic routine, focusing on the acquis, often lose sight of the fact that the European project can only be successful if countries integrate with a high standard of those characteristics of a rules-based market economy and smoothly functioning democracy. Of course, it should be pursued where the adoption of parts of the acquis is instrumental in pursuing *systemic* reforms. Where there is a conflict, for the sake of the long haul, interests of *systemic reform* should prevail over the premature adoption of the acquis.

The first hurdle is, naturally, to at least be determined to start those reforms. Some basic market reforms have, of course, emerged in the enlargement of candidate countries. However, it was nothing like the radical systemic transformation from the start, as it was implemented in a concentrated manner in Poland and the Baltic states. In the countries of the former Soviet Union (except the Baltics), the basic "role model" has been variations of the oligarchic amalgamation of political and economic power since the start of their independent existence, also connected to the lack of radical breakthroughs. Hence, now, the challenge for them is to "de-oligarchise" their economy and politics. The problem of the Balkan countries is only partially the same;[14] here, the concentration of power is typically less, although we remember the long and heavy grip on power of Djukanovic in Montenegro and that of Gruevski in North Macedonia, and

[14] Grieveson and Jovanovic (2025, in this volume) examine the Western Balkans in greater detail.

we can only hope that these systemic episodes may be already behind us for good. Here, the issues are mostly related to the fact that they did not think they needed to reform radically, starting from a relatively more advanced systemic situation. The former Yugoslavia countries had long thought that their *market* socialism was fundamentally different from the former Soviet states. However, in reality, radical reforms were as compelling, albeit somewhat different in their concrete agendas, as in the other former socialist countries. Nonetheless, most of these reforms did not happen for long. Partially, the problem was that they got engulfed in the subsequent Yugoslav conflicts that triggered different systemic evolutions, not least because of the natural centralisation tendencies and large illegal economies created by the war situation. Also, attention was not on reform but on winning those armed conflicts and nations' physical survival. Also, since Yugoslavia in the socialist times was relatively prosperous (certainly more so than the countries in the Soviet sphere of interest), their politicians were not so much aware of the need for radical systemic reforms. Most economists also had strong illusions as to the systemic problems in the Yugoslav economy in spite of its chronic hyperinflationary cycles. Hence, the *early* pressure for reforms was not strong enough in any of them.

The most notable and best counterexamples are the Baltic states and, among the countries of larger size (incidentally particularly relevant for Ukraine), Poland. These early reformers' path dependency meant that their reform trajectory had a nature of *accumulating* or *cascading* reforms towards a critical mass that is a prerequisite for convergence with the old members of the European Union. Their success was also an important gain for the entire Union. Despite these successful cases, backlash and reform retreats have happened, particularly in Poland and Hungary, the two former vanguards of East European political liberation and reform. We will discuss these two cases in the next subsection.

Still, an early good start is critical. Of all the countries of the former Soviet Union except the early reformer Baltics, Georgia is so far the only one that tried a real *systemic breakthrough*, a comprehensive, radical reform after its Rose Revolution. It entailed an agenda of radical privatisation and deregulation of the economy as well as clamping down massively on an incredibly high level of corruption that had characterised the start line before the radical reforms.[15]

[15] For an evaluation of these reforms, see Mizsei (2019).

What is important here is to underline that it has achieved a real and very rare breakthrough: Georgia's mafia state changed dramatically into a liberal market economy and democracy. Its big paradox is that exactly because it was a democracy, in 2011–12, a rich oligarch, Ivanishvili, succeeded in ousting the chief architect of these reforms, President Saakashvili and his United National Movement. Since then, reforms have stalled and, in many cases, reversed (albeit the situation did not return fully to the pre-Saakashvili period's level of cronyism). Moreover, its democratic credentials weakened, and non-transparent Russian connections were markedly strengthened. However, even this partially and temporarily successful reform effort demonstrates for the rest of the post-Soviet world that radical reform may enable countries to evolve into full compliance with the European Union values and legal system, both on paper and in implementation, that such fundamental transformation is not in the realm of fantasy. At the same time, both Moldova and Ukraine are far from the depth of systemic reforms that Georgia, maybe only temporarily, achieved in the Saakashvili era.[16] Still, radical and rapid systemic change, which in turn enables convergence, is possible.

However, except in Georgia, elsewhere in the former Soviet Union's aspiring republics, these radical early reforms did not happen. Instead, a kind of patronal political system evolved, particularly in Ukraine, although a kind of oligarchic pluralism protected the system from evolving into a full dictatorship.[17] When such a system is deeply entrenched, it is very hard for politicians not to follow the logic of patronal politics since the whole environment is gravitating towards this "systemic equilibrium". Here, a "hostile" takeover (grabbing the assets) of business empires can immediately benefit politically influential actors in a way that is hard for politicians to resist. Not doing so may even become dangerous for them because chief policymakers expect them to use political power for business acquisitions and self-enrichment. Ukraine did not achieve a breakthrough in this respect even after the two revolutions, the Orange Revolution and the

[16] With this characterisation, we do not aim to idealise the Saakashvili period; there were plenty of imperfections. However, what is important for our discussion is that this period achieved a systemic breakthrough, which is usually hard to attain.

[17] Hale (2014) discusses each electoral cycle in each post-Soviet new state except the Baltics. Within patronal politics, Ukrainian pluralism is discussed by Hale (2014) and by Magyar and Madlovics (2020). An earlier discussion of Ukraine's specific pluralistic patronal system formation is in Mizsei (2019).

Revolution of Dignity/Euromaidan.[18] Popular sentiments have become more amenable to reforms, but old habits have not died in elite politics. In other words, the logic of patronal politics is remarkably strong and inertial.

Has the war changed much? Although some analysts have been predicting the end of oligarchic politics,[19] others find the centralisation of power, natural in a war situation, and the suspension of most attributes of democratic politics, also a too great attraction to people close to the chief of cabinet of the President not to take advantage of it. Moreover, the reconstruction of the devastated country will require enormous funds—again, the challenge is to avoid using these funds in the old way. However, the immediate point is that it is remarkably complex and difficult to determine what kind of centralisation is necessary for war purposes and what part of it serves only (or predominantly) a particular elite. Again, sorting this out requires a deep, multidisciplinary analysis and a thorough understanding of Ukraine's realities. Politically, it is understandable and even laudable to give moral support to Ukraine in the form of entering membership negotiations. However, we need to realise that the task for Ukraine is much more difficult than that of other candidate countries because the country is still fighting a war and because of the size of the country, which tends to create strong systemic inertia.

Again, this is not about denying the wisdom of giving countries the candidate status. On the contrary, we think that engaging European countries for the *ultimate* purpose of accession is the appropriate approach, and it was a mistake to withhold the prospect of EU membership in the past. It may incentivise them to do the right reforms. Popular pressure may also force the elites to change. The lack of an EU perspective is making the challenge much more difficult. We could not garner enough support for this approach until the geopolitical/security situation dramatically changed and created a critical mass of support for this. However, now, we need to point out the risk involved in taking in countries without the necessary level and depth of systemic preparedness. We have already experienced a situation that is not that dissimilar to this when Romania and Bulgaria joined the EU in 2007. Political pressure made us overlook an insufficient level of systemic preparedness. Later in this subsection, we will get back to that lesson. The best approach would have been earlier and remains now to give the perspective of membership but remain very principled about

[18] A detailed assessment of this is given in Dubrovskiy et al. (2024).

[19] See, for instance, Minakov (2024).

demanding the reforms that guarantee the long-term sustainability of living in the EU and its values and standards.

So, for the three East European post-Soviet accession candidates, the challenges and perspectives vary: Ukraine is in the middle of an existential war, which necessitates the degree of centralisation of decision-making that in the future will have to be corrected as it is incompatible with the EU. Georgia has lately become a captured state by Bidzina Ivanishvili, a corrupt oligarch with deep roots and connections in Russia. In Moldova, the public attitude is the most favourable, and neighbouring Romania is a member of the EU, and the ties are very close, including about half of Moldovans now having Romanian citizenship. Moldova's path to EU membership seems now to be the smoothest. However, two major challenges are there: first, the current, very pro-Western government's *reform* record has been, at best, lukewarm: it has not yet achieved cleaning up the judicial system from corrupt, including organised criminal, interests. Also, timidity, and perhaps also a lack of competence, in economic reforms have resulted in minimal economic recovery after the devastation of the COVID pandemic and the negative economic impact of the war in neighbouring Ukraine. Thus, this is going to be a much greater challenge than we may admit, as there has not been any *breakthrough reform* during the period of the pro-European leadership. What is common is that among the creative urban classes in the three countries, there is great enthusiasm for EU accession.

Does the reform reversal in Georgia offer us any lessons? Why did it happen, and how can it be avoided in other East European accession countries? It is an important question because besides the Baltic States the only country in the former Soviet Union where breakthrough reforms happened is Georgia. Georgia traditionally had been the country with the most affinity to serious organised crime, whose agents they have also exported to other countries, primarily of the former Soviet Union (Kuzio 2015; Galeotti 2018). Even more admirably then, Saakashvili's reforms broke this tradition. They markedly improved public administration and justice institutions and put dynamism into the economy through sweeping liberal reforms. What caused the reforms' demise is different factors. Saakashvili's eight years of reign could not and did not create a perfect liberal state for objective and subjective reasons. There were shortcomings, particularly in the justice area; he presided over the judicial organisation, which he rightly deemed important, but it took too long. He left the prosecution directly under the Ministry of Justice instead of leading it towards independence. As a president, he had too much power that he often used arbitrarily, even if typically for the liberal cause. His crackdown on the protesters in November 2007 threw, disproportionately though, a long shadow on his whole reign. His popularity was also eroding because of the draconian penalties for crime. At the beginning of his period, this was a welcome change to the lawlessness of the previous Shevardnadze era. However, over time, too many relatives and acquaintances of people were in prison. As time passed, this was no longer perceived as just and welcome. Moreover, finally, and overarching, Saakashvili's larger-than-life figure towered too much over this small, brave country in the Caucasus. As a result, his informal style, which often leaned into arbitrariness, became less and less popular. Moreover, since he *institutionalised* too little in the area of the rule of law, reform reversal was easier in this area. However, the lawlessness of the Shevardnadze era has not come back since Ivanishvili took over first as prime minister more than a decade ago and established a de facto full informal control. Georgia's governance indicators are still ahead of those of Moldova and Ukraine. But reforms lost their dynamism, and, most importantly, Ivanishvili's ties to Russia dictated a quiet reorientation towards Russia, plus a gradual and steady reduction in democracy.

Integration of the Western Balkans should seemingly be easier—based on its proximity to the European Union markets, on much easier connecting infrastructure to the major markets and political partners and on most of the countries' inherited exposure to Western Europe while they had been part of Yugoslavia. Also, their governance and rule of law indicators are a bit better, and the level of economic activity is somewhat higher than for the candidate countries in the former Soviet space, of course, not counting the war-damaged Ukraine. Very importantly, the Thessaloniki Declaration explicitly offered them the prospect of full EU integration more than two decades ago.[20] In the meantime, some of these countries have become candidates—with all the financial advantages compared to those that have not gained such status in the two subregions. In that respect, the fact that none of the Western Balkans countries have achieved spectacular success in convergence with the EU cries for an explanation that, however, this chapter will not venture to deliver.

[20] EU-Western Balkans Summit Thessaloniki, 21 June 2003. Declaration. https://ec.europa.eu/commission/presscorner/detail/en/PRES_03_163

The Western Balkans has also had its fair share of near oligarchic dictatorial situations, such as Montenegro under Djukanovic, North Macedonia under Gruevski and currently Serbia as well as the tiny Republika Srpska within Bosnia and Herzegovina. However, the long reigns of Djukanovic and Gruevski were not followed by another overpowered political oligarch (or "poligarch", as Bálint Magyar aptly calls them[21]). Ultimately, strong political pluralism is a relative safeguard against consolidating undemocratic power. As much as "political fragmentation" is often criticised when the Western Balkans is discussed, a typically proportional electoral system protects these societies to some extent from the emergence of political monopolies. The only exceptions are Serbia and Republika Srpska in Bosnia and Herzegovina. Serbia is undoubtedly a serious problem as it is the country that, among the aspirants, is the relatively best prepared in terms of government and general policy capacity. However, political power is concentrated in the hands of one person and democracy is severely limited. Moreover, its recent history makes it an emotional target of Russian infiltration and a sceptical approach to the West. So, in spite of its seeming higher degree of readiness for EU membership, Serbia remains a complex case.

In economic and institutional terms, things also look a bit easier in the Western Balkans than in the candidate countries of the former Soviet Union, as Figs. 4.3, 4.4, 4.5, 4.6, and 4.7 show. For a long time, the lack (or timidity) of reforms after the Yugoslav model of employee ownership (which, in practical terms, was not real ownership of enterprises but strongly entrenched positions as employees, safeguarded from firing) resulted in astronomical unemployment rates and overall lacklustre economic performance. Over the last two decades, these rates have everywhere decreased to the 9–13 percentage point range, a very significant improvement, signalling more "normal, market-economy conform" regulatory frameworks (Fig. 4.5).

While unemployment indicators in the Western Balkans have improved, they are not better than in the former Soviet candidate states (in its negotiations, perhaps the most advanced candidate Montenegro's current rate of unemployment is 15.3%, while Moldova's 4.6%. Georgia's 16%. Ukraine's before the war was slightly below 10%). Still, the improvement signalises a distancing from the core disease of the "employee

[21] See particularly Magyar and Madlovics (2020).

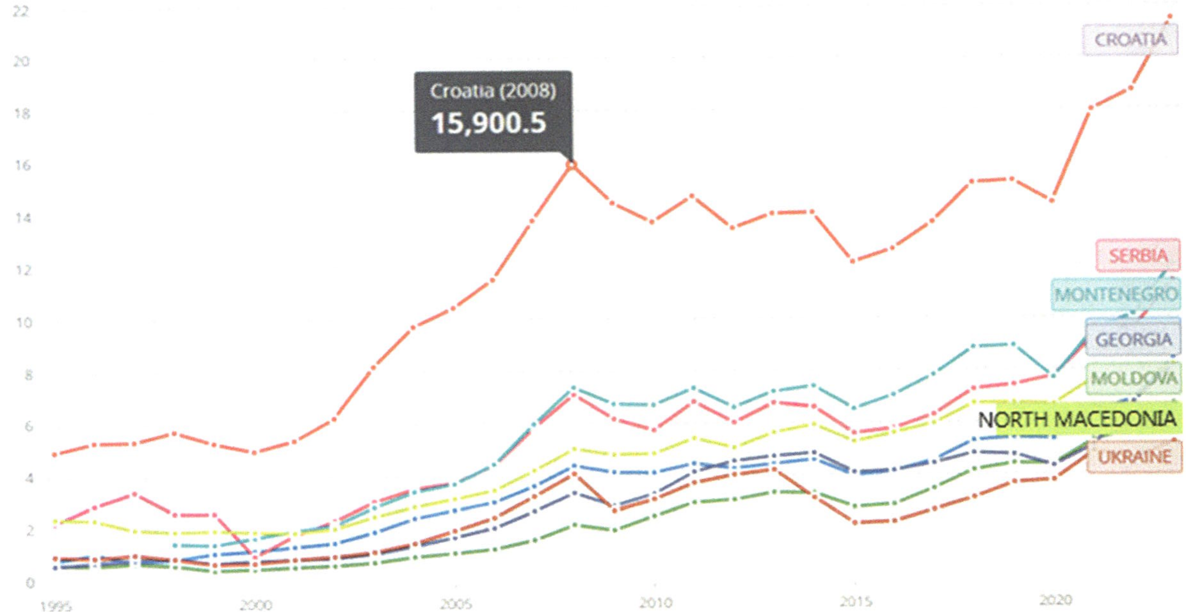

Fig. 4.3 GDP dynamics in selected candidate countries and Croatia, in thousand (current nominal USD). (Source: World Bank GDP statistics. https://data.worldbank.org/indicator/NY.GDP.MKTP.CD)

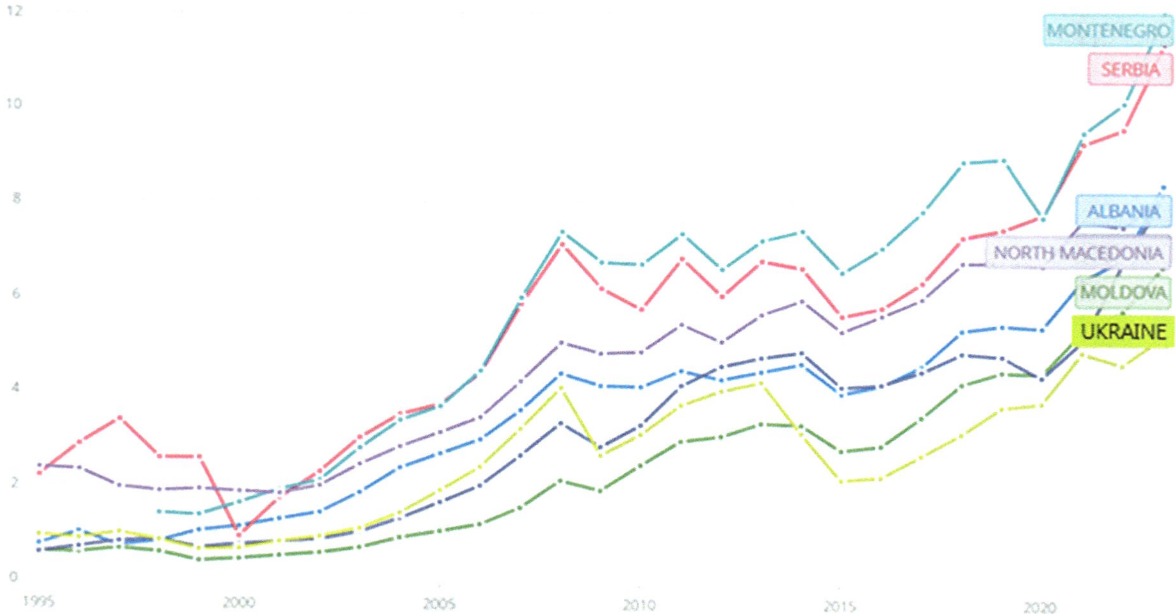

Fig. 4.4 GDP dynamics in selected EU candidate countries, in thousand (current nominal USD). (Source: World Bank GDP statistics. https://data.worldbank.org/indicator/NY.GDP.MKTP.CD)

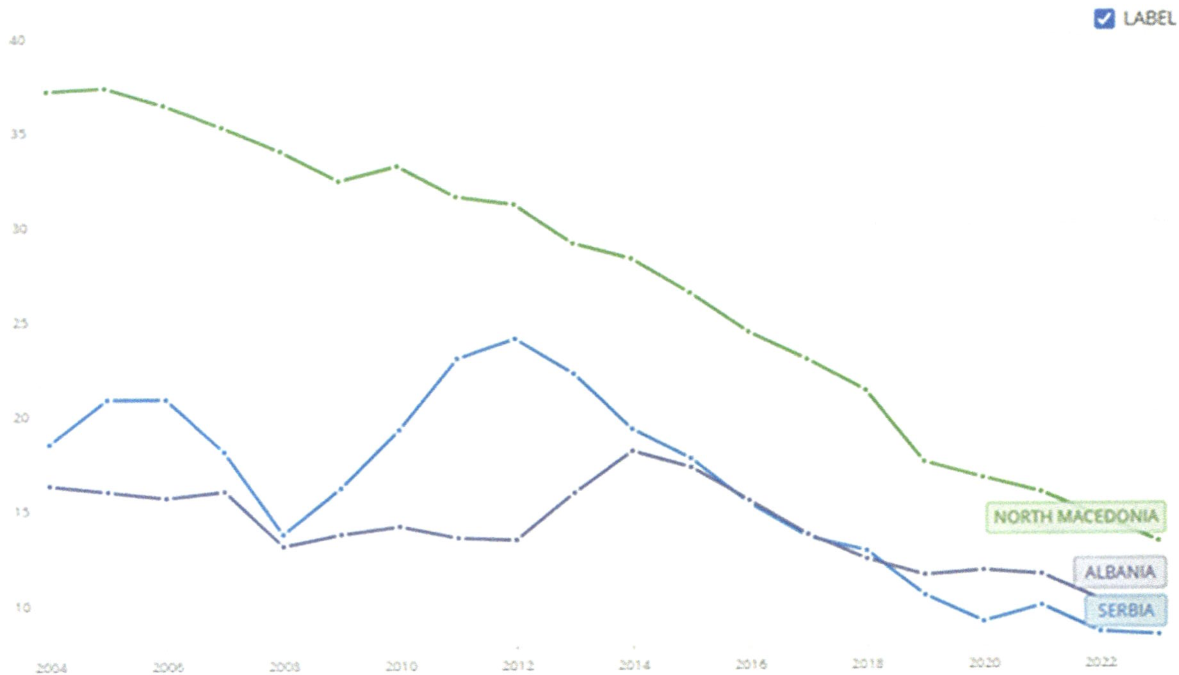

Fig. 4.5 Rate of unemployment in selected Western Balkans EU candidate countries. (Source: World Bank WDI database. Notes: Unemployment as a percentage of the total labour force. ILO model estimates. Accessed on 7 January 2025)

Fig. 4.6 Rule of Law indicators in several Western Balkans and former Soviet EU candidate countries, the Czech Republic. (Source: World Bank Doing Business 2023)

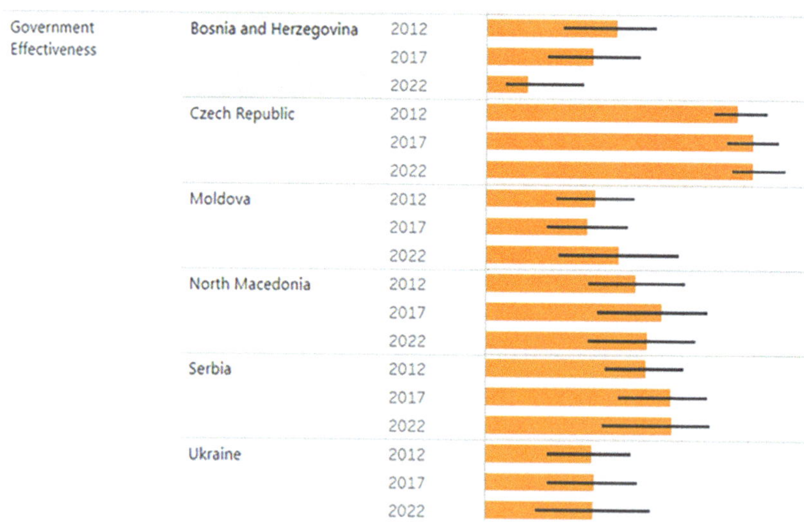

Fig. 4.7 Government effectiveness in several Western Balkans and former Soviet EU candidate countries, plus the Czech Republic

Table 4.1 Nominal per capita GDP of various accession countries in USD in 2023

Country	*Per capita GDP in USD*
Serbia	12.280
Montenegro	12.220
North Macedonia	8.620
Albania	8.580
Bosnia and Herzegovina	7.600
Kosovo	5.940
Georgia	8.280
Moldova	6.730

Source: World Bank database

self-governing" system of the former Yugoslavia, chronic high unemployment. It is an encouraging development.

The World Bank Doing Business (Figs. 4.6 and 4.7) indicators generally show some advantage to the Western Balkans over the former Soviet candidate states—but also a way to go compared to a successful Central European reformer, Czech Republic, which we have used as illustrative comparator:

Government effectiveness shows a similar picture. Moldova and Ukraine cry for radical reform in this area:

Finally, while in general per capita GDP is very low in both regions compared to the EU average (the highest in the region being about a quarter of the EU average!) in this respect the former Soviet countries also trail somewhat behind the Western Balkans (see Table 4.1).

Geopolitics should also make the situation of the Western Balkans easier, as Russia's competitive and highly destructive geopolitical pressure is weaker there. At the same time, the dynamic of expectations is also important. There has been much talk of enlargement fatigue when discussing the Western Balkans while, in contrast, the ruling elites in the new candidate countries, not having yet faced the harsh realities of inevitably lengthy negotiations for EU membership, show optimism, energy, and enthusiasm.[22] However, this enthusiasm has not yet translated into the kind of robust breakthrough reforms that we discussed in the case of post-Rose Revolution Georgia.

[22] Grieveson, Richard; Grübler, Julia; Holzner, Mario, Western Balkans EU Accession: Is the 2025 Target Date Realistic? *WIIW, Econstor*, Policy Notes and Reports, No. 22.

When managing the process of accession, the European Union, Council and Commission alike will have to be mindful of three major issues and potential pitfalls. The most important is the right approach to the issue of overarching importance, which is the *rule of law*. As mentioned earlier, these societies, both traditionally and because of their socialist past that socialised them towards inevitable hypocrisy, operate with a huge degree of informality to circumvent the law. Thus, good laws and textbook regulations for justice institutions are not enough. The classic example is the Council of Europe's advocacy, whose lead the European Union generally follows as a matter of policy; it is firm on judicial independence and self-governance. In general, this is a sound and even vital principle. However, when the judiciary, courts, and prosecution work in a mafia mode, advocating for judicial self-governance may achieve the opposite of what is desirable—context matters. Premature independence of the institutions often results in the entrenchment of mafia-like organisations, which are entirely dysfunctional from the point of view of the original reform intentions.

Further, as we argued elsewhere,[23] we need to be very clear-minded about the difference between the "fight against corruption" and the enrooting of the rule of law in any country's reforms. The fact that in many of the European countries outside the EU, justice institutions are organised partially or predominantly criminally does not mean that the "fight" against these phenomena always has to be exclusively, or even overwhelmingly, based on prosecution and repressive measures. Clamping down on large-scale corrupt, let alone organised criminal, activities should definitely be part of the repertoire. However, this, in itself, will not achieve any significant irreversible step towards the rule of law. Positive incentives are at least as, and probably more, vital. Among these crucial is public administration reform, whereby expecting and demanding professional standards is accompanied by radical salary reform, which happened in Georgia after the Rose Revolution. This should not be a piecemeal, "oh, when we have a little money in the budget" type of approach but a "radical rupture from the past" one. As it is crucial, the European Union must understand the importance of such reforms and financially help them when they are genuinely credible. Often, oligarchic politicians keep low wages to strengthen the dependence of pliant civil servants (and judges,

[23] In the aforementioned book, Dubrovskiy et al. (2024), in the chapter about the rule of law reform, I deal with this in detail.

policemen, prosecutors, and customs officials) on them. One needs breakthrough reforms here. Twenty-plus years after the Georgian successes, this elementary truth still has not quite sunken in.

Also, where institutions are rotten, one should not shy away from a complete overhaul. Naturally, it cannot succeed without massive outside help. It needs to be assessed how "rotten" the whole system is because it will determine the necessary degree of surgery. In Ukraine, after the Revolution of Dignity, parts of the governing coalition, particularly the minority coalition party Samopomich, wanted a complete replacement of prosecution and the system of judges as they assessed that these were essentially criminal organisations. Politically, it was not feasible, but it is also important to note that the Council of Europe was also firmly against a complete overhaul. Their argument was, at best, a boilerplate one that did not take into account the level of organised criminality in these institutions. Moreover, as mentioned above, relying on the self-governance of these professions in such cases is wrong and, in fact, protects and prolongs the harmful mechanisms. Such gradual self-cleaning may be possible in less acute situations, with strong political backing and financial incentives. It needs to be judged depending on the actual situation, and we will probably find more cases where gradualism is feasible in the Balkans than in the former Soviet republics.

Moldova is currently undertaking what is intended to be a comprehensive vetting process. It would be too early to judge its efficiency and whether it will produce sustainable positive outcomes. However, it seems certain that the result will depend on the process's radicalism, cleanness, and professional quality, not just the logic of the concept itself. As discussed earlier, in countries where institutions and the whole culture are tainted with corruption, substantial external input in the form of people, control, and oversight may be needed.

European officials and diplomats often repeat the mantra that solutions "need to be locally owned". It is undoubtedly the right principle, but it may not be practical in the situations discussed here. In fact, in the last few years, the Ukrainian and Moldovan governments and civil society activists have increasingly reached out to foreign officials for solutions. The reforms the international community recommends must be very well selected so that they both, professionally and ethically, become indisputably positive examples for the local professional community and the wider public and, thus, become genuine change agents. Admittedly, it is easier said than done. Similarly, in countries like Moldova and Ukraine, robust EU oversight is necessary for achieving the kind of rapid change needed to respond positively to public expectations of fast EU integration. Again, professionalism that relies on state-of-the-art knowledge of the professional practices in at least some good rule-of-law countries but can also apply that knowledge in a very different East European context is needed.

The ambition of fast integration is helpful. The long and demoralising malaise about EU integration in the Western Balkans following the Thessaloniki declaration in 2003 (more than 20 years ago) was demoralising.

However, as mentioned earlier, speed and quality are often trade-offs. Thus, we must find the optimal speed that maintains the right balance and does not water down core principles or undermine discipline. For that, the EU must possess the necessary knowledge about the movers of change in society and rule of law institutions.

So, the assessment of progress will depend not that much on the alignment of the written law to the acquis but on the daily practice of implementation. It will take time for the culture of justice to take root, even in the best of circumstances. Governments in the region will have to maintain a resolute commitment to radical reforms to implant the rule of law. Moreover, the process will have to be closely monitored to prevent backsliding. It is nearly impossible to achieve such breakthroughs in social practices by the target date of 2030 set informally by the European Commission.

In Moldova's case, the unresolved Transnistrian conflict is an additional issue. In the midst of the security crisis caused by Russian aggression against Ukraine, the European Union took the position that it could take Moldova on board without the resolution of the Transnistrian conflict. While it demonstrates a strong commitment to Moldova's integration, it may create problems later in the process. On the one hand, Transnistria constantly deteriorates Moldova's (and, incidentally, Ukraine's through its impact on, and importance to, the Odesa region) systemic characteristics. The whole model of Transnistria is essentially built on systematic illegality. Not only because it does not have an international status but also because its oligarchy lives on smuggling and a host of illegal relationships with the outside world, not to speak about its domestic oligarchic and non-democratic build-up.

On the other hand, it would be unwise to miss the opportunity European integration and the war in Ukraine offers to bring about a peaceful reunification of the illegitimate Transnistrian enclave with Moldova.

The other critical issue in the accession process is prioritisation. As mentioned, the European Commission's DNA is to negotiate the 35 chapters of the acquis communautaire and ensure the candidate complies. Historically, this approach had advantages, as Grabbe (2006) analysed, even when negotiating the Big Bang enlargement of 2004. Even now, the EU technicians involved in the process would discover many things that need fixing in the candidate country's legislation.

However, this process misses three vitally important things: first, it fails to assess what complexity of regulations a given country, typically with a lower level of government capacity, can handle. Second, how a given, usually complex, regulation would affect corruption in the bureaucracy. The more discretion and complexity there is, the more opportunity to misuse power in situations. Third, these particular chapter-by-chapter reviews do not depict the contradictions between regulations among different chapters.

Negotiators are trying to address these problems and recognise that prioritisation is important.

However, this will only work if the process is based on a deep, systemic analysis that identifies the most important reform triggers. Not only in general terms like the rule of law but also in concrete, practical measures that can induce further changes. Why do we emphasise the importance of systemic analysis so strongly? As many analysts point out[24] societies shape coherent "systems" with their economic, social, and political dimensions that mutually reinforce each other. The one that has evolved in Western Europe and the United States and that has expanded further East is called by North et al. (2009) as open access order (OAO). In our assertion, this crucial characteristic of the countries formed the nucleus of what later became the European Union, besides, of course, the post-World War 2 circumstances. However, politics would not have been enough: the glue was a shared adherence to free markets, democracy, the rule of law and humanism. These features of the open access order were crucial to make the initial six countries and then the European Economic Community so successful that it attracted more and more societies wanting to participate

[24] With my co-authors, we mainly relied on the systematic work of North et al. (2009).

and also helped to evolve from an economic integration model into something more political over time.

North et al. (2009) refer to the others as limited-access orders (LAO). There are many forms of it, and in the post-communist East European countries, what emerged is what Hale (2014) calls patronal politics in his thorough examination of each of the post-Soviet states, outside the Baltics but also involving the unrecognised ones. Magyar and Madlovics (2020) give a conceptual framework for analysing the evolution of these systems. In our book, Dubrovskiy et al. (2024), we tried to analyse, using the example of Ukraine, the arduous struggle to lift a society from one system to another. We also added a sociological component to the analysis, realising that social values and group formations significantly impact the success or failure of such perceived reform.

Our assertion is also that without this systemic transformation, countries would not be compatible with the integration model of the European Union. Since these changes can only be understood in their dynamic interactions, whether the changes are "irreversible", "radical enough", or not, replacing it with looking at the "35 chapters" without understanding the deep interactions between them may not help in guiding these countries towards the kind of radical change that is needed for EU accession. It is vital for success that the European Union develops its ability to judge the entirety of social, economic, and judicial reforms to assist the process and finally absorb countries mature enough to be members of the Union. Only countries with breakthrough changes in economic regulation, application of the rule of law, democratic order and social acceptance of all this will be able to contribute to the health of the Union in the long haul.

The immense complexity of this process is illustrated by the paradox that the two candidate countries best prepared in terms of government capacity have become the most problematic ones politically: Serbia and Georgia.

Finally, in the period leading up to accession, the EU and the candidate countries should be open to *transitional regulatory solutions*. These may be necessitated by issues I have mentioned in this subsection: the need for simplicity because of low government enforcement capacity. However, it can also be justified on the basis of tradition or justified policy concerns. An example of this can be simplified tax regulation for SMEs in Ukraine—an issue of serious earlier controversy (Cherkasyn and Dubrovskiy 2024). Incidentally, this example also shows why too much concentration on rapid, rather than thorough, adjustment to the EU could yield inferior results with adverse long-term consequences.

The need to go "light"[25] on the regulatory burden may coincide with a challenge across the Union: the European Union (and its member states) clearly suffers from *overregulation.*[26] However, it will be challenging to harmonise the regulatory reform in the whole Union and the *transitional* regulatory easing that would be advisable for the countries in the antechamber of the EU. However, it is worth thinking about because there may be synergies between the two. One of the challenges is that these two issues belong to different Directorates in the European Commission. Hence, the strategic principles this essay advocates for should be adopted at the level of the President of the European Commission as well as of the European Council.

All these challenges on the way to the necessary systemic reforms that enable the candidate countries to mature into EU members are very difficult and complex intellectual and practical challenges that also need more than just the bureaucratic routine of the apparatus of the European Commission. It cries for engaging the best professionals in the European institutions' highest echelons and beyond in Europe. It is also the best way to find the trigger points of systemic reform: it has to be fundamentally a process of the developmental discipline but avoiding its often routine approaches and aiming at defining the triggers that most often should be the priority changes that create the hope for cascading reforms; sometimes though the choice can be more banal as which area has a local leadership that offers the best chances for reform. But even in these cases, it is an important intellectual task to see what interactions the suggested changes have with other areas and how they will influence the big picture—achieving the model of the deeply rooted liberal democratic order. It should also be irreversible—the focus of the next subsection.

[25] When speaking about going "light", we do not advocate looking the other way when rules are not applied; instead, we advocate for a simpler regime that can be easily and non-corruptedly applied.

[26] See particularly the Draghi report, an official document of the European Commission: *The Future of European Competitiveness. Part A. A Competitiveness Strategy for Europe.* September 2024. https://commission.europa.eu/document/download/97e481fd-2dc3-412d-be4c-f152a8232961_en?filename=The%20future%20of%20European%20competitiveness%20_%20A%20competitiveness%20strategy%20for%20Europe.pdf

4.3 Backsliding

Evolution towards a liberal state is not, cannot, be linear. The history of the two decades of EU membership of some post-communist countries, together with the more than three decades of transition from socialism, teaches us to pay attention to this when designing the future and enlarged Europe and offers various insights. The most obvious one is that the early market reforms can be achieved fast and relatively easily as long as the ideological barrier of state socialism is resolutely lifted. Remarkably, at the very outset, some countries, most notably Estonia (but also other Baltic states) and Poland (with its considerable size and weight) achieved spectacular results with their market reforms, and the international financial institutions started to regard them as the "model" of transformation. These reforms included a rapid liberalisation of prices and trade and an easing of establishing private business. In the case of Estonia, privatisation happened particularly fast, but even in many other countries, innovative means have helped to make private ownership dominant in the economy. However, deepening the liberal state with a smoothly functioning justice provision and reform of the social spheres has proven a much more difficult challenge. Moreover, the enormous financial support by the European Union in a not-yet-sufficiently-reformed political and institutional environment has turned out to be a double-edged sword. Certainly, in Hungary, it has been an important catalyst for creating an oligarchic state with severely limited democratic space.

Things have then become even more complex as countries, namely Romania and Bulgaria, joined the European Union, whose rule of law deficit was even larger at the point of entry than of those already in, and as some initially well-performing countries' reforms undergone some sharp reversal, namely and particularly that of Hungary and Poland. In fact, the European Union introduced an innovative so-called Cooperation and Verification Mechanism (CVM) for Romania and Bulgaria. In this framework, the European Commission assessed progress in Bulgaria and Romania in this respect every six months. The mechanism was closed in 2023. It would be worth seeing an independent, impartial assessment of the actual working and impact of this innovative programme and also what lessons we should learn from it for the future, predictably even more complex situations as these lessons promise to be particularly helpful to design post-accession safeguards against reform reversals and rule of law weaknesses at the time of accession.

Hungary's case shows that not only are temporary halts and modest backsliding from the trajectory towards liberal market economies and democratic order a possibility, but severe reversals may have a major negative impact on the development of the whole of the European Union. Hence, again, the seemingly rigorous approach of the author of this essay towards accession seems to be justified. If we want to craft a successful enlargement of the European Union, we need to be very hard-nosed about the efficiency and effectiveness of the process from the point of view of quality, depth, durability and feasibility of the reform of the entirety of the political, economic, and social order.

Moreover, in cases of major structural changes in a society, it is commonplace to observe backsliding, reversals of changes, or backlash (however one calls them). It is undoubtedly true for liberalising reforms, national or wider.[27] Rapid structural changes hurt vested interests both in business and society, which triggers political organisations to reverse, derail, or at least modify those changes. That also happened in the case of post-socialist transition, and it is very likely to happen when de-oligarchisation takes place. So, temporary halts, political changes, and major backslidings are also possible in the candidate countries. As the enlargement process reaches countries with distinctly fewer rule-of-law traditions and radical reforms at the outset, reforms will be more resisted by vested interest, and backslidings will become more frequent. Hence, the EU's internal reforms must take place before the new wave of accession starts to handle those "problem" cases more effectively and smoothly. Moreover, the EU should improve its capacity to detect promptly major deviations from the common European values among the institutions of its member states.

In the first subsection, we proposed that before the next wave of the EU needs to be ready with three fundamental internal reforms, essentially it needs to be able to sanction systemic deviation from the liberal norm and that the budgetary rules should be such that the EU can act relatively fast against countries that do not oblige with the community's standards. Since the countries with likely problems with the rule of law and democratic politics will probably be the same that badly need finances, budgetary sanctions will probably be an important deterrent. The case of Hungary is an example of how the lack of sanctions over bad behaviour allowed the evolution of the situation that we now must cope with. The other

[27] Not dissimilar and not unjustified to recall the backlash against periods of globalisation. See O'Rourke and Williamson (1999).

proposed reforms—majority voting and sharpening the Article 7 procedure, would also be instrumental in a case like the one we are experiencing with Hungary.

Beyond the internal reforms proposed earlier, the EU should also develop some political safeguards for the candidate countries. The key here is not to lift conditionalities entirely as in the 2004 accession round. The year 2007 has already offered some positive adjustments in the form of CVMs. Without an exhaustive analysis, we offer two thoughts: first, stronger, binding commitments must be required from newcomers that they join the eurozone in a defined and not-too-long period. The euro offers an additional set of anchors that, at least in macroeconomic policy—and potentially more widely—binds countries to policies consistent with the liberal state. Of course, this is also not a 100% safeguard, as the recent political and rule of law backsliding in some new member states, such as Hungary, Poland, and lately Slovakia, demonstrate. However, it makes deviation from the EU norms more difficult. Second, one needs to draw political science lessons from Orbán's power grab for the region: The less opportunity for concentration of power, the better. The Hungarian designers of the post-communist political system kept the negative experiences of the Weimar Republic strongly in their minds. They created a system tilted towards government stability—but at the expense of the ability to effectively counteract efforts towards monopolising political power. This arrangement was an important, albeit not exclusive, factor that allowed a political accident to happen in 2010: Orbán gained a constitutional majority and since then used his overpower to monopolise power.

In contrast, the Baltic states run a completely proportional political system. Although it causes a degree of political instability, in this period, avoiding monopoly seems to be more important than ensuring complete political stability. To look from another angle, as experience shows, tolerating a lower degree of political stability may lead to more system stability.[28] In a similar vein, the direct election of presidents also in parliamentary systems seems to be another safeguard, as was the case most visibly in Slovakia, where the popular election of Kisko and then of Čaputová halted the march of Fico to monopolising power and contributed to the survival of pluralism even if lately this function of the presidency may have

[28] This seemingly paradoxical possibility was pointed out to me by Bálint Magyar in a private conversation.

weakened.[29] Similarly, in the Czech Republic, the popular election of the President added pluralism to the system. Claus Iohannis's victory in Romania against Victor Ponta's rising fortunes also halted a dangerous concentration of power in one pair of hands.

Interfering in the political order of countries is a touchy issue. However, as far as we know, the greatest risk of reform reversal is twofold: concentration of power that can be achieved by one overwhelming electoral victory and consequently eliminating the checks and balances in the political and judicial system. Thus, this danger should be a special concern for the European Union. Almost equally important is the degree of market competition in the economy. The oligarchic concentration of market power is a threat to the liberal order because it can lead, again, to the concentration of political power. Ivanishvili's example shows that one can hijack the political system if the person has overwhelming economic power.

Sometimes, acting upon obvious usurpation of power requires courage from the European Union. Unfortunately, such courageous action rarely happens. Ivanishvili's usurpation of power and reduction of the democratic space has been well-known for many years; this is the case now with Vucic. Similarly, the EU did not act decisively when Yanukovich imprisoned his main political opponent while negotiating an association agreement. In Moldova, after a painful period of mismanagement, from 2015 onwards, the EU did better by preferring deeds over words. This change of tack was instrumental in ending Plahotniuc's monopoly of power in 2019. Within the Union, arguably, Orbán's monopolisation of power and geopolitical turn towards Russia and then also China was tolerated for about a decade. In politics, it is always a difficult art to find the right balance between principles and *realpolitik*, and we do not advocate always acting based purely on principles. However, it is difficult not to realise that the EU has been systematically erring on the side of being soft with the enemies of liberal democracy, a core value of the EU. We can no longer afford this attitude if we want to accommodate the political desire to enlarge the European Union.

In sum, the European Union needs to be intellectually prepared to gear the current (and future) accession countries towards irreversibility. Irreversibility should not mean that none of the reforms are contested by the countries' political processes but that institutional and cultural (values-based) safeguards prevent large-scale reform reversal.

[29] Explained in much detail in Széky (2015).

4.4 In-Between Integration Mechanisms on the Way to EU Accession

The twin principles of the rule of law and democracy cherished in the European Union constitute a critical public good for the continent, including its security, which is an area that has regained importance and focus recently. At the same time, the largest incentive for reform of East and South-East European countries is the perspective of EU membership, even more so than it was for the countries involved in the two previous accession rounds. Moreover, the newly emerging sensitivity to security risks requires rethinking, first of all, the entire European security architecture from the basics, but it may have implications for other European institutions and policies. To start with the trivial: if the members of the European Union have to spend 4, not 2% of their GDP on defence, it will have implications for the welfare sector as something will have to be given in. Even if the European Union rightly mutualises some of the increases in defence spending, it will have consequences for the member states' finances. Moreover, mutualising large chunks of debt for this purpose will also have an enormous impact on the whole European Union. This, however, goes out of the scope of this essay.

The best approach is, therefore, to be open to engaging in membership negotiations with candidate countries and have a positive view for future EU membership of those who cannot yet qualify for candidate status, but also to be very hard-nosed when it comes to fulfilling the accession criteria. At the same time, the European Union needs to establish bridging or interim mechanisms to meet the aspiring countries' security, economic, and other needs in a way that helps them integrate on a broad front. Such interim mechanisms would also serve European integration well if not everything worked ideally in the next few years regarding domestic and European reforms. They would facilitate a more gradual integration of these countries into the European Union and make them feel like they are part of the European family. The latter is critical regarding security matters that have gained significance since Russia started a war in Europe. The Franko-German paper rightly points out that "a more structured and conditional methodology for sectoral integration and a staged approach to participation rights in EU institutions still needs to be developed".[30]

[30] See in Franco-German Working Group (2023).

Also, simultaneously with the European Union integration process, decision-makers need to assess the interaction of this process with two others: on the one hand, how the relationship of these countries with NATO evolves and how the role of NATO and any EU-generated security capacity and functions in providing security for Europe will change. Regarding the latter, there are many unknowns. At this stage, it is difficult to judge what the American posture will be in the long term. Again, this is a far too complex question to discuss here in sufficient detail. Nonetheless, since one of the main drivers of European integration *is* security, we cannot omit it entirely. There is a complex, sometimes less visible, but still important interaction between the security and economic and political dimensions of European integration.

In the wake of the Russian invasion of Ukraine, President Macron initiated the establishment of the *European Political Community* (EPC) in May 2022 (Greene et al. 2023). The initiative targeted multiple goals. First, it was a quick response to the dilemma of this essay: how to foster integration with countries that are not yet ready to join the European Union but would want to integrate more closely with the EU because of their security concerns. Given Angela Merkel's withdrawal from the European political scene, Macron may also have seen an opportunity to take a more central role in European leadership. The stated areas of interest of the EPC include politics, security, energy, infrastructure, investment, and migration. These are meaningful (even if very broadly defined) areas where, theoretically, one could imagine close cooperation among countries that want to cooperate continent-wide. The problem is to fill the name with useful, practical content that does not replicate the roles of the European Union and NATO, and such that would address the vital interests of the countries not yet in the European Union. The initiative does not yet have financial resources. Thus, it is challenging to foster any integration that would serve as a bridge towards full EU membership, let alone a temporary substitute for this. The EPC has already organised four summits but has had no tangible results. While such a political organisation could be filled with content, it has not yet happened in practice. Therefore, it risks becoming insignificant over time and turning out to be yet another stillborn initiative.

Since the integration of the remaining part of Europe into the EU will take much longer than expected by the most optimistic ones, it would make sense to rely on the European Political Community to develop meaningful agendas for the areas mentioned above. Also, President Trump's policies, in a way, are forcing outsiders to seek coordinated international policies, and the EPC may be yet another useful forum for that. Besides, infrastructure, energy and migration are areas where pan-European thinking and concrete action could be beneficial. Regarding security, such a pan-European approach could evolve parallel with strengthening the EU's functions in this respect. In involving the EU in managing borders, EUBAM (European Union Border Assistance Mission to Moldova and Ukraine) and, to a more limited extent, EUMM's (EU Monitoring Mission in Georgia) experience could be very useful (Freire and Simão 2013).

However, the financing mechanism could and should be thought through. Since the EU and its rich member states will inevitably be the main sponsors of the enterprise and they also possess the best governance characteristics, the best way to approach the European Political Community would be to use it as a meeting, free exchange and project designing platform as well as regular events but keep the detailed project elaboration and financing within the EU with the active involvement of the non-EU European countries affected. It would be a mistake to dilute the EU's central governance role in this process.

If properly developed, this initiative could also serve as a useful feedback mechanism for the eventual full-fledged membership of ever more countries still outside the European Union. Such projects, if properly designed and implemented, bring the "outside" countries closer, thus exposing them to the generally favourable cultural impacts of the EU that are at the core of the integration.

At the same time, the European Union should pay increasing attention to NATO. With the Russian aggression, this is already a work in progress. NATO membership in Eastern Europe is both a security guarantee and a less strong and all-encompassing but still meaningful "liberal anchor" for these countries. At the same time, the European Union needs to work out scenarios for the possible approaches the United States can take to its NATO commitment. In other words, the EU should not initiate but should be ready to take over relatively fast vital defence functions if the United States wants to withdraw from certain aspects of the security umbrella. As an inevitable starter, Europe will need to spend more on its own defence. The continent will need much more to remain safe and avoid the possibility of being blackmailed strategically.

4.5 Conclusion

The dilemma we raised in this chapter will not be easy to resolve. How can we be ambitious about integration while remaining hard-nosed and not giving up on the principles? Political inertia before the 2022 Russian aggression worked against enlargement. Now, the situation is the opposite. Bureaucratic and political inertia work towards fast integration, so fast that it may lead us to overlook deficiencies, thus creating significant existential risks for the European Union.

We see the European Union as the core integration institution and platform on the continent, with a stellar contribution to peace and development over many decades. The primary public good that the EU provides to the entire continent is that it upholds the liberal principles of the free market, the rule of law, democracy, and humanity. Current internal conflicts teach us that we cannot compromise too much on these principles without paying an unacceptably high price. There is a limit to the extent of internal conflict the Union can carry on its shoulders.

In order to fulfil the historic task of integrating ambitiously but uncompromisingly, the EU will have to develop certain skills that are out of the current scope of its bureaucratic routine. The best of developmental science, the accumulated wisdom about fast institutional development, including assessing the accession and post-accession experiences, must be made available to and applied on the strategic heights of the EU and operationalised into bureaucratic routines. The fast evolution of non-EU countries towards EU compatibility, not so much in the sense of fast adoption of the acquis communautaire but more with a focus on the essence of the liberal state, requires that this knowledge permeates the strategic heights of the Union. At the same time, the EU will have to evolve its military security function rapidly, or else a different format should be used in order to safeguard the continent from a possible drifting away of the United States. But if it is a platform different from the EU, many additional questions emerge.

To achieve this integrational goal, we need a hard commodity: leadership. Large and important bureaucracies, such as those of the EU, quite legitimately and understandably work on the basis of routine, inertia and strict legality and change things slowly. But exceptional times still need considerate but much faster moves. However, that can only happen if strong leadership emerges, which then works as an engine of the process for an extended period of time, as this will be a long-distance run.

While we have pointed out the difficulties of further enlargement, we need to end our discussion by emphasising again that, first and foremost, we should look at this challenge as a huge opportunity. More than 60 million people now, and potentially even more in the near future, and their countries want to join the European Union. We must find a way to turn this aspiration into an impetus for the whole EU instead of allowing it to become another headache. Future member states can bring the lessons they learned from failed experiences of various socialisms and the capacity to face formidable challenges and be hardened by them. Moreover, their skilled people and competitive wages can help the EU meet new geopolitical and geoeconomic challenges.

References

Cherkasyn, V. & Dubrovskiy, V. (2024) Щодо оцінки досвіду різних країн з питань застосування спеціальних спрощених режимів оподаткування мікрота малого бізнесу. March 2024. Institut socialno-ekonomichnei Transformatsii and Ekonomiichna Ekspertna griupa.

Donnachie, L. (2024). How the Draghi report on European competitiveness lines up with investor recommendations. IIGCC, 19.0.24. https://www.iigcc.org/insights/draghi-report-on-european-eu-competitiveness-investor-net-zero-climate

Dubrovskiy, V., Mizsei, K., & Ivashchenko-Stadnik, K. (2024). *Eight Years After the Revolution of Dignity. What Has Changed in Ukraine During 2013–2021?* In collaboration with Wynnyckyj, M., ibidem Press.

Franco-German Working Group (2023). Sailing on High Seas: Reforming and Enlarging the EU for the 21st Century. Report of the Franco-German Working Group on EU Institutional Reform. Paris – Berlin, 18 September 2023. https://www.auswaertiges-amt.de/blob/2617206/4d0e0010ffcd8c0079e21329bbbb3332/230919-rfaa-deu-fra-bericht-data.pdf

Freire, M. R., & Simão, L. (2013). The EU's security actorness: the case of EUMM in Georgia. European Security, 22(4), 464–477. https://doi.org/10.1080/09662839.2013.808191

Galeotti, M. (2018). *The Vory: Russia's Supermafia*. Yale University Press, New Haven and London.

Gobble, P. (2024). 1991 Borders in Post-Soviet Space No Longer 'Sacred,' Markedonov Says. 5 July 2024. https://windowoneurasia2.blogspot.com/2024/07/1991-borders-in-post-soviet-space-no.html

Grabbe, H. (2006). *The EU's Transformative Power: Europeanization Through Conditionality in Central and Eastern Europe*, Basingstoke: Palgrave Macmillan.

Greene, S., Lucas, E., & Tenzer, N. (2023). The Road to Chişinău: The European Political Community. CEPA. Insights and Analyses. 23 May, 2023. https://cepa.org/comprehensive-reports/the-road-to-chisinau-the-european-political-community/

Grieveson, R., Grübler, J., & Holzner, M. (2018). Western Balkans EU Accession: Is the 2025 Target Date Realistic? Policy Notes and Reports No. 22, The Vienna Institute for International Economic Studies (wiiw), Vienna. https://hdl.handle.net/10419/204265

Grieveson, R. & Jovanovic, B. (2025). Growing challenges and ways forward in light of the war in Ukraine and regional tensions in the Western Balkans. In: Székely, I. P. and Halmai, P. (eds) *The Future of European Integration*, Palgrave Macmillan, forthcoming.

Hale, H. E. (2014). *Patronal Politics. Eurasian Regime Dynamics in Comparative Perspective*. Cambridge University Press.

Kochenov, D., & Pech, L. (2015). Monitoring and Enforcement of the Rule of Law in the EU: Rhetoric and Reality. *European Constitutional Law Review*, 11(3), 512–540. https://doi.org/10.1017/S1574019615000358

Kuzio, T. (2015). *Ukraine: Democratization, Corruption, and the New Russian Imperialism*. Praeger.

Macron, E. (2024). Europe—It Can Die. A New Paradigm. Speech made at the Sorbonne. https://geopolitique.eu/en/2024/04/26/macron-europe-it-can-die-a-new-paradigm-at-the-sorbonne/

Magyar, B. & Madlovics, B. (2020). *The Anatomy of Post-Communist Regimes. A Conceptual Framework*. Central European University Press, 2020.

Minakov, M. (2024). War, De-oligarchization, and the Possibility of Anti-Patronal Transformation in Ukraine. In: Madlovics & Magyar (2024), pp. 141-165. https://doi.org/10.1515/9789633866641_CH05

Mizsei, K. (2019). The New East European Patronal States and the Rule-of-Law. In: Bálint Magyar, *Stubborn Structures. Reconceptualizing Post-Communist Regimes*. Central European University Press, 2019.

Mizsei, K. (2024). In the Gravitational Tensions of East and West: The Systemic and Geopolitical Integration Patterns of Ukraine and Moldova. In: Madlovics & Magyar (2024), pp. 127-163. https://doi.org/10.1515/9789633866528_CH06

North, D., Wallis, J., & Weingast, B. (2009). Violence and Social Orders: A Conceptual Framework for Interpreting Recorded Human History. Cambridge; Cambridge University Press.

O'Rourke, K. H. & Williamson, J. G. (1999). *Globalization and History: The Evolution of a Nineteenth-Century Atlantic Economy*, MIT Press, 1999.

Pech, L. (2022). The Rule of Law as a Well-Established and Well-Defined Principle of EU Law. *Hague J Rule Law* 14, 107–138. https://doi.org/10.1007/s40803-022-00176-8

Pingen, A. (2022). Key Proposals from the Conference on the Future of Europe in the Area of Values, Rule of Law & Security https://eucrim.eu/news/key-proposals-from-the-conference-on-the-future-of-europe-in-the-area-of-values-rule-of-law-security/ Accessed on 25 May 2024.

Politico (2024). European Commission maps out 'power grab' over €1.2T money pot, 5 October, 2024. https://www.politico.eu/article/european-commission-budget-economic-reforms-conditions-power-grab/?fbclid=IwY2xjawFuGoVleHRuA2FlbQIxMQABHWCPwqiplvb-UJYAgK7gidk_Sz5BJEEehdfRidKQHIg1sL5Wt4cD87lOpw_aem_pIO-ka61GTt-SI1ergxszYw

Schoenefeld, J.J., Schulze, K., Hildén, M. et al. (2019). Policy Monitoring in the EU: The Impact of Institutions, Implementation, and Quality. Polit Vierteljahresschr 60, 719–741. https://doi.org/10.1007/s11615-019-00209-2

Silenská, N. (2024). EU mulls freezing Slovakia's funds for rule of law violations, EURACTIV Slovakia, Sep 9, 2024. https://www.euractiv.com/news/eu-mulls-freezing-slovakias-funds-for-rule-of-law-violations/

Széky, J. (2015). *Bárányvakság*, Kalligram, Budapest-Pozsony.

Thisell, T. (2022). Orbán's Election Victory Sheds New Light on the 'Copenhagen Dilemma', www.idea.int, May 09, 2022. https://www.idea.int/blog/orbans-election-victory-sheds-new-light-copenhagen-dilemma

CHAPTER 5

Growing Challenges and Ways Forward in Light of the War in Ukraine and Regional Tensions in the Western Balkans

Richard Grieveson and Branimir Jovanović

5.1 Introduction

Since Croatia's accession in 2013, the EU enlargement process has rather stalled, so that some Western Balkan countries have now spent two decades in the waiting room. No country will join before 2030 at the very earliest, and for some it is likely to be much longer than that. As the EU justifiably celebrates 20 successful years following the 'big bang' enlargement of 2004, it should also reflect on why, 21 years after the promises of Thessaloniki, six Western Balkan countries remain so far away from joining the EU.

The lack of a firm accession perspective has held back the Western Balkans economically. Meanwhile regional economic integration, which once held out such promise, has delivered relatively little. The enlargement process now takes much longer than in the past, yet adequate economic measures have not been put in place to take account of this. If

R. Grieveson (✉) • B. Jovanović
The Vienna Institute for International Economic Studies (wiiw), Vienna, Austria
e-mail: grieveson@wiiw.ac.at; jovanovic@wiiw.ac.at

I. P. Székely, P. Halmai (eds.), *The Future of European Integration*, Studies in Economic Transition,
https://doi.org/10.1007/978-3-032-20186-7_5

enlargement continues to proceed at a snail's pace, there is a risk that this development gap could continue to widen, and that many of the aspirations of Ukraine and Moldova will also fail to be fulfilled. That could lead to the kind of disillusionment now evident in many Western Balkan countries. The Russian invasion of Ukraine has reinvigorated the enlargement process, yet it also brings with it fresh risks.

This chapter first examines the state of play and outlines the main ways in which the slow (or non-existent) enlargement process in the Western Balkans has contributed to the region's economic underdevelopment and its failure to make significant progress on the main territorial and constitutional disputes. Second, it looks at the new issues and challenges faced by the region, including the 'bilateralization' of the enlargement process. Third, it examines the region's past and current growth model, and identifies some of the gaps and shortcomings that need to be addressed. Fourth, it considers the impact of Russia's invasion of Ukraine on the enlargement process, taking into account the growing geo-economic competition that the EU is facing in Southeast Europe. And finally, it makes some suggestions for the way forward, including how to kick-start the enlargement process and catalyse economic development in the Western Balkans.

5.2 Old Issues

Since the 'big bang' enlargement of 2004, most of the countries that joined the EU that year and in 2007 and 2013 have made significant progress in catching up with Western Europe in terms of their economic development. In 2003, the 11 countries of Central and Eastern Europe (CEE) that are now EU members had GDP per capita (at purchasing power parity (PPP)) that was 42% of the Austrian level. By 2023 that had risen to 64%. Within this general picture, the cases of Romania (24% in 2003 to 63% by 2023), Poland (38% to 63%), Estonia (41% to 66%) and Lithuania (38% to 70%) offer particularly striking and successful examples of convergence.

The Western Balkan countries have had nothing like this kind of economic transformation over the same period (Fig. 5.1). In 2003, they averaged 20% of the Austrian GDP per capita (at PPP). Although this had risen to 31% by 2023, indicating a relative gain similar to that of the EU-CEE countries, the Western Balkan increase occurred from a much lower starting point on average. This means both that the absolute gains in economic development were much less, and that something must have gone

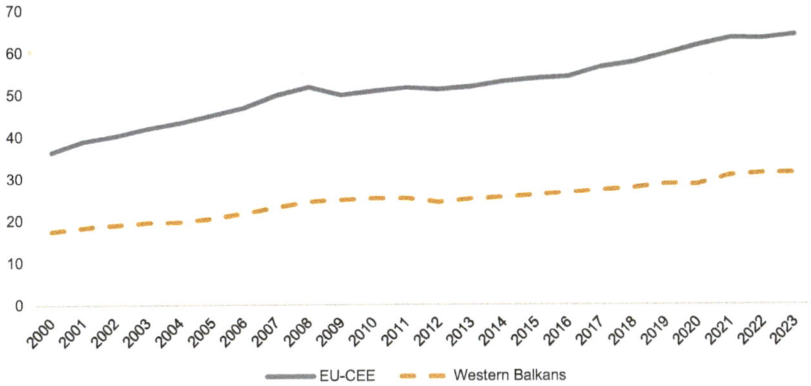

Fig. 5.1 GDP per capita at PPP, Austria = 100. Note: Simple averages. (Sources: Eurostat, national sources, wiiw)

badly wrong. Given the low level of economic development, the Western Balkans should have had much more 'low-hanging fruit' to pick; and as part of its EU integration process, the region should therefore have been able to achieve greater relative convergence than the more advanced EU-CEE countries.

The answer to this apparently confusing picture lies in the terms of the EU integration process: for the Western Balkans, those terms have been—and remain—different from those of the EU-CEE countries. EU integration and accession is an economically transformative process, as the cases of Poland and Romania emphatically underline. However, this economic transformation rests on a confluence of factors and drivers of growth, none of which has been fully applied to the Western Balkans in the same way as it was to EU-CEE. In particular, four factors stand out to explain the relative lack of economic transformation in the Western Balkans over the past two decades. All are closely related to one another.

First, the credibility of the EU enlargement process itself, which is of central importance in incentivizing the tough reforms required for the EU's *acquis communautaire* to be adopted. The reforms initiated by the 2004 joiners in the run-up to accession had a significant transformative effect on their economies, providing clear economic benefits. Especially for those 2004 joiners, EU enlargement was supported by a clear political commitment to get those countries into the EU (Anghel and Jones 2022). In the Western Balkans, that political commitment has been lacking—at least until very recently, in the wake of the Russian invasion of Ukraine. Greece's decades-long blockage of North Macedonia's accession due to the country's name; the EU's inward turn after the global financial and euro area crises, culminating in then-Commission President Jean-Claude Juncker's enlargement 'pause' speech; French President Macron's '*Non*'; subsequent Bulgarian vetoes on North Macedonia for issues unrelated to the conditions of EU accession; and the EU's acceptance of *stabilitocracy* (i.e. reducing the pressure to reform, in return for stability—see BiEPAG 2017) in countries such as Serbia—all these provide examples of this lack of commitment. As a result, the momentum towards an enlargement that all see as credible has been missing, and progress towards reform has been slow at best. As many have quipped, the countries of the Western Balkans have been pretending to follow the accession process, and the EU has been pretending to accept them. The result is that no economically transformative reforms have been achieved in the Western Balkans.

The second key factor for the Western Balkans has been the lack of transformative inflows of foreign direct investment (FDI). For the 2004 joiners, large-scale FDI inflows started to arrive in the years preceding accession, as outside investors saw the reforms being implemented and believed in the credibility of the process. This FDI-driven model has its critics, and it seems to be approaching its limits for the most advanced EU-CEE countries (Bykova et al. 2021), yet it has provided an important source of capital and has driven a serious upgrade in productivity and external competitiveness among the EU-CEE countries. Several of those countries' export sectors are now ranked among the most sophisticated in the world.[1] In the years preceding and immediately following EU accession, the EU-CEE countries generally ran big current account deficits, just as the Western Balkan countries do today. However, as high-quality FDI inflows into manufacturing led to a highly competitive export sector, those large current account deficits have all but disappeared. While the Western Balkan countries have also been able to attract a lot of FDI relative to their GDP, especially in more recent years, this has not had the same transformative impact.

In part, this is because these 'large' FDI inflows are being measured as a share of a very low GDP: the six Western Balkan countries have a combined GDP roughly equal to that of Slovakia. This can also be seen when the inward FDI stock is measured by head of population: again, the

[1] See https://atlas.cid.harvard.edu/

Western Balkan countries significantly underperform many EU-CEE countries. However, it also needs to be said that the Western Balkans have struggled to attract the same quality of FDI as EU-CEE countries (Hunya et al. 2017). The big investments in large manufacturing plants that the Visegrád countries have succeeded in attracting—investments that have created thousands of jobs and that often include some research and development (R&D) and other functions—are generally conspicuous by their absence in the Western Balkans. The main reason why the Western Balkans has struggled to attract higher-quality FDI flows is that their governments have not prioritized the quality of the FDI arriving in their countries; instead, they have focused on attracting *any and all* FDI, and have billed their countries as low-cost destinations with cheap labour and low taxes. Weak institutional factors, declining educational standards and poor infrastructure have deterred reputable companies. The lack of credibility of the EU accession process and the weak progress on reforms outlined above have not helped either.

The third key factor in the weaker economic development in the Western Balkans over the last 20 years has been the lack of EU funds. As candidate and potential candidate countries, the Western Balkans have had access to funding under the Instrument for Pre-Accession Assistance (IPA)—typically around 1% of GDP per year (Jovanović et al. 2022). By contrast, the EU-CEE countries have received flows from the EU budget of up to 5% of GDP per year, and generally in the range of 2–3%. Compounded over 20 years, this makes an enormous difference. Moreover, the inflow of EU funds into EU-CEE countries has been the main source of finance for public infrastructure, which has enabled a significant upgrading of transport infrastructure, in particular.

Beyond the direct impact on the quality of infrastructure and the level of growth, these EU funds have played two very important roles in supporting economic transformation in the EU-CEE countries. First, the prospect of EU funds on this scale was one of the reasons that EU membership was so attractive, and what made it possible to invest significant political capital in often difficult reforms pre-2004. No such 'carrot' for reforms has existed, or currently exists, to incentivize reforms in the Western Balkans. Second, the upgrading of (especially) transport infrastructure has been important in attracting large, high-quality FDI inflows, as referenced in the point above.

The final major barrier to the Western Balkans's economic transformation and EU integration over the last 20 years has been the tensions within the region itself. Resolving these issues, especially those between Serbia and Kosovo, has been set as a condition of accession by the EU. To attempt to achieve this, the EU has invested huge resources in 'regional cooperation', an umbrella term that covers thousands of initiatives that are driven both by the EU and by the people, organizations and governments of the region. The EU's goal was to achieve 'change through trade', meaning that deepening economic integration would itself be a driver of positive political change.

To be clear, although it currently has a bad name (given the shattered EU—and especially German—economic approach to Russia), change through trade can work, and it is no surprise that the EU instinctively pushes this approach. After all, the bloc is probably the most successful example in history of change through trade, starting with the integration initiatives linking France and Germany from the late 1940s.

Yet in the case of the Western Balkans, the initiatives for regional economic integration have never been followed up by similar initiatives for political cooperation; and the lack of political cooperation has often created obstacles to greater economic cooperation. As a result, despite the heavy investment of time and resources in regional cooperation initiatives, the key constitutional and territorial disputes in the region (Serbia–Kosovo and within Bosnia and Herzegovina) appear as intractable as ever. Meanwhile, in recent years regional cooperation seems to have splintered, leading to a German-led Berlin Process and a Serbian-led Open Balkan initiative. This has created a sense of overlap and of uncertain direction.

The reason this approach has not worked is that most of the prerequisites for it to work do not exist. As stated earlier, change through trade can work; but it does rely on certain political, institutional and economic prerequisites (Weiss et al. 2020).

First, politically, the countries pursuing regional cooperation need to form a unified group; and it helps to have a single outside threat to propel the process along. For Germany and France in the late 1940s, these conditions were met; but for the Western Balkans (and maybe especially for Serbia) they are not.

Second, institutionally, there needs to be a strong outside force coordinating and maintaining momentum; some degree of local ownership; an absence of territorial issues (or a realistic path to solving them); a functional political relationship and a reasonable level of trust between the partners; and decent institutional and governance standards among everyone involved. While the first two of these are somewhat true in the case of the Western Balkans, the final three clearly are not.

Finally, economically, the proposed economic area for integration should be of a size and potential to make all participants feel as though they will get something in return for their investment of political capital; current trade and investment between the parties should be low by historical standards; the importance of economic relationships within the region versus those outside the region should be roughly equal for all parties; there should be a degree of complementarity in production structures; and there should be some willingness to coordinate development and other economic policies. Again, most (or all) of these conditions have not been met in the Western Balkans over the past two decades.

In this context, it should come as no great surprise that the rather limited 'carrots' afforded by regional integration and a barely moving EU accession process have not been enough to resolve (or even to make significant progress on) the region's most intractable constitutional and territorial disputes. Of these, the two that are most serious in terms of preventing EU accession from moving forward are those within Bosnia and Herzegovina and between Serbia and Kosovo. Almost 30 years on from the Dayton Agreement that ended the war in Bosnia and Herzegovina, and 25 years after the NATO bombing of Yugoslavia that terminated the war in Kosovo, both seem intractable. While the absence of a renewed outbreak of large-scale fighting must in itself be welcome, to an extent this rests on the continued presence of NATO soldiers in the region. Serbia–Kosovo relations are, at the time of writing, at a multi-year low, while Bosnia and Herzegovina remains constitutionally paralysed. Citizens themselves do not feel any great animosity towards each other: in the 2023 Balkan Barometer, 69% of respondents from the region said they agreed that 'what brings Western Balkans citizens together is more important than what separates them'.[2] Yet many regional politicians appear to have decided that animosity suits their purposes. Here, clearly, change through trade has not worked. These issues remain a barrier to the EU accession prospects of all three countries, and indirectly of the whole region.

[2] https://www.rcc.int/balkanbarometer/key_findings/2/

5.3 New Tensions

Tensions in the region have soared in the last two years, particularly in and around Kosovo. Following the Serbs' boycott of the local elections in April 2023, ethnic Albanian mayors were installed in four municipalities with a Serb majority population. This action was met with fierce resistance from the local Serb community and with protests that escalated into violent clashes. Later in the year, a firefight in the village of Banjska resulted in four casualties, an incident that the Kosovo authorities have described as a terrorist attack. At the beginning of 2024, the Kosovo authorities decided to ban the use of the Serbian dinar throughout Kosovo—a move that encountered significant opposition from the Serbs, many of whom receive their salaries and pensions in dinars from Serbian institutions and who view this as a direct assault on their community.

At the heart of all this lies the unresolved status of Kosovo and the Serb-majority municipalities there. Kosovo, historically a province of Serbia but with a predominantly ethnic Albanian population, unilaterally declared independence in 2008. The move has been recognized by over 100 countries, including the United States and most European Union members; but Serbia, along with Russia and China, has never acknowledge the territory's independence, which has effectively prevented Kosovo from joining the United Nations and other international organizations. To address the status of the territory, the EU facilitated the so-called Brussels Agreement of 2013 between the Serbian and Kosovan authorities. This sought to normalize relations by establishing a governance framework for Serb-majority municipalities in northern Kosovo—the so-called Association of Serb-majority Municipalities (ASM). The agreement also set up cooperation mechanisms in areas such as policing, the judiciary and civil protection across the whole territory of Kosovo. It aimed to balance autonomy and protection for the Serb-majority areas with their integration into Kosovo's legal system. The move was supposed to satisfy both sides, as they were both getting something.

However, the Kosovo authorities never fulfilled their obligation to establish the ASM, citing legal obstacles. Specifically, in 2015, Kosovo's Constitutional Court ruled that certain provisions of the Brussels Agreement related to the creation of the ASM were unconstitutional, and expressed some concern about the potential it offered for the creation of an autonomous parallel structure. Behind this formal justification (which could be addressed in various ways, including by amending the constitution) lie deeper and more fundamental issues: the ethnic Albanian majority views the ASM as a potential threat to the country's territorial integrity and sovereignty. They fear that it could grant the Serb-majority regions significant autonomy, and potentially align them more closely with Serbia.

Serbia, dissatisfied with the Kosovo authorities' failure to establish the ASM—a mechanism it views as essential for protecting the cultural, political and social rights of Serbs in Kosovo –has continued to actively oppose Kosovo's attempts to gain international recognition and membership of key bodies. Leveraging diplomatic ties with allies like Russia and China, it has blocked Kosovo's entry to UNESCO and INTERPOL.

The failure of the Brussels Agreement to achieve significant progress in terms of normalizing relations between Serbia and Kosovo led to the Ohrid Agreement of 2023. This new agreement aims to overcome some of the limitations of the Brussels Agreement: it includes an undertaking by Serbia not to block Kosovo's attempts to join international organizations, while Kosovo recommits itself to working towards establishing the ASM. Although it has never officially been signed by either side, EU officials have repeatedly stated that the agreement is still legally binding on both parties. However, it has once again failed to achieve its objectives, since both sides have violated the agreement—Kosovo by still not even trying to establish the ASM, and Serbia by repeatedly obstructing Kosovo's efforts to join the Council of Europe.

While in theory the Ohrid Agreement holds out some promise, its main limitation lies in the absence of a detailed implementation plan that specifies concrete steps and deadlines. This vagueness provides leeway for both sides to potentially breach the agreement, citing non-compliance by the other party. Consequently, Serbia often accuses Kosovo of not establishing the ASM and uses this as a pretext to frustrate Kosovo's efforts to join international organizations. Conversely, Kosovo points to Serbian obstruction as a rationale for not setting up the ASM. To effectively overcome these challenges, a clear roadmap is essential. It should outline a precise sequence of steps for each party, complete with a strict timeline, and should include both rewards and sanctions for compliance or non-compliance. These incentives and penalties could be either financial—such as the release or withholding of EU funds—or non-financial, like granting Kosovo membership of the Council of Europe or influencing the progress of Serbia's EU accession negotiations by opening or closing specific negotiation chapters.

Closely related to the issue of Kosovo are the sporadic tensions in Bosnia and Herzegovina over the status of Republika Srpska. Political leaders in this Serb-majority entity occasionally voice demands for greater autonomy, or even outright secession. However, these issues differ significantly from those in Kosovo. Most of the time, the tensions in Republika Srpska serve a domestic political agenda, such as diverting attention from local issues or fostering nationalism to secure political advantage. Unlike in Kosovo, where the Serb population feels profoundly disgruntled and threatened, there is no widespread dissatisfaction among Serbs in Bosnia and Herzegovina regarding the status of Republika Srpska. Its status affords a considerable degree of autonomy and protects the interests of the Serbs there. As a matter of fact, the Kosovo authorities frequently reference Republika Srpska as a model that they wish to avoid, arguing that it grants the Serb community excessive power.

It is also very important to understand that the tensions in Republika Srpska are often influenced by the unresolved status of Kosovo. Serbs in the region perceive themselves to be treated unfairly by the international community and use Republika Srpska to air their grievances. Moreover, on a tactical political level, Serbian leaders leverage the situation there to enhance their bargaining power, hinting that unresolved issues in Kosovo could lead to problems in the wider region. Consequently, resolution of the Kosovo issue is likely to ease tensions in Bosnia and Herzegovina as well.

EU membership has substantial potential to reduce these and other regional tensions, largely by diminishing the importance of national borders and facilitating free movement, along with the adoption of common policies and regulations. However, the EU accession prospects for the region have been significantly stalled, initially by French President Macron's call in 2019 for a pause on the issue of enlargement, in order to reform the accession framework (European Council 2019; Herszenhorn 2019). This delayed the start of EU accession negotiations for Albania and North Macedonia that year, effectively halting the momentum towards enlargement. The following year, when the new framework was enforced (which incidentally did not differ markedly from the previous framework), Bulgaria vetoed North Macedonia's accession talks, citing unresolved historical and cultural disputes. That veto also delayed Albania's accession process, as the EU preferred to advance negotiations with both countries concurrently.

After a period of stagnation and intensive diplomatic efforts, 2022 saw a revival in EU accession dynamics for North Macedonia and Albania, thanks to a new initiative known as the French Proposal. As a condition for EU accession negotiations to commence, North Macedonia was required to amend the preamble to its constitution so as to recognize the Bulgarian minority. Additionally, North Macedonia had to address several Bulgarian demands regarding historical and cultural issues, and to embark on the standard reforms required for EU accession. While the agreement effectively gives the Bulgarian side the power to block North Macedonia's EU accession if it believes that some of the bilateral conditions are not being met, the government of North Macedonia accepted the proposal in July 2022. This acceptance formally restarted the accession process for both North Macedonia and Albania.

However, two years on from the French Proposal, North Macedonia is still light-years away from meeting its obligation to amend its constitution—the stumbling block being the absence of a majority in parliament in favour of the change. Furthermore, there is no indication that any such majority will emerge in the near future. And even if one were to appear and approve the proposal, that would merely herald the start of accession talks; there would be no assurance that the Bulgarian side would not potentially raise new obstacles.

This 'bilateralization' of the EU accession talks not only has stalled North Macedonia's progress towards EU membership, but also threatens to set a very dangerous precedent. If Bulgaria can weaponize its EU membership to extract concessions from North Macedonia on sensitive issues like history, language and culture, what is to prevent Croatia, for example, from doing the same to Serbia; or Hungary to Ukraine? Such exploitation of the accession process risks perverting a mechanism designed for integration and peace, so that it becomes a tool of political manipulation and coercion. One cannot help but wonder: how does this align with the EU's foundational principles of cooperation and mutual respect?

All these developments have led to rising disillusionment with the EU in Western Balkan societies. According to the Balkan Barometer public opinion survey, for years support for the EU increased steadily in the region—right up until 2021, when it peaked. That year, 62% of people in the region said EU membership would be good for their economy, and just 8% thought it would be bad. That was a significant improvement on 2016, when 41% thought the EU would be beneficial, and 21% considered it would be damaging. However, since 2021 the trend has been reversed, and support for the EU in the Western Balkans has declined steadily in recent years. In 2023 (the latest available year), the percentage of people who considered that the EU would be good for the economy declined to 59%, while the figure for those who thought it would be bad rose to 11% (Fig. 5.2). The magnitude of the decline may be small, and a majority of the people may still favour the EU; but the reversal of the trend is clear and should not be taken lightly. It could indicate that the region's EU accession may not proceed so smoothly.

Disillusionment in the region has, as in many other parts of Europe, engendered populism. However, populism is particularly challenging to define and recognize in the Western Balkans, due to both the region's socialist past and its nationalist present. During the socialist era, policies frequently invoked the 'people', understood in a socialist context as the masses or the populace. Following the fall of socialism and the emergence of nation states in the region, the term 'people' began to be used in a nationalist sense, with the narrative often framed as protecting one's own people against the perceived threats posed by others in the region. Despite

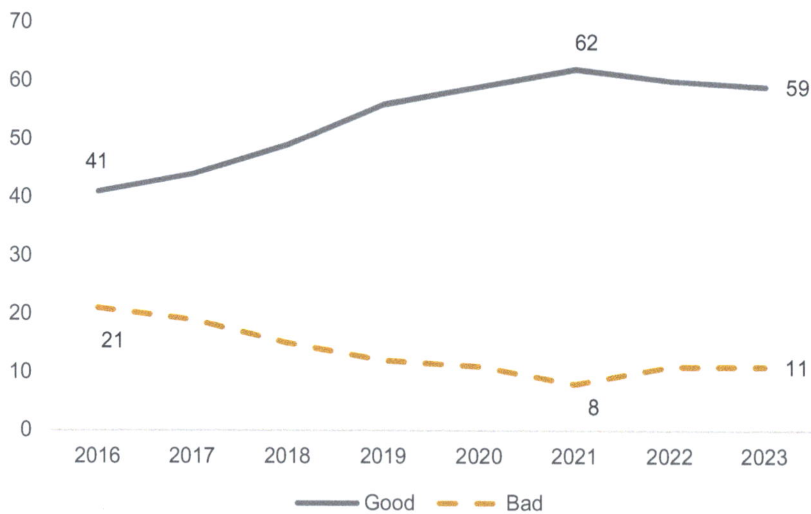

Fig. 5.2 Do you think that EU membership would be a good thing or a bad thing for your economy? % of responses, 2016–2023. (Source: Balkan Barometers 2016–2023, Regional Cooperation Council)

these complexities, it is increasingly clear that populism, as understood in the modern Western context, is on the rise in the Western Balkans as well.

The current political leadership in Serbia, Kosovo and Republika Srpska can clearly be categorized as right-wing populist, characterized as it is by language that focuses on defending the *ethnos* against others in the region and by economic policies that, at least rhetorically, oppose foreign elites. The rise of right-wing populism in the Western Balkans poses similar dangers as are visible elsewhere in the Western world: the capture of the state by ruling politicians; the abuse of public power for personal gain; the undermining of institutions; and the erosion of fundamental pillars of modern democracy, such as freedom of expression.

5.4 The Region's Growth Model

The lack of EU accession and the numerous regional tensions are not the only obstacles in the path of the Western Balkans' efforts to improve living standards. The region is also grappling with substantial economic challenges. As was already mentioned, the Western Balkan economies remain significantly less developed than their peers in Central, East, and Southeast Europe. As of 2023, only Montenegro had GDP per capita (in PPP terms) close to 50% of the EU average; the others were well below, with Kosovo, Bosnia and Herzegovina and Albania all at approximately 30% of the EU level. This is substantially lower than in neighbouring Balkan EU member states, such as Romania, Croatia and Bulgaria. Even Bulgaria, the least developed of these, had GDP per capita of 64% of the EU average, considerably higher than Montenegro's (Fig. 5.3).

Even more concerning than the level of GDP itself is the pace of convergence. Between 2000 and 2023, Montenegro (the best-performing Western Balkan country) increased its GDP per capita from 27% of the EU average to 50%—a gain of 23 percentage points. But in the same period, Croatia—the *worst-performing* EU member state in the region—saw a rise of 25 percentage points (to 76% of the EU level). Romania experienced an impressive gain of 52 percentage points, while Bulgaria improved by 35 points. In contrast, Kosovo improved by just 9 percentage points, while the other four Western Balkan economies each improved by around 15 points.

To further illustrate the slow pace of convergence: in 2000, Bulgaria had a comparable level of development as Montenegro, Serbia and North Macedonia, each hovering at around 27–29% of the EU average. By 2023,

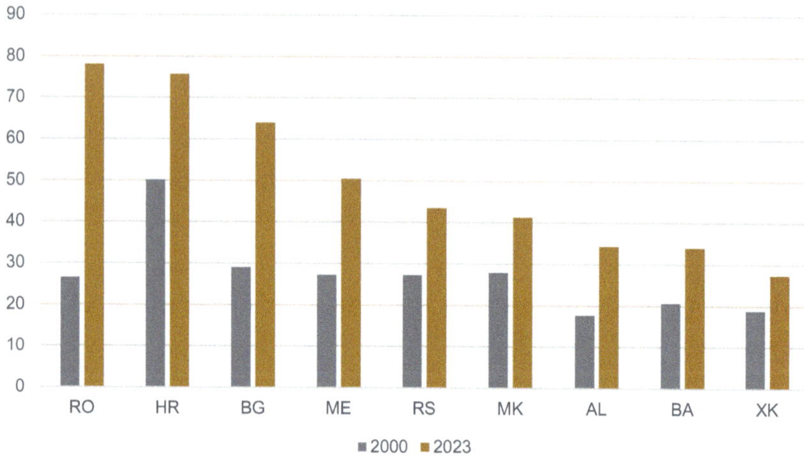

Fig. 5.3 GDP per capita PPP, as % of EU27 level. (Source: wiiw)

Bulgaria had surged to 64%, while Montenegro, Serbia and North Macedonia languished in the 40–50% range.

It is not just that growth has been low; it has also been uneven. Poverty has remained very high in the region—among the highest in the whole of Europe (see Fig. 5.4). In 2022, the share of people at risk of poverty or social exclusion in Albania was over 45%, with Montenegro on 38%. North Macedonia and Serbia also ranked poorly, with rates of between 30% and 33%. While Bulgaria, Romania and Turkey have similarly high rates of 33–35%, most other Eastern European countries have fared better, with shares of 25% or less.

Poor economic performance and a failure to improve living standards mean that the Western Balkans have experienced a significant population decline, driven primarily by emigration. Between 2000 and 2023, Serbia, Albania, North Macedonia and Bosnia and Herzegovina each lost 10–12% of their population. While some more developed Eastern European EU member states faced even more substantial declines—Bulgaria and Latvia lost over 20% of their population—the declines in the Western Balkans are nonetheless significant (Fig. 5.5). Even Montenegro and Kosovo, which overall saw population increases during this period, have recently seen a reversal of the trend and have begun to experience population decline.

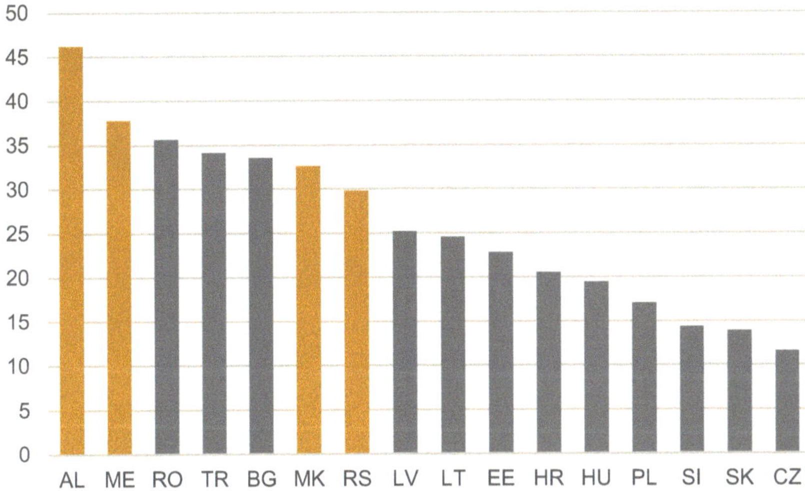

Fig. 5.4 Persons at risk of poverty or social exclusion in 2022 or last available year, as % of total population. (Source: Eurostat)

The economic, social, political and cultural consequences of population decline are profound and far-reaching, and deserve thorough examination in their own right. However, from an economic standpoint, one of the most troubling issues is the creation of a vicious cycle. Population decline restricts economic growth, on account of the reduced labour force and diminished consumer demand. It also hampers public services, as governments must allocate a larger proportion of their budgets to pensions and healthcare, in order to support an ageing population; that leaves fewer resources available for other public services. As growth diminishes and public services deteriorate, so they contribute to further emigration, which only serves to exacerbate the problem. A declining population thus contributes to lower economic growth and reduced quality of public services, which in turn accelerates population decline through increased emigration.

Many of these problems can be traced back to the economic model that the Western Balkan economies adopted after the fall of socialism. That model was based on deregulation and minimal state interference, and it relied heavily on the private sector, especially foreign investors. To attract and support these investors, policies focused on maintaining low taxation and wages. Consequently, governments have remained small, which has

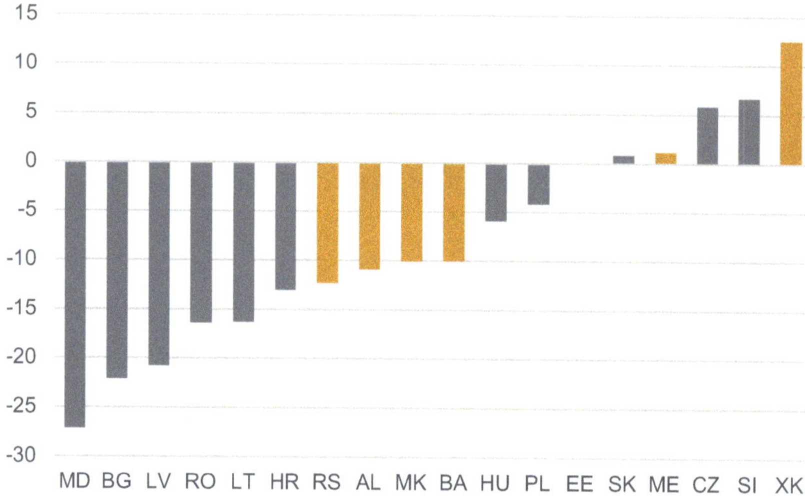

Fig. 5.5 Population change between 2000 and 2023, in %. (Source: wiiw)

resulted in limited spending on public goods, such as education, healthcare and infrastructure (Figs. 5.6 and 5.7). This has led to significant underinvestment across the region and has simultaneously stifled the development of what economists often call 'human capital', thereby restricting the potential for sustainable economic growth and development.

The primary economic focus of policy makers in the region has been to attract FDI, with the expectation that higher FDI will lead to stronger growth, increased employment, poverty reduction and overall improvements in well-being. Indeed, the Western Balkan economies have been among the best in Eastern Europe in terms of FDI inflows as a share of GDP (Fig. 5.8). While FDI inflows have brought some benefits (see, e.g., Jovanović and Hanzl-Weiss 2022), they have proved insufficient to drive significant GDP growth on their own. Those countries in receipt of the largest inflows of FDI have not been the fastest growing; and those countries with the highest growth rates have not received spectacular amounts of FDI (Fig. 5.9).

Over recent decades, as the region has striven for high economic growth, one of the perennial bugbears has been the dearth of substantial domestic investment in most of its countries. To some extent, this has been down to certain well-known institutional problems, such as the

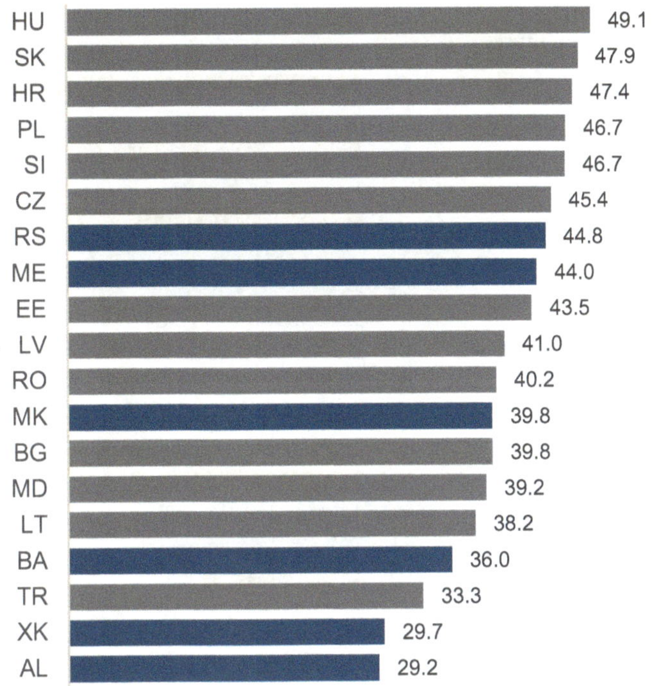

Fig. 5.6 General government expenditure in 2023, as % of GDP. (Source: wiiw)

rampant corruption and the weak rule of law; however, to a large extent it has also been due to the absence of any effective industrial policy in the region over the past 30 years. While the last decade has seen certain changes on this score, effective industrial and innovation policies are still few and far between (see Jovanović and Vujanović 2023). This continues to hamper homegrown industrial growth and innovation, both of which are essential for strong economic development.

Thus, it is perhaps time for the Western Balkan economies to reconsider their current economic model and explore alternatives. A shift towards a model centred on robust industrial and innovation policies could stimulate domestic private investment. At the same time, boosting public investment in infrastructure and green energy, along with enhanced spending on public goods and services such as education, healthcare and social

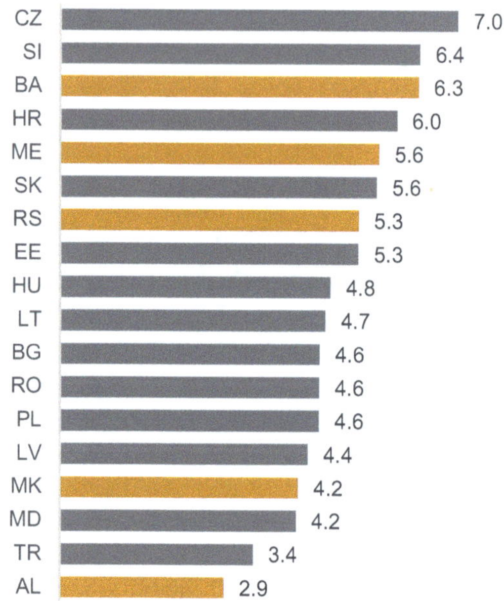

Fig. 5.7 General government expenditure on healthcare in 2017–2021, as % of GDP. (Source: World Bank)

protection, could further drive economic growth, while at the same time fostering the development of 'human capital'. To finance these initiatives, a more progressive taxation regime and greater redistribution may be necessary. Taken together, these pillars could promote more equitable growth and development across the region, potentially reversing the negative trends observed over recent decades.

5.5 The War in Ukraine

Russia's full-scale of invasion of Ukraine and its fallout have generated renewed energy around EU enlargement. EU accession is always a balance between conditionality and geopolitics, but the latter has been the driving force of enlargement over the past two years. For many in the EU, Russia's invasion has been a wake-up call and has underlined the kind of threat that the EU itself could face in an atmosphere of rising geopolitical competition. Perhaps the best illustration of this is the change in the position of French President Emmanuel Macron. Pre-invasion he described NATO as 'brain dead', vetoed the start of accession talks with North Macedonia and

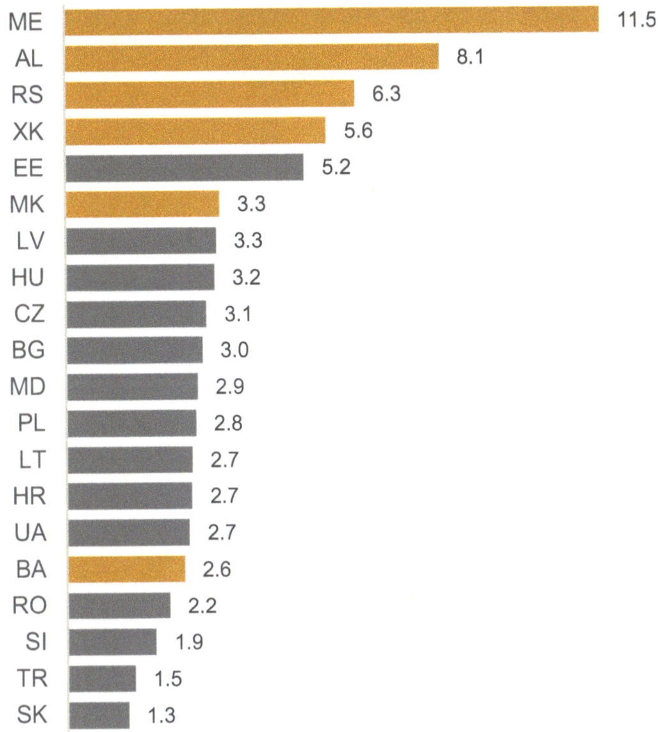

Fig. 5.8 Average annual FDI inflows 2000–2023, as % of GDP. (Source: wiiw)

Albania, and positioned himself as someone who could do business with Russian President Vladimir Putin. Only a couple of years later, he has recognized enlargement as a geopolitical necessity, and has gone further than any other Western leader in refusing to rule out sending French soldiers to Ukraine. For those who see the enlargement of the EU not only as a moral imperative, but also as a geopolitical necessity, this juncture therefore marks a crucial time to rethink the enlargement process and how best to capture and exploit the opening that Russia has provided, in order to break the deadlock of the last decade.

While the renewed energy has been provided by Russia, the countries of the Western Balkans have been swept up in this new enlargement momentum: Albania started accession negotiations in July 2022; North

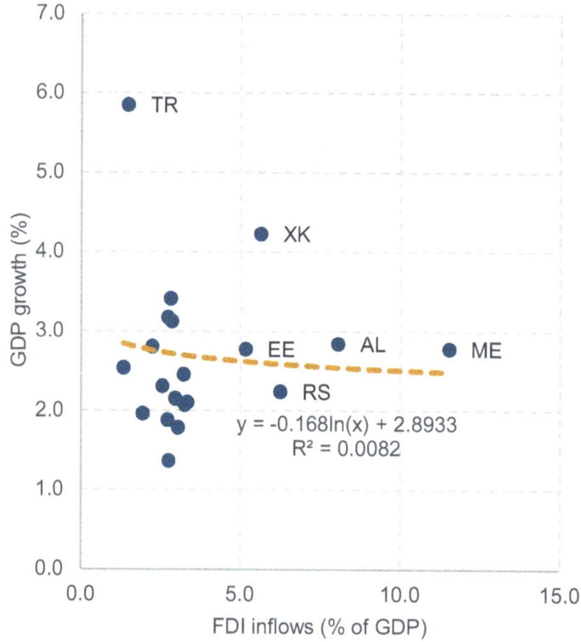

Fig. 5.9 Scatterplot of FDI inflows and GDP growth in Eastern European countries 2000–2023. Note: Annual averages for 2000–2023. (Source: wiiw)

Macedonia held the first inter-governmental conference at the same time, though it needs to change its constitution in order to start accession talks; Kosovo submitted its application for membership in December 2022; and Bosnia and Herzegovina received the status of candidate country in March 2024. Meanwhile, in October 2023, the European Commission announced its New Growth Plan for the Western Balkans. From a Western Balkan perspective, this fresh momentum—and the return of the geopolitical 'imperative' for enlargement—has both positive and negative aspects.

On the positive side, there are a number of things. First, the invasion has made it obvious that the enlargement process cannot go on as it is, with barely any progress being made and with the populations of the candidate countries losing faith (and indeed interest). In the current geopolitical environment, the EU cannot afford to 'lose' candidate countries to the influence of other powers, and most especially Russia. This has generated new thinking about the enlargement process, including a realization that the economic strategy so far hasn't worked. From all the cogitation has emerged the New Growth Plan. While we do not regard it as a game changer (more on this below), we do see it as containing some new thinking and as the first step in a different direction. Most importantly, it recognizes and makes moderate progress on the imperative to integrate the Western Balkans economically ahead of accession. It thereby provides tangible benefits in return for reforms, and increases somewhat the size of the 'carrot' available for institutional upgrading. Western Balkan accession is fundamentally different from that of the EU-CEE countries, in that it is taking much longer: in the case of North Macedonia, more than twice the average EU-CEE time (and counting). Therefore, it is natural that the process of accession should be adapted somewhat.

Second, the invasion has dramatically underscored the fact that the EU accession process is not just about reforms and box ticking, but is also about geopolitics. This has been true since at least the accession of Greece in the 1980s, and was certainly the case in 2004 and (maybe most clearly of all) in 2007. The Western Balkans is geographically surrounded by the EU. In any world where the EU wants to be taken seriously as a geopolitical actor and to be able to defend its interests and project its influence, the Western Balkans must be a part of the EU.

Third, the invasion has ensured that more attention is being paid to geo-economic competition in the Western Balkans, and the degree to which China, in particular, has gained a foothold in the region over the past 15 years or so (Astrov et al. 2023). Thanks to China's ever more central role in supporting Russia's ability to wage its war against Ukraine and the hardening geo-economic divide between China and the West in the global economy, the invasion has highlighted the potential negative implications of a strong Chinese economic presence in Southeast Europe. Here again, the relative economic failure of the enlargement process in the Western Balkans has been thrown into sharp focus, and new thinking is demanded.

Finally, the particular challenges posed by Ukraine's potential accession could benefit the Western Balkans by underlining the relatively limited economic and financial impact of the Western Balkan countries, compared to Ukraine. The impact of Ukraine's accession on the EU budget and of its agricultural sector on farmers in the EU have both come in for close scrutiny and have caused much anxiety in existing EU member states. The Western Balkans does not pose the same kind of economic and financial challenges to the EU, and that could work to the region's benefit.

On the other hand, the invasion and its fallout could also have some adverse spillovers for the Western Balkans. First, the prevalence of geopolitics in the enlargement process could have a negative side, creating the impression of progress on EU integration without the required reforms. As outlined above, the reform progress required by the EU's strict conditionality has been a key part of the economic success of EU-CEE countries. The granting of candidate country status to Bosnia and Herzegovina appears to have been driven exclusively by geopolitics, without the necessary conditions having been fulfilled.

Second, there is justifiable concern in the Western Balkans that all the focus on Ukraine could lead to the region being overlooked, and that Ukraine could even edge in front of it in the accession process (it has indeed already technically leapfrogged North Macedonia, Bosnia and Herzegovina and Kosovo). Given the scale of human suffering in Ukraine caused by the invasion, and the much bigger impact that its accession will have on the EU compared to any other candidate or potential candidate country, it is only natural that Ukraine should receive more attention. It will be important that the Commission and other EU institutions continue to pay adequate attention to the Western Balkans.

Third, there is a risk that Ukraine could heighten scepticism towards enlargement in general. While opinion polls show that most EU citizens support Ukraine, there has been some sign of cracks developing, for example, with the blockading by several EU-CEE countries of Ukrainian agricultural exports. As Ukraine's EU accession process continues, and as the potential implications of its accession become clearer, it may be the case that the scepticism increases.

5.6 Role of Russia and China

If the EU fails to integrate the Western Balkans further into its structures, disillusionment in the region will grow, creating a vacuum that external players could exploit. Over the past decade, the influence of China and Russia in the region has increased, largely owing to the EU's failure to engage more closely with the Western Balkans. With the invasion of Ukraine and rising tensions between the US and the EU on the one side, and China and Russia on the other, the situation is likely to intensify, with the concomitant risk of repercussions for the EU. At best, this would mean a greater economic footprint for actors that hold to lower standards on public procurement and the environment; this could potentially complicate the ability of the region's countries to meet the terms of EU accession. At worst, it would mean the deep penetration of Western Balkan economies by actors with malign intent, seeking to disrupt positive social and economic transformation and progress towards EU membership.

China has become an increasingly important investor in the region. Although still not at the EU level, its share of trade and FDI in the Western Balkans has been growing faster than that of any other comparable partner: especially in Serbia, Chinese investment now rivals that of the EU (Fig. 5.10). In respect of backward linkages, information and communication technology (ICT) imports, high-tech imports and certain areas of infrastructure investment, China is increasingly coming to be a direct competitor to the EU in the Western Balkans (Astrov et al. 2023). Chinese investment can, of course, bring the region positive benefits, and it is clear that—for some of the time, at least—China is meeting a need for capital that the EU has been unwilling to fulfil. However, Chinese investments in the region could potentially be a form of corrosive capital, as illustrated by two notable examples. The first is the debt crisis in Montenegro in 2021, when the country struggled to repay a loan from China that it had used to construct a highway. The second involves a corruption scandal in North Macedonia that came to light in 2015 and that was also linked to a Chinese loan for motorway construction. In this case, high-level politicians were accused of obtaining significant personal gains; the trial is still going on.

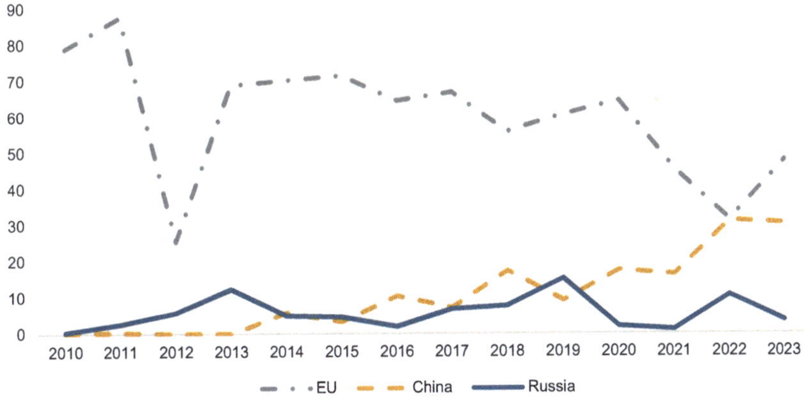

Fig. 5.10 FDI inflows to Serbia per year, 2010–2023, % of total by source. (Sources: National sources, wiiw)

These instances serve as a clear warning about the potential adverse effects of Chinese investment. The tensions between China and Lithuania over Taiwan have also underscored both how quickly China can turn on its erstwhile partners and the steps it is prepared to take to exert its influence over small economies in Central and Eastern Europe.

Russia's economic footprint in the Western Balkans is generally not as significant as China's. Figure 5.10 illustrates this well: even in Serbia, the country with which Russia has famously strong ties, its role in the economy is in no way comparable to that of the EU (or China). Along with ownership of some strategically important energy infrastructure, Russia's main role in the Balkans is political, and here it has proven adept at generating significant influence with fairly limited resources.

There is little reason to think that either China or Russia is explicitly against EU membership for Western Balkan countries per se. Indeed, for both of them it could be advantageous, in numerous ways, if countries with which they have strong economic and/or political ties end up within the EU. The main issue here has to do with the problems that could arise from the deep economic and political involvement in EU candidate countries of third powers that have very different priorities, institutional structures and ways of doing business. This could make it more difficult for the Western Balkan economies to adopt the *acquis communautaire*.

5.7 The Way Forward

The way forward should focus on three main points. First, there should be a more significant and expedited integration of the Western Balkans into EU structures, in order to eliminate any uncertainty regarding the long-term geopolitical and geo-economic orientation of the region's countries. Second, it is crucial to resolve deep-seated territorial issues that continually hinder progress in the region on even the most mundane and practical matters, such as the recognition of educational qualifications. Third, the region should consider moving away from the current neoliberal economic model towards a more interventionist and egalitarian one, in order to achieve faster and more equitable growth and development.

Regarding the first point, the EU recently adopted the New Growth Plan for the Western Balkans (see Jovanović 2024). This plan rests on four pillars, which correctly identify the main obstacles that the region faces as it strives to achieve higher growth rates and social progress. The first pillar supports economic integration within the region via the Common

Regional Market, and aims to develop a single market inspired by the EU's model. The second pillar seeks to extend this integration to the EU level. The third focuses on providing additional financial assistance to facilitate integration efforts and incentivize the necessary reforms. And the fourth is designed to expedite the essential reforms required for the region to meet EU standards, serving as a motivational tool for financial support. Collectively, these pillars address such critical challenges as weak institutions, inadequate reforms, the need for investment in infrastructure and public goods, an improvement in regional cooperation and the limited scope of the regional market.

The plan indeed introduces fresh elements to the discussion, thereby acknowledging the need for a revised EU approach towards the region. However, closer examination of its details reveals that it is largely lacking in substance and fails to tackle the primary issues within each of the four pillars.

The first pillar, the Common Regional Market, does not adequately recognize the significance of political disputes in the region. Without addressing these disputes and making greater diplomatic efforts, all attempts at regional economic integration are likely to fail. The second pillar's proposed measures for EU single market integration are too symbolic and fail to address the main obstacles that Western Balkan companies face when exporting to the EU, such as an onerous bureaucratic burden, with sheaves of documents and certificates that companies have to obtain. Nor do the measures do anything to ease the way for people from the Western Balkans who want to work in the EU: they will still face complicated and expensive permit requirements.

Regarding the third and fourth pillars, put simply the plan offers a much bigger stick, but the same-sized carrot. What the region really needs is a much juicier carrot. The proposed €6 billion over four years, including €2 billion in grants and €4 billion in loans, is only 20% of the existing Economic and Investment Plan for the Western Balkans, which totals around €30 billion. The amount does not even compensate for inflation over the period, effectively rendering it a partial inflation indexation, rather than representing any real increase in funds.

The grant component of the New Growth Plan amounts to about €500 million per year for the entire region—just 0.3–0.4% of the region's annual GDP. Such a small amount is unlikely to effect significant change. To put things into perspective, that sum *for the entire region* is just one third of the grant that Croatia receives from the NextGenerationEU fund (€6 billion), despite the fact that the region has a population four times bigger than the population of Croatia.

This financial support comes with stricter conditions, requiring Western Balkan governments to prepare and agree on a reform agenda with the European Commission. If these reforms are not implemented, the financial support will not be disbursed. While this approach may seem reasonable, the combination of a small amount of financial support and stricter conditions could backfire and fail to bring the expected changes, while potentially causing further issues.

What the EU could instead offer the Western Balkans is full access to the EU budget in the next funding round, treating candidate countries as if they were member states. That approach would significantly swell the funds allocated to the region, potentially doubling or tripling the amount to up to 3% of the Western Balkan countries' GDP. Such an increase in financial support could boost economic growth in the region by 1–2 percentage points annually. At the same time, it would come with a modest price-tag for current EU member states: just 0.04% (or less) of GDP, even for those countries that contribute most to the EU budget (Weiss et al. 2020). While there is no precedent for such an initiative, challenging times demand bold action; and given the negligible cost to current EU members, this is certainly a feasible option.

Simultaneously, the EU should immediately open its markets up to the Western Balkans, allowing the free movement of goods and people. Again, given the relatively small size of the Western Balkans—a combined GDP of less than 1% of the EU's GDP, and a combined population less than 4% of the EU's—this would have a tiny impact on the EU, but would be extremely beneficial to the Western Balkans. If such a move is difficult for political reasons, the EU should at least eliminate border controls for Western Balkan companies that enter the EU; provide direct financial and technical assistance to help those companies obtain the necessary export certificates and documentation; and reduce or eliminate work permit requirements for Western Balkan citizens seeking employment in the EU.

The two measures outlined would stop short of granting the Western Balkan countries full membership. That would protect the EU from potential institutional issues within the region and prevent possible obstacles in the EU decision-making process (similar to those currently being erected by Hungary). At the same time, the actions would send a clear message to the Western Balkan countries that the EU is committed to their integration and is supportive of them at a time of geopolitical uncertainty. These steps would also counter the influence of external players like Russia and China, by filling the vacuum they currently exploit. Ultimately, the initiatives would bring significant economic and social change to the region, accelerating growth and improving the well-being of its citizens.

The second key area on which the EU should focus is resolution of the longstanding territorial issues in the Western Balkans, particularly concerning the status of Kosovo and the Serb-majority municipalities. Accelerated EU accession should be coupled with intensified diplomatic efforts to address these disputes. The recently concluded Ohrid Agreement is essentially positive, as it offers both sides something: the Serbian side gets the Association of Serb-majority Municipalities, which it sees as a key mechanism for protecting Serbs in Kosovo, while the Albanian side gets a guarantee that Serbia will not block efforts to integrate Kosovo into international institutions. However, for the agreement to work, there must be a clear and detailed implementation plan, with concrete deadlines and specific steps that each party must take, along with a clear sequence of actions. This implementation plan should be backed by strong incentives for compliance and significant consequences for non-compliance. For instance, if the parties adhere to the agreed steps, they should be rewarded with the release of EU funds, the opening of new negotiation chapters, or enhanced membership of international organizations. Conversely, failure to comply should result in the blocking of EU funds, suspension of negotiations, or denial of participation in certain international forums.

The third key area to be addressed is not related to the EU, but is something that Western Balkan politicians and policy makers should undertake off their own bat: to move away from the current neoliberal economic model to a more interventionist and egalitarian approach. This shift could involve enhancing the role of government in economic affairs; implementing strong industrial and innovation policies to encourage domestic investment; and significantly increasing investment in infrastructure and green energy. It might also involve increased spending on public goods and services, such as education, healthcare and social protection to ensure more equitable growth and development across society.

The key ingredient here is to implement robust industrial and innovation policies. As elsewhere in Eastern Europe, industrial policy in the Western Balkans has largely been neglected over the past three decades. This may be explained by the radical about-turn in economic policy in those countries after the fall of socialism. Under socialism, they all had (to a greater or lesser extent) centrally planned economies, which can be seen as an extreme form of industrial policy. But with the transition to capitalism, in a kind of revolt against the previous system they all adopted economic models based on neoliberal premises, with minimal state intervention and deregulated markets. In addition, through the 1990s all these countries had arrangements with the IMF, which at the time was advocating Washington Consensus-type policies and was very much against industrial policy. Things have started to change a bit recently, as the countries have begun to wake up to the fact that they need to do something to ensure stronger growth and have started adopting national industrial policy strategies and smart specialization strategies; however, much more needs to be done.

As we argued in Jovanović and Vujanović (2023) and Matusiak et al. (2022), promising industrial sectors in the Western Balkans include agri-food, textiles, automotive, energy, IT and tourism. Each sector has specific areas to focus on: the agri-food industry should target premium goods; the textile sector should aim for high-quality final products; the automotive industry should focus on advanced technologies; the energy sector should prioritize renewable energy; the IT industry should foster greater innovation and final products; and tourism should offer unique alternative experiences.

Governments can support companies through various sector-specific policies, but some general measures could include:

- Supporting the adoption of new, modern and clean technologies;
- Encouraging the introduction of new premium products and own brands;
- Designing special financing schemes, such as favourable loans or loan guarantees;
- Providing direct support to meet EU quality standards;
- Facilitating technological upgrades to improve productivity and competitiveness;
- Ensuring there is enough skilled labour by enhancing vocational education and professional schools; and
- Increasing public investment in education, infrastructure and renewable energy.

Increasing investment in infrastructure and green energy is another critical component. Upgrading transport, especially the railways, will improve connectivity within the region and with the EU, thus facilitating trade and investment. Investment in public transport will also help reduce CO_2 emissions. To further combat climate change, while also supporting growth and ensuring sustainable development, governments should invest in renewable energy sources, such as solar, wind and hydroelectric power, for which there is big potential in the Western Balkans.

It is equally important to increase spending on public goods and services: boosting funding for education at all levels, improving school infrastructure, training teachers and updating the curriculum to match current societal demands are crucial steps in this. It is also vital to strengthen the healthcare system by investing in building and modernizing healthcare facilities, training medical professionals and ensuring that all citizens have access to healthcare services. And in order to reduce poverty and inequality, social protection programmes need to be expanded and a robust social safety net created, with unemployment benefits, pensions and support for vulnerable groups.

All these efforts should be accompanied by more redistributive tax regimes. The introduction of a progressive tax system, where higher earners and more profitable companies pay a larger share of their income and profits in tax, would not only reduce inequality, but also provide additional public revenue. This could then be used to fund public services, social protection programmes, investment in infrastructure, and innovation and industrial policies. As a matter of fact, most of the EU member states (21 of 27) already have progressive personal income tax (as of 2024); and while only a quarter of them have progressive corporate income tax, almost all introduced a windfall profit tax (so-called solidarity contribution) in 2023, which effectively makes their corporate income tax progressive (Enache 2023). Therefore, the adoption of a more progressive tax regime would also align the Western Balkan nations more closely with the EU's economic and social models and policies.

The introduction of these measures would lead to significant improvements in economic and social development across the Western Balkans. A more interventionist and egalitarian economic model would result in more rapid economic growth, by stimulating domestic investment and innovation, ensuring long-term sustainability through investments in green energy and infrastructure, enhancing social welfare through increased spending on education, healthcare and social protection, and fostering equitable growth by reducing inequality and promoting social cohesion. These strategies would help the Western Balkans achieve a more balanced and inclusive economic development, and would ultimately facilitate their integration into the EU, while enhancing regional stability and prosperity.

Needless to say, for these policies to work, it is crucial to acknowledge the current inefficiencies in government spending that are to be observed in many countries across the region. Poor quality of public expenditure, coupled with institutional weakness, often impedes the effectiveness of increased public spending. Therefore, any efforts to expand public expenditure and taxation should be complemented by comprehensive reforms aimed at enhancing institutional quality, reducing corruption and improving the rule of law. It is also essential to bolster the quality of public finance, in order to ensure that increased government spending effectively supports inclusive and equitable growth.

Moreover, the successful implementation of industrial and innovation policies requires a state with strong administrative capacities—something that may prove challenging for the Western Balkan countries, given their current institutional limitations. It is important to consider the capacity of these countries to effectively design and execute the policies being advocated. In addition, the fostering of innovation relies on a ready supply of highly skilled workers, which serves to underscore the importance of improving the education system. While increasing investment in education is a crucial step, it is important to recognize that such policies may take some considerable time—even decades—to filter through and finally bear fruit.

However, the challenges should not serve as excuses for inaction. Despite the longer timeframes required for these policies to yield results, it is essential to initiate them immediately. Any delay in taking action will only prolong the current problems and hinder potential progress. The region has waited far too long to see improved living standards. It cannot afford to wait any longer.

References

Anghel, V. and Jones, E. (2022) 'Failing forward in Eastern Enlargement: Problem solving through problem making', *Journal of European Public Policy* 29(7): 1092–1111. https://doi.org/10.1080/13501763.2021.1927155

Astrov, V., Grieveson, R., Hanelt, C., Jovanović, R., Kochnev, A., Kosmehl, M., Mara, I., Overdiek, M., Petersen, T., Pindyuk, O., Reiter, O., Vujanović, N. and Weiss, S. (2023) *Keeping Friends Closer: Why the EU should address new geoeconomic realities and get its neighbours back in the fold.* Vienna/Gütersloh: wiiw and Bertelsmann Stiftung. Joint Study No. 2023-02. https://wiiw.ac.at/keeping-friends-closer-why-the-eu-should-address-new-geoeconomic-realities-and-get-its-neighbours-back-in-the-fold-p-6487.html

BiEPAG (2017) *The Crisis of Democracy in the Western Balkans: Authoritarianism and EU stabilitocracy*. Belgrade: Balkans in Europe Policy Advisory Group. Policy Paper, March. https://www.biepag.eu/publication/policy-paper-the-crisis-of-democracy-in-the-western-balkans-authoritarianism-and-eu-stabilitocracy/

Bykova, A., Hanzl-Weiss, D., Hunya, G., Korpar, N., Podkaminer, L., Stehrer, R. and Stöllinger, R. (2021) *Avoiding a Trap and Embracing the Megatrends: Proposals for a new growth model in EU-CEE*. Vienna: wiiw. wiiw Research Report, No. 458. https://wiiw.ac.at/avoiding-a-trap-and-embracing-the-megatrends-proposals-for-a-new-growth-model-in-eu-cee-p-5987.html

Enache, C. (2023) *Windfall profit taxes in Europe in 2023*. Tax Foundation. https://taxfoundation.org/data/all/eu/windfall-tax-europe-2023/

European Council (2019) European Council meeting (17 and 18 October 2019) – Conclusions (EUCO 23/19). General Secretariat of the Council. https://data.consilium.europa.eu/doc/document/ST-23-2019-INIT/en/pdf

Herszenhorn, D.M. (2019) 'EU leaders deadlock over membership talks for North Macedonia, Albania', *Politico*, 18 October. https://www.politico.eu/article/eu-leaders-deadlock-over-membership-talks-for-north-macedonia-albania/

Hunya, G., Ghodsi, M., Gligorov, V., Grieveson, R., Hanzl-Weiss, D., Holzner, M. and Stöllinger, R. (2017) *CEFTA Investment Report 2017*. Brussels: CEFTA Secretariat. http://cefta.int/wp-content/uploads/2016/05/CEFTA-Investment-Report-2017.pdf

Jovanović, B. (2024) *New Growth Plan for the Western Balkans: Solid foundations, shaky extensions*. Skopje: European Policy Institute. Civil Society Forum Policy Insight. https://epi.org.mk/post/25784?lang=en

Jovanović, B. and Hanzl-Weiss, D. (2022) *Economic and Social Impacts of FDI in Central, East and Southeast Europe*. Vienna: wiiw. wiiw Research Report, No. 464. https://wiiw.ac.at/economic-and-social-impacts-of-fdi-in-central-east-and-southeast-europe-p-6407.html

Jovanović, B. and Vujanović, N. (2023) *Towards Effective Industrial Policy in the Western Balkans*. Vienna: wiiw. wiiw Policy Note/Policy Report, No. 66. https://wiiw.ac.at/towards-effective-industrial-policy-in-the-western-balkans-p-6493.html

Jovanović, B., Ghodsi, M., Grieveson, R., Hanzl-Weiss, D., Holzner, M., Weiss, S. and Zavarská, Z. (2022) *The Long Way Round: Lessons from EU-CEE for improving integration and development in the Western Balkans*. Vienna/Gütersloh: wiiw and Bertelsmann Stiftung. Joint Study No. 2022-06. https://wiiw.ac.at/the-long-way-round-lessons-from-eu-cee-for-improving-integration-and-development-in-the-western-balkans-p-6194.html

Matusiak, M., Radovanovic, N. and Rakhmatullin, R. (eds) (2022) *Analysis of Value Chains in the Western Balkan Economies: Enriching the potential for regional cooperation in priority areas.* Luxembourg: Publications Office of the European Union. https://doi.org/10.2760/47718

Weiss, S., Grieveson, R., Holzner, M., Mara, I., Pichler, D. and Vukšić, G. (2020) *Pushing on a String? An evaluation of regional economic cooperation in the Western Balkans.* Vienna/Gütersloh: wiiw and Bertelsmann Stiftung. https://www.bertelsmann-stiftung.de/en/publications/publication/did/pushing-on-a-string-en

CHAPTER 6

The Future of the Welfare State in the European Union and the Foreseen EU Enlargement

Agnieszka Chłoń-Domińczak

6.1 Introduction

One of the important achievements of the European Union is the development of European social citizenship and the approach to social rights in Europe. Initially, the Union and its *acquis* only took into account social policies in the member states to a limited extent, leaving this to the national authorities. However, after the financial and sovereign debt crisis in the early 2010s, in response to the anxiety of European citizens, who were concerned about whether national welfare arrangements and the European Union could adequately protect them, social issues became increasingly visible in the Union's policy agenda. It led, in particular, to the adoption of the European Pillar of Social Rights in 2017 and its subsequent implementation.

The focus of this chapter is the future of the welfare state in the European Union, taking into account the planned enlargement and the

A. Chłoń-Domińczak (✉)
SGH Warsaw School of Economics, Warsaw, Poland
e-mail: achlon@sgh.waw.pl

I. P. Székely, P. Halmai (eds.), *The Future of European Integration*, Studies in Economic Transition,
https://doi.org/10.1007/978-3-032-20186-7_6

social situation in the candidate countries, based on the available statistics and information. The evidence suggests that the previous enlargement and integration of the European Union have had a positive impact on social integration and development in Europe. As underlined in the last Cohesion Report prepared by the European Commission, since the 2004 accession, the average GDP per head of the member states that joined in 2004 or later has increased from 52% to nearly 80% of the EU average (European Commission 2024a). The gap with the rest of the EU has halved. The unemployment rate in these member states has decreased from an average of 13% to 4%. At the same time, future megatrends, particularly demographic changes, will affect all regions in the coming decades. Regions will have to adjust to a shrinking labour force and an ageing population. The challenges tend to be more acute in rural and thinly populated regions. Similarly, the effects of the digital transition and climate change are likely to exacerbate regional disparities in the EU. Responding to these challenges requires an efficient welfare state and social protection systems that are resilient to both shocks and long-term developments resulting from global megatrends.

There is also an increasing recognition of some less favourable trends associated with EU membership, particularly regarding inequality and demographic trends within the new member states (see, e.g., Landesmann and Székely 2021). As they demonstrate, largely due to the highly unequal distribution of FDI, a major component of investment and productivity enhancement, the overall large economic benefits of EU membership tend to be unevenly distributed among regions within new member states and social groups with different locations, skills, and mobility. Weaknesses in institutional quality and uneven quality of institutions in the new member states are generally viewed as the major sources of such negative trends regarding social fairness. Therefore, the cohesion policies should focus particularly on the most vulnerable groups and regions, also through building necessary economic and institutional capacities.

This chapter is structured as follows. First, recent developments in the area of social policy within the European Union, along with considerations related to the future of the welfare state and social protection in the European Union, are presented. The following section focuses on the megatrends that impact social development and the situation in the candidate countries in relation to these megatrends. The third section provides an overview of the social situation in the candidate countries, from the perspective of the social scoreboard, which monitors the implementation of the European Pillar of Social Rights. The final section concludes, focusing on the challenges related to the future of the welfare state in the European Union within the context of enlargement.

6.2 Development of the Social Union in Recent Years

The economic and financial crisis in the early 2010s triggered a discussion strengthening the social dimension of the European Union. As a result, the first attempts at mobilizing EU resources to alleviate the social aftershock of the crisis were implemented. In 2012, the two Employment and the Youth packages were adopted, followed by the Social Investment Package, including Communication Towards Job-Rich Recovery (European Commission 2012a), and Moving Youth into Employment (European Commission 2012a, b). Following these developments, in 2013, the European Commission presented a Communication to the European Parliament and the European Council on Strengthening the Social Dimension of the Economic and Monetary Union (European Commission 2013). This communication acknowledges that economic and monetary policies need to be complemented by appropriate institutions to address the social situation and provide adequate national safety nets. As a result, the Country Specific Recommendations formulated in the European Semester also refer to the employment, training and social policy issues. These areas are also assessed as part of the EU accession monitoring process. In 2017, the European Pillar of Social Rights (EPSR) was adopted (European Commission 2017). It was an important step in shaping the European welfare state agenda. The EPSR comprises 20 principles across three dimensions, including European-level goals that were not always reflected in earlier national policies. A crucial step towards implementing social rights is the adoption of the EPSR Action Plan in 2021 (European Commission 2021). It takes stock of the 20 principles and outlines concrete actions to implement the EPSR (Ferrera and Bruno 2023).

Since the proclamation of the EPSR, 91 measures related to its principles were adopted by the EU. It includes 48 regulations that have established power resources, understood as legal rights or tools to execute the rights for European citizens (Ferrera and Bruno 2023). However, as Ferrera and Bruno (2023) assess, there is a mixed picture regarding the implementation of the principles, with some more reflected in concrete EU-level actions than others. From the perspective of the EU accession, it is worth noting the directives that need to be implemented in the national legislations, including:

- Directive on adequate minimum wages
- Directive on transparent and predictable working conditions
- Directive on work-life balance
- Asbestos at Work Directive amended
- Proposed Directive on improving working conditions in platform work

These developments have led to the development of the European social model of social rights and social citizenship, which Ferrera et al. (2023) refer to as a "marble cake", comprising European Union, national, and sub-national government policies and regulations that establish rights and resources for Europeans.

One of the actions undertaken by the European Commission concerning the development of social protection is the establishment of the High-Level Expert Group, which prepared the Report on the Future of Social Protection and the Welfare State in the EU. The High-Level Expert Group considered the challenges for the welfare state in the European Union, related to the foreseen developments, particularly the four megatrends: demographic change, the changing world of work, digital transformation, and climate change.

These challenges have a profound impact on individuals and societies at various stages of the life course. The report of the high-level group (European Commission 2023) presents 21 recommendations that focus on the development of the welfare state and social protection in the European Union across six key areas. The first three of them are centred around the three main stages of the life course:

- Supporting children, young people and establishing families
- Ensuring inclusive social protection and lifelong learning for people of working age
- Supporting adequate income and high-quality long-term care in old age

Furthermore, there are cross-cutting recommendations that are related to societies at all ages, which include:

- Promoting inclusive and high-quality services, including inclusive and environment-friendly housing and transport, as well as social services;
- ensuring sustainable financing for a resilient welfare state, including an appropriate mix of financing social transfers through a mix of taxes and social contributions; consideration of minimum tax rate on capital, as well as a golden rule for public finances, ensuring an appropriate level of social investment;
- stepping up EU capacity to secure social protection in the future, including further legislative initiatives to fulfil the principles of the EPSR, and a guarantee of a minimum package of social rights for all EU citizens.

These developments are important for the candidate countries, which face both a challenge and an opportunity related to the enhancement of their social and welfare policies, both as a precondition and as a consequence of the EU accession.

Social policies are important for European citizens. The results of the 2024 special Eurobarometer on Social Europe (European Commission 2024b) show that 88% of Europeans consider a social Europe to be personally important to them. At least one of the recent EU initiatives related to social rights is recognized by 60% of respondents. It includes the Directive to ensure adequate minimum wages, the Work-Life Balance Directive supporting working parents and carers, as well as the EU and national contributions invested under the European Social Fund Plus to improve skills and tackle social exclusion. The key aspects of social development, according to the survey results, include a standard of living, fair working conditions, quality healthcare, and equal opportunities and access to the labour market (all with an indication of 40% or higher by the Eurobarometer respondents). These results confirm the importance of social policies and the focus on social rights at the three levels of governance, following the presented "marble cake" approach.

6.3 Facing the Megatrends

The future of the welfare state in the EU is driven, among other factors, by the megatrends that impact societies and economies. In its assessment of the future of the welfare state and social protection in the European Union, the High-Level Expert Group focused on four key megatrends: demographic developments, the changing nature of work, digital transformation, and the green transition (European Commission 2023). The challenges arising from these megatrends are also important for the candidate countries, as presented below.

6.3.1 Demographic Developments in the Candidate Countries

According to the 2024 revision of the UN population projections (as well as earlier ones), the population ageing process is most advanced in Europe (UN 2024). Population ageing will progress in most candidate countries faster than on the continent as a whole. In 2024, the old-age dependency ratio in most of the candidate countries (except Bosnia and Herzegovina and Serbia) was below the European average (Fig. 6.1).

However, according to the projections, in 2050, this indicator will be closer to the EU average in these countries, and it will exceed the EU average in all but two countries (Georgia and Moldova). The most difficult situation is expected in Albania and Ukraine, where by the end of the century, the number of people aged 65 or over will be close to or exceed the number of people of working age (25–64 years).[1]

These projections indicate that the welfare systems in the candidate countries will face significant pressure related to demographic changes in the future. This concerns their pension, long-term care, and healthcare systems in particular, as those that are most exposed to the consequences of population ageing.

[1] The UN's 2024 revision of its World Population Prospects takes into account the war in Ukraine. The revision, published in 2024, includes estimates of population changes due to Russia's invasion of Ukraine, particularly focusing on the impact on Ukraine's population and migration patterns.

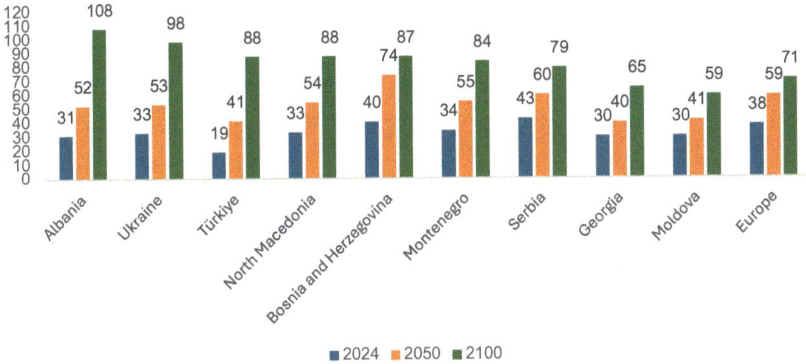

Fig. 6.1 Old-age dependency ratio in the candidate countries (65+/25–64). (Source: Authors' calculations based on the UN population projections 2024 revision)

6.3.2 *The Future of Work*

Another important megatrend is the changing nature of work and the future of work. With the demographic developments, there is a need to increase both the intensity and productivity of work. At the same time, there are increasingly diverse forms of work, including platform work, non-standard employment, telework, and others. With these developments, it is important to ensure that these developments are welfare-enhancing, and are not leading to increasing segmentation of jobs and deepening gap between more "advantageous" and more "disadvantageous" jobs, from the perspective of welfare coverage.

From this perspective, it is important to underline that the expected duration of working life in the candidate countries is, on average, shorter than in most EU countries (Fig. 6.2).

The expected duration of work of a person aged 15 in 2023 in Türkiye was less than two-thirds of the expected duration of work in Iceland. Extending working lives is an important component of delivering social rights in Europe in a sustainable manner. Social investments, which lead to a more productive and longer activity in the life course, contribute to both increased individual and societal resilience (Hemerijck et al. 2023).

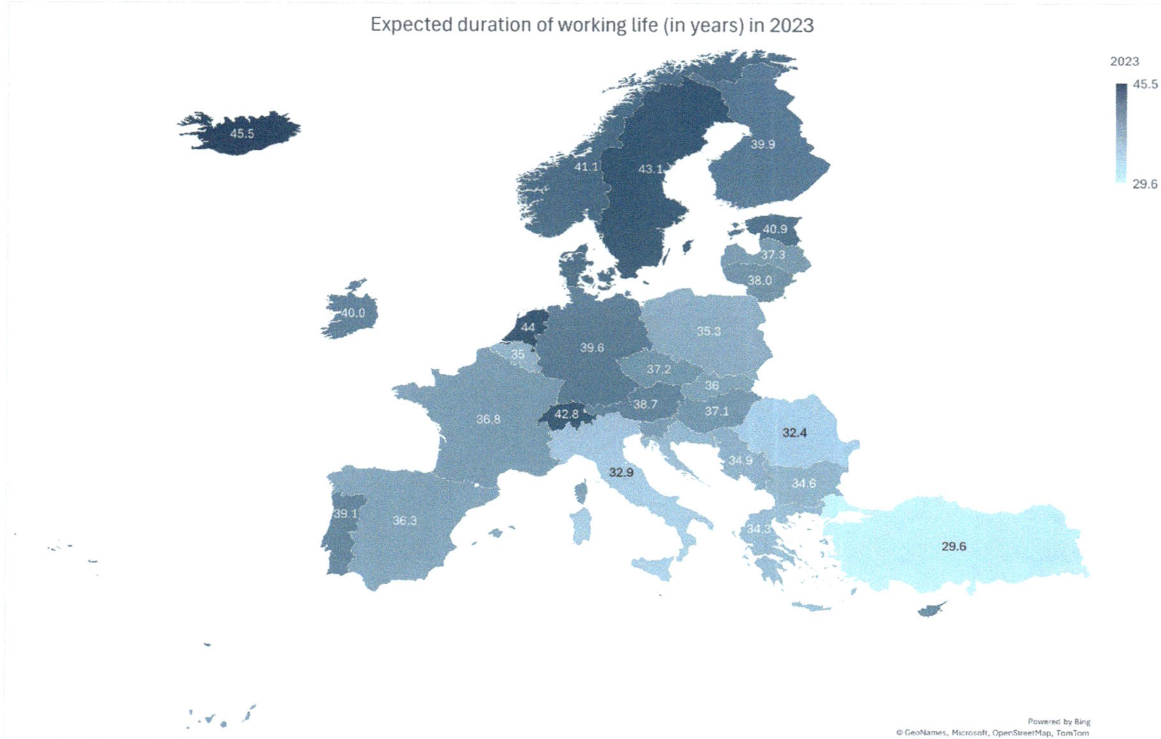

Fig. 6.2 Expected duration of working life, 2023. (Source: Author's calculations based on EUROSTAT data (lfsi_dwl_a__custom_19550925), accessed on 5 January 2026)

6.4 Delivering Social Rights from the Perspective of the Social Scoreboard in the Candidate Countries

The challenge of delivering social rights in the candidate countries can be assessed from the perspective of the Social Scoreboard. It is a tool adopted by the European Commission to monitor the employment and social performance of the countries along the dimensions of the European Pillar of Social Rights (EPSR).

6.4.1 *Equal Opportunities and Access to the Labour Market*

Figure 6.3 presents the monitoring indicators in the dimension of equal opportunities and access to the labour market, including averages for the EU-27 countries and available indicators for the candidate countries. While the EU-27 average is used as a reference, the observed developmental gap is a result of long-term divergence in economic and social development, and the reversal to convergence with the EU level is a long-term process.

The presented data indicate the diversity of challenges faced by candidate countries in the first dimension of the EPSR. This dimension focuses mainly on access to education and skills. While the candidate countries score quite well when looking at the share of early leavers from education and training, with only Türkiye significantly standing out, with one out of five young people leaving education and training early. However, the candidate countries experience a significantly higher share of young people who are neither in employment nor in education and training (NEET), compared to the EU average. This indicates a significant challenge in utilizing the potential of young people, completing their initial education, in the labour market. A relatively smaller proportion of people in the 30–34 age group (particularly in Bosnia and Herzegovina) have attained tertiary education.

Another challenge captured by the social scoreboard monitoring is digital skills. Among the candidate countries, only Montenegro has a share of individuals with basic or higher overall digital skills that is close to the EU average. In contrast, in the remaining countries, the share of people with such skills is significantly lower.

Adults in the candidate countries participate less frequently in various forms of learning—in all countries for which indicators are available, these

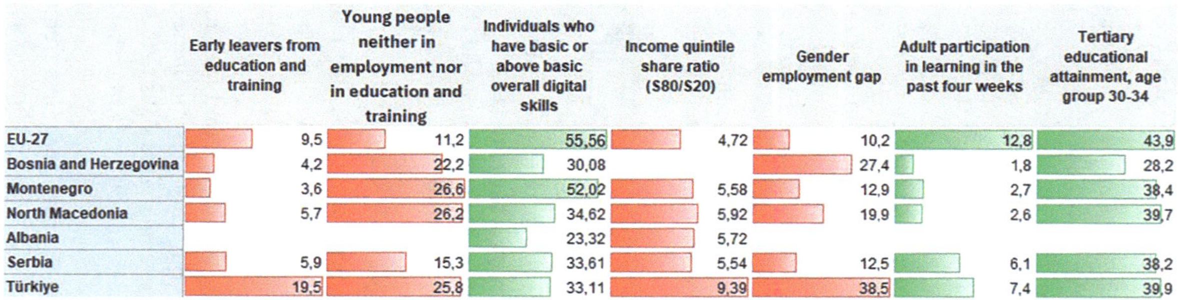

Fig. 6.3 Monitoring indicators in the dimension of equal opportunities and access to the labour market, 2023. (Notes: Indicators for Early leavers, NEET, Gender employment gap, adult participation in learning and tertiary education attainment. Data for Montenegro and North Macedonia are for 2020. Green bars indicate cases where higher values correspond to better outcomes, and red ones those where higher values correspond to worse outcomes. Source: EUROSTAT)

shares are much below the EU average. It is worth noting that a high share of NEET is combined with a low share of people participating in LLL.

With the digital transition, including the increasing role of AI tools, digital skills are important for enhancing the productivity of workers. The share of individuals with basic or above basic digital skills in the candidate countries is below the EU average. Only in Montenegro is the situation comparable to the EU average.

The development of human capital, measured by the share of young people (30–34 years) with tertiary education, is also below the EU average in the candidate countries, with the largest gap noted in Bosnia and Herzegovina, and the smallest in Türkiye. Again, this highlights the challenge for countries, but also underscores the need to utilize opportunities available after accession, among others, through Erasmus+ activities that support access to higher education.

The last important challenge for the candidate countries is the gender gap in employment. It is particularly large in Türkiye, Bosnia and Herzegovina, and North Macedonia. With the development of European regulations in the area of gender equality, including, among others, the Work-Life Balance Directive, these countries will face the societal challenge of implementing policies that facilitate the reduction of gender gaps.

6.4.2 *Dynamic Labour Markets and Fair Working Conditions*

The second dimension of the EPSR focuses on the labour market and working conditions. Figure 6.4 summarizes selected social scoreboard indicators in this dimension.

In the second EPSR dimension, the candidate countries stand behind both in terms of employment rates, particularly for women and older workers—with the largest gaps observed in Türkiye and Bosnia and Herzegovina, and the smallest ones in Serbia. The unemployment rate, including long-term unemployment and youth unemployment, is the highest in Montenegro and North Macedonia. However, it exceeds the EU average for all candidate countries for which sufficient information is available.

The in-work poverty rate is particularly high in Türkiye and Albania, while it is below the EU average in Bosnia and Herzegovina, Serbia, and Montenegro.

As the experience of the previous enlargement shows, the EU accession was an important stimulus for economic growth and labour market

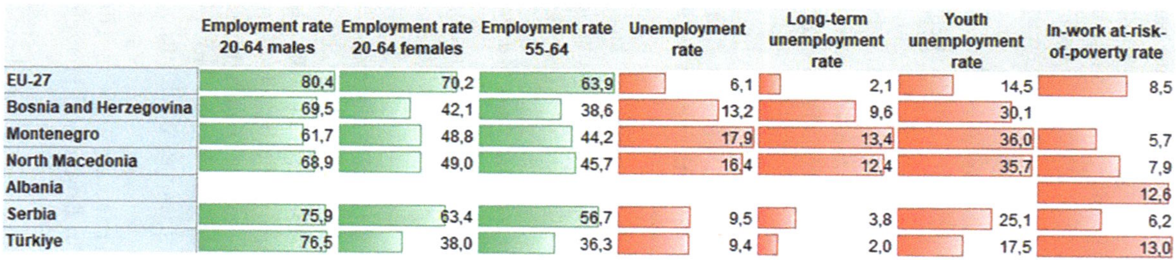

Fig. 6.4 Monitoring indicators in the dimension of dynamic labour markets and fair working conditions, 2023. (Notes: Employment and unemployment rates for Montenegro and North Macedonia are for 2020. In-work poverty rates are for 2022, Albania—2021, and North Macedonia—2020. Green bars indicate cases where higher values correspond to better outcomes, and red ones those where higher values correspond to worse outcomes. Source: EUROSTAT)

development in the countries that joined the EU in 2004 and thereafter. Hagemejer et al. (2021) estimate that EU accession led to large gains in the country's economic performance 6 and 12 years after the accession. In the case of five of the ten analysed countries (Estonia, Poland, Latvia, Lithuania, and Romania), the difference in levels of per capita gross domestic product (GDP) against the counterfactual is at least 30%. According to Eurostat, 6 out of the 26 million new jobs which have emerged across the EU in the last 20 years have been created in the ten new EU countries.[2] Caliendo et al. (2021) estimated that EU enlargement primarily benefited new member states, with increased employment rates for low-skilled workers, and yielded smaller welfare gains for existing member states. Therefore, it can be expected that the future accession will create conditions to improve the labour market dynamics and fair working conditions in the current candidate countries.

6.4.3 *Public Support, Social Protection and Inclusion*

The third dimension of the EPSR focuses on public support, social protection and social inclusion, and the monitoring indicators are summarized in Fig. 6.5.

In this dimension, the candidate countries also face challenges in several areas. The existing social transfer systems have less capacity to reduce poverty than on average in the EU countries. This is particularly visible in Türkiye, Albania and North Macedonia.

There is also a gap in the participation of children below age 3 in early childhood education and care, which is perceived as an important social investment policy. In Türkiye, North Macedonia, and Montenegro, less than 10% of children in this age group are covered by ECEC, compared to almost 36% in the EU.

Candidate countries also face a higher risk of poverty rates, both for the general population and for children. In this aspect, the biggest challenge is faced by Türkiye, Albania, Montenegro and North Macedonia. Montenegro, Albania, and Serbia have lower aggregate replacement ratios for pensions, which can indicate a lower capacity to protect older people against poverty.

[2] https://commission.europa.eu/topics/eu-enlargement/20-years-together/20-years-together-facts-and-figures-about-benefits-enlargement-eu_en

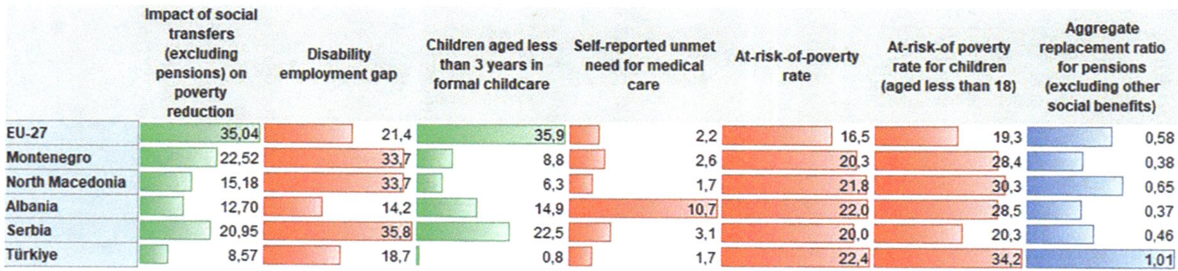

Fig. 6.5 Monitoring indicators in the dimension of public support, social protection, and social inclusion, 2022–2023. (Notes: Indicators 3–7 are for 2022, for Albania—2021, and North Macedonia—2020. Green bars indicate cases where higher values correspond to better outcomes and red ones those where higher values correspond to worse outcomes. Blue bars show indicators for which the interpretation is not one-directional. Source: EUROSTAT)

There are differences regarding the disability employment gap. While in Montenegro, North Macedonia, and Serbia, it is above the EU average, in Albania and Türkiye, this gap is smaller than in the EU.

Lastly, in most candidate countries, the unmet need for medical care does not differ significantly from the EU average, while in Albania, almost 11% of people report limited access to medical care.

6.5 Conclusion

Developments over the past few years, including the Great Recession and the COVID-19 pandemic, have proven that one of the important pillars of European integration is social policy, which must match economic and monetary ones.

The combination of European, national, and regional initiatives forms social rights that support societies in difficult times and ensure further development. The experience from the EU enlargement shows that it contributes to building social cohesion and reducing disparities among countries and societies.

The global megatrends: unprecedented demographic change, changing world of work, digital developments, including the recent expansion of artificial intelligence and its impact on economies, labour markets and societies, as well as the climate change and its influence on economies and societies, including migrations, labour markets restructuring, energy poverty and other areas of people's lives require further integration in Europe.

Adoption of the *acquis*, including the recently adopted directives and measures related to social rights, is an important challenge, as seen through the lens of the social scoreboard. The expected benefits of the integration, including the cohesion policy, can be important to strengthen and develop the social Europe in the future. However, achieving these benefits is conditional on developing the necessary institutional capacity.

As shown in the chapter, candidate countries are facing multiple challenges in the areas of employment and social policies. They are also more vulnerable to the potential negative impact of institutional weaknesses compared to most countries that joined the EU between 2004 and 2013. Hence, the challenges they will face, as well as those that the EU will face, are perhaps even greater than those observed in the case of previous enlargements. A failure to improve institutions (before and after enlargement could be particularly harmful regarding the demographic trends in the future member states, including high migration outflows following the full implementation of the free movement of people, which may further strain their welfare schemes. Therefore, the importance of institutional development is key to achieving the potential gains.

References

Caliendo, L., Opromolla, L. D., Parro, F., & Sforza, A. (2021). Goods and factor market integration: A quantitative assessment of the EU enlargement. *Journal of Political Economy*, *129*(12), 3491–3545.

European Commission (2012a) Communication from the Commission to the European Parliament and the Council, The European Economic and Social Committee and the Committee of the Regions: Towards A Job-Rich Recovery, COM(2012) 173 Final

European Commission (2012b) Communication from the Commission to the European Parliament and the Council, The European Economic and Social Committee and the Committee of the Regions: Moving Youth into Employment, COM(2012) 727 final

European Commission (2013). Communication from the Commission to the European Parliament and the Council: Strengthening the Social Dimension of the Economic and Monetary Union, COM(2013) 690 final

European Commission (2017). Communication from the Commission to the European Parliament, the Council, the European Economic and Social Committee and the Committee of the Regions on the European Pillar of Social Rights (COM(2017) 250 final)

European Commission (2021). Communication from the Commission to the European Parliament, the Council, the European Economic and Social Committee and the Committee of the Regions, The European Pillar of Social Rights Action Plan, COM (2021) 102 final, 4 March 2021.

European Commission (2023). The Future of Social Protection and of the Welfare State in the EU. Report of the High-Level Expert Group.

European Commission (2024a). Ninth report on economic, social and territorial cohesion.

European Commission (2024b). Special Eurobarometer: Social Europe.

Ferrera, M. and Bruno, F. (2023). A Resource-Based conception for the analysis of the European Pillar of Social Rights: implication for further developments, EUSOCIALCIT Working Paper D2.3.

Ferrera, M., Corti, F. and Keune, M. (2023). Social citizenship as a marble cake: The changing pattern of right production and the role of the EU, Journal of European Social Policy, 33, 5, 493–509. https://doi.org/10.1177/09589287231207333

Hagemejer, J., Michałek, J.J., Svatko, P. (2021). Economic Impact of the EU Eastern Enlargement on New Member States Revisited: The Role of Economic Institutions. Central European Economic Journal, 8(55), 126–143. https://doi.org/10.2478/ceej-2021-0008

Hemerijck, A., S. Ronchi, I. Plavgo (2023). Social investment as a conceptual framework for analysing well-being returns and reforms in 21st century welfare states, *Socio-Economic Review*, Volume 21, Issue 1, January 2023, Pages 479–500, https://doi.org/10.1093/ser/mwac035

Landesmann, M., Székely, I. P. (eds.) (2021): Does EU Membership Facilitate Convergence? The Experience of the EU's Eastern Enlargement – Volume I–II. Studies in Economic Transition, London: Palgrave, Macmillan. https://doi.org/10.1007/978-3-030-57686-8

United Nations, Department of Economic and Social Affairs, Population Division (2024). World Population Prospects 2024. UN DESA/POP/2024

CHAPTER 7

Effective Cohesion Policies to Strengthen Social Integration in the EU

Rafael de Hoyos and Michał Rutkowski

7.1 Introduction

Few projects have contributed to human well-being as much as the European Union (EU). Established in 1957,[1] it aimed to promote economic cooperation and integration among its member states to ensure lasting peace and stability in Europe. The EU has delivered much more than peace and stability—a massive contribution in a region characterized

[1] In 1957, Belgium, France, Italy, Luxembourg, the Netherlands, and West Germany signed the Treaty of Rome, which created the European Economic Community (EEC) and established a customs union to complement the European Coal and Steel Community (ECSC). The EEC and Customs Union were the precursors of what is today the European Union.

R. de Hoyos (✉)
Inter-American Development Bank, Washington, DC, USA
e-mail: rafaelde@iadb.org

M. Rutkowski
World Bank, Washington, DC, USA

SGH Warsaw School of Economics, Warsaw, Poland
e-mail: mrutkow2@sgh.waw.pl

I. P. Székely, P. Halmai (eds.), *The Future of European Integration*, Studies in Economic Transition,
https://doi.org/10.1007/978-3-032-20186-7_7

by centuries of armed conflicts. It has promoted economic growth, human and social rights, environmental protection, and democracy over an expanding territory encompassing populations with diverse cultural, linguistic, and historical backgrounds.

Since its inception, the Union went through seven expansion processes, passing from six founding countries—Belgium, France, Germany, Italy, Luxembourg, and the Netherlands—in 1957 to 28 in 2013 (27 as of today after the departure of the United Kingdom in 2020). Once a country enters the Union, its fate and well-being become part of the Union's objectives. In all expansions, the new member states have experienced a significant increase in well-being proxied by GDP per capita. For instance, the GDP per capita in Spain passed from US$17,000 in 1986, the year it joined, to US$27,500 in 2000; Romania's GDP per capita went from US$9950 in 2007 to more than US$15,000 in 2022.[2] Poorer member states—usually new entrants—experience a higher growth rate than richer ones—usually incumbent member states—resulting in convergence in average incomes between countries in the Union.

The EU's growth model, privileging convergence, has been replicated in the successive enlargements to the south, with Greece, Spain, and Portugal in the 1980s and subsequent expansions to the east in the 2000s, enabling all these countries to join the club of "high-income countries" as defined by the World Bank. As described by Raiser and Gill (2012): "It is no exaggeration to say that Europe invented a "convergence machine," taking in poor countries and helping them become high-income economies. Over the last four decades, the countries in Europe experienced a convergence in consumption levels that is unmatched. Annual per capita consumption in the poorer parts of Europe grew by 4% while in the wealthier countries, it increased at a still-impressive 2 percent." The EU's convergence machine accounts for nearly a third of all success cases of countries passing from middle- to high-income status in the last 35 years (World Bank 2018). In other words, the EU and its institutions are the best antidote for the "middle-income trap" in which many countries experience economic growth and prosperity slowdown.

Unlike other regional integration projects like the North American Free Trade Agreement (NAFTA) or the Association of Southeast Asian Nations (ASEAN), the European Union goes beyond trade. It includes the free movement of people, common principles, regulations, large,

[2] All figures in constant US dollars of 2015.

sustained over the long-term transfers to finance social policies and economic growth in lagging member states, and standard fiscal and monetary policies to reach a shared goal. The EU has created a model, a blueprint, almost a recipe for generating well-being. The uniqueness of the EU model is that its incumbents are willing to allocate financial resources to countries outside their political constituency to help them kick-start the development process, even before joining the Union. EU candidate countries receive significant financial assistance, and a roadmap of reforms needed before joining the Union, all of which contribute to some anticipation effects of Union membership on economic growth.

Despite an impressive delivery on economic growth and convergence between member states, the EU model faces significant challenges and growing dissatisfaction among its population (Rodriguez-Pose et al. 2024). Although income inequality in EU member states is among the lowest in the world, 19 out of the 27 EU member states have experienced a marginal increase in income inequality since the Great Recession of 2008 (Dalvit et al. 2023). Perhaps more relevant, most Europeans perceive that income inequality has risen recently, regardless of what is captured by conventional income dispersion statistics (Bussolo et al. 2018a). The perception of growing inequality and a sense of lack of opportunities fueled political polarization and opened the door to populist policies. In recent years, a growing share of EU voters support political platforms that oppose European integration and even favor leaving the Union (Rodriguez-Pose et al. 2024).

The Union must address growing *Euroscepticism* while dealing with aging, a green transition, and technological progress, three megatrends that could exacerbate income disparities and limit economic growth. Given its demographic structure, Europe will experience a significant decrease in the population within working age, limiting competitiveness and long-term economic growth. In addition, the green and technological transitions will increase the demand for skills, particularly transversal, fungible, or foundational skills. These are skills that university graduates usually possess, and less-educated workers, including those with a vocational or technical degree, lack them, increasing the employment opportunities and wage differential between college graduates and the rest (Dalvit et al. 2023).

The EU model is well prepared to deal with the risk of increasing income inequality during economic transitions. The Union understands the challenges of ensuring that lagging regions, particularly remote rural areas, benefit from the integration process and economic transitions. To mitigate distributional tensions, the Union created a set of funds, merged under what is known today as "Cohesion Policy," to finance social policies, innovations, economic growth, and employment creation in lagging regions. The EU's Cohesion Policy is meant to "promote harmonious progress, advancing economic, social and territorial development throughout the Union by channeling investments into regions with lower levels of development and/or specific vulnerabilities" (European Commission 2024). The EU invests significant resources through Cohesion Policies, accounting for more than 2% of GDP per year in poorer member states. Cohesion Funds can be a powerful tool to reduce income disparities, promote opportunities, and contribute to productivity and long-term economic growth if spent on effective interventions and with a well-targeted mechanism.

This essay puts forward the building blocks of a new strategy that could promote social integration and address the growing dissatisfaction among the EU population. Our proposal acknowledges the EU's model's many positive aspects, such as its emphasis on social cohesion and sustainable economic growth, while identifying its limitations in delivering an ambitious, albeit sensible, set of social rights. Our strategy rests on simplifying what can be a large set of social policies financed by Cohesion Funds to maximize their impact. In other words, Cohesion Policy funds could promote and finance fewer social programs but with more significant and measurable impacts. To have more effective social integration policies, we put forward three concrete strategies: (1) concentrate on social policies that are the most relevant for the poor, as identified by the ubiquitous "guaranteed minimum income" GMI schemes; (2) allocate resources to the generation of government capacity at the local level; and (3) innovate in the design of social policies through policy experimentation and evaluation.

The three recommendations in this chapter are based on our diagnostic of the most critical elements in an agenda to modernize and improve the effectiveness of the social policies supported by the Cohesion Funds, most of which are financed by the European Social Fund+ (ESF+). They also reflect lessons and good practices that the World Bank has accumulated while working on similar development challenges worldwide. However, these three recommendations do not represent an exhaustive list of areas that could improve the effectiveness of Cohesion Funds. Still, our recommendations are ***quick gains*** since they are relatively simple to implement given the current operational structure of Cohesion Funds.

7.2 The EU: Economic Convergence with Regional Development Traps

Many policies, regulations, and interventions form the EU model. Some of the core elements of the EU model are the following: (1) a series of pre-accession legal reforms known as the "acquis" guaranteeing the independence of their judiciary system, strengthening the rule of law, respecting human rights and the rights of minorities, and other legislation reflecting EU principles; (2) access to a large market allowing some firms in incoming member states to expand and exploit economies of scale; (3) access to cheaper and higher quality consumer products in incoming member states; (4) free movement of labor across the Union, increasing allocative efficiency; (5) direct investment flows from more affluent into poorer member states; (6) access to Cohesion Policy funds to finance social integration among lagging countries and regions.

Existing evidence shows that the economic impact of the EU model has three distinctive features: (1) it promotes economic growth among its member states, (2) poorer member states benefit from higher growth rates than richer ones, resulting in convergence on average income between countries, and (3) some regions within countries are lagging with economic growth rates close to zero. The rest of this section presents evidence supporting these three distinctive features.

7.2.1 *The EU Convergence Machine*

All accession countries have benefited enormously from joining the Union. The impact of the EU model on GDP per capital has been widely documented using the 2004 expansion when 11 Eastern European Countries joined the Union.[3] For instance, using a synthetic control analysis, Cieślik and Turgut (2021) show that GDP per capita in new member states increased by an additional US $2313 per year thanks to the EU accession. The effect is equivalent to a positive impact on GDP per capital growth rate of 2.7% per year. Using a similar methodology and period, Grassi

[3] Cyprus and Malta join the EU with eight Central and Eastern European countries—Czechia, Estonia, Hungary, Latvia, Lithuania, Poland, Slovakia and Slovenia.

(2024) shows that between 2004 and 2019, accession countries' had a cumulative increase in GDP per capita of 90%, half of which can be attributed to EU accession.

We document the impact of joining the EU on GDP per capita, the first of three features of the EU model, exploiting all seven EU expansions. We do so by running a simple regression capturing the accession effects on GDP per capita:

$$Y_t = \beta_0 + \beta_1 t + \beta_2 \left(D = 1|\text{EU}\right) + \beta_3 t * \left(D = 1|\text{EU}\right) + \varepsilon_t$$

where Υ_t is the log of GDP per capita measured in constant US dollars of 2015, "t" is a time trend (year), $(D = 1 | EU)$ is a dummy variable capturing the year of entry to the EU and ε_t is a random component. In the specification above, the parameter of interest is β_2.[4] Using GDP per capita figures in constant terms for the period 1961–2022, covering all EU expansions, we found that, on average, being part of the Union has had a cumulative impact on GDP per capita of 31% on accession countries. In other words, had the EU still be formed by its original six founding members, GDP per capital would be a third lower in the 21 countries that joined the Union subsequently. This result suggests that GDP per capita has increased for all new member states after joining the Union.

The second feature of the EU model is that while all countries in the Union experience positive growth rates, poorer members grow faster. This can be seen clearly in the convergence process triggered in members that joined the Union in 2004, who experienced an average growth rate in GDP per capita of 4.3% between 2004 and 2022 compared with a growth rate of 0.9% for incumbents, reducing the gap on average incomes between the two groups of countries (see Fig. 7.1).

What elements of the EU model explain these economic effects? Isolating the impact of each of the elements defining the EU model (set of regulations, pre-accession reforms, trade integration, migration, etc.) on economic growth would be challenging, if not impossible. However, there is some evidence of the effects of some of its most important factors. Rapacki and Prochniak (2019) identify three determinants of the

[4] This is a descriptive exercise rather than an attempt to identify the causal impact of joining the Union, which would require identifying a control group. For attempts to tease the causal effect of joining the Union on economic growth, see Cieślik and Turgut (2021) and Grassi (2024) cited above.

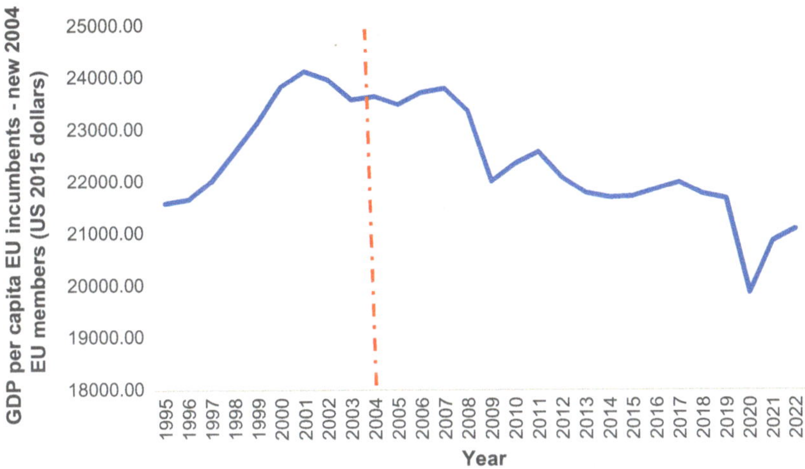

Fig. 7.1 The Convergence Machine at Work. (Source: Authors' own computation using data from the World Bank. [World Development Indicators])

convergence of incomes between the 2004 accession countries and older EU members: (1) improvements in economic freedom, business environment, and the quality of government as a result from pre-accession reforms, (2) increase in international trade and investment, and (3) EU Structural Funds (now called Cohesion Funds). Burghof and Gehrung (2022) and Orlowski (2020) show that the EU's integration of capital markets and the European single financial market played a critical role in boosting GDP per capita in new member states. Another important factor behind the convergence machine is the integration of new member states into a more extensive and more sophisticated European production network (Martínez-Zarzoso et al. 2020), which exploits its full benefits by allowing the free movement of labor (Caliendo et al. 2021). In summary, the convergence process following accession to the EU is related to improvements to the business environment, more trade and investment, more efficient production networks, free movement of people, and social and economic investments channeled through Cohesion Funds.

7.2.2 *Convergence Between Countries But Divergence Within Them?*

A potential side effect of the EU integration process is that some individuals, households, or entire communities could be left out of the convergence process. For instance, if large urban centers in new EU member states have well-functioning financial markets, a modern infrastructure, and a population with high skill levels, they could easily be inserted into European production networks. On the contrary, small towns in remote rural areas with a relatively unskilled population and few modern firms could struggle to compete and generate jobs. The integration process's regional asymmetric impact could increase income disparities within new EU member states.

Using the Gini coefficient of household per capita income as the measure of inequality within member states, we do not identify a significant change in income dispersion as a consequence of joining the Union (see Fig. 7.2). Inequality decreased in some countries that accessed the Union, but in others, it increased marginally. In the long-term, there is a divergence in within-country inequality, with countries that entered in 2004 becoming more equal, and the contrary being the case for Romania and Bulgaria, who joined the Union in 2007. Income disparities in countries

Fig. 7.2 Income Inequality within Countries Remained Constant after entering the EU. (Source: Authors' computations using data from World Income Inequality Database)

that were part of the Union before 2004 remain the same. Taking the EU as a whole, giving each citizen the same weight regardless of their country of origin, income differences have decreased since the 1990s (Lang et al. 2022). This downward trend in income dispersion is partly explained by the convergence in GDP per capita between the countries documented above.

Despite a mild and ambiguous change in income inequality post-EU accession, regional divides within countries are rising. Some regions at the "Nomenclature of Territorial Units for Statistics," levels 2 and 3, NUTS2 and NUTS3, respectively, have consistently low growth rates since the 1990s (Rodriguez-Pose et al. 2024). Surprisingly, low-growth regions are not located in the poorest EU member states. Figure 7.3 shows the cumulative GDP growth per capita from 2011 to 2022, per subnational region. Low-growth or negative-growth regions include parts of the north of France (outside Paris), most of Italy, large parts of Spain, and Greece. In contrast, most regions in Eastern Europe—where most of the 2004 and 2007 accession countries are located—show a significant increase in GDP per capita during the same period, with regions in Romania showing a remarkable performance, some of which experienced a doubling of average income in 11 years.[5]

Low-growth regions are scarcely populated, they lack economic dynamism, do not attract investment, their firms do not adopt new technologies, and their productivity is low and stagnant. They fall under a *regional development trap*, "areas facing significant structural challenges to regain their previous economic dynamism, or to improve wealth and prosperity for their residents." (Rodriguez-Pose et al. 2024).[6] Lack of economic growth and employment opportunities in regions under a regional development trap, usually small towns in rural areas, incentivizes young and

[5] Romania has made remarkable progress in poverty reduction over the past two decades. While the share of the population living below the upper-middle-income poverty line of $6.85 per day remains at 7.1% in 2021, this represents a dramatic improvement compared to 2005, when more than 40% of Romanians were poor. Strong economic growth, rising labor and pension incomes, and redistributive reforms have driven these gains, lifting millions out of poverty and transforming the country's social landscape. Yet, despite this progress, Romania continues to face persistent challenges, including high inequality, significant urban-rural disparities, and a large share of the population at risk of poverty or social exclusion by EU standards (World Bank 2018).

[6] Regional development trap: "the state of a region unable to retain its economic dynamism in terms of income, productivity, and employment, while also underperforming its national and European peers on these same dimensions" (Diemer et al. 2022).

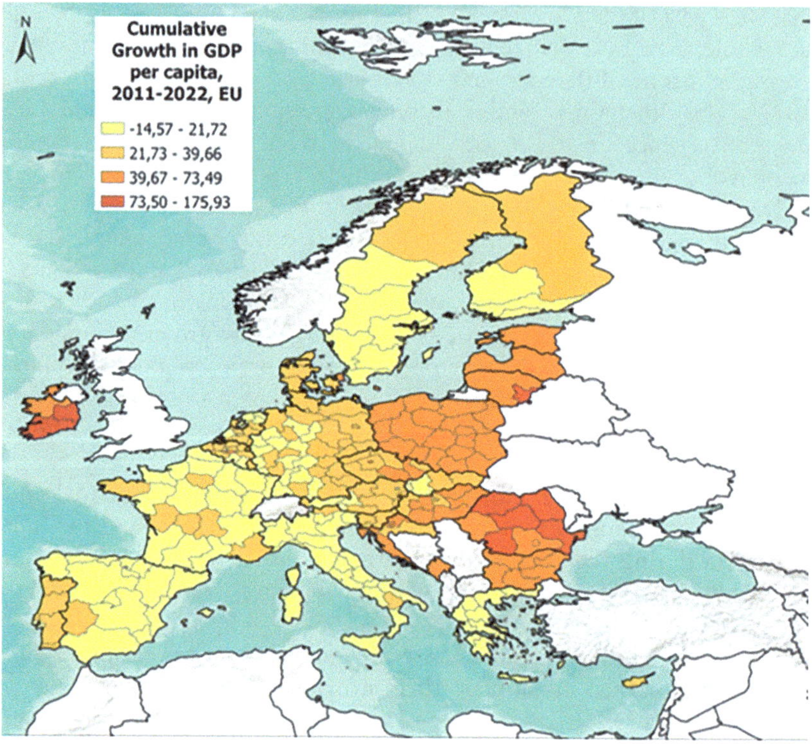

Fig. 7.3 Cumulative Growth in GDP per capita, 2011–2022, per NUTS2 region. (Source: Authors' calculations with data from Eurostat)

skilled workers to look for opportunities in large, thriving urban centers, exacerbating the development trap and creating low-productivity, low-growth equilibrium.

7.2.3 *The Regional Development Trap and Political Preferences*

In regions that have fallen into the development trap and have experienced low or no growth during the last 15 years, the prospects for intergenerational social mobility are close to zero. Employment opportunities are limited, and the expectation of having a brighter future is low. Young Europeans living in a regional development trap have low expectations of having a level of well-being above that of their parents. Lack of economic opportunities can impact political preferences. As shown in Fig. 7.4 regions with no or little economic growth during the period 2011–2017 displayed more political support for Eurosceptic parties.

This section showed that the EU model displays three distinctive features: (1) it promotes economic growth, (2) the rates of economic growth are larger among poorer member states resulting in convergence, and (3) income inequality does not increase after entering the Union, the disparities in the rates of growth do differ significantly, with some regions growing at a high-speed rate while others suffering from a "regional development trap." Therefore, the distributional concerns within the Union are not income differences between individuals or regions but differences in economic growth rates between modern urban centers and rural areas caught in a development trap. Cohesion Policy funds target low-income regions rather than low-growth regions, which might be a mismatch between the distributional challenges faced by the Union and the allocation of funds for shared economic prosperity. The EC could distribute part of the funds of the Cohesion Policy, particularly those focusing on infrastructure, competitiveness, and economic development, to areas with little or zero growth, i.e., under a regional development trap.

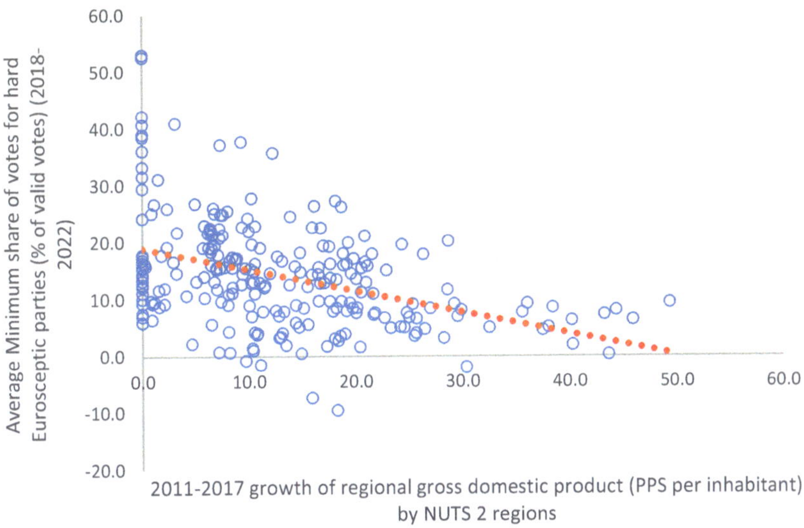

Fig. 7.4 Regional Prosperity and Euroscepticism. (Source: Authors' computation using data from Rodriguez-Pose et al. (2024) and Eurostat)

7.3 Megatrends, the Changing Nature of Work, and Income Dispersion

The development trap into which some regions in the EU have fallen and its associated political polarization could be exacerbated by the megatrends reshaping labor markets, economies, and societies. Effective and well-targeted social policies could mitigate the distributional impact of aging, the green transition, and rapid technological progress to avoid deepening the existing regional development traps or pushing new regions into economic stagnation.

The demographic structure in Europe is rapidly transforming into an inverted pyramid, with a low number of youth, a decreasing working-age population, and an expanding population above 65 years old. The EU will lose 40 million workers in the next 75 years. According to the European Central Bank, "[T]he number of people of working age is expected to drop by 19%, from 221 million in 2022 to 180 million in 2100. This will lead to a rapid increase in the old-age dependency ratio, from 34% in 2022 to around 51% in 2050 and 60% in 2100 – that is, from one elderly person for every three working-age people in 2022 to just under two elderly people in 2100." (ECB Economic Bulletin, Issue 3/2023).

A declining workforce means lower GDP growth, and with fewer young workers, the rate of innovation and technological progress could stall, limiting productivity and long-term economic growth. Regions under a development trap can experience an even more rapid decline in the number of young, highly skilled, and innovative workers who could seek better job opportunities in thriving urban centers. Therefore, aging in the EU could result in stagnant productivity, increased income inequality, and further political polarization.

The second megatrend shaping the future is the green transition. The European Green Deal (EGD) is the Union's strategy to address climate change. It establishes regulations and incentives to achieve three core objectives: (i) net-zero emissions of greenhouse gas (GHG) emissions by 2050, (ii) decoupling the economy from natural resource consumption, and (iii) leaving no person or place behind during the transition.

The EGD's general, economy-wide effects will create winners and losers—as with any other transition. One of the most important linkages between household well-being and the EGD is given through the change in the price of energy, which could rise because of removing subsidies or reducing coal-based energy production. Higher energy prices will reduce household well-being, particularly vulnerable ones that devote a significant share of income to cover energy bills. Using a general equilibrium model with ten households representing each of the deciles of the EU income distribution, Fragkos et al. (2021) show that the transition to climate neutrality within the EGD will increase marginally income inequality with poorer households experiencing a larger negative impact due to their relatively higher share of income devoted to energy consumption.

A second link between the EGD and households' well-being operates via the labor market with workers in carbon-intensive "brown" industries losing jobs and/or wages. Sanchez-Reaza et al. (2023) find that the EGD will increase the labor demand for college graduates and reduce that of less-educated workers, increasing the wage gap. The same authors show that workers in "brown" industries have lower skills than those in "green" industries. Perhaps more challenging, Sanchez-Reaza et al. (2023) document that the number of coal-related jobs to be lost in coal-producing regions such as Silesia and Wielkopolska in Poland is enough to depress the entire area, running the risk of entering into a regional development trap.

The third and most important of the megatrends, due to the speed at which it is advancing and its ubiquitousness, is technological progress. Globalization and technological change over the last 40 years have resulted in some productivity gains but also a loss of middle-class jobs in EU member states (Bussolo et al. 2018b). This process has, at least partly, contributed to the regional development traps documented above. The existing evidence shows that new technologies can result in a further deterioration of the distribution of income in the EU. Dalvit et al. (2023) show that while innovation and technological advances contribute to labor productivity, the gains will be reaped by larger and more productive firms, increasing market concentration, and decreasing the share of total national income that goes to labor. In addition, in line with the results of the European Parliament (2018), Dalvit et al. (2023) show that firms adopting new technologies increase their demand for college graduates, and therefore, wages for these workers rise while low-skilled workers may face job displacement or wage stagnation.

Technological advancements can lead to further economic disparities across regions within the EU. Dalvit et al. (2023) combine several EU firm surveys between 2014 and 2022 to show that countries and regions with higher levels of human capital, greater access to financial resources, and business-friendly regulatory frameworks promote the adoption of new technologies, enhancing productivity, and economic growth. In contrast, rural or less developed regions might lag, increasing regional income inequalities. Similarly, McKinsey (2020) emphasizes the regional differences in jobs created by technological progress: "new jobs are likely to be distributed unequally across occupations and geographies, potentially exacerbating existing strains in the social contract linking individuals and institutions."

Rapid technological progress can make existing professional competencies obsolete, posing a considerable challenge for education and training systems. If education and training systems in the EU cannot keep pace with the rapidly changing nature of work in technology-driven labor markets, relatively unskilled workers could be displaced. Dalvit et al. (2023) show that after five to seven years in the labor market, graduates with a vocational education and training (VET) degree show a labor market disadvantage compared with workers with only a general secondary diploma. In other words, VET graduates have flatter wage-income profiles than non-VET secondary graduates, which is equivalent to displaying lower returns to experience (see Fig. 7.5). This is partly explained because VET graduates are still engaged in routine and manual tasks (at a high risk of being automatized), and have low levels of foundational skills—numeracy, literacy, and social skills—which are greatly needed in dynamic labor markets characterized by constant change.

7.4 Toward a More Effective Social Policy in the EU

Social policies in the EU have as a backbone the "European Pillar of Social Rights (EPSR)," a collection of 20 principles that are the normative benchmark to promote social integration in the Union (see Fig. 7.6). The principles are organized around three broad areas: (1) equal opportunities and access to labor markets (marked in red in Fig. 7.6), (2) fair working conditions (light green), and (3) social protection and inclusion (dark green). The EPSR has an action plan that includes coordination with the EU's Cohesion Policy funds. For the programming period 2021–2027, the Cohesion Policy encompasses eight funds, supporting more than 370 programs to promote social inclusion, territorial cohesion, and a fair green and digital transition (among many others).

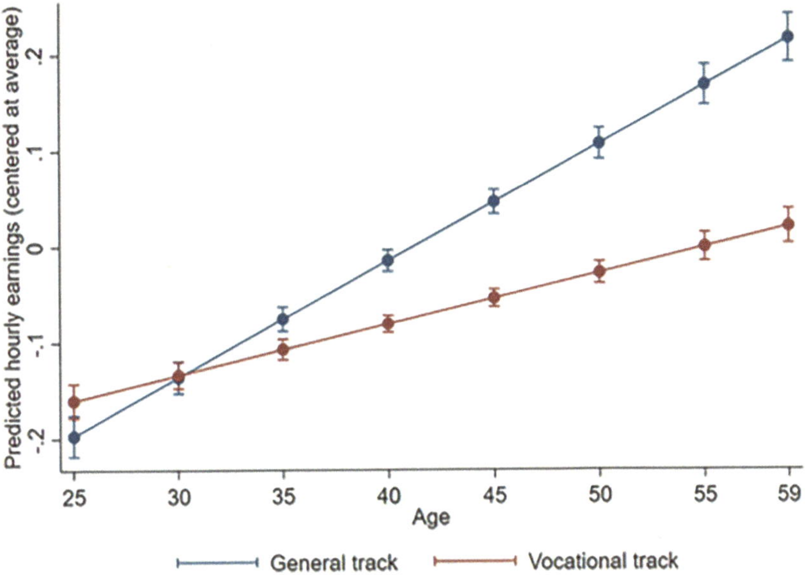

Fig. 7.5 Age profile of earnings of VET and general secondary graduates. (Source: Dalvit et al. 2023). Note: This figure plots the predicted log hourly earnings (centered at the country mean) at different ages of general secondary graduates (blue line) and VET graduates (maroon line). The values are derived from a linear regression of log hourly earnings, which includes an interaction factor between age and educational track and country, gender, parental education, numeracy, and literacy as control variables. The sample is restricted to individuals from 25 to 59 years old whose highest educational attainment is upper secondary (ISCED 3) or postsecondary nontertiary education (ISCED 4)

7.4.1 *Unleashing the Social Impacts of Cohesion Policy Funds*

The systematic revisions of the impact of Cohesion Policies have shown that while they are a useful tool that positively affects regional development, there is significant scope for improvement. Cohesion Funds are allocated based on a formula that assigns more resources to regions at the NUTS2 level with a GDP per capita below 75% of the EU average. Exploiting the exogenous threshold of 75%, Becker et al. (2010) show that Cohesion Funds positively impact regional economic growth. Cohesion Funds increase GDP per capita by 1.6% per year during the

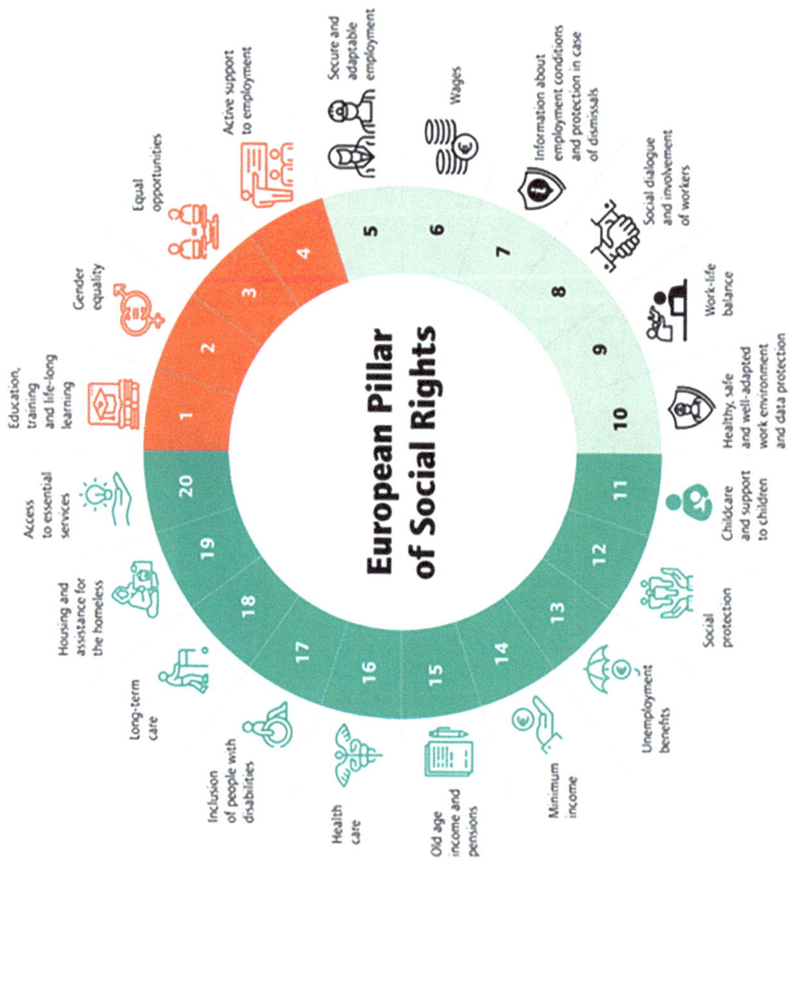

Fig. 7.6 The European Pillar of Social Rights. (Source: European Commission)

programming period for funds execution (usually seven years). However, the authors find no impact on employment, most likely due to the relatively short-term impact the Funds have on GDP, which is insufficient to address the structural constraints of regions under a development trap.

More recently, Canova (2024) analyzes the economic impact of the two largest funds within Cohesion Policy, the European Regional Development Fund (ERDF) and the European Social Fund Plus (ESF+), together accounting for close to 90% of the total budget of Cohesion Policy funds. Estimating an econometric model at the NUTS2 level, Canova (2024) finds that the ERDF positively impacts Gross Domestic Product (GDP) in the short term but this effect fades away after three years. On the contrary, the ESF+ has no short-term impact on GDP, but its effect is positive and economically relevant in the medium- to long-term. The lack of short-term effects of the ESF+ is unsurprising since the fund finances social policies and interventions to improve human capital formation among marginalized households. Most of these investments contribute to economic growth and employment creation only in the medium to long term (World Bank 2018).

One of the most important challenges of the EU's social policy under Cohesion Policy, namely, the ESF+, is that it finances many interventions and policies without devoting enough time to identify the most cost-effective options to achieve the intended objectives. The funds tend to be executed without enough time devoted to the design, identifying a theory of change, ensuring a sound targeting of the most vulnerable household, and reviewing the international evidence to find best practices. Instead, the Funds focus mainly on inputs rather than outputs (European Commission 2024). For example, one of three EPSR action plan macro targets is that at least 60% of adults should participate in training annually by 2030. However, participating in training should not be a goal in itself. Many –if not the majority—of short-term training programs that have been evaluated rigorously show a moderate impact on what matters: employability, job stability, and wages (Kluve et al. 2019; Card et al. 2018). On the contrary, the existing evidence suggests that the effectiveness of training programs is closely related to their design; programs that are tailor-made for the needs of a particular sector, have a strong collaboration with the private sector, and include a module to improve social skills are more likely to have a positive impact (Rodrik and Stantcheva 2021).

A second challenge of the social policies financed by Cohesion Funds is that the funds are administered and disbursed by the member state, in many cases, local authorities at the sub-national level, with limited administrative capacities to transform the additional resources into more well-being for the population.[7] As mentioned above, Cohesion Policy allocated more resources to subnational regions whose GDP per capita is below 75% of the EU average.[8] However, these lagging regions also have low institutional and administrative capacities, challenges that are not necessarily addressed with more financial resources. Low institutional and administrative capacities at the local level hinder the rate at which the Cohesion funds are translated into well-being, reducing the overall efficiency of social policies (Rodríguez-Pose and Garcilazo 2015; Rodríguez-Pose and Ketterer 2020; Rodriguez-Pose et al. 2024).

A third challenge not strictly related to the Cohesion Funds but a feature of social policies in most countries is the need for more innovation, experimentation, and evaluation. Labor markets and societies constantly change due to technological progress, aging, and other shocks and transitions. Nevertheless, the toolkit of social policies does not show the same dynamism. More experimentation and evaluation are needed to test the efficacy of innovative social policies. Innovations should be evaluated rigorously to identify which one works and understand why. There is no better place in the world than the EU to promote innovations in the design of social policies. The EU has the political compromise with social inclusion, the financial resources, the expertise in their universities and research centers, and the datasets to be the world leader in social policy innovation.

The rest of this section develops a strategy to address the three challenges described above and unleash the full potential of the social policies financed by Cohesion Funds. Our recommendations are focused on social policies, so they are relevant for the ESF+ and less so for other funds included in the Cohesion Policies. The proposed approach is based on the above diagnostic, existing evidence, and the World Bank's experiences implementing interventions in EU member states and many other regions worldwide.

[7] In this chapter, we follow the OECD (2013) and Eurostat. (2021) in defining well-being as a multidimensional concept that includes both material conditions and quality-of-life dimensions such as health, education, civic engagement, and subjective satisfaction.

[8] During the programing period 2014–2020, 62% of the total Cohesion Funds executed were distributed to "developing regions," i.e., with a GDP per capita below 75% of the EU average.

7.4.2 Combining Social Assistance with Social Services

EU's social policies implemented through the ESF+ attempt to achieve too many goals simultaneously, which could dilute its overall impact. The ESF+ wide range of objectives and the inclusion of numerous thematic areas could lead to a lack of focus on the needs of poor and vulnerable households, reducing the overall effectiveness and progressiveness of the funds. ESF+ could prioritize interventions that reach the poorest households (well targeted) and address their needs (relevant). This could be done by channeling more funds to help member states create a social protection system that combines well-targeted social assistance programs like the Guaranteed Minimum Income (GMI) system with relevant social services for the poor.[9] While there is no binding definition of social services in the European Union, they are broadly conceived as provisions, generally in the form of non-cash actions and activities, designed to ensure essential support and assistance to meet various social needs, fostering social inclusion for vulnerable groups, families, or individuals. Social services are provided by the government, non-profit organizations, or other entities to ensure the welfare and protection of the population, particularly the vulnerable and disadvantaged groups. They can include child welfare services, support for the older people, assistance for people with disabilities, mental health care, housing support, and poverty alleviation programs, among others. Generally speaking, social services operate as a distinct sector from mainstream health and education systems, although delivering social services to specific demographic groups, such as older people or people with disabilities, may often require a comprehensive package of multisectoral support for the delivery of which integration between sectors is crucial.

The EPSR mandates that all EU member states should have a GMI program. Although in some countries like Bulgaria, Croatia, and Romania, the GMI program is small relative to the number of families in need, building a robust and well-targeted GMI is possible. For instance, in

[9] GMI is a social welfare system that guarantees all citizens/residents or families an income sufficient to cover the minimum living costs, provided that certain eligibility conditions are met. The conditions typically include residence/citizenship and an income below a pre-established threshold (poverty line). Although the primary goal of GMI is to ensure that all citizens fulfill their social right to have sufficient income to cover minimum living costs, many schemes have "activation paths" to help the poor access the labor market and secure sufficient income to leave the minimum income program eventually.

Romania, the World Bank and the European Commission supported reforming their GMI program, building an administrative data system to identify poor and eligible households, significantly increasing the number of beneficiaries, and increasing the transfer size.[10]

A well-targeted Guaranteed Minimum Income (GMI) that covers all poor and vulnerable households is a great opportunity to understand their needs, enabling national or local governments to connect those needs with the relevant social services and labor market activation paths through a *case management* strategy. Case management recognizes that having a minimum income is important, but it's usually not enough to break the cycle of poverty. In this context, GMI is a critical poverty alleviation instrument. Poor households need access to relevant and high-quality social services to help them address the main issues causing their poverty, which, in most cases, requires access to the labor market. These issues vary from household to household, so solutions need to be personalized and tailored by the government. For example, some households might be poor because they have a family member who is sick and requires constant care, while others might be struggling due to low levels of education and skills. In such cases, the government needs to identify the specific challenges, often through assessments conducted by social workers, and then provide the relevant social services.[11]

A central element of case management is the assessment to identify poor households' constraints on a case-by-case basis—hence the name. After conducting an assessment, case managers evaluate the needs and situations of individuals or families to provide information, orientation, and intermediation for accessing available benefits and social services. This support may involve referring the beneficiary to another eligible service,

[10] For more information on the GMI reform in Romania, see: https://gov.ro/en/media/press-releases/press-release-cabinet-meeting-government-changes-the-system-of-granting-social-benefits-for-families-and-singles-in-need

[11] The World Bank developed the "Case Compass" toolkit to help governments improve case management systems—particularly in social protection and welfare services—through guidance, tools, and prototypes (www.case-compass.org). It offers a Guide that lays out best practices for case management, its enabling factors, and how to build or strengthen case management information systems; a fully functioning Prototype to help visualize a customizable case management information system; and a Learn section to support country clients through learning materials, tailored clinics, and workshop. The toolkit is meant to be a global public good: available to interested countries under World Bank support, aimed at both those wanting to introduce case management and/or case management information systems for the first time and those looking to improve existing systems.

either within the same agency or in another agency, such as employment services.[12]

Beneficiaries can enter case management interventions either directly or indirectly. People are brought into case management at the front office in direct intake. For example, in countries where municipalities provide integrated support to citizens through local social assistance units. In this case, municipalities guide beneficiaries to receive the relevant support or refer them to more specialized social work. In the indirect intake, people are brought into case management when it is provided as part of another social program or when they are referred to it by another program. For instance, case management may be provided alongside the monetary benefit of a GMI. Providing indirect intake through a well-designed GMI program has the advantage of being targeted to the poor—measured by income below the poverty line—and their needs. In all cases, the preferences of the beneficiary should play a key role in pathways offered and chosen.[13]

Most programs that combine cash transfers of GMI with case management (GMI+) have as an objective labor market activation of the beneficiaries or their reintegration in the labor market. Is there evidence that GMI+ has a positive impact on the beneficiary's well-being or their labor market outcomes? A recent paper by Marzi et al. (2024) summarizes the evidence on the effects of poverty-targeted social assistance programs with a focus on programs with a labor market activation component in high-income countries. In the remainder of this subsection, we summarize the extensive literature review discussed in Marzi et al. (2024), focusing on experiences from Chile, the UK, Norway, Denmark, and France. A central finding of Marzi et al. (2024) is the scarcity of robust evaluations on the effects of GMI+.[14] "Chile Solidario," a GMI+ program targeting households living in extreme poverty in Chile, is the only one extensively evaluated. The evaluation of "Chile Solidario" finds positive impacts on

[12] See www.case-compass.org

[13] See www.case-compass.org

[14] Three EU countries are currently conducting rigorous evaluation studies on the impact of GMIs plus social inclusion pathways to inform policymaking (Marzi et al. 2024). Spain has created a "Policy Lab" in partnership with J-PAL Europe to implement a broad range of pilot social inclusion programs targeting recipients of the IMV (MINET 2023). Next, France has been piloting and will be evaluating the results of an intensified case management model for RSA beneficiaries in 18 regions. Finally, in Italy an RCT-based impact evaluation of the Italian RdC/Adi is ongoing.

the socio-emotional well-being of the poor; however, its impact on employment is mixed.

The evidence from Chile presented in Marzi et al. (2024) shows that psycho-social support and tailored social intermediation services can be effective in increasing the poor's access to social assistance and social services and in improving their socio-emotional well-being. Quasi-experimental evaluations of "Chile Solidario" find that in the short term, the program has a strong positive impact on awareness of social services (Galasso 2011) and on recipients' take-up of family allowances and employment programs (Neidhöfer and Niño-Zarazúa 2019; Galasso 2011). Moreover, recipients of "Chile Solidario" are more likely to enroll in housing programs, adult literacy and education completion programs, pre-schools, and the public health system (Galasso 2011). There is also evidence that the program brings about a more optimistic view of their future socio-economic status among recipients (Galasso 2011). However, the evidence on the short-term impact of "Chile Solidario" on employment is mixed and not conclusive (Neidhöfer and Niño-Zarazúa 2019; Galasso 2011).

Much more evidence from Europe is available on the effects of GMI+ on labor market outcomes, according to Marzi et al. (2024). Evaluations from Norway, the UK, Denmark, and France document the impact of government-led activation programs with a case management component on labor force participation or unemployment insurance. Evidence from Norway shows that individualized intensive activation programs coupled with substantial financial benefits can have a strong and positive impact on employment prospects (Markussen and Røed 2016). Positive effects are partly explained by the integration of social services and Public Employment Services (PES), resulting in enhanced individual follow-up of recipients. The evaluation pinpoints the importance of establishing a tighter collaboration between PES and social welfare services that led to a better understanding of each other's work and of the needs of their mutual beneficiaries (Rønsen and Skarðhamar 2009). Similarly, an evaluation of the "JobCenter plus" initiative in the UK finds that the integrated model of cash benefit claiming and work placement services has a positive effect on job entry outcomes for all groups (Karagiannaki 2007).

Evidence from Denmark presented in Marzi et al. (2024) suggests that individual meetings with case managers might be effective in reducing the unemployment rate of unemployment insurance beneficiaries, although the effect is not observed for youth recipients (Graversen and van Ours

2008; Maibom et al. 2014). Evaluations of the French and UK employment pilot programs targeted at young recipients suggest that combining individualized case management with monetary assistance can improve employment outcomes (Gaini et al. 2020 for France and Blundell et al. 2004 for the UK).

Evidence from the UK on the employment impact of individualized case management and job search assistance programs addressed at people with health and disability related barriers to employment is not conclusive, according to Marzi et al. (2024). However, the evidence from the "New Deal for Disabled People" pilot, which commissioned the provision of activation services and employment advice to an external organization, suggests that tailored services lead to an increase in employment outcomes and a reduction in benefit recipiency at least for recipients who voluntary join the program (Stafford 2012). Lastly, the provision of a mandatory activation program coupled with personal advisors to facilitate claimants' return to work including with easier access to existing programs, under the "Pathways to Work" pilot might lead to an increased probability of being employed (Dorsett 2007).

The evidence presented in this section shows that GMI can be successfully linked to employment services for improved labor market outcomes, and that combining GMI with social services based on the active case management system should be considered as a promising opportunity to increase social integration in Europe through a better understanding of the constraints faced by poor households to improve their participation in the labor market. Those constraints can be matched with relevant and effective social services financed by the ESF+ within the Cohesion Funds. Effective social policies can help mitigate the increasing perception of inequality and unfairness. As Guriev (2024) described in a chapter in this same volume, "...the problem of inequality has to be urgently addressed. Europe is built on the ideas of equal opportunity. Redistribution towards the most vulnerable families and providing them with access to health and skills are crucial for Europe's success."

7.4.3 Enhancing Administrative Capacities at the Subnational Level

Although there is some evidence that EU integration improves State capacities, weak States do not fully exploit the benefits of being part of the Union (Vukov 2019). A large share of Cohesion Funds reaches regions with very low institutional and administrative capacity. Low institutional capacity limits the rate at which the Cohesion Funds are translated into people's well-being (Rodríguez-Pose and Ketterer 2020). The administrative capacity of local governments is pivotal in delivering essential services such as education, health, and social protection, which are at the core of human capital formation and, therefore, productivity and long-term economic growth. Thus, in many regions under a development trap, low government capacity is the binding constraint, which is not necessarily relaxed by additional resources.

In many EU member states, central governments have devolved administrative responsibilities to subnational entities without ensuring that there is enough institutional capacity at the local level to exercise these responsibilities effectively. Low administrative capacity at the regional level hinders their ability to manage resources effectively and deliver quality social services. The decentralization process requires complementary interventions to ensure effective managerial practices to improve the administrative capacity of subnational actors. Given the critical role played by subnational entities in the execution of Cohesion Funds, and ESF+ in particular, their staff should have the needed skills in (i) planning, (ii) budgeting, (iii) financial management, and (iv) procurement to ensure the successful execution of funds and service delivery. Mendez and Bachtler (2024) show that the quality of government at the subnational (regional) level is a significant determinant of the timely absorption of Cohesion Funds, the legality and regularity of expenditures, and the achievement of outcome targets, three core variables shaping the effectiveness of the funds.

Exploiting variation at the NUTS2 level during the period 1996–2007, Rodríguez-Pose and Garcilazo (2015) show that in most of the regions receiving Structural funds (the predecessor of Cohesion Funds), additional resources have almost no contribution to local economic growth due to low institutional capacity at the local level. The authors show that "above a threshold of cohesion expenditure—calculated at more than €120 of cohesion expenditure per capita per year—government quality improvements are a far more important and realistic option for regional development than additional public investment."

The EU should complement the distribution of funds to lagging regions with more technical support to improve their administrative capacities. Around 3% of funds are invested into technical assistance (TA) across the EU, with only 7% of the TA (i.e., 0.21% of the total funds) devoted to staff professional development—an area that has a long-lasting contribution to administrative capacities. More funds are needed to develop and implement sound instruments to measure administrative capacities at the regional level, monitor its performance, conduct policy experimentations aiming to improve administrative capacity[15] and identify and share good practices within and between member states.

A more effective ESF+ in particular and Cohesion Policy in general, must invest in improving institutional capacity at the local level, with a focus on areas with a weaker public administration. It should ensure weaker States develop administrative and managerial capacities and public sector systems and processes supporting service delivery. The starting point should be measuring administrative capacities at the local level, identifying weaker regions, and providing technical support to develop the skills and state capacity (Polverari 2023). Developing administrative capacities should be done by taking the broader national context into account, addressing the challenges in State building faced by weaker member states instead of only aiming to improve the administration of Cohesion Funds (Polverari et al. 2024).

Strengthening civil servant's managerial skills is at the core of the agenda to improve the administrative capacities of local entities. Managerial practices significantly drive public administration *productivity* or the number of projects completed and their impact. Recent evidence shows that most civil servants in middle management positions can identify the main constraint limiting the productivity in their unit (World Bank 2018). When provided with on-the-job training tailored to the binding constraint previously identified, civil servants' managerial practices improved and increased the share of projects completed (a proxy of public administration's productivity). The training itself in this type of intervention is focused on the specific challenges identified by the manager; the key element behind this approach is measuring both managerial practices and public administration's productivity.

7.4.4 Promote Social Policy Innovation and Experimentation

Thanks partly to profit-seeking, the private sector is constantly innovating, and with it, labor markets and societies are changing. The world is

[15] For an example of policy experimentation to improve State capacities, see the World Bank's "Bureaucracy Lab" https://www.worldbank.org/en/research/dime/brief/Bureaucracy-Lab

continuously evolving with new social challenges emerging due to the changing nature of work, regional development traps, aging, and the urgency of implementing the green transition. Social interventions, such as those financed by the ESF+ of Cohesion Policy Funds, do not exhibit the needed pace of innovation to keep up with the emerging challenges.

Cohesion Policy has an opportunity to expand the frontier of knowledge on effective social policies to finance interventions capable of addressing the challenges faced by the Union. Bringing more evidence into the design, implementation, and evaluation of social policies can increase the effectiveness of the funds. The generation of innovative and effective social policies requires (1) design of new interventions to address the most pressing development challenges, (2) evaluate the impact of new interventions, (3) exchange of knowledge among Member States to share interventions that have proven to be effective, and (5) scale up successful interventions using the ESF+ of Cohesion Policy.

Generating a strong link between social policy experimentation, scientific evidence, and at-scale policy implementation requires a framework, political compromise, and financing. For over 20 years, the World Bank has promoted using randomized control trials (RCTs) to complement its projects worldwide (World Bank 2018). These experiences have translated into the "trial and adopt" framework, whose main elements are summarized in Fig. 7.7. The framework moves from a pre-set policy design to an adaptive one, allowing the intervention to absorb the feedback generated by real-time results. It uses intensive administrative data and digital tools to identify the most relevant development challenges (e.g., reducing youth unemployment) and create real-time information on program effectiveness and potential changes to maximize impact (adaptation). Finally, the "trial and adopt" framework identifies the causal link between the intervention and outcomes. When a policy or intervention is proven effective, it can be scaled up and shared with other countries

Evaluating whether a policy or intervention achieved its desired objective and understanding why it worked or didn't work, is at the core of the "trial and adopt" framework. Identifying the causal relationship between a policy or intervention and its desired outcome is crucial to measuring and improving the effectiveness of public policies. For example, if significant resources are assigned to finance training programs to reduce youth unemployment—a common challenge in some EU member states—then it is only natural to test if the training programs achieve their objective and reduce youth unemployment. Such a test requires identifying the causal,

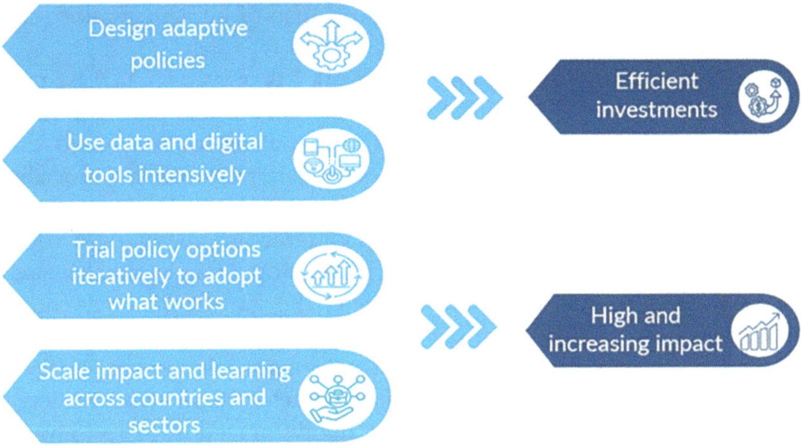

Fig. 7.7 The elements of the World Bank's "trial and adopt" framework. (Source: World Bank)

unidirectional, isolated effect of training on youth unemployment. This type of evaluation involves constructing a control group that captures a counterfactual, a scenario of how the outcome variable (in our example, youth unemployment) would look in the absence of the intervention (training programs).[16]

The "trial and adopt" framework also improves program implementation. Managing authorities and policymakers usually focus on inputs and program disbursement rates rather than assessing whether programs have achieved their goals of improving outcomes (people's well-being or a proxy of it). Even taking this somewhat limited perspective on monitoring programs, evidence-based policymaking can enhance the provision of inputs. Evidence from more than 1000 World Bank projects shows that those complemented by a robust impact evaluation had fewer delays and better disbursement rates (Legovini et al. 2015). These results are explained by having a mid-course correction based on process evaluation

[16] Constructing a valid control group can be done in many ways, using statistical methods such as matching, exploiting an exogenous discontinuity, using a natural experiment, or, more reliably, by randomizing the intervention, i.e., some individuals or households receive the intervention, and some others do not. For more technical details see Gertlet et al. (2016).

results, implementing a more detailed road map of implementation, and strengthening capacity on the ground.

Applying the "trial and adopt" framework has proven to increase program effectiveness in EU member states and in many countries worldwide (World Bank 2018). For instance, in Estonia, a trial of "enhanced care management" training doctors to use holistic care plans reduced mortality rates among chronically ill patients by 50% in two years (Rogger and Schuster 2023). An apprenticeship program targeting unemployed youth in Cote d'Ivoire designed under the "trial and adopt" framework increased the earnings of beneficiaries four years after the start of the intervention (Crépon and Premand 2019). In Mexico, a World Bank-financed project implementing a full-time school model among schools serving poor and vulnerable students improved learning outcomes by 0.15 standard deviations, with larger effects among the most disadvantaged students (Silveyra and Yañez 2018).

There are successful experiences in promoting evidence-based policy-making in the social sectors within the EU. The most recent example is the Social Inclusion Lab in Spain, a collaboration between the Government of Spain and J-PAL, a network of researchers implementing impact evaluations.[17] The close link between scientific evidence and policy design in France between 2009 and 2013 is a case of huge success in the social and other sectors (Palenberg and Paulson 2020). Finally, through DG REGIO, the European Commission is implementing the "trial and adopt" framework in technology adoption, strategies to help firms implement the green transition, and improving public sector productivity. However, more policy innovation and experimentation are needed in the social sectors. The ESF+ innovation fund finances new interventions to promote social integration but does not evaluate their impact, limiting the lessons that can be extracted from these experiences.

The growing global trend of shifting the focus from inputs to outcomes enhances accountability, can determine budget allocations to programs with more impact, and guides program design and policy decisions.

[17] For more Information see https://www.inclusion.gob.es/web/inclusion/politicas-de-inclusion

7.5 Conclusion

The European Union has been successful in improving economic performance across member states and achieving convergence in income levels, particularly for poorer countries, since its expansions began in 1957. However, this convergence at the national level masks growing disparities at the subnational level. Some regions—especially in more developed countries such as France, Belgium, Italy, and Spain—have experienced stagnation or minimal economic growth since the global financial crisis of 2008–2009. These underperforming regions, often characterized as being in a regional development trap, face compounding structural disadvantages and have been more likely to support Eurosceptic parties, fueling political polarization.

Today, one of the EU's most pressing distributional challenges lies in the divide between dynamic urban centers and lagging regions, many of which are rural and demographically aging. Megatrends—such as population aging, rapid technological change, and climate transition—risk exacerbating spatial and social inequalities unless proactively addressed. Without strong responses from the European Commission and member states, these trends could accelerate social disintegration and deepen distrust in the EU project.

Cohesion Policy—particularly the social components supported by the European Social Fund Plus (ESF+)—is a key instrument to address these territorial and social cleavages. In this chapter, we propose a three-pronged strategy to make social integration a more central and effective goal of the EU's cohesion framework.

First, more resources should be directed toward well-targeted Guaranteed Minimum Income (GMI) programs with high coverage of poor and vulnerable populations. When combined with integrated support services, as in GMI+ models featuring personalized case management, these programs improve labor market participation and broader well-being. Importantly, GMI+ also contributes to strengthening state capacity at the local level by requiring municipalities to enhance delivery systems, train case workers, and coordinate services—as evidenced by recent experiences in Italy and elsewhere.

Second, the effectiveness of Cohesion Policy depends heavily on the quality of implementation. Building administrative and institutional capacity at the subnational level is essential. Many local governments, especially in lagging regions, lack the technical expertise and systems needed to plan, deliver, and monitor programs. Strengthening local capacity is not only a goal in itself—it is a prerequisite for effective social innovation, experimentation, and scaling up of what works.

Third, the EU should invest more decisively in policy experimentation, innovation, and rigorous evaluation. Testing and learning what works—in a diverse, rapidly changing context—is critical to achieving greater impact and citizen trust. Moreover, experimentation itself can be a vehicle for capacity building, as it fosters adaptive governance, accountability, and learning at multiple levels of government.

These three priorities—better targeting, stronger implementation, and more experimentation—are deeply interconnected and mutually reinforcing. For example, delivering GMI+ at scale requires both robust administrative systems and continuous evaluation. Policy innovation often reveals gaps in local capacity or targeting that must be addressed for impact.

In addition to these programmatic improvements, we also propose revisiting the rules for allocating Cohesion Policy funds. In their current form, these rely heavily on GDP per capita. While this captures income disparities, it neglects regional economic dynamics. Incorporating indicators of economic growth performance into the allocation formula would better identify and support regions at risk of falling into—or already trapped in—a regional development trap.

Ultimately, increasing the effectiveness of Cohesion Policy—particularly its social investment components—will not only promote social integration and reduce inequality. It will also contribute to boosting productivity, resilience, and inclusive growth across the Union. In doing so, it will help preserve the legitimacy and future of the European model—a model that, despite mounting skepticism, remains a historic achievement in advancing peace, prosperity, democracy, and shared well-being.

Bibliography

Becker, Sascha O. & Egger, Peter H. & von Ehrlich, Maximilian, (2010). "Going NUTS: The effect of EU Structural Funds on regional performance," *Journal of Public Economics*, Elsevier, vol. 94(9–10), pages 578–590, October.

Blundell, Richard, Monica Costa Dias, Costas Meghir, and John Van Reenen (2004). *Evaluating the Employment Impact of a Mandatory Job Search Program.* Journal of the European Economic Association, Vol. 2, Issue 4, pp. 569–606.

Burghof, Hans-Peter & Marcel Gehrung, (2022). "One Market to Rule Them All: How Financial Integration Influenced Inequality in the European Union [Inequality and Economic Growth: The Perspective of the New Growth Theories]," *CESifo Economic Studies*, CESifo Group, vol. 68(1), pages 73–97.

Bussolo, M., Ferrer-i-Carbonell, A., Giolbas, A., & Torre, I., (2018a). "Perceptions, Reality and Demand for Redistribution." *Working Paper*, World Bank, Washington, DC.

Bussolo, Maurizio & Torre, Ivan & Winkler, Hernan Jorge, (2018b). "Does Job Polarization Explain the Rise in Earnings Inequality? Evidence from Europe," *Policy Research Working Paper Series 8652*, The World Bank.

Caliendo, Lorenzo & Luca David Opromolla & Fernando Parro & Alessandro Sforza, (2021). "Goods and Factor Market Integration: A Quantitative Assessment of the EU Enlargement," *Journal of Political Economy*, University of Chicago Press, vol. 129(12), pages 3491–3545.

Canova, Fabio (2024). "The Macroeconomic Effects of EU Regional Structural Funds," *Journal of the European Economic Association*, 2024; jvae031, https://doi.org/10.1093/jeea/jvae031.

Card, D. & Jochen Kluve & Andrea Weber, (2018). "What Works? A Meta-Analysis of Recent Active Labor Market Program Evaluations," *Journal of the European Economic Association*, European Economic Association, vol. 16(3), pages 894–931.

Cieślik, Andrzej & Mehmet Burak Turgut, (2021). "Estimating the Growth Effects of 2004 Eastern Enlargement of the European Union," *JRFM*, MDPI, vol. 14(3), pages 1–15, March.

Crépon, Bruno & Patrick Premand (2019). *Direct and Indirect Effects of Subsidized Dual Apprenticeships.* IZA Discussion Paper No. 12793. Institute of Labor Economics (IZA).

Dalvit, N., de Hoyos, R., Iacovone, L., Pantelaiou, I., Peeva, A., & Torre, I., (2023). "The Future of Work: Implications for Equity and Growth in Europe." The World Bank, Washington, DC. © World Bank.

Dorsett, Richard (2007). *The Effect of Pathways to Work on Labour Market Outcomes.* National Institute Economic Review, Vol. 202(1), pp. 79–89.

Diemer, A, S Iammarino, A Rodriguez-Pose and M Storper (2022), "The regional development trap in Europe," *Economic Geography.*

European Central Bank "Economic Bulletin," Issue 3/2023.

European Commission's Minimum Income Network (MINET) (2023). working group - Employment, Social Affairs and Inclusion: https://employment-socialaffairs.ec.europa.eu/policies-and-activities/social-protection-social-inclusion/social-protection-committee/minimum-income-network-minet-working-group_en

European Commission (2024). Directorate-General for Regional and Urban Policy, *Forging a sustainable future together – Cohesion for a competitive and inclusive Europe – Report of the High-Level Group on the Future of Cohesion Policy*, February 2024, Publications Office of the European Union.

European Parliament (2018). *The impact of new technologies on the labour market and the social economy.*

Eurostat. (2021). *Quality of life indicators—Measuring quality of life.* Publications Office of the European Union.

Fragkos, Panagiotis & Fragkiadakis, Kostas & Sovacool, Benjamin & Paroussos, Leonidas & Vrontisi, Zoi & Charalampidis, Ioannis, (2021). "Equity implications of climate policy: Assessing the social and distributional impacts of emission reduction targets in the European Union," *Energy*, Elsevier, vol. 237(C).

Galasso, Emanuela (2011). *Alleviating Extreme Poverty in Chile: The Short Term Effects of Chile Solidario.* Estudios de Economía, Vol. 38, No. 1, pp. 101–127.

Gaini, Mathilde, Marine Guillerm, Solène Hilary, Emmanuel Valat, and Philippe Zamora (2020). *Results of a Quantitative Assessment of France's Garantie Jeunes Programme: What Target Groups, What Kinds of Support, and What Beneficiary Trajectories?* Travail et Emploi, No. 2, pp. 31–52.

Gertler, P., Martinez, S., Rawlings, L. B., Premand, P., & Vermeersch, C. M. J. (2016). Impact Evaluation in Practice: Second Edition. https://doi.org/10.18235/0006529

Grassi, B (2024). "DP19114 The EU Miracle: When 75 Million Reach High Income." *CEPR Discussion Paper No. 19114.* CEPR Press, Paris & London. https://cepr.org/publications/dp19114.

Graversen, Brian Krogh & Jan C. van Ours (2008). *How to Help Unemployed Find Jobs Quickly: Experimental Evidence from a Mandatory Activation Program.* Journal of Public Economics, 92(10–11), 2042–2055. https://doi.org/10.1016/j.jpubeco.2008.03.002.

Guriev, S., (2024). The recent rise of populism and European integration. In: Székely, I. P. and Halmai, P. (eds) *The Future Challenges for European Integration, Palgrave Macmillan, forthcoming*

Karagiannaki, Eleni (2007). *Exploring the Effects of Integrated Benefit Systems and Active Labour Market Policies: Evidence from Jobcentre Plus in the UK.* Journal of Social Policy, 36(2), 177–195. Cambridge University Press.

Kluve, Jochen & Puerto, Susana & Robalino, David & Romero, Jose M. & Rother, Friederike & Stöterau, Jonathan & Weidenkaff, Felix & Witte, Marc, (2019). "Do youth employment programs improve labor market outcomes? A quantitative review," *World Development*, Elsevier, vol. 114(C), pages 237–253.

Lang, V., Redeker, N., & Bischof, D., (2022). "Place-Based Policies and Inequality Within Regions." https://doi.org/10.31219/osf.io/2xmzj.

Legovini, Arianna, Di Maro, Vincenzo and Piza, Caio, (2015). "Impact evaluation helps deliver development projects," No 7157, *Policy Research Working Paper Series*, The World Bank.

Maibom, Jonas, Michael Rosholm, & Michael Svarer (2014). *Can Active Labour Market Policies Combat Youth Unemployment?* IZA Discussion Paper No. 7912. Institute of Labor Economics (IZA), Bonn, Germany.

Markussen, Simen & Knut Røed (2016). *Leaving Poverty Behind? The Effects of Generous Income Support Paired with Activation.* American Economic Journal: Economic Policy, Vol. 8(1), pp. 180–211.

Martínez-Zarzoso I, Voicu AM, Vidovic M., (2020). "Production networks in Europe: A natural experiment of the European Union enlargement to the east." *Rev Int Econ.* 2020; 28: 11431163. https://doi.org/10.1111/roie.12484.

Marzi, Marta Serena Liliana, Marini, Alessandra, Cherchi, Ludovica, & Cenedese, Francesco (2024). *Minimum Income and Social Inclusion Pathways – A Review of Selected European Union Programs.* Social Protection & Jobs Discussion Paper No. 193099, The World Bank Group.

McKinsey Global Institute, (2020). "The future of work in Europe: Automation, workforce transitions, and the shifting geography of employment." *Discussion Paper.*

Mendez, Carlos & John Bachtler, (2024). "The quality of government and administrative performance: explaining Cohesion Policy compliance, absorption and achievements across EU regions," *Regional Studies*, Taylor & Francis Journals, vol. 58(4), pages 690–703, April.

Neidhöfer, Guido & Miguel Niño-Zarazúa (2019). *The Long(er)-Term Impacts of Chile Solidario on Human Capital and Labor Income.* Population and Development Review.

Orlowski, Lucjan T., (2020). "Capital markets integration and economic growth in the European Union," *Journal of Policy Modeling*, Elsevier, vol. 42(4), pages 893–902.

OECD (2013) "*How's Life? 2013: Measuring Well-being*," OECD Publishing. https://doi.org/10.1787/9789264201392-en

Palenberg, M., & Paulson, A. (Eds.). (2020). *The Realpolitik of Evaluation: Why Demand and Supply Rarely Intersect* (1st ed.). Routledge. https://doi.org/10.4324/9781003005162.

Polverari Laura, (2023). "How to better support administrative capacity to improve the effectiveness of Cohesion Policy." *Final report*, November, in *Rivista giuridica del Mezzogiorno, Trimestrale della Svimez* 4/2023, pp. 1161–1180, https://doi.org/10.1444/113300.

Polverari Laura & Ekaterina Domorenok & Paolo Graziano, (2024). "Empowerment via delegation? The administrative capacity-building potential of Cohesion Policy urban development strategies," *Regional Studies*, Taylor & Francis Journals, vol. 58(4), pages 733–744, April.

Raiser, Martin & Indermit S. Gill, (2012). "Golden Growth: Restoring the Lustre of the European Economic Model," *World Bank Publications – Books*, The World Bank Group, number 6016, December.

Rapacki, Ryszard & Mariusz Prochniak, (2019). "EU membership and economic growth: empirical evidence for the CEE countries," *European Journal of Comparative Economics*, Cattaneo University (LIUC), vol. 16(1), pages 3–40, June.

Rogger, Daniel & Christian Schuster (2023). *The Power of Government Analytics to Improve Public Administration*. World Bank Group.

Rodriguez-Pose, Andres & Lewis Dijkstra & Hugo Poelman, (2024). "The geography of EU discontent and the regional development trap," *Regional and Urban Policy WP 03/2023.*

Rodríguez-Pose, A. and Garcilazo, E. (2015). "Quality of Government and the Returns of Investment: Examining the Impact of Cohesion Expenditure in European Regions." *Regional Studies*, Vol. 49, No. 8, pp. 1274–1290.

Rodríguez-Pose, A. & Tobias Ketterer, (2020). "Institutional change and the development of lagging regions in Europe," *Regional Studies*, Taylor & Francis Journals, vol. 54(7), pages 974–986, July.

Rodrik, Dani & Stefanie Stantcheva, (2021). "Fixing capitalism's good jobs problem" *Oxford Review of Economic Policy*, Oxford University Press and Oxford Review of Economic Policy Limited, vol. 37(4), pages 824–837.

Rønsen, Marit & Torbjørn Skarðhamar (2009). *Do Welfare-to-Work Initiatives Work? Evidence from an Activation Programme Targeted at Social Security Recipients in Norway.* Statistics Norway, Research Department, Discussion Paper No. 597.

Sanchez-Reaza, Javier, Diego Ambasz, Predrag Djukic, and Karla McEvoy, (2023). "Making the European Green Deal Work for People: The Role of Human Development in the Green Transition." *Overview booklet.* Washington, DC: World Bank Group. License: CC BY 3.0 IGO.

Silveyra, M., Yañez, M. y Bedoya, J., (2018). "¿Qué impacto tiene el programa de escuelas de tiempo completo en los estudiantes de educación básica?: Evaluación del programa en México 2007–2016." *Banco Mundial.*

Stafford, Bruce (2012). *Supporting Moves into Work: New Deal for Disabled People Findings.* Scandinavian Journal of Disability Research, Vol. 14, Issue 2, pp. 165–176.

Vukov, V., (2019). "European integration and weak states: Romania's road to exclusionary development." *Review of International Political Economy*, 27(5), 1041–1062. https://doi.org/10.1080/09692290.2019.1645723.

World Bank (2018). The Human Capital Project. © World Bank. http://hdl.handle.net/10986/30498 License: CC BY 3.0 IGO.

CHAPTER 8

EU Anti-corruption Policies: Methods, Results, and Challenges

István János Tóth, Miklós Hajdu, and Márton Vida

8.1 Introduction

This chapter examines the efficiency and effectiveness of various anti--corruption methods by analysing international examples. We argue that additional factors influencing economic actors' behaviour should be

I. J. Tóth (✉)
SGH Warsaw School of Economics, Warsaw, Poland

KRTK KTI, Budapest, Hungary

CRCB, Budapest, Hungary
e-mail: istvanjanos.toth@crcb.eu

M. Hajdu
CRCB, Budapest, Hungary

Corvinus University of Budapest, Budapest, Hungary
e-mail: miklos.hajdu@uni-corvinus.hu

M. Vida
CRCB, Budapest, Hungary

Central European University, Vienna, Austria
e-mail: vida_marton@alumni.ceu.edu

I. P. Székely, P. Halmai (eds.), *The Future of European Integration*, Studies in Economic Transition,
https://doi.org/10.1007/978-3-032-20186-7_8

considered beyond traditional approaches—such as reducing the financial incentives for corruption, increasing the likelihood of detection and conviction, and reinforcing the moral costs and ethical satisfaction associated with rejecting corruption. In particular, increasing the perceived likelihood of detection and the perceived likelihood of replacement among economic and political actors can serve as powerful deterrents. Incorporating these perspectives introduces new, previously underutilised methods in the fight against corruption, thereby expanding the strategic toolkit of anti-corruption organisations.

We also examine the possible correlations between trends in corruption risk and anti-corruption policies through two examples related to public procurement in EU countries between 2007 and 2023. In the first example, we look at how corruption risk in the public procurement of New Member States could approximate the lower corruption risk levels of developed Western European countries or Southern European countries. In the second example, we examine how the corruption risk of public procurements financed by EU Funds evolved between 2007 and 2023 compared to those financed nationally.

In the trend of corruption risk among New Member States, we observe that the corruption risk in public procurements significantly decreased between 2007 and 2023. Undoubtedly, this trend is related to the EU's anti-corruption efforts, especially their intensification after 2010, although we cannot provide precise quantitative analysis. We cannot statistically substantiate the percentage contribution of the EU's anti-corruption measures to the improving trend in public procurement corruption risk. To do this, we would need data that accurately shows the effects of the EU's anti-corruption policy on the corruption risk in public procurement, isolated from other influences. Without such data, we can only demonstrate how public procurement corruption has evolved in different groups of EU countries following the EU's anti-corruption measures. We use the data from the EU TED public procurement database between 2007 and 2023, the annual reports of OLAF and EPPO, and the European Semester country reports in the analysis.

The examination of the corruption risk of EU-funded procurements between 2007 and 2023 shows that this significantly exceeds that of nationally financed public procurements. This correlation holds for New Member States, Southern European countries, and Western European countries, where the proportion of EU-supported public procurements is much lower than in the previous two country groups. This result highlights that the EU should take further steps beyond current measures to reduce the corruption risks of public procurements realised through EU support.

The chapter is structured as follows. In the second part, we argue for the subjective (perceived) probability of detection as an important new aspect of combating corruption among the factors influencing the behaviour of economic actors concerning corruption. In the third part, we review the experiences of empirical studies on the effectiveness of various anti-corruption measures. In the fourth part, we examine the results, challenges, and possible new methods of the EU's anti-corruption efforts based on two examples. Finally, we summarise the policy implications derived from the study's results.

8.2 A Factor Affecting Corrupt Behaviour: The Perceived Probability of Conviction

According to the economic theory of crime, the three most important factors determining the benefits of criminal behaviour are (i) income from the crime, (ii) the probability of conviction, and (iii) the severity of punishment (Becker 1968). Increasing the probability of conviction, ceteris paribus, reduces the probability of committing a crime. Becker also showed that a 1 per cent increase in the probability of punishment has a more significant negative effect on criminal activity than a 1 per cent increase in the severity of punishment if the offender is a risk lover. In contrast, if he is risk-averse, the reverse is true. On a rational choice model, a criminal weighs the expected reward from criminal activity against its expected costs, where, assuming full rationality, agents take the expected value of punishment dependent on the probability of punishment as well as its severity. Most relevant studies on the economics of corruption use models analogous to the above to describe an actor's corruption-related behaviour. The literature underscores the pivotal role of income generated from corruption, the expected punishment, and the moral cost of corruption in the actors' decision-making regarding corruption (Rose-Ackerman 1975; Rose-Ackerman 1978; Klitgaard 1988; Andvig et al. 2001; Lambsdorff 2007; Dhillon and Nicolò 2023).

Beyond the above, abstaining from corruption involves moral satisfaction. When actors decide to abstain from corruption, they can record the income they have legally obtained. Moreover, there is a moral surplus:

they will feel more satisfied with their position and workplace (Kim et al. 2024; Tanner et al. 2022).

Actors considering corruption must also account for the possibility of losing their office. This outcome entails a disadvantageous consequence: the loss of income. It is essential to distinguish loss of office due to corruption from the penalties incurred when caught, as the two events are unrelated. A politician convicted of corruption may not be removed from office by voters, as most voters might tolerate corruption. Conversely, a politician against whom there is sufficient public evidence of corruption but has not been convicted by the court may still be removed from office and lose their position.

Secondly, beyond the income loss due to the loss of office, another factor worth considering in anti-corruption efforts is the cost of establishing a corrupt transaction and maintaining a corrupt system. Corrupt actors may need to create and operate companies or organisations and integrate individuals (fronts) into the corrupt transaction and system to conceal the transaction and the identities of the actual participants (della Porta and Vannucci 1999; della Porta and Vannucci 2012; Dolan 2024). The greater the need to hide the actual participants and conceal the corrupt transaction, the higher these costs may become. These increased costs reduce the net benefits of corruption. Therefore, it is crucial to implement anti-corruption policies that effectively increase the costs of establishing corrupt transactions and maintaining corrupt systems, thereby reducing the attractiveness of corruption.

An actor—whether a politician, public or corporate manager, or individual—considering initiating or accepting a corrupt transaction weighs the decision based on the expected value they attribute to the illicit income, the probability of being caught, and the potential penalties for engaging in corruption.

However, as discussed in criminological literature, individuals involved in criminal justice rarely base their decision to commit a crime on the actual likelihood of being caught (Nagin 2013). As we will argue, would-be criminals care more about the probability of punishment than its severity, and their perceived (or subjective) probability of punishment is often independent of its objective probability. This has important implications for anti-corruption legislation too.

When looking at anti-corruption measures, these policies, assuming that corrupt actors are risk-averse, mainly focus on raising the probability of conviction. They see the increasing control and investigative activity of state institutions as a valuable tool to increase the likelihood of detection, which deters actors from corruption. However, because actors are not perfectly informed, it is worth considering the perceived likelihood of detection by economic actors besides increasing the likelihood of conviction.

Several empirical and experimental criminology papers find, in accordance with the rational choice model, that the probability of punishment influences criminal behaviour (Klepper and Nagin 1989a, b; Lochner 2007). In departure from this model, it has been found that the probability of punishment matters more than the severity of punishment (Becker 1968; Bachman et al. 1992; Nagin and Paternoster 1993; Nagin and Pogarsky 2003; Durlauf and Nagin 2011; Nagin 2013), although some contested these findings (Grasmick and Bryjak 1980). A plausible explanation for why the probability of punishment matters more than its severity is that would-be criminals already attach shame and stigma to the scenario in which they are detected; hence, changes in the severity of punishment have little marginal effect (Blumstein and Nagin 1977).

Importantly, not only is it the case that the perceived risk of punishment drives the deterrent effect of criminal law, but numerous authors have also found that the perceived probability of detection is largely independent of its objective probability (Apel 2013; Hjalmarsson 2009; Kleck et al. 2005; Lochner 2007; MacCoun et al. 2009). It has also been found that criminals systematically underestimate the risk of detection (Pogarsky and Piquero 2003), while the police perceive the severity of punishment as higher than citizens (Erickson and Gibbs 1979). One paper argues that the inconsistency in criminals' perception of the risk of detection has been overstated when objective risk is measured as the ratio of detected criminal activity to all criminal activity for each individual criminal (Horney and Marshall 1992).

In the context of white-collar crime, the criminology literature often questions whether deterrence (the prospect of punishment) or legitimacy (moral beliefs, ethical culture, trust in institutions) matters more for decreasing crime. While few studies have investigated this question specifically in the context of corruption, it has been found both in a developing (Tankebe 2009, 2019) and developed (Tsushima and Hamai 2015) country setting that deterrence is more important than legitimacy. Hence, the focus on the deterrence channel via influencing perceived detection risk is warranted. However, as we will show, legitimacy ought not to be neglected either, as it may also influence perceptions of detection risk.

In regards to deterrence via influencing perceptions of detection risk, the literature is inconclusive in regards to whether arrests increase perceived risk (Anwar and Loughran 2011; Apospori and Alpert 1993; Bridges and Stone 1986; Pogarsky et al. 2017). However, some studies point to the fact that providing information to citizens about the risks of criminal activity influences perceived risk (Pickett et al. 2016). This is consistent with the argument that criminals update their perceived risk via a Bayesian probability model (Matsueda et al. 2006). However, others argue that this updating process is less consistent (Pogarsky et al. 2017). Lastly, a paper finds that informal gossip among criminals matters a lot for the perceived risk of detection (Dickinson and Wright 2015).

Regarding legitimacy, multiple authors argue that the moral beliefs of citizens are relevant for restraint from criminal activity (Bachman et al. 1992; Nagin and Paternoster 1993; Tittle 1977). Consistently, a paper found that criminal activity is decreased as a result of punishment only conditionally on the blameworthiness of the punished (Farrar and King 2023). A related body of literature finds that procedural fairness matters for citizens' compliance with the law (Bradford et al. 2015; Murphy et al. 2016). This finding is relevant as it contradicts policy suggestions that law enforcement could exploit potential criminals' risk aversion by generating uncertainty about the risk of detection (Loughran et al. 2011). Lastly, a body of literature argues that certain extra-legal factors, such as peer pressure (Meier and Johnson 1977; Pogarsky et al. 2004), ethical culture (Suh et al. 2018) or psychological factors (Warren and Schweitzer 2021) are also relevant.

The emphasis on legitimacy besides deterrence in reducing corruption is important for two reasons. First, it shows that reducing corruption by deterring criminals through influencing their perceived risk of detection must observe rules of procedural fairness, as otherwise, the intrinsic motivation to refrain from corrupt activity may be crowded out. Second, some authors have found that the perceived risk of detection often corresponds to what individuals believe should be the case, instead of what actually is (Williams et al. 1980). Hence, positively influencing citizens' moral beliefs about the severity of corruption may also lead to a higher perceived risk of detection.

8.3 Anti-corruption Measures

According to analyses by international organisations regarding anti-corruption policies, effective anti-corruption strategies are necessarily multifaceted, encompassing governance measures, legal reforms, education, and technological innovations (Huther and Shah 2000; United Nations 2003, 2004; African Development Bank Group 2004; Bajpai and Myers 2010; International Monetary Fund 2018, 2023; European Commission 2023; OECD 2024). The success of these policies depends on how well they can deter economic actors from participating in corruption. The preconditions for this success include the political will to implement anti-corruption policies and the active involvement of civil society in holding governments accountable.

In the following, we will review empirical research findings on the effectiveness of specific anti-corruption measures.

8.3.1 Wages and Selection of Bureaucrats

Extensive literature discusses the question of whether increasing the wages of bureaucrats leads to lower corruption. In their groundbreaking work, Becker and Stigler argue for a pay rise for public employees to discourage illicit behaviour (Becker and Stigler 1974). Authors who argue the affirmative often point to the fact that higher relative wages in the public sector attract better candidates from the private sector (Demirgüç-Kunt et al. 2021; Dal Bó et al. 2013), who in turn make the bureaucracy more efficient (Gagliarducci and Nannicini 2013). Relying on an unexpected wage cut in Romania, this negative relationship between wages and corruption has been verified (Borcan et al. 2014).

A cross-country analysis also supports this relationship, though it notes that very high wages would be necessary to eradicate corruption solely via this channel (Van Rijckeghem and Weder 2001).

Other authors dispute the claim that higher wages of bureaucrats lead to lower corruption. Another cross-country analysis argues that it is not higher wages per se that reduce corruption but meritocratic performance-related pay (Dahlström et al. 2012). This is consistent with the idea that public sector employees have high intrinsic motivation (Barfort et al. 2015; Kwon 2014), which can be crowded out by unconditionally higher wages (Navot et al. 2016). An alternative mechanism by which higher wages may increase corruption is that it increases the bargaining power of the bureaucrat over the citizens, which may lead to higher bribe payments (Khan et al. 2016).

The literature has also discussed selecting bureaucrats via means other than wages. Analysing the German federal government's staff rotation policy, one paper confirmed that regularly rotating bureaucrats has a desirable effect on corruption (Abbink 2004). Another paper found that employing more women in the public sector also decreases corruption (Dollar et al. 2001).

8.3.2 Decentralisation of Bureaucracy

Numerous empirical cross-country analyses suggest that a more decentralised bureaucracy leads to lower corruption (Arikan 2004; Fisman and Gatti 2002). One paper adds that decentralising state functions leads to lower corruption only if officials are adequately monitored via means such as a free press (Lessmann and Markwardt 2010). Another group of authors using cross-country data found that changes in the level of centralisation have a desirable effect on the level of corruption with an estimated lag of three years (Fiorino et al. 2015). Analysing the effects of multiple types of decentralisation and relying on survey data about direct experiences with bribery, a paper concludes that government complexity increases corruption (Fan et al. 2009).

Some authors dispute the claim that decentralisation reduces corruption. The theory behind this claim is that when a firm faces multiple public officials instead of a single one, it has to pay bribes to each. Consequently, as verified in a sample of former communist countries (Diaby and Sylwester 2014), decentralisation may lead to higher bribe payments, that is, higher corruption.

8.3.3 Law Enforcement and Monitoring

There is mixed evidence on the positive effect of law enforcement and monitoring on corruption. On the one hand, such measures should deter officials and market actors from engaging in corruption, but on the other hand, this deterrent effect often fails to materialise. The former argument is supported by a paper analysing the spillover effects of anti-corruption campaigns. It finds that crackdowns on mafia-related officials in Italian municipalities lead to a reduction in public investment in neighbouring municipalities, which in part is because they reduce financial misconduct (Galletta 2017). Likewise, audits were found to reduce corruption (in

Brazilian municipalities Avis et al. 2018). One paper analysing Puerto Rican data adds that auditing municipalities affects corruption only temporarily and only if done before elections (Bobonis et al. 2016).

A pair of authors question the deterrent effect of crackdowns on corruption. They find that while increasing resources in the persecution of corruption led to more convictions in the US, its deterrent effect is limited (Alt and Lassen 2014). As the authors note, this may, in part, be because deterrence depends on the probability of being detected as perceived by the would-be criminal, which is often independent of the actual probability of detection (Nagin 2013).

A paper relying on lab experiments from the US and Pakistan finds that crackdowns on corruption affect behaviour only at best in the short run but not in the long run (Banuri and Eckel 2015). Another paper using empirical evidence from China adds that increased monitoring of bureaucrats may have the undesirable side-effect of lower productivity (Wang 2018). Lastly, analysing the effects of the OECD Anti-Bribery Convention of 1997, a paper finds that international bribery is reduced only if countries respond in a coordinated fashion (Cuervo-Cazurra 2008).

8.3.4 Government Size and Regulation

It has been argued, relying on state-level US data, that government size—measured as spending by local governments—increases corruption (Goel and Nelson 1998). Consistently, another paper relying on cross-country data found that countries with more stringent regulations on start-up entry have higher corruption and larger unofficial economies (Djankov et al. 2002). Utilising survey data from multiple post-socialist countries, an author adds that it is not a heavy regulatory policy per se but rather the unofficial means of implementing such policies that causes corruption (Duvanova 2014). Lastly, it has been found that countries with protectionist trade policies experience higher levels of corruption (Dutt 2009).

8.3.5 Political Institutions

The effect of different political institutions on corruption has been widely studied. Intuitively, it has been found that higher levels of democracy translate to lower corruption (Billger and Goel 2009; Lederman et al. 2001). Likewise, in more focused settings, it has been shown that institutions that promote electoral accountability reduce corruption. An empirical analysis of Brazil found that municipalities where mayors can get re-elected experience lower corruption (Ferraz and Finan 2011). Another study using US state-level data found that elected state supreme court justices, rather than appointed ones, entail lower corruption (Alt and Lassen 2014). Other authors relying on cross-country data argued that lower barriers to entering elections via smaller district size and higher individual accountability via a lower share of candidates selected from party lists lead to lower corruption (Persson et al. 2003). Lastly, a paper found that proportional electoral systems are associated with higher corruption than plurality ones, which they attribute to the fact that voters need to coordinate more in the former systems to punish corrupt incumbents (Jana Kunicová and Rose-Ackerman 2005).

The empirical corruption literature has also studied different aspects of political institutions. One paper argues that the relationship between incumbent stability and corruption is U-shaped, given two competing effects: at low stability, incumbents have high incentives to extract rents while in office, while for high stability, private actors have a larger incentive to bribe the incumbent (Campante et al. 2009). In a long-run cross-country analysis, it has also been found that regulating political finance can also help reduce corruption (Hummel et al. 2021). Lastly, anti-corruption campaigns have been found to increase political trust among the citizens (Kang and Zhu 2021).

8.3.6 *Media and Information Disclosure*

Cross-country empirical studies have long argued that greater press freedom translates to lower corruption (Bhattacharyya and Hodler 2015; Brunetti and Weder 2003). Social media has also been found important in Russia's non-democratic setting, where blog posts exposing corruption had a negative causal impact on the targeted companies' returns (Enikolopov et al. 2018). It has also been argued that the emergence of the Internet has led to decreased corruption (Andersen et al. 2011).

As a related matter, freedom of information laws have also been analysed regarding their impact on corruption. Cross-country studies disagree on whether freedom of information laws decrease corruption: some argue in favour (Djankov et al. 2010; Vargas and Schlutz 2016), while others are against (Costa 2013; Escaleras et al. 2010). A possible synthesis of these results is offered by a paper arguing that freedom of information laws, on the one hand, make the detection of corruption easier for authorities, thereby increasing measured corruption. However, on the other hand, they increase the probability of detecting corrupt officials, thereby decreasing actual corruption. Using US data, the authors of this paper find that even when controlling for the former effect, freedom of information laws still decrease actual corruption (Cordis and Warren 2014).

Several other questions have been studied relating to citizen awareness and corruption. In the US, it has been found that greater awareness of whistleblower laws entails lower corruption (Goel and Nelson 2014). Relying on survey data from South Korea, a paper argued that civil servants who are aware of ongoing anti-corruption policies are less corrupt than their unaware counterparts (Lee et al. 2022). Using survey data from Costa Rica, the hypothesis that one's beliefs about the level of corruption in one's environment influence one's choice of whether to engage in corruption has also been verified (Corbacho et al. 2016). It was also found that US states with spatially isolated capitals experience higher corruption as citizens far from the capital are less informed about state politics (Campante and Do 2014).

8.3.7 Digitalisation and AI

The creation and online publication of large databases (such as the EU's Tender Electronic Daily system or Ukraine's ProZorro) allow anomalies (including corruption and cartels) to be detected (Colman 2020; European Parliament 2021; Open Contracting Partnership 2024). As part of digitalisation, such tools can increase the effectiveness of the fight against corruption (López Acera 2023). In general, open databases have the potential to act through multiple channels to help fight corruption (Granickas 2014). However, it should be added that the production of open data can also be biased, reducing its positive role in fighting corruption (Martinez and Whitley 2023).

A few papers have analysed whether the digitalisation of bureaucracy leads to lower corruption. A cross-country analysis has found that e-governance reforms effectively reduce corruption (Elbahnasawy 2014). Another paper analysed a specific e-governance reform in India and found that it effectively decreased financial leakages (Banerjee et al. 2020). Collecting and statistically analysing municipal land sales in a database can significantly reduce corruption in countries with high corruption levels. Statistical analysis of more than one million Chinese municipal land sales between 2004 and 2016 found a strong correlation between selling prices and political connections (Chen and Kung 2019). Where local governments were the only sellers, firms linked to China's top political elite—the Politburo—received 55–60 per cent discounts compared to those without such connections. Based on the results of the analysis, the Chinese authorities increased controls and investigations, which resulted in a significant reduction in corruption. Lastly, a study analysing e-procurement in India and Indonesia found that while these policies did not lead to price reductions, they led to higher-quality projects implemented (Lewis-Faupel et al. 2016).

Within digitalisation, artificial intelligence is a relatively new area that can help fight corruption, and its use dates back only a few years. Accordingly, empirical results based on a systematic analysis of how much AI improves the effectiveness of anti-corruption measures have yet to be available, except for a few studies (Aarvik 2019; Odilla 2023; Gerli 2024). The behaviour of corrupt actors and transactions follows specific patterns if we can observe them. Detecting them can be much faster and more accurate with AI. On the other hand, corrupt actors also adapt to newer detection techniques to evade them. AI can also detect, predict, and extract such adaptivity from corrupt actors. The use of AI requires (i) cross-sectional databases describing the characteristics of the actors and the transactions between them, reproduced over time (day/week/month or year) and (ii) functions and models describing the behaviour of the actors and (iii) the IT knowledge to develop models based on AI. All three conditions are already in place in areas critical to corruption, such as public procurement, and there is no technical barrier to building AI-based anti-corruption technologies. The use of AI technologies is already quite widespread in the literature on corruption detection and prevention (Berrú et al. 2020). The authors investigated different types of corruption (bribery, embezzlement, misappropriation, fraud, abuse of discretion, favouritism, and nepotism) and distinguished six AI techniques (classification, regression, clustering, prediction, outlier detection, and visualisation). One of the lessons from their research is that we are likely on the verge of a breakthrough: using AI to accelerate the adoption of digital solutions at an unprecedented rate. This breakthrough is because of AI solutions' speed, accuracy, and flexibility, as well as because the cost of developing AI-enabled methods is orders of magnitude lower than the budgetary savings achieved by reducing corruption.

8.4 Corruption Risk and EU Policies

Since 1999, the EU has been combating corruption through various steps, including (i) adopting laws and directives, (ii) monitoring their implementation, (iii) creating new organisations, and (iv) funding research on related topics.

We highlight two of these steps in the next part of the analysis: (i) the establishment of OLAF in 1999 and EPPO in 2017 and (ii) the "European Semester" programme launched by the EU Commission in 2010, which annually monitors Member States and publishes country reports. We examine how these steps impacted the corruption risks in public procurement. In the third section, we address to what extent the more frequent use of the electronic auction (e-auction) in public procurement could reduce the level of corruption risk in public procurement.

We cannot directly measure the impact of these steps with statistical tools. However, it is possible to compare these steps with the trends of objective indicators that characterise the Member States and may be related to them. Such indicators can assess the corruption risk in public procurement (Fazekas and Tóth 2016; Tóth and Hajdu 2021).

In 2018, around 12 per cent of the global GDP was spent on public procurement (Bosio et al. 2022). Corruption in public procurement is a critical area of corruption in transactions. Estimates for EU countries based on public procurement data for 2010, 2012, and 2014 put the cost of corruption in EU public procurement at around €5.3 bn per year (Hafner et al. 2016).

8.4.1 Monitoring and Investigations

An essential part of the EU's anti-corruption policy includes (i) the formulation of EU-level directives and their implementation at the Member State level[1]; (ii) coordination, monitoring of Member States' anti-corruption institutional and legal procedures and formulation of country-specific anti-corruption recommendations within the framework of the European Semester[2]; (iii) setting up and funding organisations at the EU

[1] See: https://home-affairs.ec.europa.eu/policies/internal-security/corruption/eu-legislation-anti-corruption_en; https://www.europarl.europa.eu/legislative-train/package-anti-corruption-package/file-directive-on-combating-corruption and https://finance.ec.europa.eu/financial-crime/anti-money-laundering-and-countering-financing-terrorism-eu-level_en

[2] See: https://commission.europa.eu/business-economy-euro/european-semester_en

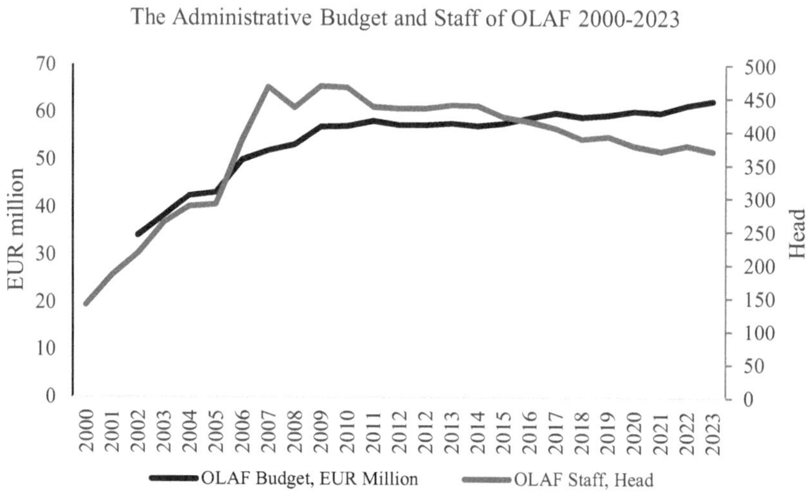

Fig. 8.1 The administrative budget and staff of OLAF 2000–2023

level to investigate anomalies and corrupt activities in the EU (European Anti-Fraud Office[3]; European Public Prosecutor's Office[4]).

The European Anti-Fraud Office (OLAF) was founded on April 28, 1999,[5] and the establishment of the EPPO was approved by the European Council in 2017,[6] officially starting its operations on June 1, 2021.[7] OLAF's staff and budget grew significantly between 2000 and 2017, followed by a slight decrease in staffing, while its budget continued to increase modestly until 2023 (see Fig. 8.1). Between 2021 and 2023, the EPPO's budget grew by 50 per cent from €44 million to €66 million (see Fig. 8.2). A clear indicator of the EU's increasing anti-corruption efforts is the combined budget of these two organisations: in 2002, the EU spent €34 million on OLAF, while in 2023, it allocated almost €130 million to

[3] See: https://anti-fraud.ec.europa.eu/index_en

[4] See: https://www.eppo.europa.eu/en

[5] See_ https://eur-lex.europa.eu/LexUriServ/LexUriServ.do?uri=OJ:L:1999:136:0020:0022:EN:PDF

[6] See: https://eur-lex.europa.eu/eli/reg/2017/1939/oj

[7] See: https://ec.europa.eu/commission/presscorner/detail/en/ip_21_2591

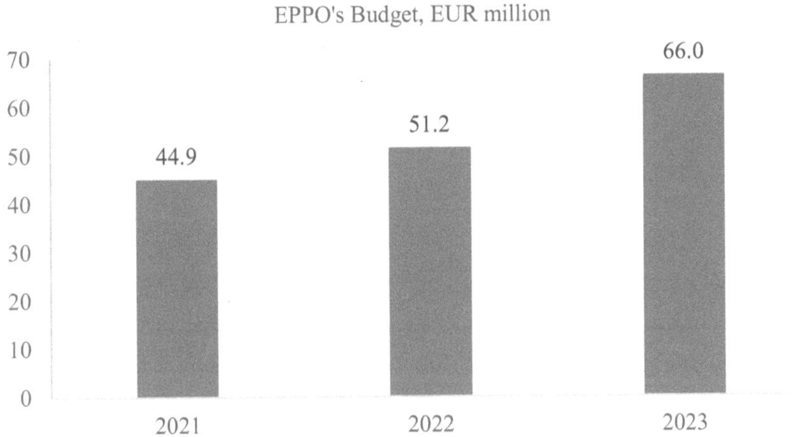

Fig. 8.2 The administrative budget of EPPO 2021–2023

both anti-corruption organisations. In other words, the EU has nearly quadrupled its dedicated anti-corruption budget over the past 20 years.

The fight against corruption has gradually moved to the forefront of the EU's agenda. This process accelerated following the 2004 and 2006 EU enlargements, as many of the new Member States (NMS) ranked among the most corrupt countries in Europe. After the enlargement, it became increasingly evident that the persistently high levels of corruption in most of the NMS were jeopardising the proper and efficient use of EU cohesion funds.

The success of this EU anti-corruption policy can be demonstrated through the analysis of corruption risks in public procurement. This type of analysis provides valuable insight into the strength of institutional convergence (Tóth & Hajdu, 2021). A review of public procurement data from 2007 to 2023 reveals a reduction in corruption risks and a convergence towards levels observed in Western European countries (WEC) for both New Member States (NMS) and Southern European countries (SEC). Figures 8.3 and 8.4 illustrate this convergence trend, which we attribute to the EU's intensified anti-corruption efforts. However, it is important to note that while this convergence trend is encouraging, the NMS remains relatively far from the WEC level regarding institutional

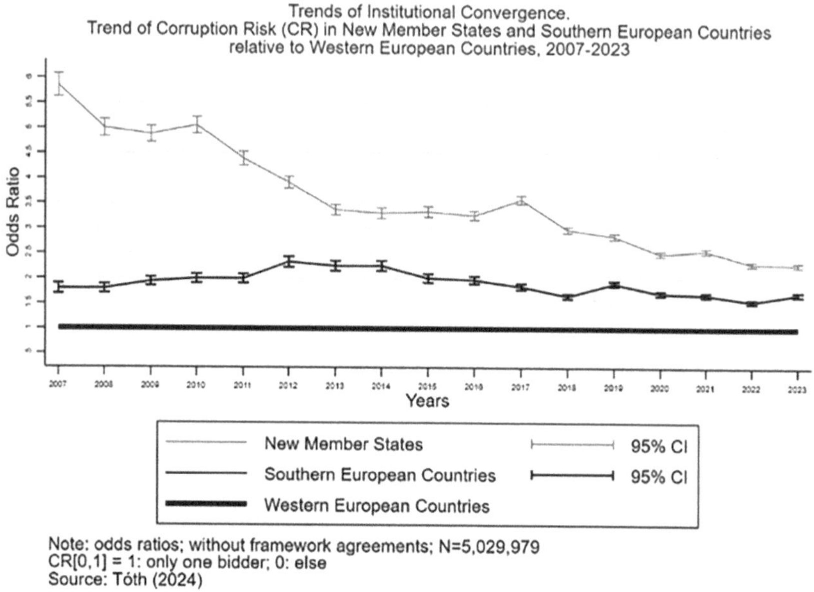

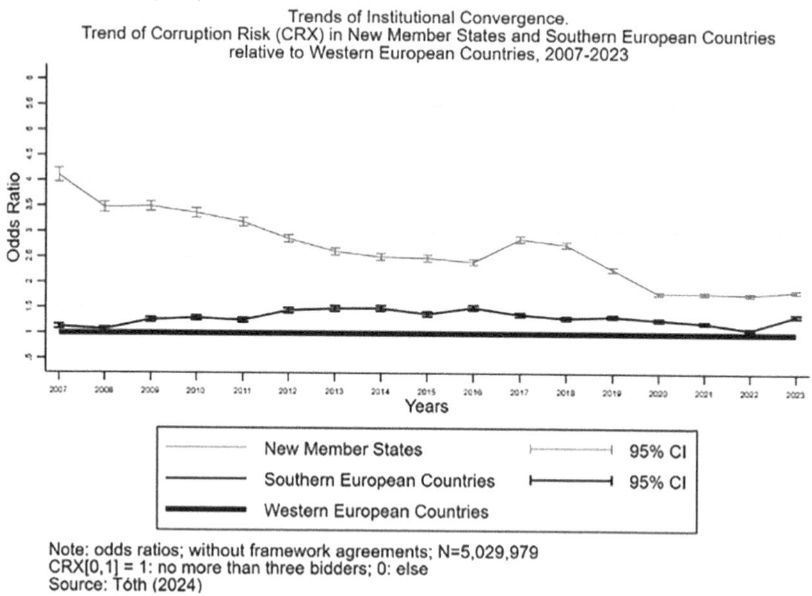

Figs. 8.3 and 8.4 Trends of institutional convergence 2007–2023

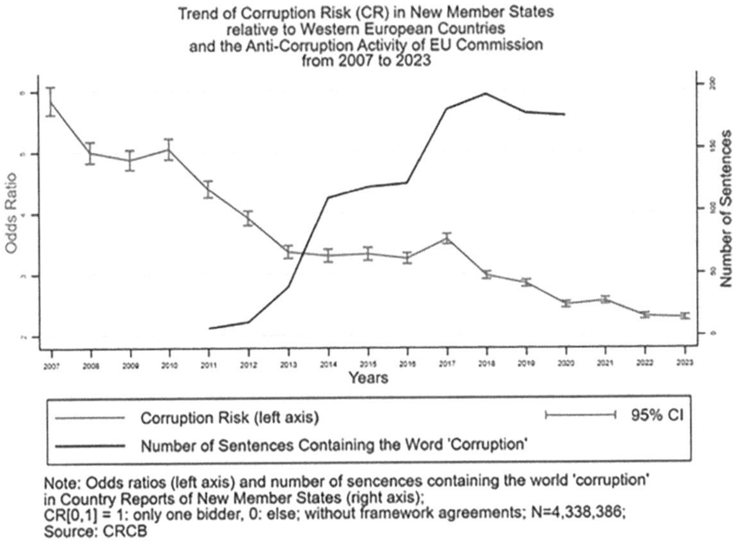

Fig. 8.5 Trends of corruption risk in New Member States relative to Western European countries and the number of sentences containing the word "corruption" in the EU Country Reports of New Member States

convergence. As of 2023, the corruption risk in the NMS is still 2.5 times higher than in the WEC.

The European Semester country reports also show the EU's increasing anti-corruption efforts. Over the years, EU experts responsible for drafting and editing these reports have increasingly addressed the issue of corruption in their assessments of the New Member States. This trend can be seen by tracking the frequency of the word "corruption" in the country reports produced between 2011 and 2020 (see Fig. 8.5). In 2011, the topic was barely mentioned, with only six sentences containing the word "corruption". By 2013, this number had risen to 39 sentences, and by 2020, it had reached 176 sentences, even though the reports' structure and length remained unchanged over this period. We believe that, in addition to the establishment of OLAF and the EPPO, the annual consultations under the European Semester—along with the monitoring, evaluation, and recommendations regarding Member States' anti-corruption policies have contributed to the observed reduction in corruption risk.

8.4.2 *Corruption Risk in EU-Funded Contracts*

A deeper data analysis reveals that the EU still faces significant challenges. One of the EU's most essential policy objectives is to support the economic convergence of New Member States, partly by providing financial assistance through cohesion funds. It is important to note, however, that EU funds are accessed not only by New Member States but also by South European countries and relatively less developed regions within Western European countries. From 2007 to 2023, excluding framework agreements, the share of the net contract value in EU-funded contracts as a percentage of the total net contract value is 21.4 per cent for the New Member States, 12.0 per cent for the Southern European Countries, and 3.7 per cent for the Western European Countries. Similarly, the share of EU-funded contracts in the total number of contracts is 9.2, 9.0, and 3.3 per cent, respectively (see Table 8.1). Therefore, any assessment of corruption risk in using EU subsidies should encompass the entire EU, not just the New Member States.

An analysis of corruption risk in EU-funded public procurement (Tóth 2024) indicates that, between 2007 and 2023, the corruption risk associated with EU-funded public procurement was consistently higher than

Table 8.1 The share of EU-funded contracts across three specific country groups from 2007 to 2023

Country Groups	*Share of EU-funded contracts in total net contract value* %	*Share of EU-funded contracts in total number of contracts* %
New Member States	21.4	9.2
South European Countries	12.0	9.0
Western European Countries	3.7	3.3

Note: Without framework agreements

that of nationally funded procurement across the entire EU, except in 2018 (see Figs. 8.6 and 8.7).

This trend is evident in both the New Member States and Western European countries, where the corruption risk associated with EU-funded public procurement was significantly higher than that of nationally funded public procurement in most years between 2007 and 2023 (see Figs. 8.8, 8.9, 8.10, and 8.11).

The results presented in Figs. 8.8 and 8.9. clearly show that the differences in corruption risk between EU-funded and nationally funded public procurement are most pronounced not in the New Member States but in Western European countries, where the share of EU-funded contracts is relatively small. This observation highlights the need for the EU to focus on reducing the risk of corruption in public procurement not only in the New Member States and Southern European countries but also in Western European countries.

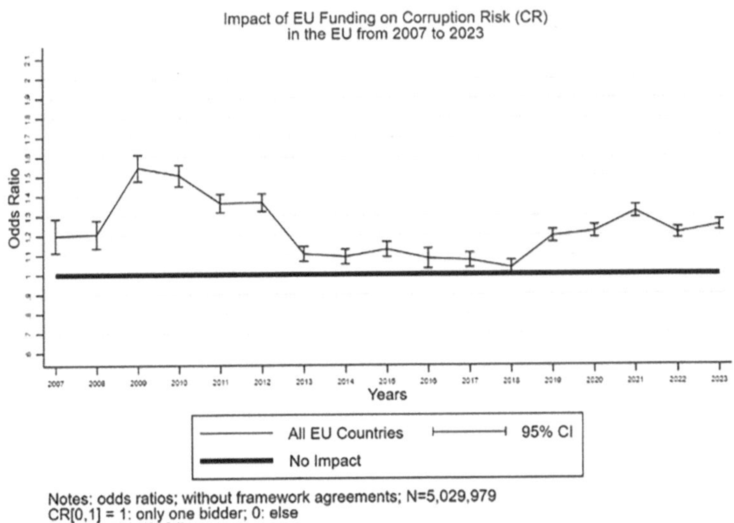

Figs. 8.6, 8.7, 8.8, 8.9, 8.10, 8.11, 8.12, and 8.13 Trends of corruption risk in EU-funded public procurement relative to nationally funded ones 2007–2023

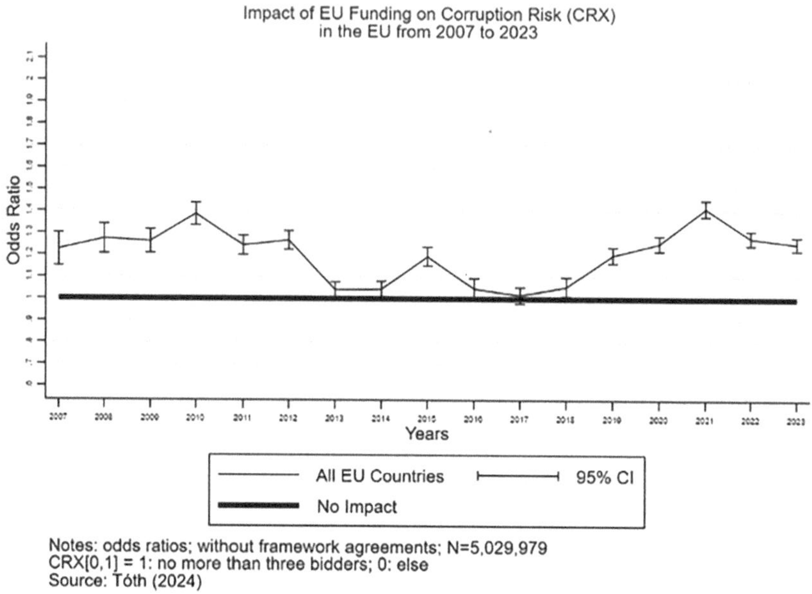

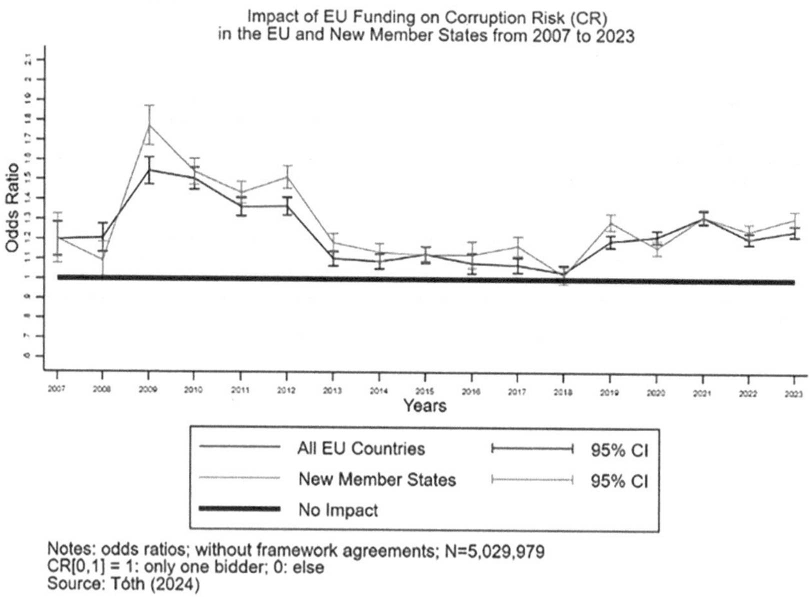

Figs. 8.6, 8.7, 8.8, 8.9, 8.10, 8.11, 8.12, and 8.13 (continued)

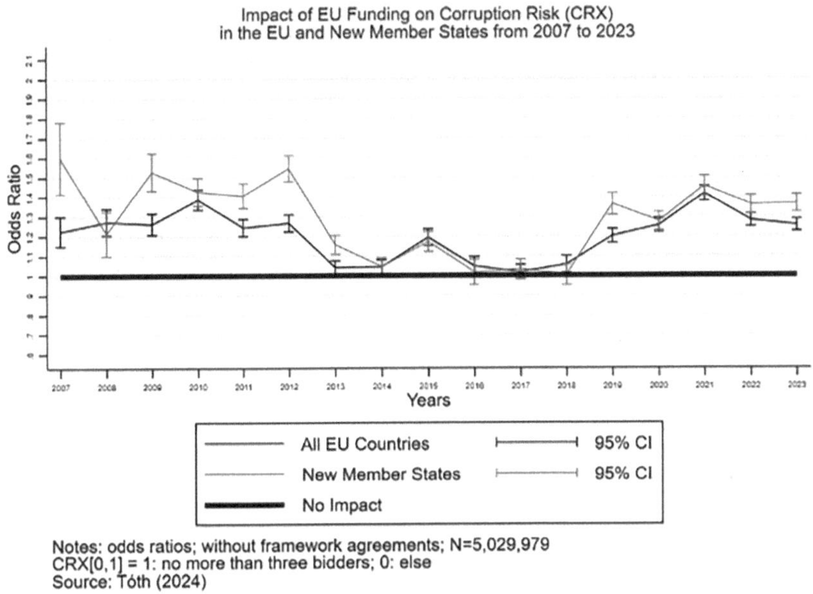

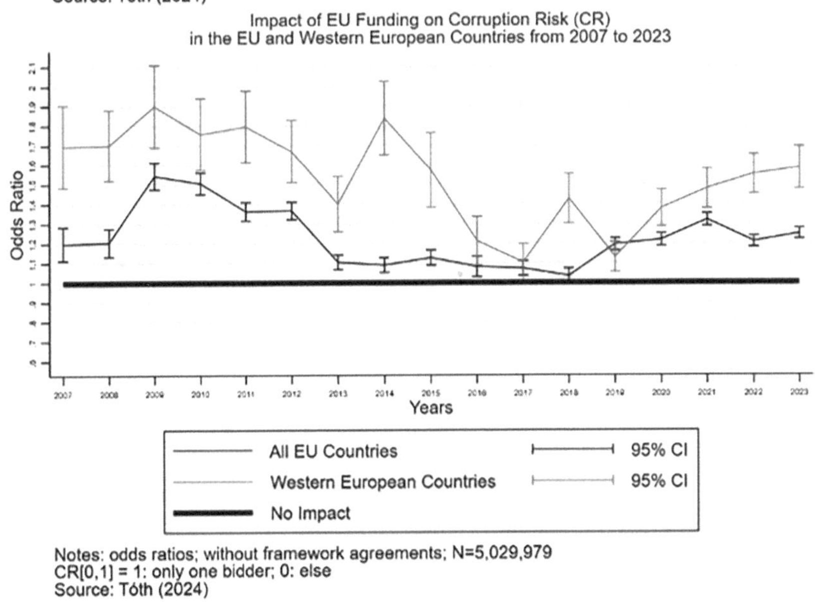

Figs. 8.6, 8.7, 8.8, 8.9, 8.10, 8.11, 8.12, and 8.13 (continued)

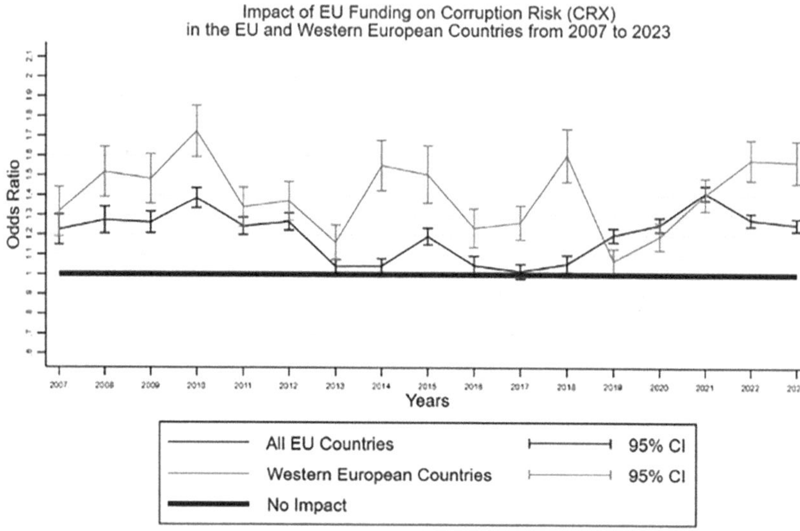

Notes: odds ratios; without framework agreements; N=5,029,979
CRX[0,1] = 1: no more than three bidders; 0: else
Source: Tóth (2004)

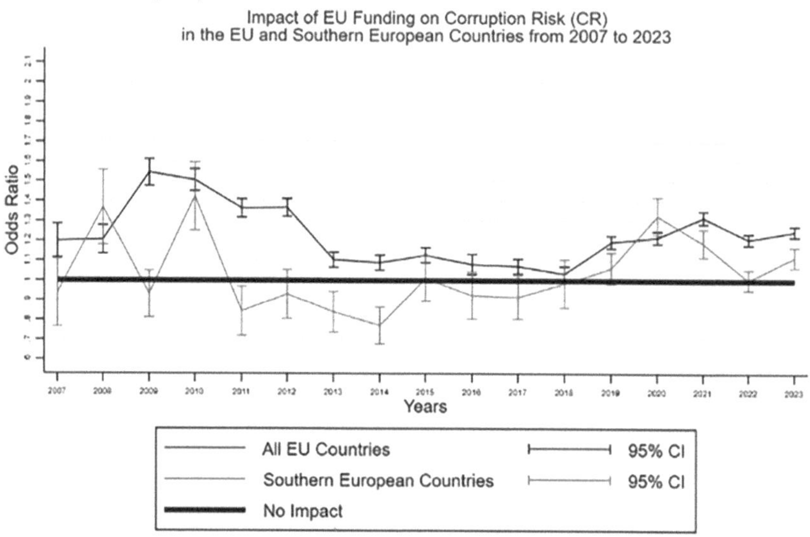

Notes: odds ratios; without framework agreements; N=5,029,979
CR[0,1] = 1: only one bidder; 0: else
Source: Tóth (2024)

Figs. 8.6, 8.7, 8.8, 8.9, 8.10, 8.11, 8.12, and 8.13 (continued)

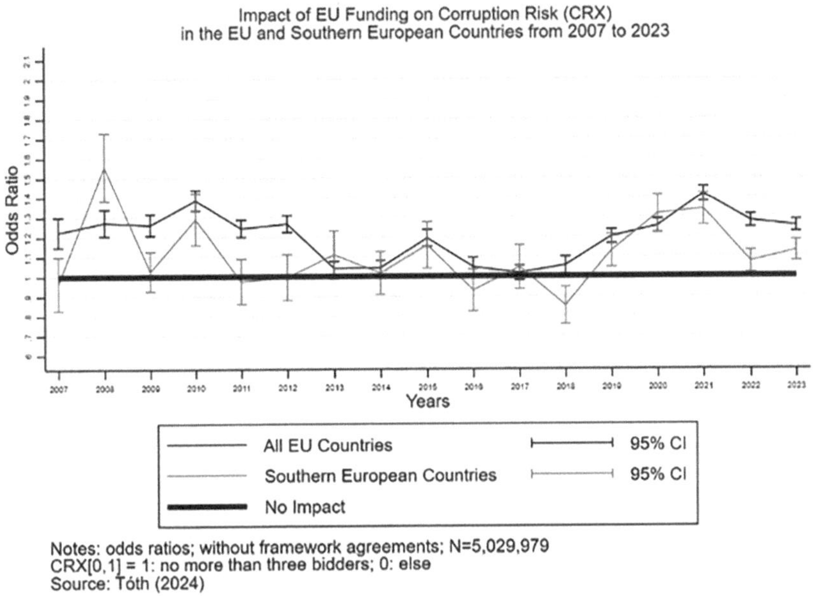

Figs. 8.6, 8.7, 8.8, 8.9, 8.10, 8.11, 8.12, and 8.13 (continued)

8.5 Summary and Policy Implications

According to some estimates (Hafner et al. 2016), corruption costs the EU between €179 billion and €990 billion per year in social, economic, and political losses. So effective action against corruption can bring significant social benefits. It is therefore important to find adequate anti-corruption tools to achieve this social objective.

Anti-corruption efforts require the simultaneous application of multiple strategies that influence economic actors' decisions regarding corruption through various mechanisms. These tools aim to reduce the prevalence of corrupt transactions by either decreasing the expected gains from corruption or increasing the expected costs, primarily by raising the likelihood of detection, increasing transaction costs, and highlighting the moral consequences of corrupt behaviour. Together, these factors reduce the expected net income from corruption for economic actors.

Methods such as raising bureaucrats' wages, decentralisation, enhancing law enforcement monitoring, strengthening political institutions, publishing state-controlled databases, promoting open data and open government initiatives, applying modern detection tools based on digitalisation and statistical analyses, and encouraging oversight from civil society and the media all contribute to these efforts.

In this study, we argue that both the EU and its Member States should intentionally leverage the fact that, beyond the actual probability of detection, the subjective (or perceived) likelihood of getting caught plays a significant role in economic actors' decisions regarding corruption. Anti-corruption policies should aim to increase this perceived likelihood of detection and strengthen public trust in anti-corruption institutions. This is not just about increasing the budgets and activities of anti-corruption institutions, which would indeed raise the actual probability of detection and discourage corrupt transactions, but also about actively publicising the results of these efforts. Doing so would elevate economic actors' subjective fear of detection beyond what the actual rise in detection probability might accomplish.

The EU and its Member States must collaborate in this effort, as joint action is essential in the fight against corruption. Merely publishing and disseminating annual reports from investigating authorities like OLAF or the EPPO is not enough. Transparent, consistent, and regular communication with economic actors—through scientific analyses, case studies, media engagements, and conference presentations—is vital. This will help convince economic actors that engaging in corruption is not worthwhile because anti-corruption organisations are equipped with modern tools that will inevitably lead to their exposure. It is crucial to instil confidence that these modern anti-corruption methods significantly increase the likelihood of being caught.

Additionally, it is essential to build trust in the integrity of anti-corruption organisations. Economic actors must believe that these institutions operate impartially, in accordance with the law, and are committed to using all available tools to combat corruption.

From this perspective, the integrity of organisations fighting corruption must be unquestionable. There can be no cases where members of the European Parliament are involved in corruption scandals,[8] and it is espe-

[8] See the "Cash-for-Laws" scandal or the "Qatargate" scandal. Some links about the former scandal, see: https://www.againstcorruption.eu/articles/timeline-of-mep-corruption-scandal/; https://www.thetimes.com/article/insight-euro-mps-exposed-in-cash-for-laws-scandal-g8w93bql3v0; https://www.youtube.com/watch?v=JTS4rpIuwAE; https://www.euractiv.

cially unacceptable for any leader of the European Commission or EU anti-corruption institutions to be caught breaking the law or convicted of corruption.[9] Such events not only deeply undermine public trust in EU institutions (the European Parliament, the European Commission, or EU anti-corruption organisations), but also contribute to reducing economic actors' subjective, perceived probability of getting caught, leading them to underestimate the actual probability of detection related to corruption. This outcome could form the basis for an increase in corruption.

The empirical literature on specific anti-corruption measures generally supports the theoretical assumptions, indicating that factors such as higher wages, careful selection of bureaucrats, decentralisation of bureaucracy, competitive organisations, solid political institutions, a free press, data disclosure, digitalisation, and modern technologies all contribute to reducing corruption. However, the results for law enforcement and monitoring are more mixed.

com/section/justice-home-affairs/news/ex-austrian-mep-imprisoned-in-lobbying-scandal/ https://www.euractiv.com/section/future-eu/news/ex-mep-to-serve-prison-in-cash-for-laws-scandal/; https://www.politico.eu/article/ex-mep-convicted-of-accepting-bribes/ And for the actors and history of the latter scandal, see: https://www.lesoir.be/482080/article/2022-12-09/info-le-soir-le-qatar-soupconne-de-corruption-en-plein-coeur-de-leurope; https://time.com/6240539/eva-kaili-european-union-eu-corruption/; https://www.nytimes.com/2022/12/11/world/europe/eu-parliament-bribery-qatar.html; https://www.france24.com/en/live-news/20221211-greek-mep-held-as-qatar-graft-probe-expands-1; https://www.france24.com/en/europe/20230121-corruption-cash-and-confessions-who-are-the-key-suspects-in-the-qatargate-scandal; https://en.wikipedia.org/wiki/Eva_Kaili; https://en.wikipedia.org/wiki/Antonio_Panzeri; https://www.euractiv.com/section/politics/news/qatargate-teary-eyed-tarabella-reiterates-innocence-before-media/;https://www.politico.eu/article/qatargate-belgium-parliament-waive-immunity-meps-tarabella-cozzolino/

[9] For instance, the "Dalligate" scandal. For the actors and history of the scandal, see:https://www.maltatoday.com.mt/news/court_and_police/123906/expolice_chief_john_rizzo_details_discrepancies_in_john_dallis_statements_on_bribery_allegations; https://timesofmalta.com/article/Dalligate-for-Dummies.441699; https://projects.icij.org/investigations/pandora-papers/power-players/en/player/john-dalli; https://www.maltatoday.com.mt/news/court_and_police/116032/john_dalli_held_private_meetings_with_tobacco_lobbyists_former_olaf_chief_tells_court; https://tobaccotactics.org/article/tpd-dalligate-timeline/; https://tobaccotactics.org/article/swedish-match/; https://www.alter-eu.org/sites/default/files/ALTER-EU%20Lessons%20from%20Dalligate.pdf; https://www.euractiv.com/section/justice-home-affairs/news/former-eu-commissioner-dalli-charged-with-bribery-in-malta-court/; https://www.politico.eu/article/hello-again-dalli/. Here, we would like to thank Dávid Kristóf for his help in collecting articles on the "Cash-for-Laws" scandal, the "Qatargate", and the "Dalligate" scandal.

It is also worth noting that there is a shortage of studies measuring corruption based on objective indicators rather than perception-based indicators like the Transparency International Corruption Perceptions Index (TI CPI) or expert surveys. Moreover, empirical studies examining the effectiveness of the EU's anti-corruption measures are almost non-existent. This fact highlights the need for research that measures the impact of anti-corruption efforts using objective indicators and analyses how these measures influence the decisions of economic actors involved in corruption.

The analysis of EU public procurement data from 2007 to 2023 shows that both New Member States and Southern European countries have experienced a reduction in corruption risk, moving closer to the lower levels observed in Western European countries. This fact is seen as a sign of institutional convergence, and the positive trend is undoubtedly linked to the EU's strengthened anti-corruption efforts. Key steps, such as the creation of OLAF and the EPPO, the increase in their budgets, and the growing focus on corruption and anti-corruption measures in the European Commission's country reports, may have contributed to these improvements.

However, the analysis of corruption risk for EU subsidies indicates that, despite these efforts, the corruption risk associated with EU-funded public contracts remained significantly higher than that of nationally funded ones between 2007 and 2023, not only in the New Member States but also in Western European countries. This suggests a weak and inefficient use of EU funds. These findings underscore the need for EU institutions to take further action to address the challenges of effectively managing EU funds and reducing corruption risks.

References

Aarvik, P. (2019). Artificial intelligence – a promising anti-corruption tool in development settings? *U4 Anti-Corruption Resource Centre.*

Abbink, K. (2004). Staff Rotation as an Anti-corruption Policy: An Experimental Study. European Journal of Political Economy, 20(4), 887–906. https://doi.org/10.1016/j.ejpoleco.2003.10.008

African Development Bank Group. (2004). *Guidelines for Preventing & Combating Corruption & Fraud in Bank Group Operations.* African Development Bank Group. https://www.afdb.org/fileadmin/uploads/afdb/Documents/Policy-

Documents/15-EN-Guidelines_for_preventing_and_combating_corruption_and_fraud.pdf

Alt, J. E., & Lassen, D. D. (2014). Enforcement and Public Corruption: Evidence from the American States. The Journal of Law, Economics, and Organization, 30(2), 306–338. https://doi.org/10.1093/jleo/ews036

Andersen, T. B., Bentzen, J., Dalgaard, C.-J., & Selaya, P. (2011). Does the Internet Reduce Corruption? Evidence from US States and across Countries. The World Bank Economic Review, 25(3), 387–417. https://doi.org/10.1093/wber/lhr025

Andvig, J. Ch., Fjeldstad, O-H., Amundsen, I., Sissener, T., & Søreide, T. (2001). Corruption. A Review of Contemporary Research. *Chr. Michelsen Institute.* http://bora.cmi.no/dspace/bitstream/10202/225/1/R%202001%207.pdf

Anwar, S., & Loughran, T. A. (2011). Testing a Bayesian Learning Theory of Deterrence Among Serious Juvenile Offenders. Criminology, 49(3), 667–698. https://doi.org/10.1111/j.1745-9125.2011.00233.x

Apel, R. (2013). Sanctions, Perceptions, and Crime: Implications for Criminal Deterrence. Journal of Quantitative Criminology, 29(1), 67–101. https://doi.org/10.1007/s10940-012-9170-1

Apospori, E., & Alpert, G. (1993). Research Note: The Role of Differential Experience with the Criminal Justice System in Changes in Perceptions of Severity of Legal Sanctions Over Time. Crime & Delinquency, 39(2), 184–194. https://doi.org/10.1177/0011128793039002004

Arikan, G. G. (2004). Fiscal Decentralisation: A Remedy for Corruption? International Tax and Public Finance, 11(2), 175–195. https://doi.org/10.1023/B:ITAX.0000011399.00053.a1

Avis, E., Ferraz, C., & Finan, F. (2018). Do Government Audits Reduce Corruption? Estimating the Impacts of Exposing Corrupt Politicians. Journal of Political Economy, 126(5), 1912–1964. https://doi.org/10.1086/699209

Bachman, R., Paternoster, R., & Ward, S. (1992). The Rationality of Sexual Offending: Testing a Deterrence/Rational Choice Conception of Sexual Assault. Law & Society Review, 26(2), 343–372. https://doi.org/10.2307/3053901

Bajpai, R. & Myers, C. B. (2010). Enhancing Government Effectiveness and Transparency : The Fight Against Corruption. The World Bank Group. http://documents.worldbank.org/curated/en/235541600116631094/Enhancing-Government-Effectiveness-and-Transparency-The-Fight-Against-Corruption

Banerjee, A., Duflo, E., Imbert, C., Mathew, S., & Pande, R. (2020). E-governance, Accountability, and Leakage in Public Programs: Experimental Evidence from a Financial Management Reform in India. American Economic Journal: Applied Economics, 12(4), 39–72. https://doi.org/10.1257/app.20180302

Banuri, S., & Eckel, C. (2015). Cracking Down on Bribery. Social Choice and Welfare, 45(3), 579–600. https://www.jstor.org/stable/i40146981

Barfort, S., Harmon, N., Hjorth, F., & Olsen, A. (2015). *Dishonesty and Selection into Public Service in Denmark: Who Runs the World's Least Corrupt Public Sector?* University of Copenhagen Department of Economics. https://www.economics.ku.dk/research/publications/wp/dp_2015/1512.pdf

Becker, G. S. (1968). Crime and Punishment: An Economic Approach. Journal of Political Economy, 76(2), 169–217. http://www.jstor.org/stable/1830482

Becker, G. S., & Stigler, G. J. (1974). Law Enforcement, Malfeasance, and Compensation of Enforcers. The Journal of Legal Studies, 3(1), 1–18. http://www.jstor.org/stable/724119

Berrú, Torres Y., Batista, López V. F., Torres-Carrion P. V. and Jimenez, Maria Gabriela (2020). Artificial Intelligence Techniques to Detect and Prevent Corruption in Procurement: A Systematic Literature Review. *Computer and Information Science*. 1194(2), 254–268. https://doi.org/10.1007/978-3-030-42520-3_21

Bhattacharyya, S., & Hodler, R. (2015). Media Freedom and Democracy in the Fight Against Corruption. European Journal of Political Economy, 39, 13–24. https://doi.org/10.1016/j.ejpoleco.2015.03.004

Billger, S. M., & Goel, R. K. (2009). Do existing corruption levels matter in controlling corruption? Cross-country quantile regression estimates. Journal of Development Economics, 90(2), 299–305. https://doi.org/10.1016/j.jdeveco.2008.07.006

Blumstein, A., & Nagin, D. (1977). The Deterrent Effect of Legal Sanctions on Draft Evasion. Stanford Law Review, 29(2), 241–276. JSTOR. https://doi.org/10.2307/1228240

Bobonis, G. J., Cámara Fuertes, L. R., & Schwabe, R. (2016). Monitoring Corruptible Politicians. American Economic Review, 106(8), 2371–2405. https://doi.org/10.1257/aer.20130874

Borcan, O., Lindahl, M., & Mitrut, A. (2014). The impact of an unexpected wage cut on corruption: Evidence from a "Xeroxed" exam. Journal of Public Economics, 120, 32–47. https://doi.org/10.1016/j.jpubeco.2014.08.003

Bosio, E., Djankov, S., Glaeser, E., & Shleifer, A. (2022). Public Procurement in Law and Practice. American Economic Review, 112 (4), 1091–1117. https://doi.org/10.1257/aer.20200738

Bradford, B., Hohl, K., Jackson, J., & MacQueen, S. (2015). Obeying the Rules of the Road: Procedural Justice, Social Identity, and Normative Compliance. Journal of Contemporary Criminal Justice, 31(2), 171–191. https://doi.org/10.1177/1043986214568833

Bridges, G. S., & Stone, J. A. (1986). Effects of Criminal Punishment on Perceived Threat of Punishment: Toward an Understanding of Specific Deterrence. Journal of Research in Crime and Delinquency, 23(3), 207–239. https://doi.org/10.1177/0022427886023003002

Brunetti, A., & Weder, B. (2003). A free press is bad news for corruption. Journal of Public Economics, 87(7), 1801–1824. https://doi.org/10.1016/S0047-2727(01)00186-4

Campante, F. R., & Do, Q.-A. (2014). Isolated Capital Cities, Accountability, and Corruption: Evidence from US States. American Economic Review, 104(8), 2456–2481. https://doi.org/10.1257/aer.104.8.2456

Campante, F. R., Chor, D., & Do, Q.-A. (2009). Instability and the Incentives for corruption. Economics & Politics, 21(1), 42–92. https://doi.org/10.1111/j.1468-0343.2008.00335.x

Chen, Ting, and James Kai-sing Kung. 2019. "Busting the 'Princelings': The Campaign Against Corruption in China's Primary Land Market". *The Quarterly Journal of Economics* 134 (1): 185–226. https://doi.org/10.1093/qje/qjy027.

Colman, R. (2020, September 10). FUNES, the corruption-detecting algorithm that "never forgets". *Open Contracting Partnership.* https://www.open-contracting.org/2020/09/10/funes-the-corruption-detecting-algorithm-that-never-forgets/

Corbacho, A., Gingerich, D. W., Oliveros, V., & Ruiz-Vega, M. (2016). Corruption as a Self-Fulfilling Prophecy: Evidence from a Survey Experiment in Costa Rica. American Journal of Political Science, 60(4), 1077–1092.

Cordis, A. S., & Warren, P. L. (2014). Sunshine as disinfectant: The effect of state Freedom of Information Act laws on public corruption. Journal of Public Economics, 115, 18–36. https://doi.org/10.1016/j.jpubeco.2014.03.010

Costa, S. (2013). Do Freedom of Information Laws Decrease Corruption? The Journal of Law, Economics, and Organization, 29(6), 1317–1343. https://doi.org/10.1093/jleo/ews016

Cuervo-Cazurra, A. (2008). The effectiveness of laws against bribery abroad. Journal of International Business Studies, 39(4), 634–651. https://doi.org/10.1057/palgrave.jibs.8400372

Dahlström, C., Lapuente, V., & Teorell, J. (2012). The Merit of Meritocratization: Politics, Bureaucracy, and the Institutional Deterrents of Corruption. Political Research Quarterly, 65(3), 656–668. https://doi.org/10.1177/1065912911408109

Dal Bó, E., Finan, F., & Rossi, M. A. (2013). Strengthening State Capabilities: The Role of Financial Incentives in the Call to Public Service. The Quarterly Journal of Economics, 128(3), 1169–1218. https://doi.org/10.1093/qje/qjt008

della Porta, D. & Vannucci, A. (1999). Corrupt Exchanges. Actors, Resources, and Mechanisms of Political Corruption. Routledge. https://doi.org/10.4324/9781315080284

della Porta, D. & Vannucci, A. (2012). The Hidden Order of Corruption. An Institutional Approaches. Routledge. https://doi.org/10.4324/9781315557267

Demirgüç-Kunt, A., Lokshin, M., & Kolchin, V. (2021). Effects of Public Sector Wages on Corruption: Wage Inequality Matters. The World Bank. https://documents1.worldbank.org/curated/en/387481619624669061/pdf/Effects-of-Public-Sector-Wages-on-Corruption-Wage-Inequality-Matters.pdf

Dhillon, A., & Nicolò, A. (2023). Moral Costs of Corruption: A Review of the Literature. In: Basu, K., Mishra, A. (eds) Law and Economic Development. Palgrave Macmillan. https://doi.org/10.1007/978-3-031-24938-9_5

Diaby, A., & Sylwester, K. (2014). Bureaucratic competition and public corruption: Evidence from transition countries. European Journal of Political Economy, 35, 75–87. https://doi.org/10.1016/j.ejpoleco.2014.04.002

Dickinson, T., & Wright, R. (2015). Gossip, Decision-making and Deterrence in Drug Markets. The British Journal of Criminology, 55(6), 1263–1281. https://doi.org/10.1093/bjc/azv010

Djankov, S., La Porta, R., Lopez-de-Silanes, F., & Shleifer, A. (2002). The Regulation of Entry. The Quarterly Journal of Economics, 117(1), 1–37. https://doi.org/10.1162/003355302753399436

Djankov, S., La Porta, R., Lopez-de-Silanes, F., & Shleifer, A. (2010). Disclosure by Politicians. American Economic Journal: Applied Economics, 2(2), 179–209.

Dolan, C. (2024, February 13). The Myth of Strategic Corruption. European Democracy Hub. https://europeandemocracyhub.epd.eu/the-myth-of-strategic-corruption/

Dollar, D., Fisman, R., & Gatti, R. (2001). Are women really the "fairer" sex? Corruption and women in government. Journal of Economic Behavior & Organization, 46(4), 423–429. https://doi.org/10.1016/S0167-2681(01)00169-X

Durlauf, S. N., & Nagin, D. S. (2011). Overview of "Imprisonment and crime: Can both be reduced?" Criminology & Public Policy, 10(1), 9–12. https://doi.org/10.1111/j.1745-9133.2010.00681.x

Dutt, P. (2009). Trade protection and bureaucratic corruption: An empirical investigation. Canadian Journal of Economics/Revue Canadienne d'économique, 42(1), 155–183. https://doi.org/10.1111/j.1540-5982.2008.01503.x

Duvanova, D. (2014). Economic Regulations, Red Tape, and Bureaucratic Corruption in Post-Communist Economies. World Development, 59, 298–312. https://doi.org/10.1016/j.worlddev.2014.01.028

Elbahnasawy, N. G. (2014). E-Government, Internet Adoption, and Corruption: An Empirical Investigation. World Development, 57, 114–126. https://doi.org/10.1016/j.worlddev.2013.12.005

Enikolopov, R., Petrova, M., & Sonin, K. (2018). Social Media and Corruption. American Economic Journal: Applied Economics, 10(1), 150–174. https://doi.org/10.1257/app.20160089

Erickson, M. L., & Gibbs, J. P. (1979). On the Perceived Severity of Legal Penalties. The Journal of Criminal Law and Criminology, 70(1), 102–116. https://doi.org/10.2307/1142970

Escaleras, M., Lin, S., & Register, C. (2010). Freedom of information acts and public sector corruption. Public Choice, 145(3/4), 435–460.

European Commission. (2023). *Joint Communication on the fight against corruption.* European Commission. https://commission.europa.eu/document/download/b6888f6a-45ed-4af7-b85a-6712dfe8952c_en?filename=JOIN_2023_12_1_EN.pdf

European Parliament. (2021). *Proceedings of the workshop on use of big data and AI in fighting corruption and misuse of public funds – good practice, ways forward and how to integrate new technology into contemporary control framework.* Policy Department D for Budgetary Affairs, Directorate General for Internal Policies of the Union. https://www.europarl.europa.eu/RegData/etudes/STUD/2021/691722/IPOL_STU(2021)691722_EN.pdf

Fan, C. S., Lin, C., & Treisman, D. (2009). Political decentralisation and corruption: Evidence from around the world. Journal of Public Economics, 93(1), 14–34. https://doi.org/10.1016/j.jpubeco.2008.09.001

Farrar, J., & King, T. (2023). To Punish or Not to Punish? The Impact of Tax Fraud Punishment on Observers' Tax Compliance. Journal of Business Ethics, 183(1), 289–311. https://doi.org/10.1007/s10551-022-05061-w

Fazekas, M., & Tóth, I. J. (2016). From Corruption to State Capture: A New Analytical Framework with Empirical Applications from Hungary. Political Research Quarterly, 69(2), 320–334. https://doi.org/10.1177/1065912916639137

Ferraz, C., & Finan, F. (2011). Electoral Accountability and Corruption: Evidence from the Audits of Local Governments. American Economic Review, 101(4), 1274–1311. https://doi.org/10.1257/aer.101.4.1274

Fiorino, N., Galli, E., & Padovano, F. (2015). How long does it take for government decentralisation to affect corruption? Economics of Governance, 16(3), 273–305. https://doi.org/10.1007/s10101-015-0156-y

Fisman, R., & Gatti, R. (2002). Decentralisation and corruption: Evidence across countries. Journal of Public Economics, 83(3), 325–345. https://doi.org/10.1016/S0047-2727(00)00158-4

Gagliarducci, S., & Nannicini, T. (2013). DO Better Paid Politicians Perform Better? Disentangling Incentives from Selection. Journal of the European Economic Association, 11(2), 369–398.

Galletta, S. (2017). Law Enforcement, Municipal Budgets and Spillover Effects: Evidence from a Quasi-experiment in Italy. Journal of Urban Economics, 101, 90–105. https://doi.org/10.1016/j.jue.2017.06.005

Gerli, C. (2024). How Public Organisations Can Use AI in Anti-corruption: What We Know So Far and Why We Need to Learn More About It. *Hertie School Centre for Digital Governance. https://www.hertie-school.org/en/digital-governance/research/blog/detail/content/how-public-organisations-can-use-ai-in-anti-corruption-what-we-know-so-far-and-why-we-need-to-learn-more-about-it.*

Goel, R. K., & Nelson, M. A. (1998). Corruption and Government Size: A Disaggregated Analysis. Public Choice, 97(1/2), 107–120.

Goel, R. K., & Nelson, M. A. (2014). Whistleblower laws and exposed corruption in the United States. Applied Economics, 46(20), 2331–2341. https://doi.org/10.1080/00036846.2014.894633

Granickas, Karolis. 2014. "Open Data as a Tool to Fight Corruption". 2014/04. European Public Sector Information Platform.

Grasmick, H. G., & Bryjak, G. J. (1980). The Deterrent Effect of Perceived Severity of Punishment. Social Forces, 59(2), 471–491. JSTOR. https://doi.org/10.2307/2578032

Hafner, M., Taylor, J., Disley, E., Thebes, S., Barberi, M., Stepanek, M., and Levi, M. (2016). The Cost of Non-Europe in the area of Organised Crime and Corruption Annex II – The Cost of Non-Europe in the Area of Corruption. European Parliamentary Research Service, European Added Value Unit. https://www.europarl.europa.eu/RegData/etudes/STUD/2016/579319/EPRS_STU%282016%29579319_EN.pdf

Hjalmarsson, R. (2009). Crime and Expected Punishment: Changes in Perceptions at the Age of Criminal Majority. American Law and Economics Review, 11(1), 209–248. https://doi.org/10.1093/aler/ahn016

Horney, J., & Marshall, I. H. (1992). Risk Perceptions Among Serious Offenders: The Rore of Crime and Punishment. Criminology, 30(4), 575–594. https://doi.org/10.1111/j.1745-9125.1992.tb01117.x

Hummel, C., Gerring, J., & Burt, T. (2021). Do Political Finance Reforms Reduce Corruption? British Journal of Political Science, 51(2), 869–889. https://doi.org/10.1017/S0007123419000358

Huther, J. & Shah, A. (2000). *Anti-Corruption Policies and Programs: A Framework for Evaluation.* The World Bank. http://hdl.handle.net/10986/19753

International Monetary Fund. (2018). *Review of 1997 Guidance Note on Governance – A Proposed Framework for Enhanced Fund Engagement.* International Monetary Fund. https://www.imf.org/-/media/Files/Publications/PP/2018/pp030918govpaper.ashx

International Monetary Fund. (2023). *Review of Implementation of the 2018 Framework for Enhanced Fund Engagement on Governance.* International Monetary Fund. https://www.imf.org/-/media/Files/Publications/PP/2023/English/PPEA2023015.ashx

Kang, S., & Zhu, J. (2021). Do People Trust the Government More? Unpacking the Distinct Impacts of Anti-corruption Policies on Political Trust. Political Research Quarterly, 74(2), 434–449. https://doi.org/10.1177/1065912920912016

Khan, A. Q., Khwaja, A. I., & Olken, B. A. (2016). Tax Farming Redux: Experimental Evidence on Performance Pay for Tax Collectors. The Quarterly Journal of Economics, 131(1), 219–271. https://doi.org/10.1093/qje/qjv042

Kim, S., Rho, E., & Teo, Y. X. J. (2024). Citizen satisfaction research in public administration: a systematic literature review and future research agenda. The American Review of Public Administration, 54(5), 460-485. https://doi.org/10.1177/02750740241237477

Kleck, G., Sever, B., Li, S., & Gertz, M. (2005). The Missing Link in General Deterrence Research. Criminology, 43(3), 623–660. https://doi.org/10.1111/j.0011-1348.2005.00019.x

Klepper, S., & Nagin, D. (1989a). Tax Compliance and Perceptions of the Risks of Detection and Criminal Prosecution. Law & Society Review, 23(2), 209–240. https://doi.org/10.2307/3053715

Klepper, S., & Nagin, D. (1989b). The Deterrent Effect of Perceived Certainty and Severity of Punishment Revisited. Criminology, 27(4), 721–746. https://doi.org/10.1111/j.1745-9125.1989.tb01052.x

Klitgaard, Robert. 1988. *Controlling Corruption*. University of California Press. http://www.jstor.org/stable/10.1525/j.ctt1pnj3b.

Kunicová, J., & Rose-Ackerman, S. (2005). Electoral Rules and Constitutional Structures as Constraints on Corruption. British Journal of Political Science, 35(4), 573–606. https://www.jstor.org/stable/4092413

Kwon, I. (2014). Motivation, Discretion, and Corruption. Journal of Public Administration Research and Theory, 24(3), 765–794. https://doi.org/10.1093/jopart/mus062

Lambsdorff, Johann Graf. 2007. *The Institutional Economics of Corruption and Reform: Theory, Evidence and Policy*. Cambridge: Cambridge University Press. https://doi.org/10.1017/CBO9780511492617.

Lederman, D., Loayza, N., & Soares, R. R. (2001). *Accountability and Corruption: Political Institutions Matter.* The World Bank. https://doi.org/10.1596/1813-9450-2708

Lee, D. S., Meyer-Sahling, J.-H., & Park, S. (2022). Learning effects of anti-corruption reform in public organisations: Explanations from social psychological theory. Public Management Review, 1–22. https://doi.org/10.1080/14719037.2022.2051064

Lessmann, C., & Markwardt, G. (2010). One Size Fits All? Decentralisation, Corruption, and the Monitoring of Bureaucrats. World Development, 38(4), 631–646. https://doi.org/10.1016/j.worlddev.2009.11.003

Lewis-Faupel, S., Neggers, Y., Olken, B. A., & Pande, R. (2016). Can Electronic Procurement Improve Infrastructure Provision? Evidence from Public Works in India and Indonesia. American Economic Journal: Economic Policy, 8(3), 258–283. https://doi.org/10.1257/pol.20140258

Lochner, L. (2007). Individual Perceptions of the Criminal Justice System. The American Economic Review, 97(1), 444–460. https://doi.org/10.1257/aer.97.1.444

López Acera, A. (2023, November 21). Artificial intelligence and the fight against corruption. *Blog-AVAF-En*. https://www.antifraucv.es/en/artificial-intelligence-and-the-fight-against-corruption/

Loughran, T., Paternoster, R., Piquero, A., & Pogarsky, G. (2011). On ambiguity in perceptions of risk: Implications for criminal decision making and deterrence. Criminology, 49, 1029–1061. https://doi.org/10.1111/j.1745-9125.2011.00251.x

MacCoun, R., Pacula, R. L., Chriqui, J., Harris, K., & Reuter, P. (2009). Do Citizens Know Whether Their State Has Decriminalised Marijuana? Assessing the Perceptual Component of Deterrence Theory. 5(1), 347–371. https://doi.org/10.2202/1555-5879.1227

Martinez T. M., Whitley E.A. (2023). Open data as an anti-corruption tool? Using distributed cognition to understand breakdowns in the creation of transparency data. *Data & Policy*, (5) e13. https://doi.org/10.1017/dap.2023.10

Matsueda, R. L., Kreager, D. A., & Huizinga, D. (2006). Deterring Delinquents: A Rational Choice Model of Theft and Violence. American Sociological Review, 71(1), 95–122. https://doi.org/10.1177/000312240607100105

Meier, R. F., & Johnson, W. T. (1977). Deterrence as Social Control: The Legal and Extralegal Production of Conformity. American Sociological Review, 42(2), 292–304. JSTOR. https://doi.org/10.2307/2094606

Murphy, K., Bradford, B., & Jackson, J. (2016). Motivating Compliance Behavior Among Offenders: Procedural Justice or Deterrence? Criminal Justice and Behavior, 43(1), 102–118. https://doi.org/10.1177/0093854815611166

Nagin, D. S. (2013). Deterrence in the Twenty-First Century. Crime and Justice, 42(1), 199–263. https://doi.org/10.1086/670398

Nagin, D. S., & Paternoster, R. (1993). Enduring Individual Differences and Rational Choice Theories of Crime. Law & Society Review, 27(3), 467–496. JSTOR. https://doi.org/10.2307/3054102

Nagin, D. S., & Pogarsky, G. (2003). An Experimental Investigation of Deterrence: Cheating, Self-Serving Bias, And Impulsivity. Criminology, 41(1), 167–194. https://doi.org/10.1111/j.1745-9125.2003.tb00985.x

Navot, D., Reingewertz, Y., & Cohen, N. (2016). Speed or Greed? High Wages and Corruption Among Public Servants. Administration & Society, 48(5), 580–601. https://doi.org/10.1177/0095399715623313

Odilla, F. (2023). Bots against corruption: Exploring the benefits and limitations of AI-based anti-corruption technology. Crime Law Soc Change (80), 353–396. https://doi.org/10.1007/s10611-023-10091-0

OECD. (2024). Anti-Corruption and Integrity Outlook 2024. OECD Publishing. https://doi.org/10.1787/968587cd-en

Open Contracting Partnership. (2024). *Better Public Procurement for People & The Planet.* Open Contracting Partnership. https://www.open-contracting.org/wp-content/uploads/2024/03/OCP2024-Strategy.pdf

Persson, T., Tabellini, G., & Trebbi, F. (2003). Electoral Rules and Corruption. Journal of the European Economic Association, 1(4), 958–989. https://doi.org/10.1162/154247603322493203

Pickett, J. T., Loughran, T. A., & Bushway, S. (2016). Consequences of legal risk communication for sanction perception updating and white-collar criminality. Journal of Experimental Criminology, 12(1), 75–104. https://doi.org/10.1007/s11292-016-9254-2

Pogarsky, G., & Piquero, A. R. (2003). Can Punishment Encourage Offending? Investigating The "resetting" Effect. Journal of Research in Crime and Delinquency, 40(1), 95–120. https://doi.org/10.1177/0022427802239255

Pogarsky, G., Piquero, A. R., & Paternoster, R. (2004). Modeling Change in Perceptions about Sanction Threats: The Neglected Linkage in Deterrence Theory. Journal of Quantitative Criminology, 20(4), 343–369. https://doi.org/10.1007/s10940-004-5868-z

Pogarsky, G., Roche, S., & Pickett, J. (2017). Heuristics and Biases, Rational Choice, and Sanction Perceptions. Criminology, 55(1), 85–111. https://doi.org/10.1111/1745-9125.12129

Rose-Ackerman, S. (1975). The Economics of Corruption. Journal of Public Economics,4(2),187-203.https://doi.org/10.1016/0047-2727(75)90017-1

Rose-Ackerman, S. (1978). Corruption. A Study in Political Economy. Academic Press. https://doi.org/10.1016/C2009-0-22067-8

Suh, J. B., Shim, H. S., & Button, M. (2018). Exploring the impact of organisational investment on occupational fraud: Mediating effects of ethical culture and monitoring control. International Journal of Law, Crime and Justice, 53, 46–55. https://doi.org/10.1016/j.ijlcj.2018.02.003

Tankebe, J. (2009). Public Cooperation With the Police in Ghana: Does Procedural Fairness Matter? Criminology, 47(4), 1265–1293. https://doi.org/10.1111/j.1745-9125.2009.00175.x

Tankebe, J. (2019). Cooperation With the Police Against Corruption: Exploring the Roles of Legitimacy, Deterrence and Collective Action Theories. The British Journal of Criminology, 59(6), 1390–1410. https://doi.org/10.1093/bjc/azz030

Tanner, C., Linder, S., & Sohn, M. (2022). Does moral commitment predict resistance to corruption? Experimental evidence from a bribery game. Plos One, 17(1), e0262201. https://doi.org/10.1371/journal.pone.0262201

Tittle, C. R. (1977). Sanction Fear and the Maintenance of Social Order. Social Forces, 55(3), 579–596. JSTOR. https://doi.org/10.2307/2577457

Tóth, I. J. (2024). *Corruption Risk of EU-Funded Contracts and in the EU 2007-2023.* CRCB. https://www.crcb.eu/?p=3577

Tóth, I. J. & Hajdu, M., (2021). Corruption, Institutions and Convergence. In M. Landesmann & I. P. Székely (Eds.), *Does EU Membership Facilitate Convergence? The Experience of the EU's Eastern Enlargement – Volume II*, (pp. 195–248). Palgrave Macmillan. https://www.springerprofessional.de/en/corruption-institutions-and-convergence/18869574

Tsushima, M., & Hamai, K. (2015). Public Cooperation With the Police in Japan: Testing the Legitimacy Model. Journal of Contemporary Criminal Justice, 31(2), 212–228. https://doi.org/10.1177/1043986214568836

United Nations. (2003). *UN Guide on Anti-Corruption Policy.* United Nations. https://www.unodc.org/pdf/crime/corruption/UN_Guide.pdf

United Nations. (2004). The Global Programme Against Corruption. An Anti-Corruption Toolkit. 2nd Editions. United Nations. https://www.unodc.org/documents/corruption/Toolkit_ed2.pdf

Van Rijckeghem, C., & Weder, B. (2001). Bureaucratic corruption and the rate of temptation: Do wages in the civil service affect corruption, and by how much? Journal of Development Economics, 65(2), 307–331. https://doi.org/10.1016/S0304-3878(01)00139-0

Vargas, G. A., & Schlutz, D. (2016). Opening Public Officials' Coffers: A Quantitative Analysis of the Impact of Financial Disclosure Regulation on National Corruption Levels. European Journal on Criminal Policy and Research, 22(3), 439–475. https://doi.org/10.1007/s10610-016-9320-3

Wang, J. (2018). The State as a Vehicle of Technological Change: Economic Openness, Technological Catching-up, and Indigenous Innovation in Chinese Firms. Perspectives on Global Development and Technology, 17(4), 373–407. https://doi.org/10.1163/15691497-12341485

Warren, D. E., & Schweitzer, M. E. (2021). When Weak Sanctioning Systems Work: Evidence from Auto Insurance Industry Fraud Investigations. Behavioral Field Evidence on Ethics and Misconduct, 166(9), 68–83. https://doi.org/10.1016/j.obhdp.2019.04.003

Williams, K. R., Gibbs, J. P., & Erickson, M. L. (1980). Public Knowledge of Statutory Penalties: The Extent and Basis of Accurate Perception. The Pacific Sociological Review, 23(1), 105–128. https://doi.org/10.2307/1388805

CHAPTER 9

Domestic Acceptability as a Condition for Ambitious Climate Policies

Simone Borghesi, Albert Ferrari, and Lea Heinrich

9.1 Introduction

Since 2019, the European Union has significantly increased its ambitions with regard to climate protection by comprehensively revising its climate legislation in order to be the first continent to become carbon neutral by 2050. The EU Emissions Trading Scheme has been reformed and expanded to accelerate emission reductions in the sectors covered. Important changes have also been introduced for the sectors covered by the Effort Sharing Regulation, innovation and industrial policy, renewable energy and energy efficiency policy. As climate policy measures gain traction, it is essential to carefully assess their impact on the economy and

A. Ferrari (✉) · L. Heinrich
Florence School of Regulation, European University Institute, Florence, Italy
e-mail: lea.heinrich@eui.eu

S. Borghesi
Florence School of Regulation, European University Institute, Florence, Italy

Department of Political and International Sciences, University of Siena, Siena, Italy
e-mail: simone.borghesi@eui.eu

I. P. Székely, P. Halmai (eds.), *The Future of European Integration*, Studies in Economic Transition,
https://doi.org/10.1007/978-3-032-20186-7_9

society. While it will take many years to confirm the impact of the new policy package under the European Green Deal, further climate action will likely be needed to meet the EU's climate targets. In the meantime, citizens and businesses are already affected by the (perceived) costs of the transition, including the consequences of rising carbon prices, pressure to adopt new production and consumption patterns and to invest in low-carbon technologies.

Particularly in the context of the recent crises, opinions on climate policies have become increasingly polarised. There is a serious risk that climate action will lose democratic support if this issue is not properly addressed. This could be due to fears that carbon pricing measures will increase inequality and energy poverty by placing a disproportionate burden on low-income households, as well as concerns about the inclusiveness and scientific foundations of climate action due to the prevalence of top-down governance and insufficient participation and integration of scientific evidence into policymaking.

There are solutions that should be considered when designing publicly acceptable climate policies that fairly distribute the benefits and costs of the transition, allow for inclusive decision-making and are scientifically sound. Carbon pricing can be a highly positive example as it generates a significant amount of revenue, which can be re-invested in redistributional and climate measures. This is the case for the Social Climate Fund, which will come into force in 2027. In general, distribution policy will be an important part of a successful transition. To keep costs down and preserve environmental incentives, compensation measures need to be better targeted. A look at the emergency measures introduced by Member States during the recent energy crisis shows that financial support can prioritise the most vulnerable businesses and households. Digitalisation and the use of new context-specific indicators can increase the economic and environmental effectiveness of support measures.

Finally, participatory approaches such as climate citizens' assemblies and energy communities can improve the quality and acceptability of climate policy while creating local added value. This, together with the better integration of scientific knowledge into policymaking, for example, through scientific advisory boards, can strengthen the impact of climate action in times of controversy.

9.2 State-of-Play and Prospects of the European Climate Policy Mix

9.2.1 The EU Emissions Trading System(s)

In 2007, the landmark study Stern Review described climate change as "the greatest market failure the world has ever seen" (Stern 2007). This failure results from the fact that the exploitation and pollution of common resources are generally not reflected in the market. Climate policy measures can correct this market failure, for example, by pricing emissions according to the damage they cause. This is the aim of emissions trading systems (ETS), which create a carbon market and a carbon price that offers an economic incentive for emission reduction and low-carbon innovations. ETSs rely on the forces of the market rather than on legal restrictions or bans, which is why economists have long argued in favour of emissions trading as the most cost-effective climate policy instrument for reducing GHG emissions.

Almost 20 years after the introduction of the European Union Emissions Trading System (EU ETS), the figures are indeed promising. According to the European Commission (2024a), the EU ETS has helped to reduce emissions from the sectors it covered by 47% and raised auction revenues of over EUR 152 billion for the Member States (European Commission 2023a). Emissions trading is set to play an even more important role in the EU's policy mix in the coming years, as achieving the intermediate climate target for 2030 largely depends on further emission reductions in the EU ETS sectors. The EU ETS Directive[1] envisages an extension of the ETS to the maritime sector as well as a 62% reduction in emissions by 2030 compared to 2005. In addition, a new separate ETS covering the road transport and buildings sectors will be introduced. This raised level of ambition implies a significant increase in the carbon price over the next two decades, which has direct implications for acceptability and competitiveness.

While higher carbon prices are needed to incentivise emission reductions, it is important to reassess their effects on the economy and society. For instance, a higher carbon price may impact the competitiveness of the

[1] Directive 2003/87/EC of the European Parliament and of the Council of 13 October 2003 establishing a scheme for greenhouse gas emission allowance trading within the Community and amending Council Directive 96/61/EC.

EU industry, and cause higher levels of carbon leakage, i.e., the relocation of industries to countries with less stringent climate policies. It will also affect households in a more pronounced way, which may, in turn, have impacts on the public perception and acceptability of emissions trading. This section addresses the question of whether the EU ETS is fit for the low carbon transition, considering the state of play of the current legislation as well as the prospects for its development until 2050 and beyond.

9.2.1.1 Introducing the EU ETS

The EU ETS, established in 2005 after the failed attempt to adopt an EU-wide carbon tax, aims to implement the 'polluters-pay-principle'. Companies regulated by the ETS must acquire an emission allowance, known as EU Allowance (EUA), for each ton of CO_2-equivalent they emit. The EUAs are auctioned or handed out for free and then eventually traded among companies. Entities with lower emissions can sell their surplus allowance to those with higher emissions, promoting efficiency and emissions reductions. EU policymakers set an overall ceiling (cap) on GHG emissions and thus limit the amount of EUAs on the market. Emission reduction targets are achieved via the progressively decreasing cap.

9.2.1.2 The Cap, the Allowances, and the Market Stability Reserve

The velocity with which the cap decreases is determined by the Linear Reduction Factor (LRF), which is expressed as a percentage of the 2010 total cap. In theory, the shrinking cap should lead to increasingly scarce and costly EUAs, thereby incentivising companies to lower emissions. However, this has not been the case in the early years of the EU ETS, among other reasons, due to the insufficiently high LRF, which from 2013 to 2020 was set at 1.74% and from 2021 to 2024 at 2.2%. To increase ambition and align the EU ETS with the EU's overall emissions reduction target of −55% by 2030, the LRF increased to 4.3% for the period from 2024 to 2027 and will be set at 4.4% from 2028 onwards. Moreover, the cap will be rebased twice, by 90 million EUAs in 2024 and by 27 million EUAs in 2026. The new provisions present a significant reform of the EU ETS emission trajectory, and it is forecasted that, without regulatory changes, the cap will hit zero by 2039 as noted in the report of the European Scientific Advisory Board on Climate Change,hereafter "ESABCC" (2024).

In 2019, the Market Stability Reserve (MSR) was implemented to prevent a growing surplus in allowances. The so-called Total Number of

Allowances in Circulation (TNAC) determines the number of allowances that the MSR withdraws or releases for auction, thereby stabilising the market. Until 2030, the MSR withdraws 24% of the TNAC annually.

9.2.1.3 *Scope Expansion and the EU ETS 2*

In addition to the cap, the scope of the EU ETS has significantly changed over the years. It currently applies to the EU Member States (MS), Iceland, Lichtenstein, and Norway as well as Northern Ireland for electricity generation. It generally covers carbon dioxide emissions from electricity and heat generation, from energy-intensive industries (e.g., oil refineries, steel works, and production of iron, aluminium, cement, and paper), from aviation within the European Economic Area and, since 2024, from maritime transport (specifically 50% of maritime transport emissions from voyages starting or ending outside the EU and 100% from voyages between EU ports or while in EU ports). Additionally, the system applies to nitrous oxide and perfluorocarbon emissions from specific activities and methane emissions from maritime transport will be included in the EU ETS in 2026.

Furthermore, during the recent EU ETS revision, a new EU ETS 2 for carbon dioxide emissions from road transport, buildings and small-scale industrial emitters was established. The EU ETS 2 is meant to come into force in 2027 or in 2028 if energy prices are considered exceptionally high and is designed to bring down emissions in the defined sectors by 43% by 2030 compared to 2005 levels.

The scope extension is a major reform of the system, and the extension of carbon pricing to other industry sectors remains a topic of discussion. For example, the recent assessment of the ESABCC (2024) suggested extending the EU ETS to the agricultural, forestry, and land use sectors which currently lack sufficient incentives to reduce emissions. At the same time, resistance to environmental reforms has been particularly strong in these sectors as farmer's protests in many European countries have shown in 2023 and 2024.

9.2.1.4 *Carbon Leakage, Free Allocation, and the Carbon Border Adjustment Mechanism*

Another important variable to describe the evolution of the EU ETS is the allocation of allowances. While allowances were largely allocated for free in the first two trading phases (Phase I from 2005 to 2007 and Phase II from 2008 to 2012), auctioning has been the default method since the third trading phase (Phase III from 2013 to 2020 and ongoing Phase IV from 2021 to 2030) and the rules for the remaining free allowances have been revised. Free allowances have been mainly a tool to prevent carbon leakage in the industrial sectors (other motivations apply to the aviation sector and to the power sector in low-income Member States). While the power sector has received nearly no free allowances since 2013, industrial sectors deemed at risk of carbon leakage, as determined by the European Commission, continue to receive 100% of their allowances for free. Free allowances for less vulnerable sectors were decreasing over time and will be phased out until 2030.

Until today, there is little scientific evidence that supports the hypothesis that the EU ETS is causing carbon leakage (Ekins et al. 2024). This is because past carbon prices have been too low to significantly affect investment decisions, and other factors, including labour, local taxes, and energy costs, play a more important role (ERCST 2023). At the same time, the free allocation of allowances seriously undermines the stringency of the EU ETS. During Phase III, industrial installations deemed at risk of carbon leakage (i.e., included in the so-called carbon leakage list) were entitled to receive 100% of the allowances for free. According to Carbon Market Watch (2022), "in 2017, 2018 and 2019, free allocation covered 98.8%, 96.8% and 97.5% of industrial [verified] emissions respectively", and the industry accumulated 966 million surplus allowances between 2006 and 2020 (p. 25). Comparing the emission reductions in the industrial and aviation sectors with the ones in the combustion sector may indicate the counterproductive effect of the free allocation policy. While the emissions from heat and electricity generation steadily decreased until 2020, emissions in the industrial sector stagnated and even increased in the aviation sector (see Fig. 9.1). The subsequent COVID-19 pandemic and the energy supply crisis had strong temporary effects on all sectors.

To protect the competitiveness of certain industry sectors and incentivise other countries to increase their climate ambitions, the EU established the Carbon Border Adjustment Mechanism (CBAM), which places a tariff on carbon-intensive imports into the EU, thereby applying a carbon price to imports and levelling the playing field for European producers. The mechanism will come into full effect in 2026 and will coincide with the phasing out of free allowances in the sectors covered by it. Even though CBAM has received much criticism, particularly from EU trading partners, it can be part of the solution to level international competition without undermining the integrity of the EU ETS. Elements for a successful

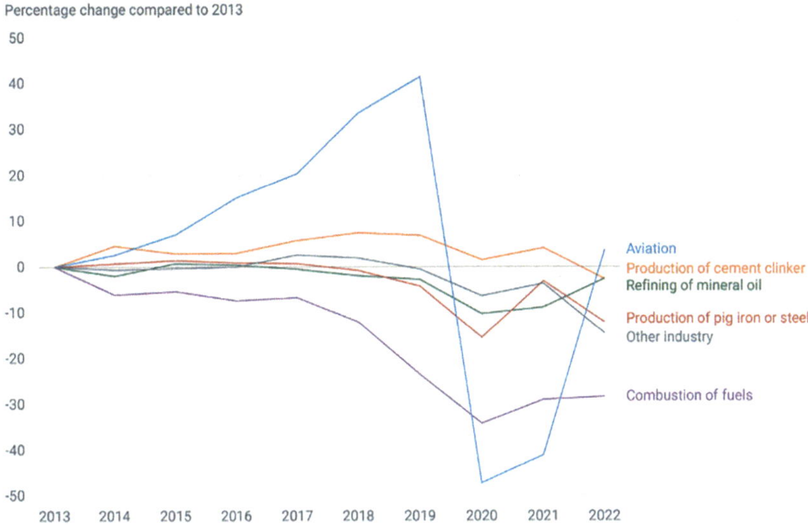

Fig. 9.1 Greenhouse gas emissions under the EU ETS. (Source: European Environment Agency (2023). Greenhouse gas emissions under the EU ETS. (https://www.eea.europa.eu/en/analysis/indicators/greenhouse-gas-emissions-under-the?activeAccordion=546a7c35-9188-4d23-94ee-005d97c26f2b). CC BY 4.0)

implementation could be the expansion of the mechanism to more products and sectors, increased diplomatic efforts to move towards global carbon pricing and the use of CBAM proceeds for climate-related investments (ESABCC 2024). In addition, more attention should be paid to the overall restructuring of the economy to compensate for the decline of Europe's carbon-intensive industry with growth in other sectors based on green technologies and know-how. Without effective industrial, innovation and just transition policies, entire regions risk falling behind in the path to decarbonisation, exacerbating regional disparities in Europe.

9.2.1.5 *The Use of Revenues*

While ETSs are recognised as cost-efficient climate policy tools, they depend on further investments and policies to facilitate the low-carbon transition and to support Member States (MS), regions or individuals that are disproportionately affected by higher carbon prices. The ETS revenues that are generated via the auctioning of allowances are an important source of income in this regard. In the EU ETS, a part of the auctioning revenues feeds into (1) the Innovation Fund, for the investment in projects focusing on the demonstration of innovative low-carbon technologies, (2) the Modernisation Fund, supporting the energy systems modernisation and energy efficiency in lower-income Member States, and, from 2026, (3) the Social Climate Fund, for investments in more efficient buildings and lower-emission mobility and to finance direct temporary income support to vulnerable households, transport users and micro-enterprises. The Fit-for-55 revision increased the amount of revenues used for the existing funds, i.e., for the period from 2020 to 2030, revenues from the auctioning of an additional 125 million allowances for the Innovation Fund and an additional amount of 2,5% of the Union-wide quantity of allowances for the Modernisation Fund. Accompanying the establishment of the EU ETS 2 for the road transport and buildings sector, the Social Climate Fund is expected to raise 65 billion EUR from the new ETS during the period from 2026 to 2032, supplemented bythe revenues from the auctioning of 50 million allowances under the old EU ETS for the initial year. Including the 25% of own resources that will be added by MS, the fund will be equipped with a total of around 86.7 billion EUR.

The remaining lion's share of revenues—approximately 400–500 billion EUR (Borghesi and Ferrari 2023)—is then distributed to the EU Member States, whereby a tenth of the revenues are redistributed to lower-income Member States. While it was previously recommended that countries use 50% of auctioning revenues for climate action, this share of revenues used for climate purposes has been increased to 100% and made mandatory in 2023. According to the ERCST 2023 State of the EU ETS Report, MS spent revenues mainly on climate-related expenditures (see Fig. 9.2), i.e., in the areas of green transport (20%), energy efficiency (17%), and renewable energy sources, hereafter "RES" (12%). The main non-climate-related area reported by MS in 2022 was energy bill support to protect consumers from high energy prices after the energy crisis (Marcu et al. 2023). However, the guidelines concerning revenue spending and reporting leave a lot of leeway to national governments. It has been criticised that the reporting has been "vague and of very low quality", making independent verification of revenue spending difficult (Carbon Market Watch 2022, p. 29). It has therefore been recommended to transparently earmark revenues for specific climate-related measures. While it would generally be more efficient to count the revenues towards

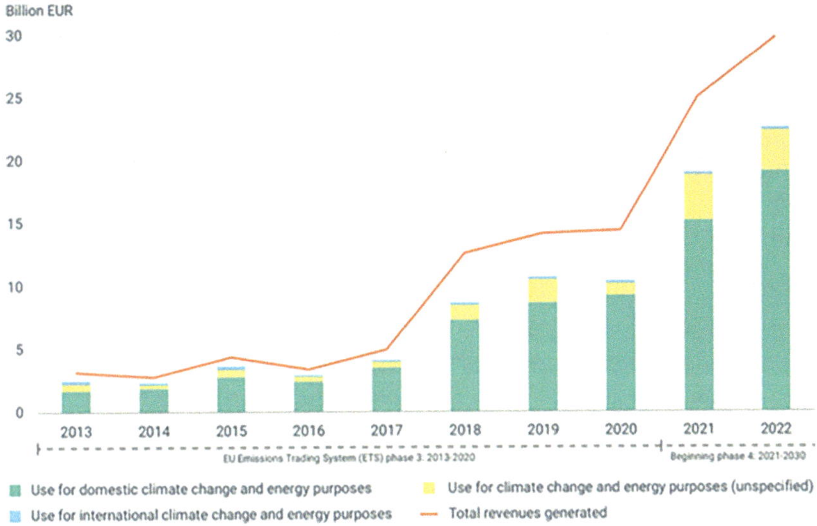

Fig. 9.2 Use of auctioning revenues generated under the EU ETS. (Source: European Environment Agency (2023). *Use of auctioning revenues generated under the EU ETS*. (https://www.eea.europa.eu/en/analysis/indicators/use-of-auctioning-revenues-generated). CC BY 4.0)

the overall budget, earmarking might prove crucial for the public acceptability of carbon pricing.

The transparent and efficient use of revenues is even more important as fiscal returns have been increasing significantly over the past years, and the trend is expected to continue. An important aspect to consider is the different capacities of governments to effectively manage and reinvest the funds. Increasing revenues from carbon pricing in the coming years should incentivise represent an opportunity only if governments have built the capacity to finance the most appropriate technologies, infrastructures and projects. It should also be kept in mind that ETSs are not a long-term source of income. As prices increase, the demand for allowances should decrease since firms are incentivised to invest in emission abatement. Mazzarano and Borghesi (2024) suggest that there is an optimal price between EUR 86 and EUR 125 per ton of CO_2eq, where revenues are highest. Surpassing this price range, demand and revenues shrink, describing what can be defined as a carbon pricing Laffer curve.

9.2.1.6 *Emissions Trading Beyond 2030: Making the System Fit for the Future*

The EU has revised the EU ETS to align with its ambitious 2030 climate target. However, challenges remain in ensuring the system's efficacy beyond 2030. Questions concern the liquidity in the market as the cap tightens, the inclusion of carbon dioxide removals, and the future relationship between the EU ETS 1 and the EU ETS 2, as well as with third-country and voluntary carbon markets.

Pahle et al. (2023) explore the possible effects of an increasing allowance scarcity on the market. Under the assumption that there will be no further legislative changes, they predict more rapid emission reductions but also anticipated investments and banking of EUAs. As the cap tightens, the number of allowances available would be too limited, and the allowance price could become increasingly volatile. The options to prevent what has been coined as the "EU ETS endgame" include the revision of the Market Stability Reserve to adjust it to a situation of increasingly high prices, to include carbon dioxide removals into the EU ETS, to increase liquidity by expanding the EU ETS to other sectors and/or by linking it with the newly established EU ETS 2, and finally by linking it to other carbon markets.

There are currently barriers to all options, e.g., ensuring that carbon removals are permanent and additional, public resistance to regulatory changes in the agricultural sectors and practical barriers to linking carbon markets of different sizes and designs, and all of them need to be considered carefully in order not to compromise the integrity of the EU ETS as a climate policy instrument. However, since the EU ETS works with long-term incentives for companies and individuals, it is key to creating **a forward-looking policy environment**.

9.2.2 *Other Companion Policies*

Since the adoption of the Energy & Climate Package of 2007 by the European Union, energy and climate policies have been driven by three main targets: a greenhouse gas emissions target, a renewable energy production target, and an energy efficiency target. The EU climate policy mix aims to achieve all these targets contemporarily. It relies on mechanisms at different levels of governance, between European, national, and local levels.

While the EU ETS represents the cornerstone of European climate policies, it is accompanied by other major building blocks supporting the decarbonisation of the European economy. The other policy instruments, hereafter companion policies, have their own motivations, scope, and impacts on climate policy. They are all to consider in the prospect of how they affect the acceptability of climate policies. In this section, we will give a first overview of how these support policies work and relate, directly or indirectly, to acceptability.

9.2.2.1 Effort Sharing

The EU ETS stands still today as the flagship of European climate policies. As the EU ETS cannot cover all sectors, part of the emissions reduction competencies and obligation is left to the MS. Effort sharing is, hence, a fundamental principle of EU climate policy aimed at ensuring a fair distribution of emission reduction efforts among EU MS for sectors not regulated at the EU level, namely domestic transport (excluding aviation), buildings, agriculture, small industry and waste.[2] It builds upon the current situation of heterogeneity among Member States, in which different countries have varying levels of economic development, industrial structure, and historical emissions, which necessitates a differentiated approach to climate action.

In other words, each MS is responsible for meeting its individual targets and can decide how to reach its targets. In addition, cooperation mechanisms such as the trading of emission allocations and the sharing of best practices can help optimise overall cost and facilitate a smoother transition to a low-carbon economy. This heterogeneity, and autonomy, allow Member States to explore their own paths, but also take advantage of this diversity of approaches to learn from each other.

The Effort Sharing Regulation (EU) 2018/842 (ESR), as updated in 2023, sets binding emission reduction targets for sectors such as transportation, buildings, agriculture, and waste. Until the European Green Deal, these sectors collectively accounted for 60% of the EU's greenhouse gas emissions and will continue to represent a major source of emissions in Europe. However, by 2030, only 23% of the EU emissions will not be regulated by an EU carbon price with the creation of an EU ETS 2 for road transport, buildings and small industrial emitters, a de-facto reduction of the scope of the ESR and increase in the Europeanisation of climate policy (Pisani-Ferry et al. 2023).

[2] See https://climate.ec.europa.eu/eu-action/effort-sharing-member-states-emission-targets/effort-sharing-2021-2030-targets-and-flexibilities_en (accessed on 22 April 2024).

Figure 9.3 illustrates the share of each sector under the ESR (and the Effort Sharing Directive before 2020) and the projects of emissions reductions and targets. It shows the relatively limited emission decrease in agriculture and transport so far. Effort sharing implies coordination between the EU and national level and is not without its challenges and debates on governance. One key issue still discussed is the method used to allocate efforts among MS. The selection of the various indicators, including GDP per capita, emissions intensity, and historical emissions, taken into account when determining the distribution of the emission reduction efforts are quite subjective and often criticised.

As Europe aims to transition to a climate-neutral economy by 2050, the role of effort-sharing becomes more critical since it will become imperative to abate faster emissions in these non-EU ETS sectors. MS will have to ramp up their commitments to achieve emission reductions across all sectors while ensuring a just transition for affected communities and

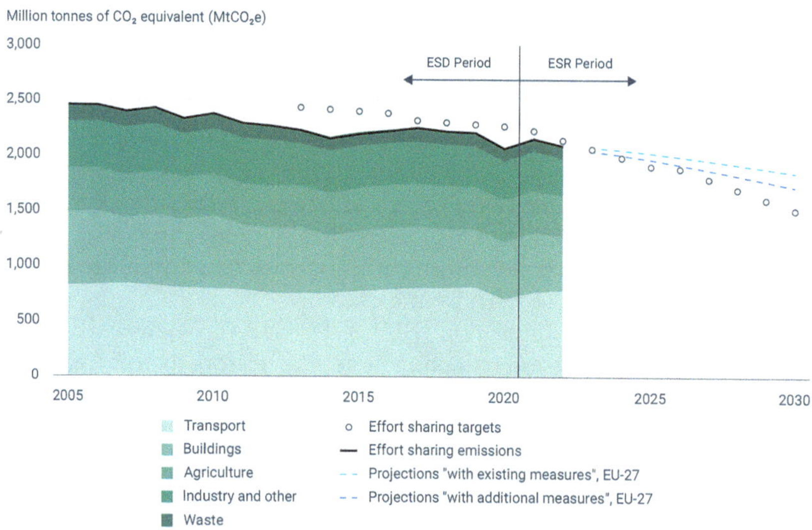

Fig. 9.3 Greenhouse gas emissions trends and projections under the scope of the Effort Sharing legislation at the EU-27 level. (Source: European Environment Agency (2023). *Greenhouse gas emissions trends and projections under the scope of the Effort Sharing legislation, EU-27.* (https://www.eea.europa.eu/data-and-maps/figures/eu-27-ghg-emission-trends-2). CC BY 4.0

industries. At the same time, new measures, such as the implementation of the EU ETS 2 after 2027, represent a step forward towards more stringent climate policies at the EU level in these sectors.

9.2.2.2 Innovation and Industrial Policies

Innovation and industrial policies play a pivotal role in European climate policy. They aim to foster the development and deployment of innovative technologies to reduce emissions, enhance energy efficiency, and promote the adoption of decarbonising materials and practices across industrial sectors.

Over the years, the EU has implemented several initiatives to support innovation and industrial transformation in the context of climate action. One such initiative is Horizon Europe, the EU's flagship research and innovation funding programme. Horizon Europe provides funding for research and technological projects that contribute to different EU priorities, including breakthrough technologies and solutions to address climate change and environmental challenges.

Other notable components of European climate policy are the Innovation Fund and Modernisation Fund, which use revenues from the EU ETS to fund innovation for low-carbon technologies and modernisation of the industrial and energy systems. With the recent adoption of the Green Industrial Plan, these funding mechanisms are now supported by broader strategies to secure the decarbonisation and competitiveness of the European industry. The Green Industrial Plan will support the EU in accessing and producing specific raw materials and technologies that are identified as strategic for the European Green Deal.[3]

Innovation and industrial policies in Europe are characterised by a collaborative approach involving governments, industry stakeholders, research institutions, and civil society. Stakeholder engagement through public-private partnerships, knowledge-sharing networks, and collaborative research projects is fundamental in driving innovation and industrial transformation across the EU. This is also key in making the transition acceptable. By providing stakeholders with financial means to decarbonise and accompany the transition, the European Union contributes to decarbonising the hard-to-abate sectors in an inclusive and rapid manner.

[3] See https://fsr.eui.eu/the-green-deal-industrial-plan/ (accessed 23 April 2024).

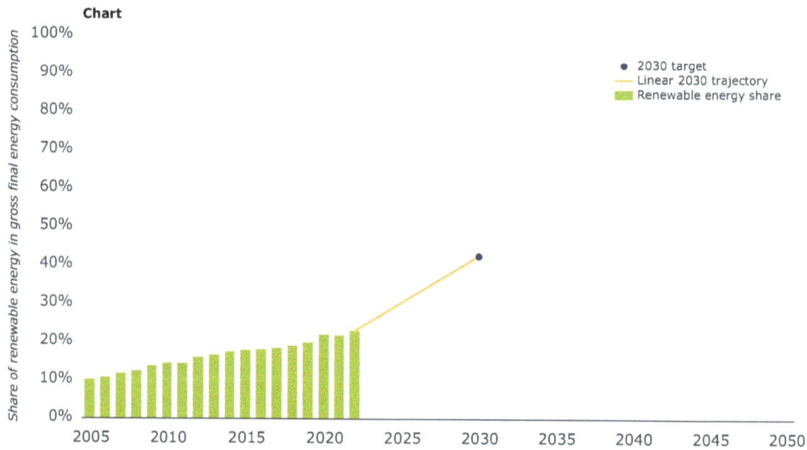

Fig. 9.4 Progress towards renewable energy source targets for EU-27. (Source: EEA) (Source: European Environment Agency (2023). *Progress towards renewable energy source targets for EU-27.* (https://www.eea.europa.eu/data-and-maps/daviz/actual-res-progress-indicative-trajectory-17#tab-chart_3). CC BY 4.0

9.2.2.3 Renewable Energy Production and Consumption

As the energy sector, including the combustion of energy for other sectors, represents 77% of the EU emissions (ICAP 2024), decarbonising the entire value chain from production to final consumption of energy is crucial. This passes primarily by renewable energy production and energy efficiency.

The Renewable Energy Directive (EU) 2018/2001, as amended in 2023, is the key legislative instrument to promote RES deployment. The EU aims to produce at least 42.5% but aiming for 45% of its final energy consumption covered by RES by 2030. This implies almost doubling the yearly deployment rate of technologies like wind and solar power (ESABCC 2024; Fig. 9.4). The directive establishes binding targets and provides a framework for supporting renewable energy production, including financial incentives and regulatory mechanisms. Moreover, Member States are asked to deploy renewables acceleration areas and consider RES projects of overriding public interest.

EU MS implemented various support mechanisms to incentivise RES production, such as feed-in tariffs, auctions, contracts for difference and green certificates. These support schemes aim to stimulate investment in

RES, facilitate market integration, and ensure a level playing field for renewable energy producers compared to traditional energy sources, namely fossil and nuclear.

Infrastructure, in particular access to and investment on the grid, and digitalisation are crucial for RES policies, enabling the integration of variable sources into the energy system. The EU supports the development of smart grids, interconnections, and storage technologies to enhance grid flexibility and reliability (European Commission 2023d).

This exceptional need to deploy decentralised infrastructure across the continent can only succeed if the population and stakeholders accept it. At a time when RES is becoming cost-competitive with fossil fuels installations, the recent EU action has been focusing on incentivising consumers' engagement in their deployment through self-consumption, energy communities and long-term power purchase agreements between RES producers and consumers.

9.2.2.4 Energy Efficiency and Demand Reduction

Energy efficiency policies are pivotal in European climate action, aiming to optimise energy use, reduce greenhouse gas emissions, and enhance energy security. The EU has established ambitious targets for improving energy efficiency, including a binding target to achieve at least 11,7% energy consumption reduction by 2030 compared to projections of the expected energy use for 2030.

The Energy Efficiency Directive 2012/27/EU, as amended in 2018 and 2023, is one of the key legislative instruments that sets out measures to promote energy efficiency in buildings, industry, transport, and public services. It mandates energy efficiency obligations for MS, establishes the principle of energy efficiency first (i.e., as the first step prior to considering investing in green energy) and puts forward energy audits and energy management systems as solutions to implement cost-effective energy-saving measures.

This is accompanied by building energy performance standards and regulations. The Energy Performance of Buildings Directive 2010/31/EU, as amended in 2018 and 2024, sets minimum energy and performance requirements for new and existing buildings, promotes energy-efficient building design and renovation, and supports the deployment of RES in buildings.

Furthermore, energy efficiency policies include standards that mandate constructors to reduce the emissions intensity of their products (e.g., cars) and labels to inform consumers about the energy efficiency of appliances (e.g., fridges). The EU also offers financial support for energy efficiency investments through the European Structural and Investment Funds (ESIF), the European Investment Bank (EIB), and the European Fund for Strategic Investments (EFSI). These funding mechanisms help overcome financial barriers and stimulate private sector investment in energy efficiency projects.

These policies contribute to reducing energy consumption, lowering GHG emissions, and building a sustainable energy future for Europe. To achieve that, they rely mostly on the consumers' capacity to adopt new technologies and habits and reduce their consumption needs. The energy efficiency target was the only EU target for 2020 that was not met. Therefore, to reach the new target by 2030, we need to ensure that consumers are enabled to reduce their energy consumption without compromising their comfort (for households) or capacity to compete in markets (for enterprises).

9.2.2.5 Prospects to 2040 and 2050

Although 2050 is the end goal, recent proposals from the European Commission and reviews by the ESABCC (2024) show that the energy sector needs to be almost entirely decarbonised by 2040. The different scenarios provided in the Impact Assessment of the European Commission's proposal of climate targets for 2040 foresee a share of RES in the final energy consumption between 65% and 75%, to reach 89% by 2050, and a final energy consumption reduction between −34% and −36% in 2040 compared to 2015, so that by 2050, it reaches −40% (European Commission 2024b).

Gradually, as the capacity to reduce emissions or energy consumption or to increase the share of RES in the energy system gets more and more limited, the issue of acceptability of such policies will become more acute.

Regulation of the effort-sharing sectors and industrial and energy decarbonisation is a key element of the European climate policy. Interactions between instruments of climate policy, as identified above, affect the overall emissions reduction. Such interactions take the form of negative, zero or positive synergistic effects. Studies have shown that the EU ETS can be strengthened if accompanied by a supportive policy mix (van den Bergh et al. 2021). At the same time, such support policies may have a negative impact on the EU ETS if they are not properly calibrated: they can lead to waterbed effects or carbon leakage (Verde et al. 2021).

9.3 Critical Challenges to Reach Net-Zero Emissions

9.3.1 Ensuring Acceptability

The EU's climate policy has been effective in reducing the continent's emissions and has particularly stepped-up reductions in the past years. Yet, while many of the effects of the European Green Deal legislation have yet to materialise, a rapid acceleration in the pace of emissions reductions is needed to meet climate targets. Meanwhile, businesses and citizens are already beginning to feel the costs of the transition. As mentioned above, EU climate policy has a greater impact on businesses but also affects individuals more directly. For example, rising carbon prices will likely be passed on to consumers, and in the case of the new EU ETS 2, investment decisions such as energy renovations or the purchase of electric cars will be borne by households rather than businesses.

At the same time, resistance to further climate action is growing in many MS, threatening to delay the implementation of the European Green Deal. The 2022 Eurobarometer survey found that 88% of EU citizens polled are in favour of further emission reductions to achieve a climate-neutral economy by 2050 (European Commission 2023b). Nevertheless, citizens seem less inclined to bear the costs of the transition and change their consumption and lifestyle habits. In Germany, for example, a legislative proposal to phase out gas and oil heating in 2023 was met with strong opposition, and a proposal to phase out tax breaks for agricultural diesel sparked protests from farmers across the country in 2024. There were similar protests across Europe: in the Netherlands, where a regulation to reduce nitrogen emissions provoked strong opposition in 2019, and in Czechia, where farmers protested high energy prices, the EU Green Deal and cheap imports from Ukraine in 2024.

It is still unclear how EU climate policies will be affected by these challenges in the long run. Policy priorities are set by various actors, and the climate issue has become polarised on both ends, also causing vocal protests in favour of climate action. Nonetheless, it is safe to say that climate policies may receive less public support at a time when accelerated emission reductions are needed to prevent the most dramatic consequences of climate change.

Generally, the public acceptability of a policy describes a positive public attitude towards a measure before it is implemented (Schuitema and Bergstad 2018). Research suggests that public acceptability for carbon pricing remains generally low (Klenert et al. 2018) and that taxation is the least favoured measure compared to other climate policies (Drews and van den Bergh 2016; Fairbrother 2022). An important aspect is that the perceived effects of climate policies may be more important than their actual effects, and research has shown that citizens often overestimate their costs and underestimate their benefits (Drews and van den Bergh 2016; Carattini et al. 2018). Whether a policy is perceived as effective and fair is decisive for its acceptability (Maestre-Andrés et al. 2019; Douenne and Fabre 2022). This concerns not only the perceived personal consequences—for example, a particularly low level of acceptability for carbon pricing has been shown among car owners and citizens living in rural areas—but overall social fairness, too. Likewise, in the case of carbon pricing, many studies demonstrate that perceived distributional fairness importantly enhances public acceptability (Dechezleprêtre et al. 2022; Douenne and Fabre 2022; Ewald et al. 2022; Sommer et al. 2022). Furthermore, resistance to climate policies seems to be especially high when individuals feel excluded from decision-making (Carattini et al. 2019). Therefore, public participation has been identified as an important factor in increasing the acceptability of climate action.

As climate change policies become more controversial and the public debate on climate change becomes more polarised, policymakers need to pay more attention to designing policies that are acceptable to the public. Research points to two important ways to achieve more acceptable policies: balancing distributional effects, ensuring fair policy outcomes and involving stakeholders in the decision-making process.

9.3.2 Compensating for the Distributional Impacts

Overall, the low-carbon transition is expected to create net employment gains (Eurofound and EEA 2023), to have, if at all, modest effects on GDP (European Parliamentary Research Service 2022), and to create many co-benefits of a healthier environment. However, there may be regional mismatches between labour supply and demand; some skills may become more relevant than others, and GDP composition may change considerably, affecting some socio-economic groups more than others. Many studies have shown that climate policies without mechanisms for social compensation can have regressive effects, meaning that lower-income groups are affected disproportionately (Fragkos et al. 2021). Compensating for the distributional effects of climate policy has become a recent policy focus in Europe, with many policymakers emphasising the importance of a "just transition". Concerns over the socio-economic effects of climate policies are growing because fairness has been identified as a precondition for more comprehensive and sustainable climate action. Thus, a growing body of literature looks at approaches to environmental, climate and energy justice (e.g., Mohai et al. 2009; Jenkins 2018; Sovacool and Dworkin 2014).

The inequalities of climate policies can be worsened in times of energy crisis where the most vulnerable households are also those most dependant on fossil energy. The surge in energy prices following the recovery in energy demand after the coronavirus pandemic and the war in Ukraine has worsened an already difficult situation in terms of energy poverty for many EU citizens (European Commission 2023c). Meanwhile, income inequality, measured as the disproportionate allocation of income among groups, is influenced by a multitude of factors, such as changes in the labour market, globalisation and trade, wealth distribution and redistributive policies (Fragkos et al. 2021). Income inequality is most commonly measured with the Gini coefficient, indicating the extent to which income distribution deviates from a perfectly equal distribution. A Gini value of 0 implies that income is distributed equally, whereas higher values indicate an increasingly unequal distribution. According to Eurostat (2023), in 2022 the EU's Gini coefficient was 29.6 with the highest income disparities in Bulgaria (38.4), Lithuania (36.2) and Latvia (34.3) and the most even distribution in Slovakia, Slovenia, Czechia and Belgium, where the Gini coefficient was less than 25.0. Fischer and Filauro (2021) analyse the inequality between all EU citizens across individual Member States and find that "inequality among EU citizens is significantly lower than among US citizens but slightly higher than in countries with established welfare models such as Australia and Japan". One important aspect of the analysis is that while EU market incomes are distributed highly unequally, showing a Gini coefficient of around 54% in 2019, the Gini coefficient drops significantly to 35% in the same year when looking at the distribution of EU disposable income. This demonstrates the redistributive effect of taxes and social transfers in broad terms. When it comes to climate policies, without redistributive mechanisms, such policies may risk increasing inequality because poorer households spend a larger share of their income on energy-related expenses (Labandeira 2022) and because jobs in energy-intensive industries will decline, affecting particularly lower-income segments.

Closely related is the concern that levels of energy poverty will increase due to climate policies. According to the European Commission (2023c), “energy poverty occurs when a household must reduce its energy consumption to a degree that negatively impacts the inhabitants’ health and wellbeing”. It is caused by a combination of factors, including a high proportion of household expenditure spent on energy, low income, and low energy performance of buildings and appliances. The percentage of Europeans who were unable to keep their homes adequately warm was 9.3% in 2022 (European Commission 2023c). Furthermore, almost 7% of EU citizens had payment arrears on their utility bills, and nearly 15% lived in housing with leak, damp, or rot in 2020. Particularly, high levels of energy poverty have been measured in eastern and southern Europe, with Bulgaria and Greece being the most affected.

Whereas the EU has rather reinforced its climate policy as a reaction to the energy crisis, critics fear that ambitious climate policies may overburden low-income households and Member States at times of economic pressure. Indeed, climate policies need to be assessed not only by considering their environmental but also social outcomes. So far, research has largely focused on the distributional and, to a lesser extent, employment effects of carbon pricing. Other policies and other dimensions, such as age, gender, health and ethnicity, have received less attention. Most studies find that carbon pricing, including emissions trading systems and carbon taxes, has regressive effects if revenues are not redistributed (Gancheva et al. 2023). Other studies highlight that people living in rural areas with poor public transport connections are especially affected by higher energy prices (Eurofound and EEA 2021). Overall, the distributional effects vary from policy measure to policy measure. A study commissioned by the European Parliament summarises that taxes on electricity and heating tend to be regressive, while subsidies, feed-in-tariffs and standards disproportionately benefit high-income households, which have the capital to invest in and make use of low-carbon technologies (Gancheva et al. 2023). Public investment programmes, on the other hand, seem to reduce inequality and poverty by increasing the accessibility and affordability of energy and transport services (Zachmann et al. 2018). The implementation of EU climate policies will likely also trigger a restructuring towards a high-skill and capital-intensive economy (Fragkos et al. 2021), significantly affecting jobs in carbon-intensive industry sectors, for example, in the coal, chemicals, pulp, paper, and plastics industries.

However, the picture changes drastically when revenue spending is considered. The redistribution of revenues via lump-sum transfers or support schemes mostly benefits lower-income households and changes distributional effects from regressive to progressive (Borghesi and Ferrari 2023). Furthermore, a more comprehensive look at structural causes for economic disparities is needed. Preexisting levels of inequality and poverty are better addressed by accompanying labour market and fiscal policies, for instance, via education and health spending, tax reforms and social transfers. Finally, most of the analyses of the distributional effects of climate policies do not yet consider the costs of inaction. The economic costs of a climate crisis are estimated to greatly outweigh the costs required to mitigate emissions in line with the 2 °C target of the Paris Climate Agreement (Kotz et al. 2024). Climate change itself is a driver of social inequality (Albu and Albu 2020), bearing great risks for the economy, public health, and national safety. Lower-income households and low-skilled workers have a lower ability to adapt to economic changes and are more vulnerable to climate disasters, including increasingly frequent temperature extremes, floods, storms, and health pandemics. The cost of inaction thus needs to be considered when estimating the cost of climate policies for society.

9.3.3 Strengthening Energy and Climate Policymaking

Despite significant progress in promoting renewable energy and energy efficiency, past climate policies in Europe have faced several challenges and shortcomings, hindering the achievement of carbon neutrality by 2050. A critical gap in climate policies has been the inadequate integration of scientific evidence and projections into policy development and implementation. Many policies may not have been sufficiently grounded in the latest scientific understanding of climate change, its impacts and solutions to tackle it in an effective, efficient and acceptable way. Although not considered so far as a critical issue, this gap has led to possible mismatches between policy objectives and the necessary measures to achieve them, resulting in suboptimal outcomes and missed opportunities for effective climate action. This becomes more critical as policies for net zero shall combine stringency with effectiveness, efficiency, and acceptability. To do so, it may have to rethink how policies are shaped and grounded in science and participation.

Furthermore, the EU climate policy landscape has been characterised by insufficient cohesion and alignment that can hamper collective action and undermine the efforts against climate change. Harmonising policies and enhancing European governance and policymaking is crucial for achieving meaningful progress towards carbon neutrality (ESABCC 2024).

In addition, traditional climate policies in Europe have been overly focused on short-term objectives, prioritising immediate economic or political considerations over long-term sustainability goals (OECD 2023). This approach does not address the structural changes and transformative measures needed for a successful transition to a low-carbon economy.

Addressing these shortcomings is essential for accelerating progress towards carbon neutrality and achieving Europe's climate objectives. This calls for a series of considerations, in particular as technical efforts will have to be accompanied by a new policymaking approach, better taking into account society, science and crisis management.

Future climate policies must prioritise science-based decision-making, enhance coherence and coordination among policies pursuing sometimes diverging objectives, and adopt long-term perspectives that align with the urgency of the climate crisis. By adopting a more holistic and forward-thinking approach, Europe can overcome these challenges and lead the way towards a sustainable and resilient future.

Drawing from these conclusions, the European Climate Law (Regulation (EU) 2021/1119), which sets net-zero emissions by 2050 and the target of 55% greenhouse gas emissions reduction by 2030, acknowledges this need. One of its motives highlights that "scientific expertise and the best available, up-to-date evidence, together with information on climate change that is both factual and transparent, are imperative and need to underpin the Union's climate action and efforts to reach climate neutrality by 2050".

Furthermore, reaching carbon neutrality implies embarking all users, beneficiaries, consumers and regulated entities on a collective journey. While this may have been overseen until recently, it has now become an integral part of the policymaking process. The effect of ambitious climate policies is perceived as much more impactful towards households (although there may not always be such a direct impact). By engaging directly with citizens and stakeholders in the formal processes of assessing, designing, and implementing policies, useful insights can emerge, and inclusiveness

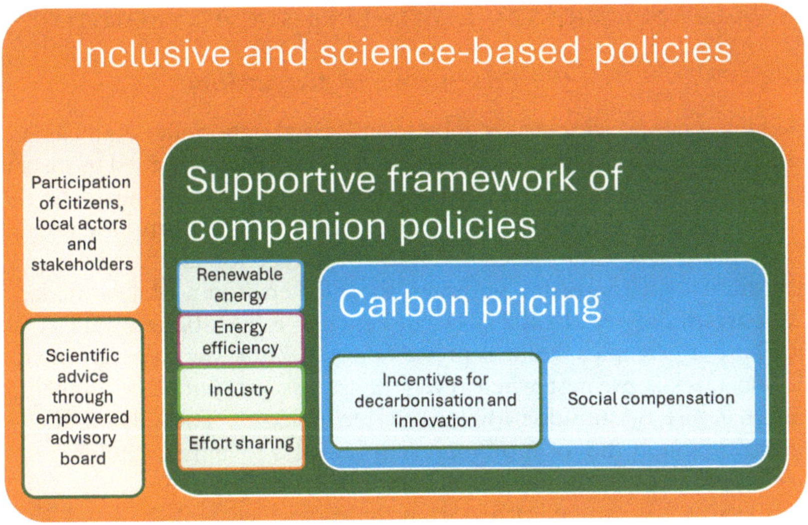

Fig. 9.5 The policymaking environment enabling the acceptability of ambitious climate policies

can be key in crafting perceptions. Besides, EU policies themselves should rely more on democratic or participative initiatives on the ground.

As illustrated in Fig. 9.5, the carbon price is at the core of climate policies and can play two roles: it incentivises economic actors to reduce emissions and, at the same time, allows for compensation for its adverse effects, including distributional and competitiveness impacts, when revenues are redirected through this channel. This already provides enabling conditions for its acceptability. Furthermore, carbon price is accompanied by a set of supportive policies that enable decarbonisation while keeping direct carbon prices at acceptable levels. However, since the interactions of such policies do not always provide for positive synergies, the governance and institutional level should facilitate the scientific and citizen contributions to the design and assessment of policies.

9.4 Solutions to Enable Domestic Acceptability

9.4.1 Perceptions and Acceptability

Designing fair policies is of economic and moral importance and will also lead to more acceptable policies. Broad public support is needed to sustain the long-term climate efforts to prevent and, regrettably, adapt to the drastic effects of climate change. Carbon pricing instruments have proven to be more acceptable when revenues were recycled and used for pre-determined environmental purposes, so-called environmental earmarking (Maestre-Andrés et al. 2021; Dechezleprêtre et al. 2022; Ewald et al. 2022). For example, Dechezleprêtre et al. (2022) show that support for carbon taxes is greatest when revenues are used to fund environmental infrastructure or subsidise low-carbon technologies. They also find that redistribution in the form of lump-sum transfers to all households is one of the least popular options for the use of revenues.

A lesson that can be learned from the experience with the EU ETS is the merit of experimentation and gradual implementation. The EU ETS has evolved over four trading periods, the first one being a trial phase to allow market participants to adapt to the system and allow regulators to observe the functioning of the market and draw lessons for the second trading period.[4] Even though the delivery fell short of the environmental ambitions set, the testing phase allowed stakeholders to gain experience and build trust in the system. This increased the acceptability of subsequent reforms (Carattini et al. 2018).

Unsurprisingly, the availability of information and transparency are important preconditions for public acceptance and support of climate measures. It is, therefore, crucial that the benefits of climate policies are better communicated. Environmental and financial gains need to be made visible, and the use of revenues should be more transparent, either by introducing the earmarking of revenues or by updating the reporting rules on national revenue spending. Research shows that it can be fundamental to present emission reductions not only as a goal per se but to emphasise the co-benefits of climate policies (Baranzini and Carattini 2017), including improved air quality, noise reduction, reduced costs due to renewable

[4] During the initial trial phase of the EU ETS, regulators gained practical experience with the system leading to later reforms of the system. This includes, for example, the later permission of the banking of allowances as well as the introduction of the Market Stability Reserve to reduce price fluctuations.

energies and improved energy efficiency, reduced dependency on fossil fuel imports, more urban green areas, biodiversity, landscape preservation and improved mental and physical health.

Another crucial precondition for policy acceptability is democratic decision-making. Options for local solutions and inclusive decision-making processes should be prioritised where possible. Carbon pricing policies are technology-neutral, allow for low-carbon innovation and incentivise emission reductions where they are least costly. Yet, the transformations that are caused by carbon pricing policies should be accompanied by collective action at the local, regional, national, and international levels.

9.4.2 *Fair and Just Policies Through Redistribution*

There is a growing awareness that climate policies can have significant distributional consequences. Higher energy and fuel prices and a shift in labour markets may present a particular burden for low-income households. However, as mentioned above, carbon pricing policies raise revenues that can be spent for social and climate purposes, thereby turning regressive into progressive effects, provided they are well targeted. In fact, some studies (e.g., Berry 2018) suggest that using only a small share of carbon pricing revenues is sufficient to compensate for the distributional effects on households. According to ICAP (2024), in 2023, the EU ETS generated USD 47,098 billion (about EUR 44,2 billion), and revenues are expected to increase, even if for a limited period of time.

As Borghesi and Ferrari (2023) summarise, "auction proceeds can be used in different ways: (1) funding climate action by investing in renewable energy, low-carbon technologies, adaptation, energy efficiency, forestry, or transport; (2) contributing to the public budget by reducing other taxes, financing other public priorities, or reducing debts; and (3) financial assistance to disadvantaged groups" whereby an inclusion into the general budget would be the optimal solution from an economic point of view. Research has shown that revenue spending on carbon mitigation and support of vulnerable households increase the acceptability of the policy (Maestre-Andrés et al. 2019; Douenne and Fabre 2020; Dechezleprêtre et al. 2022).

The EU's Social Climate Fund (SCF) is a prime example of such a redistributive policy instrument since it will channel part of the revenues from the EU ETS to support vulnerable groups affected by higher energy or transport costs. The fund, which is meant to come into force in 2027, allows for temporary direct income support and for investments in energy efficiency, renovation of buildings, clean heating and cooling, as well as low emission mobility, including public transport. Results from the Life Coase project[5] highlight that some challenges persist in the effective spending of SCF revenues. First, more data and indicators are needed to identify individuals most at risk of being impacted by rising energy and transport costs. While the evidence indicates that, on average, low-income households are disproportionately affected, significant disparities within income groups remain. Factors like rural or urban residence, the energy efficiency of homes, and commuting requirements all influence how households are impacted. Second, governments need to choose wisely how to spend the revenues. Green investments, such as energy-efficient renovations, rural transport initiatives, and electric vehicle adoption, are preferred as these not only reduce long-term costs for households but also contribute to climate targets. Direct income support to households, in contrast, may be useful to grant but not as effective, which is why its use has been limited to 37.5% in the SCF. Generally, carbon pricing raises large amounts of money that, spent wisely, can benefit poor households and accelerate the green transition.

The planned creation of the SCF is a sign that the distributional effects of climate policies are gaining more attention in policy and research. The SCF can be an example for climate policies in general, showcasing the potential of market-based measures but also highlighting the challenges related to the improved targeting of financial assistance.

9.4.3 *Targeting of Financial Assistance During the Energy Crisis*

Of course, EU climate policies are not designed and implemented in a political vacuum, but always compete with other policy priorities. To sustain environmental objectives in difficult economic times and even throughout crises, it is helpful to draw lessons from the emergency measures taken by the EU and its MS during the energy crisis in 2021–2023. In the EU, wholesale gas and electricity prices started rising in 2021 and peaked in 2022, which contributed to high inflation rates and a cost-of-living crisis (OECD 2022). In reaction to the economic consequences of

[5] For further information see LIFE COASE—Collaborative Observatory for ASsessment of the EU ETS—Florence School of Regulation (eui.eu).

the coronavirus pandemic, the EU agreed to a Recovery and Resilience Facility (RRF) for MS economic assistance, whereby 37% had to be used to contribute to the energy transition. In May 2022, the EU adopted the REPowerEU Plan, setting out measures to compensate for the phase-out of Russian fossil fuels, thereby increasing the ambition of several Fit for 55 legislative proposals. Likewise, European countries increased their spending on RES and energy efficiency to reduce dependencies on Russian oil and gas after the Russian invasion of Ukraine. Furthermore, the spike in energy prices led many governments to implement significant compensation measures for businesses and consumers, such as reduced energy taxes, transfers, and credits. According to a Bruegel study, between September 2021 and January 2023, EU governments collectively earmarked EUR 646 billion to shield households and firms from high energy prices (Sgaravatti et al. 2023).

Yet, recent findings show that most of these measures were untargeted, meaning that they benefitted all households or firms rather than targeting the most vulnerable. Only a third of the fiscal measures put in place by European governments (including Norway and the UK) were targeted to benefit vulnerable groups (Sgaravatti et al. 2023). A recent OECD study analysing 41 countries (Hemmerlé et al. 2023) confirms that untargeted measures accounted "for 77% of the estimated total gross fiscal cost of support in 2022–23 as governments responded to the necessity of providing a rapid policy response that protected households' purchasing power and the viability of firms" (p. 15). Policies have thus too often been expensive, have disproportionately benefitted high-income households and in many cases have reduced environmental incentives. However, allocated funding varied largely from country to country as well as the share of the total value of support measures that has been allocated to vulnerable households which ranged from 2% in Germany, 5% in Spain, 11% in Poland, 15% in France and 16% in the Netherlands to 31% in Portugal, 36% in Italy and 41% in Ireland (Hemmerlé et al. 2023).

Among other institutions, the European Central Bank has repeatedly called for emergency measures that are temporary, tailored (not to weaken environmental incentives) and targeted. Some of the positive examples of better-tailored and targeted solutions include the Austrian "Clean heating for all" programme, which offered coverage of the costs for the replacement of fossil fuel with climate-friendly heating systems depending on income level and household size (Bruegel 2023). Similarly, France approved lump-sum energy payments based not only on income but also on household size and age structure and the Italian social bonus considered serious health conditions next to an income level threshold (Hemmerlé et al. 2023). The OECD study highlights that, overall, digitalisation of the public administration and energy systems has allowed for better identification of vulnerable households, the facilitation of payments, and the development of novel indicators to identify context-specific vulnerabilities. Countries should carefully analyse the effects of their support measures and draw lessons from successful examples that better target those in need, reduce overall costs and maintain environmental incentives throughout economic turbulence.

These crisis situations and how European governments responded to them also taught other lessons. As outlined below, they embed some good practices that can be replicated in climate policies, such as scientific advisory boards. Furthermore, they also demonstrated that the EU and its Member States are capable of acting swiftly and collectively to tackle urgent situations much faster than previously imagined. Nonetheless, in many cases the quick reaction has led to costly and untargeted policies, which call for better preparedness going forward. Sadly, the capacity to handle such crises will be crucial in facing future extreme weather events and climate impacts, be it local or on a larger scale.

9.4.4 Policies Building upon Participation and Science

The current policies for the energy transition, including carbon pricing, clearly affect citizens: this impact can be economic but also social, political, cultural, or visual when wind farms impact landscapes. The more ambitious the policies are, the more citizens will be affected. Locally, they can be impacted by new infrastructure deployment, including RES installations such as wind farms. Politically and nationally, they can be impacted by the implementation of new policies or simply consider they are negatively impacted, though this may not be the case.

After the Yellow Vest movement in France, other vocal groups, such as farmers, regularly criticised the alleged negative impact of excessive environmental regulation, with a certain success. Better inclusion of individuals in climate decision-making can improve regulation and prevent opposition to climate action. Public participation has been shown to enhance the quality (Few et al. 2007) and acceptability (Heyen and Wicki 2024) of climate policies. As argued above, awareness and information contributed to the adoption of more environmentally friendly behaviours.

Furthermore, public participation enhances the likelihood of successful policy implementation.

9.4.4.1 Citizen Climate Assemblies

Beyond merely attending meetings or providing opinions, citizens can play an active role in proposing alternative options. Forums allowing stakeholders to exchange information, perceptions, and concerns contribute to engaging all citizens in ambitious policies towards achieving net-zero ambitions by 2050. Policymakers can leverage transparency, equity, and trust to enhance public involvement.

Such examples of public participation nationally, but also locally, are citizen climate assemblies (CCA). According to the Knowledge Network on Climate Assemblies,[6] citizen climate assemblies bring together a diverse group of everyday people selected by democratic lottery to learn, deliberate and make recommendations on aspects of the climate crisis. Let's illustrate this process with an informative example. In France, as a response to the Yellow Vests movement, a representative panel of citizens was appointed by the government in 2019–2020. Around 150 citizens were selected randomly according to criteria of gender, age, education, socio-professional and geographical representativity. It proceeded to a series of hearings to inform its opinion.

Building upon this understanding, they formulated 149 proposals gathered in a report addressed to the government, which was expected to transform their proposals into actual policies. The final report was approved at 95% by the members of the CCA. At the end of the process, although most proposals were taken into consideration, French President Emmanuel Macron retained the option to discard three of their proposals. Out of the 146 proposals, the Government declared in February 2021 that 75 were implemented and 71 were being implemented. Among the proposals that had to pass through a legislative process, the members of the national parliament further amended the initial proposals. At the end of the same month, 96 of the 150 CCA members gave notes of appreciation for the transposition, in general, of their proposals. The average of these scores was 3.3 out of 10 about the transposition process: this low score illustrates the dissatisfaction of the members of the CCA about the way their proposals were followed up by the government.

[6] See https://www.knoca.eu/about-knoca (accessed on 23 April 2024).

A survey run in Germany confirmed that a citizen assembly could increase public support for climate policies (Kuntze and Fesenfeld 2021). However, this positive effect strongly depends on how the citizen assembly is designed and on the degree of public awareness and information about the assembly. The French experience emphasises that the process needs to be anchored in a solid institutional framework clear from the outset. Governments would gain credibility by explaining from the beginning how the proposals emanating from the assembly will be taken into consideration by the policymakers and stick to the declared process. This policy proposal appropriation is crucial and would provide trust among participants and citizens.

Studies such as Galván Labrador (2023) show a remarkable citizen empowerment taking place during the French Citizens' Convention, which nevertheless vanished during the joint elaboration of the law, allowing certain political and economic interests to impose their vision. Although they do not necessarily have a direct impact by truly being citizen-centred policymaking processes, they have at least an indirect impact on policymaking by creating momentum around climate action and supporting the introduction of pre-planned or pre-existing policies (Wells 2021).

9.4.4.2 Local Action and Energy Communities

By actively participating in energy communities, advocating for sustainable policies, and making eco-conscious choices in their daily lives, citizens collectively pressure governments and corporations to prioritise climate action. RES are, in essence, projects that can be decentralised and accessible to citizens individually or collectively since they can be small-scale and installed at different levels of the grid. Locally, from a concrete point of view, RES deployment is hindered by two main obstacles. On the one hand, the capacity and the structure of the current grid are not fit for a vast and fast RES deployment. On the other hand, like any major infrastructure project, RES are often hindered by the local acceptability of projects. This may lead to some backlash if a consultation or involvement of local stakeholders does not accompany this deployment. Meanwhile, the EU internal energy market and open competition in the retail market only in terms of prices did not bring as many benefits to EU consumers as planned.

Since the Clean Energy Package for all Europeans, the EU has put forward new tools to engage consumers with the double objective: make the transition happen locally and allow consumers to reap the benefits of the internal markets directly. Among the main concepts introduced, one can name the framework set up for active consumers, self-consumers, and energy communities. The Repower EU initiative, as the EU energy response to critical energy security concerns raised after the war of aggression of Russia towards Ukraine, has considerably reshuffled the energy policy priorities towards saving energy, producing clean energy and diversifying its energy supplies. More importantly, policymakers and citizens came to realise that domestic green energy was, after all, not cheaper and more reliable than importing fossil fuels. The plan for Europe to decarbonise its energy system relies on the vast deployment of RES onshore and offshore and the deployment of renewables acceleration areas.

CE Delft (2016) highlighted that by mid-century, nearly half of all EU citizens (households and energy communities) could be producing their own electricity and meeting approximately 45% of the EU electricity demand. Acting jointly, consumers can have better leverage to consume their own energy not only by splitting the investment costs but also by sharing their own energy. The concept of energy communities allows consumers and local stakeholders to get together as a legal entity to develop their RES assets that allow them to supply part of their energy needs, renovate their buildings or get more active in electricity markets. Another perk of energy communities is the capacity it has to turn passive consumers into social entrepreneurs or investors taking part in a business that is more driven towards environmental and social concerns rather than financial value while sometimes being able to benefit from actual dividends.

The literature has primarily examined the societal impacts of community renewable energy projects, focusing on areas such as the local economy, energy systems, acceptance of energy transition, and individual energy-related behaviours. Given the significance of this topic, a fast-growing amount of research has been conducted. Current evidence suggests that energy communities have positive impacts on the local economy and job creation, although the nature and magnitude of these impacts vary depending on the specific characteristics of the community. Research findings clearly support the expectation that energy communities enhance local acceptance of RES and garner general support for climate action. Additionally, participation in renewable energy communities projects tends to correlate positively with increased energy-efficient behaviours, enhanced knowledge and skills, and to some extent, greater social trust and capital (Verde et al. 2020).

However, policymakers shall consider barriers hindering citizen action against climate change and acceptance of climate policies. Factors such as time constraints and economic resources limit individuals' acting ability (Steg and Vlek 2009).

9.4.4.3 Science-Informed Policies

While European policies often rely on extensive open consultations of experts, industry players and NGOs, these may not be sufficient to develop credible and impacting policies. Policymakers should further ensure the proposed policies are anchored in scientific evidence. The impact assessments and modelling exercises upon which the European Commission's proposals are based would gain at expanding the scope of scientific disciplines that can inform decision-making. So far, climate policies have been mostly reviewed from legal and economic perspectives, but the challenges ahead call for their analysis from different disciplines simultaneously.

9.4.4.3.1 Focus on Enlightenment 2.0

Polarisation, complexity and uncertainty make policymaking very delicate. As the Commission's in-house scientific service, the Joint Research Centre (JRC) provides independent scientific advice, evidence-based policy support, and technical expertise to inform EU policymaking across a wide range of areas, including climate change, energy, environment, health, and digital transformation. According to the JRC, a better understanding of and explanation of the drivers that influence policy decisions and political decision-making will help to optimise the way that evidence is used in policymaking.

To do so, the JRC deployed "Enlightenment 2.0", a multi-annual research programme to provide the interdisciplinary scientific underpinning to optimise this evolution of the political decision-making process. Understanding what is behind this research programme can help understand how science can improve climate policymaking.

Enlightenment 2.0 represents a vision to harness the power of science, technology, and innovation to address the complex challenges facing society in the twenty-first century. It builds upon the principles of the Enlightenment period, which relied on reason, science, and progress to drive social and intellectual advancement. Enlightenment 2.0 invites to apply these principles to tackle contemporary issues, such as climate change.

At the core of Enlightenment 2.0 is a commitment to evidence-based decision-making. In other words, rigorous scientific research, data analysis, and empirical evidence are put at the core of the mission to inform both policy development and implementation. By grounding decisions in what are considered "objective" facts and analysis and by fostering dialogue, policymakers can make more informed decisions that are likely to yield positive outcomes for society. Collaboration with citizens, civil society, and other stakeholders can help build trust, legitimacy, and accountability in decision-making processes.

In addition, Enlightenment 2.0 emphasises the importance of interdisciplinary collaboration, bringing together experts from diverse fields to develop comprehensive and effective solutions to multifaceted problems. Moreover, innovation and technological advancement are seen as central: societies can unlock new opportunities for economic growth, social progress, and environmental sustainability through research, development and innovation. The JRC research programme also promotes openness, transparency, and public engagement as essential components of democratic governance (see above).

Through its activities associated with the development and implementation of evidence-based policies, the JRC puts at its core the values of Enlightenment 2.0. This can bridge the gap between science and policy, driving progress towards a more sustainable, inclusive, and resilient future for Europe and beyond. In the specific context of EU climate policies, more systematic and context-specific impact assessments and ex-post evaluations would help reinforce synergies between EU social and climate policies and improve climate policy narratives (ESABCC 2024).

Environmental regulation is about changing behaviours or practices, with the goal of encouraging or discouraging people or legal entities from doing an action. Viewing environmental problems from a behavioural perspective can help policymakers to make effective regulations. A comprehensive grasp of behaviour dynamics is imperative in the pursuit of environmental objectives since it enables policymakers to tailor policy interventions addressing complex environmental challenges (OECD 2023). This consideration applies to the targeted beneficiaries of policies, but not only. For instance, the way policymakers perceive climate science, uncertainty or the public opinion of such policies can influence how policies are shaped.

9.4.4.3.2 The Role of Scientific Advisory Boards

More than any other recent event in the twenty-first century, COVID-19 highlighted the need for policies to be grounded on scientific evidence. All over the world, it profoundly challenged the resilience of public health systems and governance structures, demanding rapid and evidence-informed responses from policymakers. Scientific advisory boards (SAB) re-emerged as pivotal spaces in this context, providing technical and scientific guidance to inform policies. Drawing from the experiences of these SABs, several salient insights emerged from COVID19 that hold relevance for the development and execution of climate policies.

Scientific advisory boards played a fundamental role in synthesising evidence and modelling projections to provide recommendations and inform policy deliberations. Similarly, in the domain of climate policy, leveraging the insights of climate scientists and researchers is imperative for crafting robust, evidence-informed strategies to reduce greenhouse gas emissions, adapt to climate change, and foster resilience. In fact, already before COVID19, several MS set up climate advisory bodies to provide expert scientific advice on climate policy to the national authorities.

The urgency of addressing a pandemic implies swift and proactive measures motivated by the need of timely action to respond to emergent threats. Similarly, the urgency of addressing climate change requires prompt action to anticipate, avert or limit the impacts of climate disasters. These policy decisions are to be grounded on solid scientific evidence rather than political concerns to ensure the problems are addressed at their roots.

These boards play a pivotal role in identifying the best policies and technologies for decarbonisation, ensuring that those are effective and efficient and prevent any lock-in effects. The allocation efficiency of EU funds, including the RRF, across and within countries remains an open question. SABs can support this endeavour by providing inputs for an efficient allocation of green investments. This is critical to making climate change policies not only effective but also widely supported and sustainable in the long term.

Furthermore, the health crisis underscored the importance of interdisciplinary collaboration and knowledge integration in addressing multifaceted challenges. SABs that convened experts from different disciplines, including epidemiology, virology, public health, economics, and social sciences, provided holistic insights into the pandemic's dynamics and societal ramifications. Analogously, climate policy formulation would much benefit from interdisciplinary collaboration, drawing upon insights from climate scientists, economists, psychologists, political scientists and sociologists, among others, to develop comprehensive strategies that account for the complexity of climate change challenges and societal responses. Savin et al. (2023) invite us to consider the exploitation of agent-based models by policymakers as those allow to integrate methods, dynamics and effects from different disciplines in one comprehensive model.

In addition, as highlighted above in the chapter and during the COVID-19 crisis, transparent communication and meaningful public engagement are fundamental to converting policies into behavioural changes, fostering trust, comprehension, and adherence to public directives. To be more impactful, the SABs should also rely on transparent, clear, and qualitative communication. This also contributes to combating fake news. Similarly to the COVID-19 situation, in the context of climate policy, communication and public engagement are indispensable.

The COVID-19 SAB experience provides invaluable insights for informing the formulation and execution of climate policies. Building upon scientific expertise, timely action, interdisciplinary recommendations and transparent communication, policymakers can develop and implement evidence-based and effective climate policies.

This is why the European Climate Law establishes the ESABCC as a point of reference for scientific knowledge relating to climate change by virtue of its independence and scientific and technical expertise. The way the ESABCC will be integrated into the policymaking process—how binding and impactful will be their recommendations—will determine its success. The design of selection processes and governance structures for SABs is critical. To a certain extent, if the ESABCC become influential, politicians may seek to influence its selection, work or recommendations. Additionally, since the climate measures required to meet the ambition become costly for citizens and businesses, those negatively affected, including those owning stranded assets, will likely lobby "harder" policymakers and scientific advisers. Therefore, the selection process based on scientific excellence should also avoid any possible risk of conflicts of interest with the policy world or civil society. Also, randomness, rotating responsibility of subject files, non-renewables mandates, and a peer-reviewing process are all possible solutions to limit the risk of SABs being affected negatively by lobbying.

9.5 Conclusion

If the EU is committed to being the first carbon neutral continent by 2050, it should design policies combining effectiveness and efficiency to reduce emissions, decarbonise its economy while ensuring acceptance. The latter aspect has been overlooked until recently, but science has much to say.

Carbon pricing is expected to remain the flagship of European climate policies, but the narrative around it should build on its capacity to change behaviours positively while inherently providing the means to compensate its distributional impacts thanks to the auctioning of its revenues. This, together with communication, will be fundamental to provide acceptability. To illustrate that, it is worth noting that several US States are now implementing emission trading systems labelling them "cap-and-invest" rather than "cap-and-trade".

To optimise its price, a supportive policy environment should be developed together with carbon price. Other decarbonisation policies, including for effort sharing, renewables, energy efficiency and industrial policies, are part of this enabling framework for decarbonisation. Those should be properly calibrated to ensure positive synergies and avoid counterproductive impacts on incentives to decarbonise. Ex-post studies and ex-ante studies can be informative on how different policies can affect the desired outcomes (Ekins et al. 2024).

Two grave crises shook up the world since 2020, the COVID-19 pandemic and the Russian invasion of Ukraine. The traumatic experiences also provided good and bad practices around how to handle crises, identify impactful measures inspired by scientific recommendations and react swiftly to a given situation. New policies fostering acceptability should strike a clear balance between effectiveness, efficiency, and speed of decision-taking.

Moreover, independent and multidisciplinary policy assessment directly feeding into a clear policy process would ensure a diligent monitoring of the various impacts of climate policy. Furthermore, economic regulation should pay closer attention to science and citizen participation in the policymaking, institutionalising participative fora such as scientific advisory boards and citizen assemblies, and in the policy solutions that build upon local innovations to address climate challenges.

Acknowledgements S.B. and A.F. acknowledge funding from the European Union's Horizon Europe research and innovation programme for the project CAPABLE—ClimAte Policy AcceptaBiLity Economic framework—under grant agreement number 101056891. Views and opinions expressed are however those of the authors only.

References

Albu, A., Albu, L. (2020). The Impact of Climate Change on Income Inequality. Evidence from European Union Countries. Studies in Business and Economics 15(3):223–235. https://doi.org/10.2478/sbe-2020-0055

Baranzini, A., & Carattini, S. (2017). Effectiveness, earmarking and labeling: Testing the acceptability of carbon taxes with survey data. Environmental Economics and Policy Studies, 19(1), 197–227. https://doi.org/10.1007/s10018-016-0144-7

Berry, A. (2018), "Compensating Households from Carbon Tax Regressivity and Fuel Poverty: A Microsimulation Study", FAERE Policy Paper 2017–08.

Borghesi, S., & Ferrari, A. (2023). Can the EU ETS and its revenues tackle the impact of high carbon prices? Cadmus EUI. https://cadmus.eui.eu/handle/1814/76127

Carattini, S., Kallbekken, S., & Orlov, A. (2019). How to win public support for a global carbon tax. Nature, 565(7739), 289–291. https://doi.org/10.1038/d41586-019-00124-x

Carattini, S., Carvalho, M., & Fankhauser, S. (2018). Overcoming public resistance to carbon taxes. WIREs Climate Change, 9(5), e531. https://doi.org/10.1002/wcc.531

Carbon Market Watch. (2022). EU ETS 101- A beginner's guide to the EU's Emissions Trading System. https://carbonmarketwatch.org/publications/eu-ets-101-a-beginners-guide-to-the-eus-emissions-trading-system/

CE Delft (2016). The potential of energy citizens in the European Union. CE Delft, Publication 16.3J00.75, Delft.

Dechezleprêtre, A., Fabre, A., Kruse, T., Planterose, B., Sanchez Chico, A., & Stantcheva, S. (2022). Fighting climate change: International attitudes toward climate policies. Working Paper No. 30265, National Bureau of Economic Research. https://doi.org/10.3386/w30265

Douenne, T., & Fabre, A. (2022). Yellow Vests, Pessimistic Beliefs, and Carbon Tax Aversion. American Economic Journal: Economic Policy, 14(1), 81–110. https://doi.org/10.1257/pol.20200092

Douenne, T., & Fabre, A. (2020). French attitudes on climate change, carbon taxation and other climate policies. Ecological Economics, 169, 106496. https://doi.org/10.1016/j.ecolecon.2019.106496

Drews, S., & van den Bergh, J. C. J. M. (2016). What explains public support for climate policies? A review of empirical and experimental studies. Climate Policy, 16(7), 855–876. https://doi.org/10.1080/14693062.2015.1058240

Ekins, P., Osorio, S., Doda, B., Wildgrube, T., Raude, M., Ferrari, A., Heinrich, L., & Borghesi, S. (2024). Impacts and evolution of emissions trading systems: Insights from research and regulation. Research Project Report No. 2024/01, Florence School of Regulation, European University Institute, LIFE COASE. https://hdl.handle.net/1814/76438

ESABCC (2024). Towards EU climate neutrality: Progress, policy gaps and opportunities. European Scientific Advisory Board on Climate Change, Report, Copenhagen.

European Commission (2024a). Record reduction of 2023 ETS emissions due largely to boost in renewable energy. Retrieved from: https://climate.ec.europa.eu/news-your-voice/news/record-reduction-2023-ets-emissions-due-largely-boost-renewable-energy-2024-04-03_en, last accessed on 24.04.2024.

European Commission (2024b). Impact Assessment Report accompanying the Communication "Securing our future: Europe's 2040 climate target and path to climate neutrality by 2050 building a sustainable, just and properous society", Staff Working document. European Commission, Brussels.

European Commission (2023a). REPORT FROM THE COMMISSION TO THE EUROPEAN PARLIAMENT AND THE COUNCIL on the functioning of the European carbon market in 2022 pursuant to Articles 10(5) and 21(2) of Directive 2003/87/EC, COM/2023/654 final. https://op.europa.eu/en/publication-detail/-/publication/f6ffaa05-77cf-11ee-99ba-01aa75ed71a1/language-en

European Commission (2023b). Citizen support for climate action. Retrieved from: https://climate.ec.europa.eu/citizens/citizen-support-climate-action_en, last accessed 24.04.2024.

European Commission (2023c). Energy poverty. Retrieved from https://energy.ec.europa.eu/topics/markets-and-consumers/energy-consumer-rights/energy-poverty_en, last accessed on 24.04.2024.

European Commission (2023d). Report on the State of the Energy Union, Staff Working document. October 2023, European Commission, Brussels.

Eurofound and EEA (2023). The transition to a climate-neutral economy: Exploring the socioeconomic impacts. Publications Office of the European Union, Luxembourg.

Eurofound and EEA (2021). Exploring the social challenges of low-carbon energy policies in Europe. Retrieved from https://www.eea.europa.eu/publications/exploring-the-social-challenges-of, last accessed on 24.04.2024.

European Parliamentary Research Service (2022). Briefing: Economic impacts of the green transition. Retrieved from: https://www.europarl.europa.eu/thinktank/en/document/EPRS_BRI(2022)733623, last accessed on 24.04.2024.

Eurostat (2023). Living conditions in Europe – income distribution and income inequality. Retrieved from https://ec.europa.eu/eurostat/statistics-explained/index.php?oldid=481137#Income_inequality, last accessed 24.04.2024.

Ewald, J., Sterner, T., & Sterner, E. (2022). Understanding the resistance to carbon taxes: Drivers and barriers among the general public and fuel-tax protesters. Resource and Energy Economics, 70, 101331. https://doi.org/10.1016/j.reseneeco.2022.101331

Fairbrother, M. (2022). Public opinion about climate policies: A review and call for more studies of what people want. PLOS Climate, 1(5), e0000030. https://doi.org/10.1371/journal.pclm.0000030

Fragkos, P., Fragkiadakis, K., Sovacool, B. K., Paroussos, L., Vrontisi, Z., & Charalampidis, I. (2021). Equity implications of climate policy: Assessing the social and distributional impacts of emission reduction targets in the European Union. Energy, 237, 121591. https://doi.org/10.1016/j.energy.2021.121591

Few, R., Brown, K., & Tompkins, E. L. (2007). Public participation and climate change adaptation: avoiding the illusion of inclusion. Climate Policy, 7(1), 46–59. https://doi.org/10.1080/14693062.2007.9685637

Fischer, G., Filauro, S. (2021). Income inequality in the EU: General trends and policy implications. Retrieved from https://cepr.org/voxeu/columns/income-inequality-eu-general-trends-and-policy-implications, last accessed 24.04.2024.

Galván Labrador, A., & Zografos, C. (2023). Empowerment and disempowerment in climate assemblies: The French citizens' convention on climate. Environmental Policy and Governance, 1–13. https://doi.org/10.1002/eet.2093

Gancheva, M., Akbaba, M., Geraci, M., Ludden, V., Donkova, R., Beghelli, S., Neumann, T., Finello, F., Laine, A. (2023). Policy instruments to tackle social inequalities related to climate change. Retrieved from https://www.europarl.europa.eu/thinktank/en/document/IPOL_STU(2023)740081, last accessed 24.04.2024.

Hemmerlé, Y., et al. (2023), "Aiming better: Government support for households and firms during the energy crisis", OECD Economic Policy Papers, No. 32, OECD Publishing, Paris, https://doi.org/10.1787/839e3ae1-en.

Heyen, D. A., & Wicki, M. (2024). Increasing public support for climate policy proposals: a research agenda on governable acceptability factors. Climate Policy, 1–10. https://doi.org/10.1080/14693062.2024.2330390

Kuntze, L. & Fesenfeld, L. P. (2021. Citizen assemblies can enhance political feasibility of ambitious climate policies. Working Paper, https://doi.org/10.2139/ssrn.3918532

ICAP (2024). Emissions Trading Worldwide: Status Report 2024. Berlin: International Carbon Action Partnership.

Jenkins, K. (2018). Setting energy justice apart from the crowd: Lessons from environmental and climate justice. Energy Research & Social Science, 39, 117–121. https://doi.org/10.1016/j.erss.2017.11.015

Klenert, D., Mattauch, L., Combet, E., Edenhofer, O., Hepburn, C., Rafaty, R., & Stern, N. (2018). Making carbon pricing work for citizens. Nature Climate Change, 8(8), 669–677. https://doi.org/10.1038/s41558-018-0201-2

Kotz, M., Levermann, A., & Wenz, L. (2024). The economic commitment of climate change. Nature, 628(8008), 551–557. https://doi.org/10.1038/s41586-024-07219-0

Labandeira, Xavier (2022). *Taxation and ecological transition during climate and energy crises: the main conclusions of the 2022 Spanish White Book on tax reform.* WP 09-2022, Real Instituto Elcano. https://www.realinstitutoelcano.org/en/work-document/taxation-and-ecological-transition-during-climate-and-energy-crises/

Maestre-Andrés, S., Drews, S., Savin, I., & van den Bergh, J. (2021). Carbon tax acceptability with information provision and mixed revenue uses. Nature Communications, 12(1), Article 1. https://doi.org/10.1038/s41467-021-27380-8

Maestre-Andrés, S., Drews, S., & van den Bergh, J. (2019). Perceived fairness and public acceptability of carbon pricing: A review of the literature. Climate Policy, 19(9), 1186–1204. https://doi.org/10.1080/14693062.2019.1639490

Marcu, A., López Hernández, J. F., Romeo, G., Alberola, E., Faure, A., Obienu, C., Qin, B., O'Neill, M., Caneill, J., Schleicher, S. (2023). 2023 State of the EU ETS Report – ERCST. https://ercst.org/2023-state-of-the-eu-ets-report/

Mazzarano, M., & Borghesi, S. (2024). Searching for a Carbon Laffer Curve: Estimates from the European Union Emissions Trading System. Metroeconomica. https://doi.org/10.1111/meca.12458

Mohai, P., Pellow, D. N., & Roberts, J. T. (2009). Environmental justice. Annual Review of Environment and Resources, 34(1), 405–430. https://doi.org/10.1146/annurev-environ-082508-094348

OECD (2023). Better Regulation for the Green Transition. OECD Public Governance Policy Papers, number 40 https://doi.org/10.1787/c91a04bc-en.

OECD (2022). Income support for working-age individuals and their families. Retrieved from https://www.oecd.org/social/Income-support-for-working-age-individuals-and-their-families.pdf , last accessed on 24.04.2024.

Pahle, M., Günther, C., Osorio, S., & Quemin, S. (2023). The emerging end-game: the EU ETS on the road towards climate neutrality. Social Science Research Network. https://doi.org/10.2139/ssrn.4373443

Pisani-Ferry, J., Tagliapietra, S., & Zachmann, G. (2023). A new governance framework to safeguard the European Green Deal. Policy brief, Bruegel, https://www.bruegel.org/policy-brief/new-governance-framework-safeguard-european-green-deal

Savin, I., Creutzig, F., Filatova, T., Foramitti, J., Konc, T., Niamir, L., Safarzynska, K., & van den Bergh, J. (2023). Agent-based modeling to integrate elements from different disciplines for ambitious climate policy. WIREs Climate Change, 14(2), e811. https://doi.org/10.1002/wcc.811

Schuitema, G., & Bergstad, C. J. (2018). Acceptability of Environmental Policies. Environmental Psychology: An Introduction, 295–306. https://doi.org/10.1002/9781119241072.ch29

Sgaravatti, G., S. Tagliapietra, C. Trasi and G. Zachmann (2023). National policies to shield consumers from rising energy prices. Bruegel Datasets. https://www.bruegel.org/dataset/national-policies-shield-consumers-rising-energy-prices

Sommer, S., Mattauch, L., & Pahle, M. (2022). Supporting carbon taxes: The role of fairness. Ecological Economics, 195, 107359. https://doi.org/10.1016/j.ecolecon.2022.107359

Sovacool, B. K., & Dworkin, M. H. (2014). Global Energy Justice. https://doi.org/10.1017/cbo9781107323605

Steg, L., & Vlek, C. (2009). Encouraging pro-environmental behaviour: An integrative review and research agenda. Journal of Environmental Psychology, 29(3), 309–317. https://doi.org/10.1016/j.jenvp.2008.10.004

Stern, N. (2007). The Economics of Climate Change. https://doi.org/10.1017/cbo9780511817434

van den Bergh, J., Castro, J., Drews, S., Exadaktylos, F., Foramitti, J., Klein, F., Konk, T. & Savin, I. (2021). Designing an effective climate-policy mix: accounting for instrument synergy. Climate Policy, 21(6), pp. 745–764. https://doi.org/10.1080/14693062.2021.1907276

Verde, S. F., Rosetto, N., Ferrari A. & Fonteneau T. (2020). The future of renewable energy communities in the EU: an investigation at the time of the Clean Energy Package, Technical Report, Florence School of Regulation, Florence. https://hdl.handle.net/1814/68383

Verde S., Galdi G., Alloisio I., Borghesi S. (2021). The EU ETS and its companion policies: any insight for China's ETS?. Environment and Development Economics, 26, 302–320

Wells, R. H.-C. (2021). Are citizen juries and assemblies on climate change driving democratic climate policy-making? An exploration of two case studies in the UK. Climatic Change 168, 5.

Zachmann, G., Claeys, G., Fredriksson, G. (2018). The distributional effects of climate policies. Retrieved from https://www.bruegel.org/book/distributional-effects-climate-policies, last accessed on 24.04.2024.

CHAPTER 10

EU Industrial Policy in the Evolving Geopolitical and Geo-economic Environment

Michael A. Landesmann

10.1 Introduction: Aims and Conduct of Industrial Policy

A chapter on industrial policy (IP) should start with a definition of what exactly is meant by it. We suggest the following: Industrial policy covers policy instruments that are geared towards influencing the 'structural' composition of an economy, whereby 'composition' can refer to technologies, sectors, the compositions of firms and labour forces working in these sectors, and patterns of economic activity across geographic space. Since this naturally covers a very wide range of structural features of economies, we should narrow down the scope of IP by saying that these instruments also need to aim to achieve the goals of IP.

10.1.1 What Are the Aims of Industrial Policy?

Traditionally, IP has been used—through its 'structural' impact—to improve the growth performance of an economy and, in an open economy

M. A. Landesmann (✉)
Vienna Institute for International Economic Studies (wiiw), Vienna, Austria
e-mail: landesmann@wiiw.ac.at

I. P. Székely, P. Halmai (eds.), *The Future of European Integration*, Studies in Economic Transition,
https://doi.org/10.1007/978-3-032-20186-7_10

context, the 'competitiveness' of an economy. From this, it is clear that an IP pursuing such aims will be dependent on the developmental state of an economy. We can distinguish here between three situations: First, there is the use of IP in economies that are far behind when it comes to employing state-of-the-art technologies. Such economies will direct IPs towards developing institutions and using policy instruments that allow technologies and business practices to be efficiently and effectively transferred from other economies that are already more advanced than themselves. Second, on the other side of the spectrum, there are economies that are already close to the global technology frontier. These will have to direct policies (and design institutions) that are themselves contributing to the advancement of that frontier, thereby reaping the benefits of being a leader in technological development. Then there is a third situation—and one which has become particularly important in the present geo-economic context: when advanced economies are challenged in their technological leadership positions by fast-moving catching-up economies, with China being the most prominent among the latter in today's global economy. It is this third situation that has given particular impetus to the revival of IP in advanced economies and prompted strategic behaviour that is no longer simply guided by the traditional analytical concepts of IP aimed at correcting market failures. Such strategic behaviour increasingly also includes geopolitical considerations that go beyond purely economic considerations and that also factor in political/international relations.

The use (and the potential for the effective use) of IP instruments will therefore depend on the international context in which an economy finds itself. This is particularly relevant in the context of the European Union (EU), where an economy that is an EU member state can make use of the coordination possibilities that the bloc's deeply integrated market and institutional policy-making framework provides. This allows it to participate in the setting of common goals, to orientate policies towards providing 'public goods' at the cross-national level, and to reap the benefits of economies of scale and scope in the context of a policy space that is wider than would be possible for a country operating on its own. On the other extreme, there are economies that are isolated in an international context or find themselves in a conflict situation between major economies (e.g. the current US-China relationship) in which IPs can only be coordinated to a very limited extent, if at all. In this case, IP would be seen as operating mostly in a 'win-lose' context.

10.1.2 What About Aims Other Than 'Growth' and 'Competitiveness'?

'*Growth*' itself can include narrower or wider definitions. For example, while a narrow definition would refer mostly to growth in GDP per capita, wider definitions could include a number of social targets, such as general health, more widespread levels of education across the population, or access to 'cultural capital', which have been included and operationalised in 'beyond GDP' concepts of growth (see Stiglitz et al. 2009). More recently, ecological/environmental criteria of sustainability have also been emphasised in assessing growth and industrial strategies.

Furthermore, macroeconomic criteria of sustainability will have to be kept in mind when the design and impact of IP are considered. This particularly refers to the development of public and external debt situations that are linked to public expenditure programmes and, hence, to IP as well. However, in both of these domains, IP should be able to alleviate sustainability issues related to both public debt and external accounts through its (intended) impact on growth and competitiveness.

'Competitiveness' is traditionally defined using trade indicators (e.g. growth in market shares of tradable goods and services), but it is often also measured in other ways, such as earning high ranks in various types of 'scorecards' based on indicators such as patenting, citations, R&D expenditures, or the levels of training and skills of the workforce, which would lead to high rates of innovation and more advanced capabilities to work with advanced technologies. It can also refer to the effectiveness of managerial and organisational structures in the private or public sectors (think of the role such structures play in the success of large US or Chinese digital companies or of publicly provided services, such as health or digital infrastructure, in different countries).

10.1.3 What About the Range of Policy Instruments That Could Be at the Disposal of Industrial Policies?

Bringing the definition and the goals of IP together, one would delineate instruments of IP as those that are aimed at affecting the 'structural composition' of an economy to achieve 'growth' and 'competitiveness' goals. This could, in principle, include a very wide array of instruments, since we have mentioned many categories of 'structures' (e.g. sectors, products, technologies, skills of the labour force, types of companies, and regions), all of which might impact growth and competitiveness in one way or another. And, indeed, researchers' attempts to compile an inventory of IP instruments have come up with a wide array of instruments used (for one of the most recent compilations of such a database, see IMF 2024a).

Traditionally, a distinction has been made between 'horizontal' and 'vertical' instruments. Both of these can influence the 'structure' of an economy aimed at growth and competitiveness. As an example of a horizontal policy, one could cite the incentivisation of R&D spending across the board through tax incentives. Although designed as part of a 'horizontal' policy, such incentives will be taken up in a differentiated manner by different sectors of the economy, by different types of companies, and by different regions, depending on how well-positioned the sectors, companies and regions are to benefit from such tax incentives to drive their innovation and, thereby, their productivity and competitive performances. Looked at it this way, all 'horizontal' policies—be they general tax incentives, provision of infrastructure, training and R&D support, measures to facilitate exports, etc.—will have an impact on 'structural' change.

Apart from this, there are naturally also policies that explicitly single out specific sectors, technologies, types of companies, regions, or segments of the labour force for specific types of support, including preferential subsidies, access to cheaper finance, support for small and medium-sized enterprises (SMEs), specific training and research programmes, trade and international investment policies, etc. This is what is considered the core of 'industrial policies', which are now compiled in various international databases, such as the New Industrial Policy (NIPO) database (IMF 2024a; see also Juhasz et al. 2023 for a text-based approach that compiles such a database).

Since policies that aim to achieve the goals of IP will have impacts on economic and social developments that are also the targets of other policies (e.g. competition and regional or social policies), trade-offs and conflicts between these different policy aims will have to be explicitly considered. Thus, for example, regional policy might be aimed at the convergence of income levels across regions, while the use of some IPs (e.g. innovation policy) might give impetus to agglomeration tendencies and thereby contribute to the divergence of regional developments. Similarly, competition policy is aimed at constraining the power of leading companies on EU markets, while IP might want to encourage the emergence of European 'big players' in certain sectors that are able to compete with international competitors of a similar size. Furthermore, R&D and training policies aimed at strengthening innovation capabilities will support differentiated skill and remuneration developments, which might conflict with a more egalitarian thrust of social policies.

Another issue of importance in the EU context relates to the policy instruments being deployed at different levels of governance (EU, national and regional), given the multi-level governance structure that characterises the EU. The EU's ability to deploy policy instruments at such different levels and to coordinate them effectively may be one of the great advantages it enjoys compared to other global competitors for which the cross-country integration and coordination of policies is either absent or has reached a much lower level than in the case of the EU. In this respect, a careful elaboration of the principles that should guide the allocation of the domains of IP to different levels of governance is important in addition to putting in place the administrative and monitoring structures that could effectively leverage this potential advantage.

10.2 The Evolving Geo-economic and Geopolitical Context of the EU's Industrial Policy

We currently find ourselves in a period of rapidly changing geo-economic and geopolitical constellations, and the increased amount of attention that policy makers are paying to IP reflects these changes to an important extent.

10.2.1 The Competitive Challenges of China and the US

First, the dynamics of global economic developments over the past decades (i.e. the 'geo-economics') have themselves led to 'multipolarity'. There is no longer an unrivalled dominance by 'the advanced West' (including—without being exhaustive—the US, Canada, the EU, the UK, Japan, South Korea and Australia) in technology and in commanding global market shares in trade and international investment. This is particularly true in the case of the rise of China, which—in the earlier phases following Deng Xiaoping's liberalising reforms—has mostly benefited from technology transfer and from 'Western' multinationals, which have played a major role in its successfully becoming the dominant global manufacturing powerhouse and exporter of 'Made in China' products. But this stage has been superseded by China's rapid development of its own technological capabilities, which has made it into a major force in some of the most advanced technological fields—as, most recently, in artificial intelligence (AI). Indeed, China now occupies a prime position in international patenting activity and has achieved dominance in a wide range of 'green technology' fields, such as the production of solar panels, batteries and electric vehicles (EVs).

Of course, challenges from fast-moving catching-up economies have also arisen before. In particular, Japan, South Korea and other Southeast Asian economies have closed technology and product-quality gaps with US and European producers in the period following the Second World War. However, China's closing of the gaps has been different, specifically in relation to the scale of its production capacity thereby reaping very significant economies of scale. This has given it relatively unparalleled dominance in a number of product areas and allowed it to produce goods at costs that give it a competitive advantage with which European producers cannot effectively compete. For countries in Europe (in particular, Germany) that saw themselves as dominant high-quality producers in many areas of equipment manufacturing (e.g. mechanical, electrical and transport equipment), this challenge is very serious. One should note, however, that this challenge has to date been concentrated on the manufacture of goods but not on tradable services, for which 'the West' (especially the US and the UK) continues to enjoy a strong competitive advantage (Fig. 10.1).

Over roughly a similar period, beginning in the mid-1990s and especially since the global financial crisis (GFC) of 2008/2009, the EU's position vis-à-vis the US has deteriorated. As is well documented in the so-called Draghi Report (Draghi 2024), Western Europe's efforts to catch up with the US in terms of income and productivity levels were successful during the period between the end of the Second World War and roughly 1995, when it reached 95% of the (labour) productivity level of the US. But then the gap in productivity levels began to widen again (and is currently estimated to be about 80% of the US level; see Draghi 2024: 15). Since the 1990s, a number of studies (see van Ark et al. 2008; Aiginger and Landesmann 2007) have pointed out that Europe lagged behind the US in the initial digital revolution—specifically in terms of the production and diffusion of information and communication technology (ICT)—in a way that is similar to how it is now lagging behind in the current wave of AI as well as cloud and quantum computing. In these fields, not a single major European company ranks among the top players,

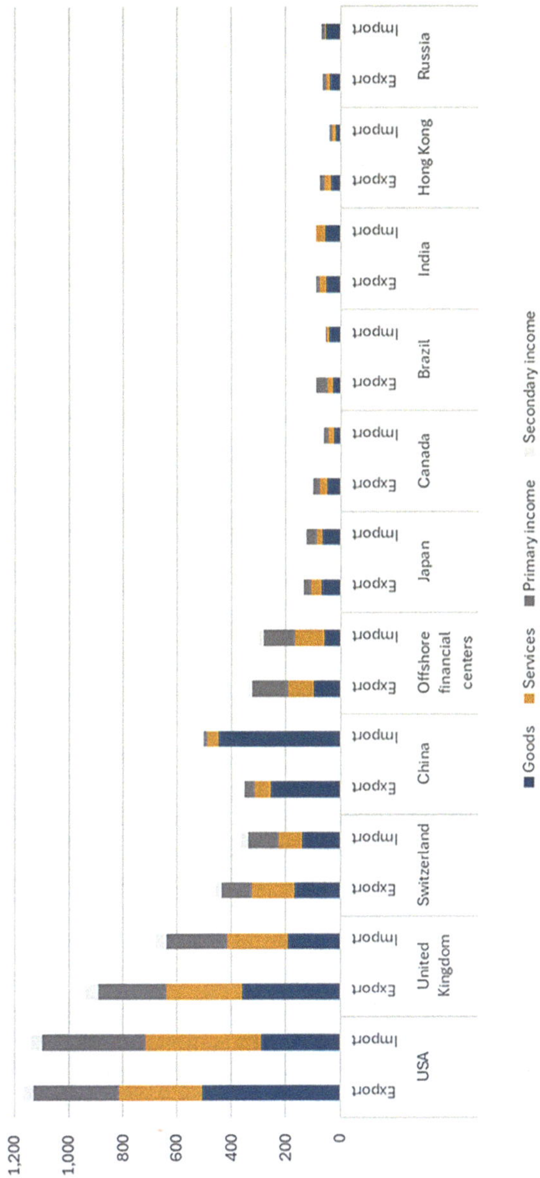

Fig. 10.1 Balance of payments of the top ten trading partners of the EU 2023, EUR bn. (Source: Eurostat, own illustration)

which predominantly come from the US and China. This points to a major failure of Europe's innovation and IP over the past decades (see e.g. publications of Veugelers[1]). The evidence presented in the Draghi Report shows a lack of structural change in European industry, with little change in the composition of the main sectors accounting for the bulk of European spending on R&D and patenting activity, while the major productivity growth gaps relative to the US can specifically be found in the ICT sector and in digital services. A number of analysts now speak of the 'middle technology trap' in which Europe's industry, as well as the scale and direction of its innovation activity, is currently caught (see Fuest et al. 2024).

10.2.2 Can Europe Successfully Counter the Enormous Scale and Network-Externality Advantages of China and the US?

In China, the EU and Western economies in general are facing an economy with a persistent savings rate of about 50% of GDP, which means that it can afford a lot of inefficient/wasteful investment yet still achieve some of its IP goals. This occasionally gives rise to significant excess capacities, which can exert strong price pressures on international markets. Furthermore, while China's single party-dominated governance structure used to be judged incapable of efficient decision-making in comparison to liberal market economies, it has turned out to be effective in steering the economy towards a successful catching-up path while pursuing an IP that has made it a major force in innovation and put it at the forefront of the most recent wave of industrial, green and IT innovations. It remains, however, still an open question whether weaknesses in China's governance structure—which sometimes strongly interferes in the affairs of domestic companies (e.g. Alibaba and Tencent)—will emerge over time and dampen the innovative capacity of its economy.

In comparison with China, Europe and the US have a much lower aggregate savings rate, from which both public and private investments have to be financed. Although international borrowing is an important additional source of finance for the US, this is not true for the EU, which is a net capital exporter. Furthermore, public investment in European economies often falls victim to episodes of fiscal consolidation. Public infrastructure investment projects (which have long gestation periods but

[1] https://www.bruegel.org/people/reinhilde-veugelers

are vital public inputs for a well-functioning economy) are often scaled back during such episodes. Hence, when it comes to mobilising the volume of needed investment, Europe faces a clear disadvantage not only to remain competitive in areas of long-term capacity-building in general, but also to deal with the long-term challenges of industrial structural transformation and the build-up of technological capabilities.

Linked to this is also the disadvantage that the EU faces with respect to the expected return on (public and private) investment both in comparison to China and the US, and this has to do—amongst other factors—with the scale of expected sales and of potential users of the output that results from public and private investment. Since the European market is more fragmented, the expected (private and social) returns from such investments are lower. This also explains the lower interest of international capital markets in investing in European equities. Although the importance of deepening the integration of the EU's Single Market is the core topic of the so-called Letta Report (Letta 2024) and has been emphasised in numerous European Commission strategy papers, not much progress has been made to date. Furthermore, while there has been continuous emphasis on developing a joint approach to public infrastructure (e.g. by enhancing cross-border transport infrastructure and linking energy grids; see European Commission 2024a, b), the resources devoted to these efforts have been limited and the users of public infrastructure still encounter more segmented access to such assets in Europe than is the case in the US and China.

From a European perspective, it is unlikely—as well as not desirable—to aim to achieve investment rates comparable to those of China. At the same time, however, we do agree with the Draghi Report's recommendation that a significant increase (say, of 4–5 percentage points) in the investment rate (i.e. investment as a share of GDP) would be important to direct Europe's economy to achieve the necessary industrial transformation and to facilitate the required change in technological trajectories (see Sects. 10.3.1 and 10.4 below). The emphasis must be on the efficient use of savings and investment. Recent considerations to mobilise untapped savings in the European markets to support private and public investment efforts as well as innovation activity that requires risk capital go in this direction (see Walther 2024a, b; Draghi 2024: Chap. 5).

10.2.3 *Is Industrial Policy a 'Win-Lose' Game? Or Can the EU Aim to Strike a Balance Between Cooperation and Rivalry?*

With multipolarity comes tensions, rivalries and outright conflicts, but also the potential for forming coalitions and cooperation. In such an international environment, the conduct of IP must take into consideration the positions, interests, resources and strategies of a multiplicity of actors as well as the spill-over effects that the EU's conduct of IP has on them and, vice versa, that their strategies have on the EU (see also IMF 2024b).

There are a number of actors or groups of actors that the EU has to consider when it thinks about the consequences of the conduct of its own IP on these actors, how they might react to these consequences, and the actors' conduct of their own IPs.

First of all, there are the two actors already mentioned above: the US and China. How should the EU approach the conduct of IP in a global context that is increasingly shaped by the US-China rivalry, which may in many instances be seen as a non-cooperative conflictual relationship? Should the EU pursue a double-sided cooperative strategy with these two major strategic players while the latter conduct industrial, trade and technology policies that are non-cooperative in nature?

At this stage, it is difficult to predict the evolving characteristics of the US-China rivalry. If it develops into an outright conflict (such as one triggered by a Chinese invasion of Taiwan), it will be hard for the EU to avoid taking a position strongly aligned with the US in strategic terms. This could include a sharp turn away from the EU's current careful adjustment of trade and investment policies towards China, which encompasses a 'diversification' strategy to be less dependent on Chinese imports and its market as well as to more strictly monitor Chinese inward investment. Under deteriorating conditions, it could even go so far as following the heavily restrictive trade and investment policy of the US combined with a strong military alliance with the US, which would also dominate the strategic steps taken by such an alliance.

Although it is difficult to see which scenario will evolve over the coming years, the EU is currently trying to maintain an 'in-between' position—although one not characterised by 'equal distance'—that serves its economic interests in terms of both EU businesses with strong linkages with China as well as EU consumers, who benefit from Chinese imports. Over the medium to longer term, policy will also be driven by the EU's concerns about a possible technology gap opening up—not only with the

US but also with China—and about losing further fields in which it has traditionally held comparative advantages.

Second, there are mid-sized emerging powers, with some being in the EU's immediate neighbourhood (e.g. Turkey) and some being farther away (e.g. Brazil, Saudi Arabia and India, with the latter being in the process of becoming a major power). These countries have increasingly been gaining some 'strategic power', which means that they can play a significant role in influencing geopolitical alliances and, through their actions, generate positive or negative spill-over effects in the areas of trade policy, access to raw materials, or supporting mutually beneficial migration and mobility schemes (including for skilled workers). Through the choice of their alliance partners, they influence the global supplies of energy and critical raw materials as well as the development and security of global value chains (GVCs), which makes them important to European business strategies. A conflictual relationship with these countries would have negative impacts on Europe's geo-economic position, including its industrial strategy, which has to rely on international linkages. Cooperation vs. non-cooperation with these economies is not just a function of the EU's strategy in a world of 'big power' geopolitics and geo-economics, as it also depends on strategies directed specifically at these countries.

In this context of alliances and rivalries, the EU is manoeuvring in a manner unlike the other two big powers (i.e. US and China). While it must rely mostly on instruments of economic incentives and 'soft power', the other two are also motivated by geo-strategic interests beyond economic interests and can also project military might. This can also be an advantage for the EU, as non-economic geo-strategic interests are not interfering with economic interests, which might even be welcomed by these emerging powers. On the other hand, it might also dent the relative bargaining position that the EU can project.

Third, there is a large number of other countries in the 'Global South' and, again, some are in the EU's neighbourhood and others are farther away. In many cases, these are low-income countries that have very limited strategic power themselves. They are mainly so-called policy takers, meaning that they are affected by the policies of others, be they regional or global powers, while their own policies do not have much impact on the economic or political destinies of others. Nonetheless, a cooperative relationship with countries of the 'Global South' can be of significant importance for industrial cooperation, as it can provide scope for mutually beneficial relationships in the areas of trade relationships, allow the EU to benefit from supporting countries in their development processes as well as support them in their efforts to adjust their economies to meet various challenges (e.g. climate change). Furthermore, as an ageing continent, Europe has a strong interest in exploiting demographic complementarities for mutual benefit and, given the numbers of votes that the 'Global South' commands in international organisations (e.g. the United Nations and the World Trade Organization), it can support or negatively counteract Europe's strategic interests through their collective voting share.

10.2.4 Can the EU's Design of Industrial Policy Better Exploit the Potential of Its European and Non-European Neighbourhood and Benefit from Intensifying the EU's Interactions with the 'Global South'?

At present, the EU is not properly exploiting the potential of its relationship with its European as well as with its non-European neighbourhood to further the aims of its IP. This is apparent in the distinct difference in the pattern of income and institutional catching-up between those countries that have joined the EU and those countries that remain outside the EU but are still strongly linked to it, especially through international trade.

Let us first deal with the group of European neighbourhood countries that includes the Western Balkan countries, Moldova, Georgia, Ukraine and Turkey (we intentionally leave out Russia and Belarus because including them would necessitate a separate analysis, as the current situation indicates a strong economic decoupling given the antagonistic relationship). All of the included countries are candidate countries for EU membership, but the time horizon of accession—and even whether it will finally materialise—is far from clear. Nonetheless, these neighbourhood countries could be much better supported in their development processes than they currently are and, at the same time, they could be drawn more tightly into the EU's IP strategy.

For starters, while these countries are beneficiaries of significant pre-accession support programmes, there is still a big gap in terms of the resources made available to the countries that are not members of the EU compared to those that are. This is not surprising in itself. After all, non-members are not participants in the main expenditure programmes of the EU (e.g. the common agricultural policy, regional policy, innovation policy and the European Social Fund). All these programmes support the pursuit of the goals of IP in one way or another, and for those countries that have become EU members, these programmes contributed significantly to their growth and catching-up processes (see the evidence provided in Landesmann and Szekely 2021).

Given these circumstances, we would support the proposals found in Mihajlović et al. (2023) for a staged accession process, whereby candidate countries can gradually fully participate in such programmes as soon as they have positively concluded negotiations on the linked chapters of the acquis. In addition to supporting their development processes, this would also allow them to contribute to the EU's industrial strategy, which would thereby cover a wider economic space, thereby encouraging their full integration into regional production networks, into training and labour market programmes, as well as into the EU's transport and energy systems (see also Grieveson and Jovanovic 2026 in this volume).

As regards the non-European neighbourhood programmes, access to the large expenditure programmes of the EU will not be feasible. Nevertheless, tailored support for their economic and institutional development could be intensified, as there is a lot of scope for a more intensive integration of trade and production structures, for exploiting comparative advantages, and for mobility and training schemes that build on demographic complementarities and upgrade human capital and labour market prospects in the EU's non-European neighbourhood, thereby also reducing unwanted migration pressures (for more on this issue, see Sect. 10.3.2 below).

10.3 Structural Challenges of the EU's Industrial Policy

We are currently living in an era in which the challenges to be addressed by EU IP are particularly intense and varied. In what follows, we will discuss three particular challenges in turn: (i) the challenge of technological and industrial transformation; (ii) the challenge of designing an 'appropriate industrial policy' that takes into account the very differentiated capabilities and potentialities of the main addressees of IP (i.e. companies, countries/regions, and segments of the labour force); and (iii) the challenge of how to conduct IP in a complex, competitive, conflictual and evolving international environment.

10.3.1 *The Challenge of Technological and Industrial Transformation*

At this historical juncture, the EU is confronting the challenge of a multiplicity of technological and industrial transformations: the green transition, the digital/AI technological transition, and the need to adjust to Europe's security challenge. Why is guidance needed from IP to facilitate the required industrial transformation in all three of these areas?

Each of these involves (or, as economists would sometimes say, 'traverses'[2]) rather fundamental industrial transformation processes. However, the IP instruments to be used will be somewhat different, the resistances to be overcome might be different, and the main actors involved (e.g. governments and the private sector) as well as their methods of coordination (e.g. EU-level vs. national- and regional-level interventions) will also be different.

The green transition: Much has been written about the 'green transition', and it is probably the area in which the most work has been done by the European Commission in its various directives to guide EU policies towards this transition (European Commission 2019, 2023, 2025; for a critical evaluation, see Tagliapietra and Veugelers 2021, 2023; Tagliapietra et al. 2023a, b). The last Commission developed the Green Deal as a core policy programme (for an overview of the development of the EU's green industrial policy, see Landesmann 2025). More recently—owing to the more immediate pressures of an energy price shock as well as given the evidence of falling behind in competitiveness terms—there are indications that the EU is backsliding on its strong commitment to the Green Deal.

The green transition encompasses a range of domains of industrial transformation: of the energy system; of production processes across the spectrum of industries, especially those that are intensive in terms of energy requirements and CO_2 emissions; and, finally, of the basket of commodities/inputs purchased by consumers and producers, as these commodities directly or indirectly require inputs whose production is intensive in terms of energy requirements and CO_2 emissions.

All of these areas require changes in 'structures': changes in the composition of different forms of energy generation; changes in the composition of industries that are consuming energy in different forms and emitting

[2] A 'traverse' refers to the move from one structural composition of an economy to another. The concept was introduced into economics by J.R. Hicks (1973).

CO_2 to different degrees; changes in the techniques of production used (reducing energy intensity and changing the energy mix away from those that emit the most CO_2 all the way to a shift towards renewables); and, finally, changes in the commodity baskets consumed.

The difficulty of industrial transformation lies in the 'rigidity of structures'. This involves three things: (i) fixed capital invested, which reflects the existing composition of industries and the use of specific techniques of production; (ii) infrastructure installed as well as the acquired skills of the labour force that are used to work in those industries and with those technologies; and (iii) habitual consumer expenditure patterns. There are important 'sunk-cost' advantages that these existing structures have in comparison to developing new industries, working with different techniques of production, or changing acquired skills. Sunk-cost advantages lead to a 'path dependency' along existing lines of industrial structures, as investments in new industries, production techniques and skills acquisition still have to be made. The bigger the gap between 'old' and 'new' structures (requiring different types of capital equipment, different skills, new or adapted infrastructure, etc.), the stronger the incentive to move along an old trajectory of energy use, composition of industries, production techniques and skills. This explains why 'older' industrial powers or those that were particularly successful in an older set of industries or with an older set of technologies (e.g. Germany in mechanical engineering industries or in fuel combustion technology in the automotive sector) stay on an existing industrial and technological trajectory for longer than would be the case if the sunk-cost advantages of 'older' structures were not present.

The shift towards a new trajectory involves changeover costs that deter such a shift. IP can (and does) intervene in a number of ways. For example, various tax and subsidy schemes can be (and are) used that make the continued operation of old structures (e.g. energy systems and production techniques) more expensive, such as by imposing CO_2 emission charges and/or subsidising the instalment of the 'new' structures (e.g. with preferential financing schemes to install new equipment and to subsidise skills acquisition), both of which are meant to reduce or compensate for the sunk-cost advantages of the 'old' structures. Public authorities can also fully shoulder some of these costs, such as by paying for worker training, investing in or operating new energy systems, providing new infrastructural facilities and financing, and (at times) even operating new start-ups in new industries. However, the pursuit of an 'efficient traverse' by policy makers must counter lobbying powers, which in many instances represent the interests of well-established incumbent industries—a phenomenon well known from the literature on trade policy (see e.g. Grossman and Helpman 2002).

A further important rationale for intervention by public authorities is related to innovation (and learning) processes. Here, too, it amounts to countering features of 'path dependency', as innovation and learning (i.e. skills acquisition) are cumulative processes and innovation, along new technological trajectories, have the comparative disadvantage of being less able to draw on the cumulative advantages of older technological innovation processes. Thus, such changeover processes in innovation also require incentives, subsidies and/or public goods provision (publicly supported research and training facilities) to support the switchover to new innovation trajectories. Here, as well, the further the new technological trajectory is in terms of being able to draw on the cumulative knowledge stock of the older innovation trajectory, the higher the costs of such a switchover to compensate for the advantages that older technological innovation trajectories have over new ones (see Acemoglu et al. 2023; Aghion et al. 2016, 2019).

We can see that sunk-cost advantages of old structures and technological innovation trajectories are an important reason for IP intervention in processes of industrial transformation, such as the 'green industrial transformation'. It also points to an advantage enjoyed by countries in which 'old structures' and old technological innovation trajectories are not in place and therefore public intervention to incentivise such a switchover might not be needed. This is the advantage of 'greenfield' sites and of catching-up economies, which might be well positioned to 'leap-frog' the more arduous industrial transformation processes in more advanced economies. At times, there is also an advantage enjoyed by older industrial powers that have previously gone through a profound process of 'deindustrialisation' (e.g. the US and the UK as compared to, say, Germany). In such places, since building on older industrial trajectories was no longer feasible, the switch to new activities (e.g. digital industries) has not faced the sunk-cost advantages and lobbying powers of older industries.

Innovation and industrial transformation: IP thus has an important role to play when there is the challenge to achieve a major shift in technological trajectories (e.g. decarbonisation or the use of AI in many forthcoming applications), both in innovation but also in overhauling industrial structures (including invested capacities and skill/training structures). We have argued above that this is the case with the green transition. But it also applies more generally to other types of transitions that require a shift in industrial structures, technological trajectories and qualifications in addition to physical infrastructure and institutions (e.g. new types of regulatory bodies and educational institutions).

Europe has not been very effective in a number of technological innovation waves over the past decades (especially digital technologies) and, more recently, in what seems to be a major technological revolution in the field of AI. Especially in Germany, which occupies a crucial position in European manufacturing production, there has been insufficient intervention to facilitate an overhaul of industrial structures in light of the new technological trajectories, as the timely shift to digital technologies, information technology and EVs was missed. The power of sunk-cost advantages led to the continued investment of a high share of industrial R&D in traditional technologies (e.g. the combustion engine) and the industries in which Germany has traditionally held a comparative advantage (motor vehicles maintained the top position in the share in industrial R&D spending) (see also Tordoir and Setser 2025). Furthermore, as discussed above, the lobbying power of incumbent firms in traditional industries also leads public R&D and IP instruments to be skewed towards powerful incumbent firms and industries.

The relatively weak position of the EU as a whole in supporting innovation can be seen in overall R&D spending. The figures for 2022 show that the share of R&D in GDP in the US is about 3.5% compared to 2% in the EU (China's R&D share in GDP of 2.4% was already above the EU's). If we look at the breakdown of public vs. private spending on R&D, we find that the discrepancy between the US and the EU lies almost exclusively with private-sector funding: while government-financed R&D amounted to 0.66% percent in the EU and 0.6% in the US, business-financed R&D was 1.22% in the EU and 2.4% in the US (see Veugelers 2024).

To explain this difference, analysts specifically point to four factors: (i) the factor already discussed above, namely, the insufficient market integration, as emphasised in the Letta Report (Letta 2024; also European Commission 2021); (ii) the different financing structures of European capital markets, especially the under-provision of venture capital (for a recent assessment, see Walther 2024a, b); (iii) the tighter and more effective relationship in the US between research institutions, universities and innovation activity in the business sector; and (iv) the role the military sector plays through public procurement and innovation spill-overs for the innovation process in the civilian sector (see Mazzucato 2013). While the four items above have been well explored when it comes to comparing the EU with the US, the comparative analysis of the Chinese system in relation to these factors (especially (iii) and (iv)) has been less explored.

We would also like to mention two additional items that are important for a sustained dynamic of innovation in these three economies: (v) competition policy and (vi) migration policy and international attractiveness for highly skilled workers.

Competition policy has been much discussed in relation to a new direction of European IP (see EPSC 2019 and Bundesministerium für Wirtschaft und Energie/Ministère de l'Économie et des Finances 2019). The issue here is one of a distinct trade-off that the EU is facing in the evolving geo-economic and geopolitical environment. On the one hand, there is the important role of competition policy to constrain the market power of incumbents, thereby supporting the entry and growth of new innovative companies (see Veugelers and Cincera 2010). On the other hand, there is the tendency in the global economy—and especially in the most high-tech digital and AI industries—for oligopolistic market structures to emerge in which a handful of companies dominate the industry.

This is not a new phenomenon, as the international car industry, the pharmaceutical industry, the duopoly of aircraft production, and the computer industry (think of IBM) have also shown such high levels of concentration in the past. Hence, European competition policy must adjust to the reality of this global competitive pressure, especially in high-tech industries.

The dominance of the 'global players' in high-tech industries is currently very strong, and a breakthrough for European producers to be present in such industries with their own 'champions' will only happen if a coordinated effort is made at the cross-national European level (as happened with the Airbus project). However, it does not have to mimic the US or the Chinese model in this respect, as the EU can design its own way of nurturing highly competitive companies that have the innovative capacity and can achieve sufficient scale to contend with global competitors.[3]

The European model can thereby rely on its own comparative advantages. For example, there could be a more state-guided cooperative effort at the EU level (e.g. the already ongoing Important Projects of Common

[3] For an initiative to build a stronger presence in the area of micro-chips, see European Commission (2022).

European Interest (IPCEIs)), support for 'infant industries' through financing schemes, a continuous effort to bring down barriers within the Single Market, the incentivisation of much closer university-business linkages, the utilisation of public procurement policies, the provision of infrastructure, and the establishment of state-sponsored training and 'innovation labs', all of which can support efforts to reach the required scale and innovative capacity to meet the global competitive challenge.

Since many of the 'knowledge-based' industries are characterised by strong 'network externalities', breaking into these markets with well-established incumbents requires up-front support from a differentiated but targeted portfolio of IP measures. This does not exclude cooperative joint ventures with some of Europe's global competitors, and the pooling of resources through cross-European IPCEI business ventures and EU support packages should provide the basis for negotiating such joint ventures not from a subordinate position.

Nevertheless, competition policy will continue to have a role to play in controlling the power of nascent 'European champions' on the European market to ensure that innovative new entrants, especially in highly innovative branches, are protected from early takeovers. They could be supported through (competitive bids for) finance and venture capital, the encouragement of university spin-offs, and a migration policy that eases the hiring of highly qualified international personnel (both technical and commercial). Competition policy will also remain important to make sure that one of the strengths of European industry—namely, the medium-sized companies (the 'Mittelstand') that are prevalent in Germany, Austria and some countries in Northern Europe—continue to receive support, as quite a few of them are technology leaders in global market niches.

Migration policy, and especially providing conditions to attract highly qualified personnel (i.e. the so-called race for international talent), is also one of the relevant factors for a successful EU IP. Given the demographic dynamic, with a declining labour force as a share of the population and the already visible labour shortages in important fields, it will become an even more important factor for growth, productivity and innovation performance in the decades to come—not only in Europe, but also in the US. A policy that follows the rationale of economic necessity, however, is countered by political processes that are increasingly dominated by populist pressures; these enforce an increasingly restrictive stance on migration policy. To date, policy makers have not found a recipe for successfully resolving this contradiction.

The security dimension of industrial policy: Over the post-war period, Europe has benefited from a military-industrial security umbrella provided by the US, which has allowed most EU member countries (with the exceptions being France and, when still an EU member, the UK) to neglect to build up and maintain a robust defence industry of their own. With the Russia-Ukraine war and the intensified pressure from the US (especially with the second Trump presidency) for Europe to meet a much higher share of its security needs, the situation has changed. There is now a general acknowledgement that significant resources must be devoted to this task. In addition to the mobilisation of more (public and private) resources, this will also require much more intensified coordination efforts—not only among EU member countries, but also with European allies that have joint security interests (e.g. the UK, Switzerland, Norway and—in future—Ukraine, with Turkey being a more complex case).

The target of moving towards 2.5% or 3% of GDP in defence spending is not the only issue here, as achieving some degree of independence from the US in terms of security policy- related decision-making will also entail developing production and innovation capacities in the security field in areas that are currently not sufficiently covered in Europe (e.g. satellite and intelligence capacities). This also goes back to the importance of pooling resources and strongly increasing coordination and cooperation within Europe. Alternatively, a significant share of the spending would go towards purchasing weapons and relying on innovation in the defence field from other partners, most prominently the US.

How does EU IP in the defence field differ from the conduct of IP in other areas, such as innovation policy more generally or the public-private efforts to achieve industrial transformation in areas like the Green Deal?

First, there is the issue of how to deal with technology transfer outside the EU and restrictions related to supplying defence equipment (including 'dual use' goods and services) to countries that are potential foes in geostrategic relationships.

Second—and this also applies at the domestic and intra-EU level—public authorities need to have stricter control over the defence industry, as allowing private actors to have fundamental decision-making authority (take the example of Elon Musk's SpaceX Starshield) would not be acceptable.

Third, harmonisation and scale are likely to play more important roles in many parts of the defence industry than in other areas of industrial production and innovation. The 'love of variety', which is an important feature of differentiated demand in civilian areas of production (both consumers' expenditure, but also in the demand for tailor-made intermediate inputs and capital equipment), plays much less of a role in defence and is, in many cases, a hindrance to achieving efficiency in this sector. Hence, exploiting scale and making strategic decisions with respect to production sites at the European level can play a particularly important role in this area compared to other fields in which EU IP has to be active.

Apart from direct public procurement at the European level, the relatively successful concept of coordinating cooperation among European businesses through IPCEIs applies here as well. Just like in the successful Airbus project, there are a number of important similarities: (i) long lead times will be required for planning, and there will be a significant gap between when initial investments (in innovation and production facilities) are made and when returns on that investment materialise; (ii) cooperation can and should exploit comparative advantages across European partners in innovation and production capabilities; and (iii) effective coordination at each stage (e.g. long-term planning of defence requirements as well as the development and use of defence capabilities) is important (see also Engberg 2025).

The defence sector is not isolated from other sectors of the economy, and this applies to both innovation and production. There are spill-overs in both directions, and these have to be encouraged and exploited, although due attention has to be paid to the issue of overall public (state or EU-level) control of decision-making over sensitive aspects of such spill-overs. In the current context, since the expected spill-overs of AI development between military and civilian uses will be particularly high, it will be important to have robust monitoring and effective control mechanisms in place.

10.3.2 The Challenge of Designing an 'Appropriate Industrial Policy'

Heterogeneity and differentiation across the European continent and its neighbourhood can be seen as an important advantage, a characteristic which it shares with the Asian continent (particularly South and Southeastern Asia). It is a continent with widely diverse productivity levels (as reflected in income and wage levels), resource endowments, climate conditions and demographic characteristics (the latter with the non-European Middle Eastern and African neighbourhood). Together with this also comes a constrained diversity of institutional structures due to the impact of the EU on its member states as well as on associated and candidate countries. Although the EU's well-known 'Unity in Diversity' motto mainly applies to its members, it can also be extended to the European continent as a whole (though the conflict with Russia limits the scope to include this country as well as Belarus). While the institutional anchorage is definitely much looser, from an economic-integration point of view, this concept can also apply to Europe's neighbourhood, the Middle East and Northern Africa (and, beyond that, to the African continent as a whole), which are all strongly linked with the EU through trade, although in different ways and to different degrees.

This differentiation in resource endowments, demographics and production conditions across a wide economic space gives Europe an enormous opportunity in a geo-economic/geopolitical environment in which there is a strong trend towards 'regionalism'. This refers to tighter economic linkages across a neighbouring group of countries supported by preferential trade and investment policies within a wider global region. At the same time, the linkages across these regionalist entities become subject to geopolitical tensions, potentially leading to 'regional bloc' formations, which go against a world ruled by multilateralism.

The conceptualisation of IP across a continent (and its neighbourhood) that is characterised by such diversity in income, productivity levels and institutional/political economy conditions has to take into consideration that the design and application of any IP factors in the different conditions in the different parts of this economically highly integrated continent (plus its neighbourhood). Roman Stoellinger and I (Landesmann and Stoellinger 2019) have coined the concept of '*appropriate industrial policy*', which is analogous to the concept of '*appropriate technology*' that is well known in development economics (e.g. Los and Timmer 2005). There, it refers to the importance of having technology transfer from more advanced to developing countries take into account the conditions and levels of economic development in the countries that should be the beneficiaries of this technology transfer. In the same way, the design and application of the instruments of IP across a differentiated regionalist economy must factor in the differentiated requirements of participating economies and regions.

In the following, we first discuss the differentiated use of IP programmes across the EU member states. As already discussed, IP programmes are financed and implemented at both the national and EU levels. Let us first look at the differences across EU member countries regarding national- vs. EU-level funding of IP.

Although we are already in the midst of the 2021–2027 Multiannual Financial Framework (MFF), which outlines the detailed expenditure plans of the EU's budgetary spending for the current period, we have to limit ourselves here to the previous financing period (2014–2020), as information regarding actual (rather than planned) spending is not yet available for the current period (here we draw on an earlier analysis by Landesmann and Stoellinger 2020a, b; for details on how the data were compiled, see Appendices 1 and 2). An important feature that is apparent from an analysis of *financing of industrial policy at the EU and national levels* is that different EU member countries rely to very varying degrees on EU policy programmes to support their own efforts. Figure 10.2 shows that, over the 2014–20 financing period, the lower-income countries (i.e. those in Eastern and Southeastern Europe as well as the Southern European countries) drew to a much higher degree on EU funding for their IP efforts than was the case for the more advanced EU member states. This is a particular consequence of the important role that EU Structural and Investment Funds (ESIF) programmes play in EU-level financing of IP. In this respect, the 'cohesion' aspect does play an important role when considering EU-level financing of IP.

In Fig. 10.3, we then show the *composition of spending from EU programmes*: spending from programmes other than the ESIF programmes in panel a) and spending from ESIF programmes—i.e. regional policy—in panel b). This again shows significant differences between the more advanced EU member countries (the UK is still included in the 2014–2020 financing period) and the lower-income countries, especially those in Eastern and Southeastern Europe. What is most striking is that, as regards funding from central and ESIF budgets, the advanced economies spend a considerably higher share of EU funding on R&D and technology support than the lower-income economies in Eastern and Southeastern Europe (ESEE). Although this is what one might expect, it nevertheless conflicts with the aim of closing gaps in 'innovation capacities' between the two groups of economies. Also evident is the high share of spending on infrastructure by the ESEE group of economies, with relatively little spending on SME support from ESIF funding (see panel b) compared with the more advanced economies.

Our first conclusion from this analysis of spending on IP efforts by EU member states is that, regarding the distribution between national- and

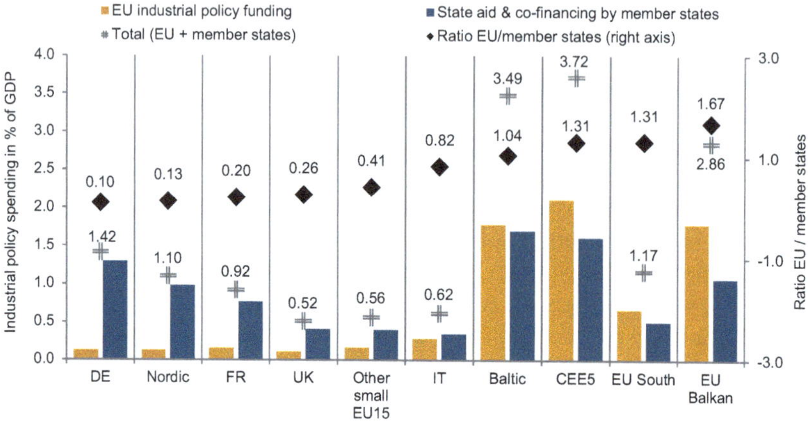

Fig. 10.2 Spending on industrial policy by the EU and its member states, by country group, average for the 2014–2020 period. (Note: EU Balkan = HR, BG, RO; Other small EU15 = AT, BE, NL, LU, IE; CEE5 = HU, CZ, SK, PL, SI; Baltic = EE, LT, LV; EU South = CY, EL, ES, MT, PT. For the EU regional funds, the total actual financing flows are assigned to individual funds by the European Structural and Investment Funds (ESIF) using the shares of these funds in the planned budget allocations in the MFF 2014–2020. Co-financing amounts by member states are calculated using the ratio of planned allocation of EU spending to actual spending by member states in the MFF 2014–2020. National state aid by member states is the subsidy element contained in national state aid, which is also expressed as a percentage of GDP. Sources: European Commission (various sources; for details, see Appendices 1 and 2.) The calculations have already been compiled in Landesmann and Stoellinger (2020a, b)

EU-level funding, there is much more dependence of the 'cohesion countries' (i.e. countries that are distinctly stronger beneficiaries of ESIF programmes) on EU-level funding than is the case for the more advanced economies, which finance a greater part from national sources. In this respect, there is evidence that IP funding through EU-level programmes supports the lower- and medium-income countries to different degrees and, therefore, that the cohesion aspect is reflected in the allocation of EU funds for IP purposes. The second conclusion, however, is that a more detailed analysis of different countries' participation in the sub-components of overall EU-financed programmes shows that the less advanced economies spend considerably less (in share terms) on R&D-related programmes

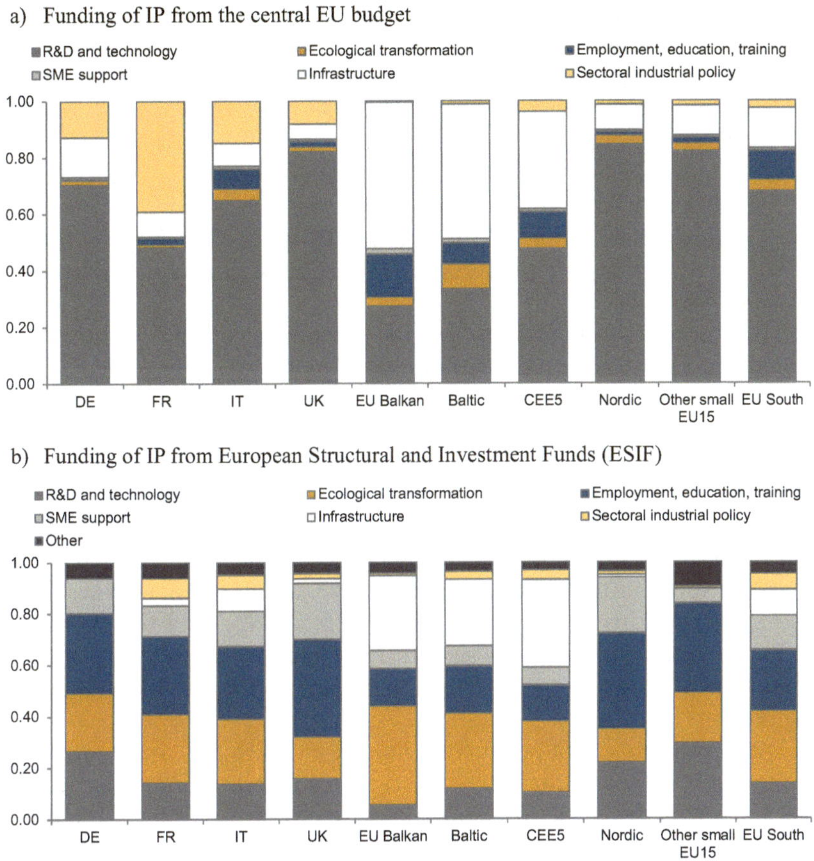

Fig. 10.3 Spending on industrial policy from the EU budget, by country group and theme, average for the 2014–2020 period. (**a**) Funding of IP from the central EU budget. (**b**) Funding of IP from European Structural and Investment Funds (ESIF). (Note: EU Balkan = HR, BG, RO; Other small EU15 = AT, BE, NL, LU, IE; CEE5 = HU, CZ, SK, PL, SI; Baltic = EE, LT, LV; EU South = CY, EL, ES, MT, PT. The numbers are the shares of the respective IP theme in a country or country group's total EU policy spending, funded by either the central budget or the ESIF. Sources: European Commission (various sources; for details, see Appendices 1 and 2.) The calculations have already been compiled in Landesmann and Stoellinger 2020a, Fig. 4)

than the more advanced ones. Thus, this aspect reveals that EU funding that targets the build-up and support of innovation capabilities across the EU member states is more skewed towards the advanced economies and therefore potentially reinforces agglomeration tendencies of such capabilities in those economies.

Let us now turn to the issue of integration with the EU's neighbouring regions (both within and outside of Europe), which we partly covered in Sect. 10.2 when we addressed the question '*Can the EU's design of industrial policy better exploit the potential of its European and non-European neighbourhood?*'

These neighbouring regions have the potential to be more tightly integrated into a development strategy that exploits complementarities between them and the European economy along a set of different dimensions: through trade, international production linkages, foreign direct investment (FDI), and education and labour mobility programmes, including training schemes.

The opportunities that—from an economic point of view—exist for a wider region with considerable differentiation within it and strong complementarities (most importantly demographic complementarities, but also in terms of natural resource endowments, skills, and technological and organisational know-how) should also shape the design of IP not only within the EU itself, but also across the continent and with its neighbouring regions.

Deepening trade and production integration with this wider region is of mutual benefit, and there are still considerable protectionist barriers in place, particularly as regards exports of agricultural goods from the non-EU neighbourhood, which is an important sector with considerable potential for quality upgraded food production. Bringing down such barriers will incentivise more FDI and a more intensive integration into international production networks, which can extend to a wider range of industries, including manufacturing but also tradable services. This, in turn, will stimulate employment possibilities in the region, which suffers from considerable youth unemployment, including of the better educated. Combined with circular mobility and training schemes, this could make an important impact on the labour market situation in these neighbouring regions, which currently suffer from a brain drain of the young and more highly educated. This is also true for the EU neighbouring region, in the Balkans and in Ukraine (where there are special circumstances due to the war, but we expect this to persist even after the war), as is the case in the non-EU neighbouring regions of Northern Africa and the Middle East.

Among the well-known constraining factors are institutional deficiencies, including poorly functioning legal and administrative structures, which act as a deterrent to international investment and a more intensive inclusion in international production networks (this particularly affects sectors where reliance on the rule of law is important). If this is not tackled, international trade specialisation is distorted, which leads neighbouring regions to remain stuck in a development trap of supplying mostly raw materials and commodities that cannot otherwise be sourced along with low chances for upgrading in the direction of processing, higher value-added stages of production, and more extensive global value chain (GVC) integration.

The use of IP instruments in EU neighbouring regions is also important when it comes to linking up their energy systems and transport infrastructure with those of the EU as well as reducing regional trade and (business) entry barriers within the regions to provide a wider and more attractive economic space for international investors. But it is also important in terms of nudging these regions to improve their legal and administrative structures through monitoring and incentive mechanisms. In some cases, it might be necessary to set up dual structures that cover export processing zones (EPZs) with better functioning and monitored administrative and fast-track legal mechanisms.

An important additional lesson, which has been learnt from past development processes in pre-accession countries, is that while FDI-led industrial development has made important contributions to economic upgrading, the spill-overs to the domestic company sector were rather low and—at times—negative, as resources were withdrawn from the domestic business sector and concentrated in multinational corporations (MNCs). Here, it is important to use instruments to also strengthen the domestic business sector through public support for the supply of skilled labour, supporting spin-offs from the operations of MNCs, managerial and technical training programmes, etc.

10.3.3 *The Challenge of How to Conduct Industrial Policy in a Complex, Competitive, Conflictual and Evolving International Environment*

The global environment has become much more challenging for the EU. How does EU IP adapt to such an environment? The more challenging environment involves:

- Much less power of multilateral organisations
- Fragmentation of international trade and GVC relations (regional bloc formation)
- Developing policies of 'resilience' and 'open strategic autonomy'
- The requirement to build up military capacities (part of industrial transformation)
- The 'competition for talent' and the need for a migration and integration policy

Since the failure of the Doha Round of international trade negotiations, the world has moved away from multilateral trade agreements, and regional and bilateral trade agreements are now prevalent. The EU has been very active in moving in this direction, reflecting its importance as—what continues to be—the largest trading bloc, although China now rivals it in terms of the number of countries for which it is the most important trading partner (see Fig. 10.4, though note that it only covers trade in goods). China is now the largest trading partner (in goods) of 71 countries (data for 2023), whereas the figure for the EU is 68 and that for the US is 32.

Two longer-term structural issues will dominate the perspective for the future of the EU's position in the global economy. One is the worry about the persistence of a trajectory of low productivity growth and innovation compared to its two main global rivals (i.e. the US and China); this also does not equip it well in relation to the expected additional pressures from other catching-up economies (e.g. India) that are challenging Europe's economies in their traditional areas of comparative advantage. The other is that the EU, in the currently evolving global setting of strategic actors, does not speak with a forceful and unified voice. This means that it is at a disadvantage compared to unitary nation states (specifically the US and

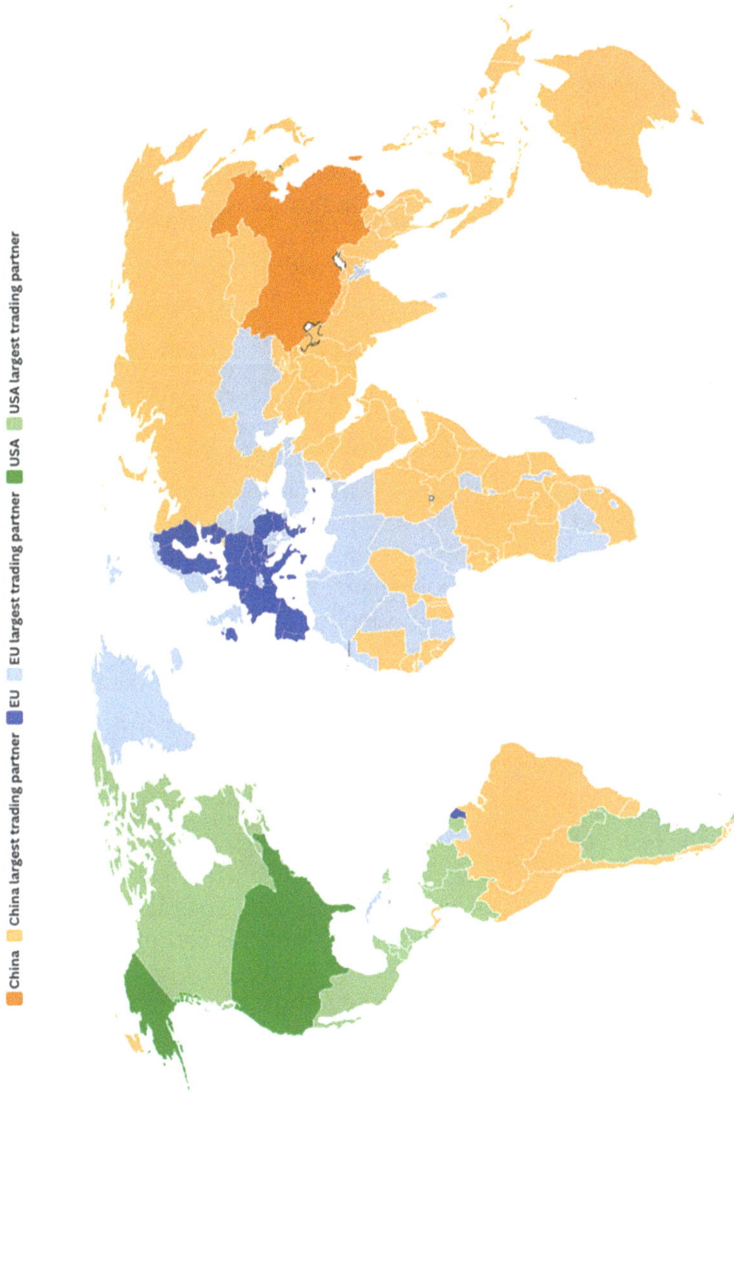

Fig. 10.4 Countries for which the EU, the US or China is the top trading partner, 2023, goods only (sum of imports and exports). (Source: own calculations based on UN Comtrade, wiiw calculations. Sum of imports and exports (2023))

China[4]) to act in a world that is increasingly characterised by strategic policy-setting and that has moved away from an international rules-based setting as multilateral organisations (e.g. the World Trade Organization) have been severely weakened. The heterogeneity and differences in positions of EU members on crucial issues of international relations (e.g. its stances towards China or the Ukraine-Russia conflict) prevent the EU from acting with the same power and determination as these unitary nation-states. To complicate things further, this problem is becoming much more severe during the second Trump presidency.

The EU has responded to a number of 'shocks' (e.g. the global financial crisis of 2008/2009, the COVID-19 pandemic, the energy crisis, cyber-attacks and IT/AI-generated fake news challenges) by strengthening its regulatory frameworks as well as developing and operationalising concepts of 'resilience' and 'open strategic autonomy'.

On the issue of '*resilience*': During the COVID-19 crisis, it became apparent that the cost-minimising strategies pursued by internationally operating companies in their effort to establish and maintain global supply chains showed severe signs of vulnerability. It was not only the pandemic, with its lockdowns and interruptions of supply lines, but also the behaviour of suppliers of strategically important inputs that revealed that strong dependency relationships can be problematic. Hence, the policy response was three-fold: (i) diversification of supplies from multiple potential sources; (ii) more friend- and near-shoring; (iii) and building up a safety margin of production facilities in critical product areas within the EU. All of these meant that one moved away from a pure cost-minimising strategy of supply lines built on the principle of comparative advantage. This involved changes in the strategies of internationally operating companies and—in a number of areas—the need for state subsidies, with the latter falling into the realm of IP. Furthermore, the thinking went that in important, sensitive areas (e.g. medical equipment and pharmaceuticals), one had to rethink the importance of investing in domestic (or EU-wide) production facilities that had previously been outsourced as part of the earlier globalisation drive.

International trade policy is now dominated by bilateral (or group and regional) trade agreements rather than multilateral agreements, which

[4] The US is, of course, a federal state. However, when it comes to foreign and security policy, it acts as a unitary state, which is a far cry from how decisions are being taken at the EU level in these crucial areas.

have not been revived after the failed Doha Round. Countries are now increasingly employing instruments of strategic IP to influence industrial developments and the innovation dynamic in their countries or regions. These are not coordinated at the international level and lead to counter-actions by other global players, such as the EU's reactions to the measures undertaken during the Biden presidency, specifically the Inflation Reduction Act (IRA), which attempted to support the return of manufacturing capacities to the US, and the CHIPS and Science Act (European Commission, 2022). Retaliatory measures in response to Chinese subsidies (e.g. to support EV and battery production) led to protectionist trade policy reactions and battery-support programmes by the EU (two rounds of IPCEI initiatives[5]). The shift towards IP is thus strengthened by having to react to other countries' use of industrial and trade policy instruments. The actions of all three global actors (i.e. the US, China and the EU) have led to a situation in which the active use of trade and IPs plays an increasingly prominent role in shaping the system of international economic relationships.

In this context, the concept of '*open strategic autonomy*' (OSA) is directed towards the strategic build-up of technological and production capabilities that would allow some degree of self-reliance in strategic areas. Here are two quotations from EU documents that highlight the complexity in the design and implementation of this concept, which is still at an early stage of operationalisation in the EU context:

> *[…] the EU should pursue a model of 'Open Strategic Autonomy'. This simply means strengthening the EU's capacity to* ***pursue its own interests independently and assertively, while continuing to work with partners around the world to deliver global solutions to global challenges****. It is as unlikely that the EU would be self-sufficient in producing certain complex critical health products, as it is impossible to tackle global climate and environmental challenges on our own.* (Author's bolding) (Source: European Commission 2020: 3)

> *The Commission will …* ***make full use of trade defence instruments (TDI) to defend the Single Market****, and rules-based international trade, from unfair trade practices like dumping and distortive subsidies.* (Author's bolding) (Source: European Commission 2023: 2)

[5] https://competition-policy.ec.europa.eu/state-aid/ipcei/approved-ipceis/batteries-value-chain_en

International production and trade relationships are thus subject to probably the most fundamental changes since the Second World War, for both longer-term economic and strategic political reasons. The longer-term economic factors are changing comparative advantages following the dynamics of productivity and catching-up processes in product quality and innovation capabilities of emerging economies and particularly of China. The strategic political factors generate conflictual relationships in which trading partners rethink dependency relationships regarding reliance on specific supply lines and critical inputs.

The shift in strategies also manifests itself specifically in the intensification of competition in the development of high-tech industries. In addition to being at the forefront of the innovation process, these are crucial for the diffusion of new technologies across a wide range of industries and, thus, are highly relevant for overall longer-term productivity performance. While international cooperation in the area of scientific development used to be widespread and international businesses could draw on an evolving pool of scientific knowledge, stronger restrictions are now imposed on access to such a pool. The issue of technology transfer is no longer just seen as of general benefit for global development but also in terms of how it affects the strategic (and military) capacities of countries. Reducing or severing international production and technology linkages will negatively impact global growth performance, and it will especially affect countries that have traditionally been net beneficiaries of such knowledge transfer. In the more advanced countries, international competition in technology races leads to manifold duplication of efforts. Those who have missed the early advances in crucial areas of technological developments—as European producers are now experiencing with their attempts to catch up with the AI advances made by the US and China—can only recoup technology leads that they have lost to one of the other actors with the help of highly resource-intensive public supports.

The deteriorated geopolitical scenario is apparent in a number of areas: more trade conflicts, more regionalist bloc formation, frictions in international scientific research collaboration and knowledge transfer, and a strong increase in resources devoted to expanding and upgrading military capacities. All of these pose major challenges to the EU economy, as it has traditionally relied on trade openness and the effectiveness of multilateral agreements, in addition to having benefited from having opted out of the international arms race in the past.

10.4 Fiscal Issues Related to the Conduct of EU Industrial Policy

Like (almost) any policy area, IP requires fiscal resources. Thus, a careful assessment must be made regarding which of these resources should be mobilised, allocated and employed at the cross-national (i.e. EU), national and regional levels.

First of all, there is the question regarding the scale of the financial resources needed to conduct an effective IP at the cross-European level. This depends on what we want to include within the realm of 'industrial policy'. We have taken a wider view of what would be included here, which includes the tasks of: (i) tackling the major three challenges of industrial transformation that were discussed in Sect. 10.3.1 (e.g. the continued push towards the Green Deal); (ii) making the innovation system in the EU more effective so as to enable the bloc to become a serious contender in the most advanced technology areas (e.g. AI and quantum computing) and to remain at the innovation frontier in some of the areas in which European economies are or used to be leaders (e.g. pharmaceuticals and transport equipment); and (iii) building up an effective military industry that can look after the security interests of Europe without a strongly asymmetric dependence on US armament supplies. Of course, the three areas are related and, in many ways, there will be synergy effects of supporting one area on the other areas (e.g. green transformation and the build-up of military capacities inducing new innovation trajectories), and these in turn will initiate patterns of new lines of industrial production and employment. Furthermore, the impact of these innovation trajectories will impact price and cost structures and, as a result, affect the evolution of demand.

The above three areas of industrial structural transformation—which includes substantial support for basic and applied research, start-up costs, and needs associated with scaling up new production lines until they become fully self-supporting—will require a substantial net investment push. I concur with the recommendation of the Draghi Report (Draghi 2024) that a 4–5 percentage point increase in the investment share in GDP over the coming ten years (from currently about 22% to 27%) would be an appropriate target to reach such a goal. The Draghi Report makes the point that the savings volume in Europe would be available to reach such a target (EU household savings were EUR 1390bn compared to EUR 840bn in the US in 2022; ibid.: 55), and that could be mobilised.

The Report also makes a number of recommendations regarding how reforms in capital markets could lead to a more effective mobilisation of such savings to achieve the ambitious goals of industrial transformation and overhauling the innovation systems in Europe.

The Draghi Report also discusses the role of public vs. private investment in such a major sustained investment push:

> *Historically in Europe, around four-fifths of productive investment has been undertaken by the private sector, and the remaining one-fifth by the public sector. Delivering [additional] private investment of around 4% of GDP through market financing alone would require a reduction in the private cost of capital – by approximately 250 basis points in the European Commission model. Although improved capital market efficiency* (e.g. *through the completion of the Capital Markets Union) is expected to reduce private financing costs, the reduction will likely be substantially smaller. Fiscal incentives to unlock private investment therefore appear necessary to finance the investment plan, in addition to direct government investment.* (Draghi 2024: 63)

Apart from the many reforms in capital markets that the Draghi Report mentions to mobilise financial resources and specifically also risk capital, there is the additional demand for public investment and, specifically, the type of public investment that supports projects at the EU level:

> *Joint funding for specific projects will be key to maximise the productivity gains of the strategy, such as investing in breakthrough research and infrastructures to embed AI into the economy. At the same time, there are other public goods identified in this report – such as investing in grids and interconnectors, and financing the joint procurement of defence equipment and defence R&I – that will be undersupplied without common action and funding. Finally, for Member States to converge more closely in their policies – be it the Single Market or more generally in the policies described in this report such as climate, innovation, defence, space and education – both regulation and incentives will be required. Incentives will also require common funding.* (Ibid.: 64–65)

To achieve the ambitious goals outlined in the Report, there will also be the need for more public borrowing at the EU level, along the lines of the Next Generation EU (NG-EU) programme,[6] which responded to the emergencies triggered by the COVID-19 pandemic. This will also include

[6] https://next-generation-eu.europa.eu/index_en

the issuing of common debt instruments to finance joint investment projects, which will also have the positive side effect of creating a deeper and more liquid market in EU bonds, which in turn will play an important role in the integration of Europe's capital markets (ibid.: 66). The issuing of more debt at the European level will be all the more important, as the earlier EU borrowing for the NG-EU programme will have to start being repaid beginning in 2028, which would unduly constrain the envisaged EU expenditure programmes for the next MFF.

The bulk of Europe's economics experts have argued in favour of such recommendations, which implies pursuing reforms of fiscal arrangements at the EU level and continuing along the paths of strengthening the coordination of fiscal policies between the EU and national levels that had already been set in motion during the InvestEU[7] and the NGEU programmes. Both of these programmes tried to address the issue of financing 'common public goods' but also to counter centrifugal tendencies linked to the uneven 'fiscal capacity' faced by different EU economies, which require joint financing schemes.

10.5 Social Inclusion and Industrial Policy

The task of industrial restructuring while also boosting the innovation performance of the EU involves significant demands for a changed skill/qualification set and for educational/training institutions that equip the labour force with such qualifications. This is a traditional area in which public investment is needed, as private human capital investment would be sub-optimal, especially in areas that are at the risky early stages of innovation and then production. We emphasise that this area has to be seen as an integral component of an 'appropriate industrial policy' and should aim at exploiting the potential of training, education and employment possibilities across the entire spectrum of capabilities of the labour force and across all age groups. Furthermore, tailoring such policies to the differentiated needs across the spectrum of companies (with different technological capabilities) and across regions should be seen as a central concern of such a policy.

The use of instruments of IP has to be sensitive to the distributional and 'social cohesion' implications of the impact of IP. There are two

[7] https://investeu.europa.eu/investeu-programme_en

dimensions of a ‘cohesion-sensitive IP’ (CS-IP): (i) the regional aspect and (ii) the social-structural aspect.

The *regional aspect* is, in principle, well covered by EU Cohesion Policy. This policy has been an important pillar of the EU’s policy-making framework for a long time, accounting for about one-third of spending from its community budget, and it has been going through multiple stages of reform. At present, EU Cohesion Policy centres around the concept of ‘smart specialisation’ (S3), which requires (NUTS 2) regions to submit plans regarding the direction in which they see their economic structure evolving in the context of the intra-European and global division of labour. In this way, EU Cohesion Policy builds on existing capabilities (endowments) of the regions and interacting with the various stakeholders within the region in designing such a plan (Foray 2013; Foray et al. 2009). Regional policy should thus be directed towards strengthening physical and human capital infrastructure, providing support to businesses and the regional innovation systems, and assisting the labour market through active labour market policy. The European Commission has gained a lot of experience in the domain of regional policy over the years, and the implementation of the S3 strategy shows that the ‘competitiveness’ target is now foremost in its design. Nonetheless, there is the issue that ‘backward regions’ often do not have the institutional capacity to design and effectively implement S3 plans, which is why we also find critical assessments of the strategy in the literature, such as:

> *[...] the regions which appear to be the most conducive and favourable for the operation of smart specialisation-type processes are the buoyant core regions, and as such precisely the types of regions which EU Cohesion Policy does not prioritise.* (McCann and Ortega-Argilés 2015: 12)

In our own analysis in Sect. 10.3.2, we also pointed out that EU financing schemes that particularly target innovation activity are much less used in the countries of Central-Eastern and Southern Europe than in the more advanced Northern and Central European countries, which means that EU Cohesion Policy does not necessarily foster convergence in the area of regional innovation capacity. Agglomeration of top-level research and innovation might be a necessary feature of an efficient innovation policy, but it would detract from the ultimate goal of boosting overall productivity performance if sufficient attention is not paid to designing a policy in such a way that it also supports (and specifically targets) the innovation and productivity potentials across the entire spectrum of regions and businesses.

The *social-structural aspect* has to be covered not necessarily by IP itself but in part by accompanying policies. The EU has provided some policy initiatives to deal with the social challenges posed by the industrial transformation process involved in the Green Deal, such as through the so-called Just Transition Fund.[8] However, the resources devoted to these efforts have been relatively small, and the visible tendencies of social disparities emerging in most European economies have clear political implications, as evidenced by the strong rise of right-wing populist parties (see Rodriguez-Pose 2018 and Guriev 2026 in this volume). This demonstrates that the tasks of dealing with the social implications of industrial structural change and adjusting to the challenges of rapid technological change are very formidable. As the use of AI will speed through many sectors of the economy, such challenges will only grow more daunting. A stronger emphasis on industrial and accompanying policies on tackling these social-structural aspects of industrial transformation will definitely be necessary both from a social cohesion point of view as well as when it comes to providing sustainable support to address the core targets that industrial and innovation policy aims to achieve (i.e. boosting the growth and competitiveness performance of the EU's economy).

10.6 Concluding Remarks: How Should EU Industrial Policy Be Directed?

It is clear that EU IP is operating in a world that has been changing significantly over the past decades both in economic terms and—in an accelerated manner more recently—in geopolitical terms.

In economic terms, over the past few decades, we have witnessed a significant decline in the share that 'the West'—but particularly the European economy—accounts for in global GDP, global trade, and global (inward and outward) investment. This comes along with an even longer-run decline in its share in the global population. From a once dominant bloc, Europe now only represents one of the larger regional entities in the global economy, albeit still a significant one. These trends are likely to continue over the coming decades.

[8] https://commission.europa.eu/funding-tenders/find-funding/eu-funding-programmes/just-transition-fund_en

More worrying are the trends in productivity and in Europe's contribution to global technological dynamism, which has been well pointed out in the Draghi Report. This is exactly the area that industrial and innovation policy is supposed to target (at the EU, national and regional levels). The worrying trends seem to point to a less-than-satisfactory record of these policies in Europe.

The factors behind this track record have been addressed in numerous studies over the past few decades. These include: (i) the insufficient completion of Single Market integration, which affects particular sectors (e.g. services and public utilities) more than others, as these sectors in particular suffer from not being able to exploit the potential of a large and integrated domestic market;[9] (ii) the ineffective mobilisation of Europe's considerable savings volume for productive investment purposes and particularly for investments with a high innovation potential, such as through venture capital finance; (iii) the insufficient interaction between research undertaken in universities and research institutions and the business sector (note, for example, that high patenting rates in Europe are not reflected in the volume of start-ups in high-tech areas); and (iv) barriers to the growth of 'yollies' (young leading innovators; Veugelers and Cincera 2010), which again is a function of having less access to finance and up-scaling opportunities in European markets.

All of this is reflected in a rather slow transformation of industrial structures in Europe, with the principal traditional sectors (and incumbent companies) accounting for the bulk of R&D spending, as well as in the lethargic adaptation of Europe's industrial specialisation and international trade performance to new technological opportunities, as compared to a faster change in the dynamic and reallocation of resources across sectors (and companies) in the US and China. The end result is that Europe is lagging behind in the innovation, production and diffusion stages of important waves of essential new technologies, most prominently digital technology and AI. In these technologies, Europe has missed out on taking leading positions in pushing the technological frontier, and there are

[9] Furthermore, in many of the 'knowledge-based industries and services', network externalities are very important, and exploiting these determines the market power of then-dominating companies in high-tech industries.

also indications that Europe's position is weakening in fields in which it has traditionally been strong (e.g. pharmaceuticals).[10]

Although, some observers would also point to the factor of 'over-regulation', I would argue that the real issue is not the extent of regulation but the need for careful screening and for designing a regulatory framework that can reconcile the achievement of various targets (e.g. consumer protection, health and safety, and environmental concerns) with contributing to achieving competitiveness. Since this has definitely become more difficult than it was in the past, as fierce competitive pressures have intensified in an increasingly fragmented global setting, Europe's strategy has to adapt and confront this new reality. The reduced geo-economic weight of Europe, combined with the decline of multilateralism, means that the power of the so-called Brussels effect, which led trading partners to adopt European regulations due to the incentive effect of Europe's large market, has become weaker (Bradford 2020). The trends are globally heading in the direction of a multiplicity of regulatory frameworks (e.g. technical standards) that are in competition with each other and are adopted by different regionalist entities in different combinations. In addition, geopolitical pressures are increasingly influencing this adoption process.

Coming to the issue of Europe's presence in geopolitical terms, we have pointed out that the EU is a collection of nation-states with a commitment to economic integration and the coordination of economic policies in important areas. This kind of coordination happens to a very high degree in some areas, such as competition, trade and monetary policy (for members of the Economic and Monetary Union) and much less in other areas (e.g. social policy). There are attempts to move further in the direction of harmonisation and coordination in other policy areas (e.g. migration/asylum, foreign and security policy), but we have seen that this is not an easy task. The cumbersome decision-making processes, complexities of voting procedures, and blocking/vetoing powers of individual member states all lead to a constrained ability to act in a decisive way in an era of 'big power' politics. On the other hand, the slow-moving evolution of legislative structures and institutional set-ups (to which the EU has committed itself through the various treaties and delegations of powers to the supra-national level) also means that rolling these back would be very

[10] The Draghi Report points out that EU public-sector spending on pharma R&I currently stands at less than half the level of the US, while total private R&I investment is about a quarter as large as that of the US (Draghi 2024: 24).

difficult. This, in turn, makes it a more predictable player in the international sphere (in contrast to the erratic shifts of the Trump administration in foreign policy positions).

The current set-up of the EU (in comparison to, say, the US or China) also means that the resources allocated for policy conducted at the supra-national/EU level are very small compared to those still commanded at the national levels (about 1% of gross national income (GNI) at the EU level compared to 40–45% at the national levels). This not only means that the financing of EU-level projects faces severe restrictions (e.g. to engineer a major boost to cross-European public investment), but also means that strategies that are commonly designed and agreed upon will very often have to be financed from resources at the national level, which means that different countries are then constrained to different extents by the fiscal and financial resources they have at their disposal. This is why most economists now agree that the budgetary resources that are allocated to the supra-national level to support the financing and supply of 'Europe-wide public goods' as well as common industrial and geopolitical/geo-economic strategies should be increased (by another 1–2 percentage points of EU GDP). A wide range of proposals have been put forward on how to finance such an expansion of the EU budget (e.g. increasing own resources taxation, issuing common bonds, and expanding the lending possibilities of the European Investment Bank).

There is both an economic and geopolitical rationale for such a move. Making more resources available at the EU level and extending 'qualified majority voting' to a wider set of policy fields would give the Commission more room for more effective strategic action in a world in which less complex and quick decision-making is required, which in turn would more effectively translate Europe's economic power into influence in geopolitical terms. In the current global geopolitical context, the urgency for more streamlined coordination, quick decision-making and joint financing in a number of policy areas at the EU level has undoubtedly increased. Although the time horizon of IP should be long, there are areas (e.g. trade policy, adapting and responding to pressures on regulatory frameworks, and responding to international refugee and migration crises) where decisive and quick action may be required.

Pointing to the above-mentioned weaknesses should, however, not deflect from the fact that Europe also has important comparative advantages that could help it to succeed in today's changing geo-economic and geopolitical context.

Let us start with an advantage that the EU enjoys precisely because of the constitutional and institutional nature of its construction, and that (in the discussion above) has also been interpreted as constituting a disadvantage: appearing on the global stage mostly as a 'soft power' allows the EU to display a more differentiated behaviour towards global partners that are worried about the increased use of 'hard power'. This might particularly be an advantage in relation to countries in the 'Global South' that do not want to be coerced by the exercise or threat of 'hard power' to comply with the interests (e.g. in trade, investment, finance, regulations and security) of other global or regional powers.

Furthermore, the heterogeneity of the EU's membership (and of Europe more generally) can be beneficial in a number of ways. First, it can help the EU to exploit comparative advantages for production location and specialisation within the European continent, thereby reaping 'gains from trade' of cross-continental value chains, which is of particular benefit in a world that fragments into 'regional bloc' formations. Second, differences in institutional structures can also lead to differentiated experimentation of what works better or worse[11] and, in a highly integrated market, this would combine with competitive selection pressures enforced by capital flows and the mobility of people. The other side of the coin, however, is that such competitive processes could also lead to a cumulative divergence of performances and the emergence of regions and countries trapped in a 'low equilibrium' situation from which it is hard to escape. Assistance for the transfer of 'best practices' as part of EU Cohesion Policy is therefore a necessary component of such a strategy.

A multi-level governance structure is, in principle, an important feature of the EU and, through the application of the 'subsidiarity principle', it could be a major advantage in terms of the efficient operation of the EU. However, an effective application of this principle has to be continuously reviewed in light of changing (economic, technological and geopolitical) circumstances. It is clear that certain areas will require efforts to harmonise and mobilise resources at the pan-European level, such as an overhaul of cross-European energy and transport systems as well as the selection and support of world-class research infrastructure. Other areas will require a bottom-up design and implementation of innovation and IP

[11] Analyses of Chinese development processes have pointed out that experimentation with policies tried out in different regions has also played an important role in developing policy strategies at crucial stages in the country's development (see Weber 2021).

at the local levels in order to exploit the location and evolving comparative advantages of regions and interconnected districts. In this field, the S3 strategy is the appropriate one, although insufficient attention has been given in its implementation to support and strengthen institutional capacities of weak regions so that the intended structural change and growth targets can be achieved as a result of the design and execution of these strategies. Stronger EU-level technical and financial support, as well as careful monitoring of the different phases of execution, could boost the performance of these regions. The multi-level monitoring ability of the three-tier governance structure (EU, national and regional) should be seen as an important lever for controlling the proper use of resources as well as for ensuring that regional S3 programmes are embedded in a wider strategy regarding specialisation structures and growth trajectories across European regions. After all, regional development processes are interlinked through spill-over effects, supply interdependencies, and the mobility patterns of labour and capital.

The European economy is still a large entity (especially if the potential of Europe's neighbourhood regions is also included), and economies of scale and scope could be exploited as well or even better than they are in the other major competing regions (principally North America as well as East and Southeastern Asia). This will require efforts aimed at the increased pooling of resources, boosting the efficiency of administrative structures to implement policies, and pushing back against the lobbying power of entrenched incumbent interests to allow the shift of resources towards new, innovative areas. These efforts should also be directed towards working to establish a consensus and implementing a persistent strategy in support of the three areas of industrial transformation that Europe has to pursue: implementing the green transition and catching up on the digital (and now AI) transformation, regaining a leadership position in innovation related to cutting-edge technologies, and supporting the necessary build-up of European defence capacities.

Below, we provide a summary of recommendations that the EU's IP should follow as guiding principles in the currently evolving geopolitical context:

- Use the EU's multi-level governance structure effectively in addition to flexibly exploiting the heterogeneity of the economic and institutional space of the European continent.

- Focus on boosting productivity growth and innovation performance (in a manner that follows the recommendations found in the Draghi Report) while persistently implementing programmes that have been (or will be) launched and—at times—increasing their resources.
- Innovation policy will continue to be characterised by the tension between the need to support 'centres of excellence' (which goes in the direction of agglomeration) as well as the importance to exploit the innovation (and technology diffusion) potentials across the entire spectrum of firm segments and of regions that are currently operating below the technology frontier. Hence, it is important that innovation policy takes both of these—at times—conflicting targets into account, as diffusion processes are as important to overall productivity improvement as is innovation at the technology frontier.
- Following from this, we emphasise to design and implement an 'appropriate industrial and innovation policy' (AIIP) that aims at mobilising the competencies and potentialities of the different segments of firm, regional and labour force distributions.
- Take up the recommendations found in the Draghi Report to utilise the considerably under-tapped savings volume in Europe to support innovation policy as well as technological and industrial transformation. This involves making urgently needed progress in capital market integration as well as providing support to underdeveloped segments (e.g. venture capital) and instruments of finance.
- View elements of migration policy as an integral part of a successful European industrial and innovation policy, particularly in the area of the mobility of highly skilled/highly qualified migrants. This should include schemes of circular migration combined with cooperative training/educational and labour market policy initiatives in source countries (and especially in EU neighbouring countries).
- Include EU neighbouring countries—to different degrees—in the IP schemes of the EU. Doing so should be an important component of a strategy of intensified trade, investment and security relationships with the non-European neighbourhood.
- Given that the development of military capabilities in Europe resulting from the current conflictual geopolitical context will definitely play an important role in the coming phases of European industrial and innovation policy, target spill-over effects in innovation and production relations between the civilian and military sectors when designing policies in this field.

Appendix 1: Mapping of Budget Items in the MFF 2014–2020 to the Industrial Policy Themes

The discussion of the EU's budgetary expenditure on IP-related issues during the 2014–2020 period is based on a selection of items within the Multiannual Financial Framework (MFF) 2014–2020 that are subsumed in the realm of IP. Table 10.1 lists all budget items that were selected to qualify as being related to IP.

Appendix 2: Mapping of Thematic Objectives in the ESIF to the Industrial Policy Themes

For the budget items representing expenditure of the European Structural and Investment Funds (ESIF), additional information on the 'thematic objectives' of the funds was used. However, for these targets, only the figures from the projected expenditure (as allocated in the MFF 2014–2020) were available. This information was used to assign the regional policy expenditures to individual targets/objectives. The implicit assumption here was that the actual disbursements (both from the EU budget and from national co-financing) have the same distribution across objectives as the projected amounts in the MFF 2014–2020. Since the classification of the MFF 2014–2020 does not allow a distinction to be drawn between expenditure under the European Social Funds (ESF) and the European Regional Development Fund (ERDF), these are treated together, although distinguished by objectives. The data on regional fund allocations can be found at: https://ec.europa.eu/regional_policy/EN/funding/available-budget/

Spending under the Cohesion Fund that was not found in the budget allocations is assigned to infrastructure, as it must be assumed that this spending is made in connection with the Connecting Europe Facility (CEF), which is also included in this budget item.

Table 10.1 Industrial policy item within the MFF 2014–2020

Section in MFF	*Description*	*Assigned IP category*
1.1.10	European Fund for Strategic Investments (EFSI)	Infrastructure
1.1.11	Implementation and exploitation of European satellite navigation systems (EGNOS and Galileo)	Sectoral policy
1.1.13	European earth observation programme (Copernicus)	Sectoral policy
1.1.31	Framework Programme for Research and Innovation (Horizon 2020)	RDI
1.1.4	Programme for the Competitiveness of Enterprises and Small and Medium-sized Enterprises (COSME)	SME
1.1.6	EU Programme for Employment and Social Innovation (EaSI)	Employment, education, training
1.1.81	Energy	Infrastructure
1.1.82	Transport	Infrastructure
1.1.83	Information and communications technology (ICT)	Sectoral policy
1.1.9	Energy projects to aid economic recovery (EERP)	Infrastructure
1.2.5	Youth Employment Initiative (specific top-up allocation)	Employment, education, training
1.2.6	Contribution to the Connecting Europe Facility (CEF)	Infrastructure
2.0.4	Programme for the Environment and Climate Action (LIFE)	Ecological
1.2.11	Less developed regions (regional convergence)	Regional—for breakdown, see Table 10.2
1.2.12	Transition regions	Regional—for breakdown, see Table 10.2
1.2.13	More developed regions (competitiveness)	Regional—for breakdown, see Table 10.2
1.2.14	Outermost and sparsely populated regions	Regional—for breakdown, see Table 10.2
1.2.15	Cohesion fund (incl. contribution to the CEF)	Regional—for breakdown, see Table 10.2

Source: European Commission (http://ec.europa.eu/budget/graphs/revenue_expenditure.html)

Table 10.2 Categorisation of the thematic objectives in the ESIF into industrial policy themes

Code	*Target objective of structural funds*	*Assigned IP category*
1	Research & innovation	RDI
2	Information & communication technologies	Sectoral policy
3	Competitiveness of SMEs	SME
4	Low-carbon economy	Ecological
5	Climate change adaptation & risk prevention	Ecological
6	Environment protection & resource efficiency	Ecological
7	Network infrastructures in transport and energy	Infrastructure
8	Sustainable & quality employment	Employment, education, training
9	Social inclusion	Social
10	Educational & vocational training	Employment, education, training
11	Efficient public administration	Institutions
12	Outermost & sparsely populated regions	Social
TA	Technical assistance	Institutions
DM	Discontinued measures	Not assigned

Source: European Commission (https://ec.europa.eu/regional_policy/EN/funding/available-budget/)

References

Acemoglu, D., Aghion, P., Barrage, L. & Hémous, D. (2023). Green innovation and the transition toward a clean economy. Peterson Institute for International Economics, Working Paper 23–14.

Aghion, P., Dechezleprêtre, A., Hémous, D., Martin, R. & Van Reenen, J. (2016). Carbon taxes, path dependency, and directed technical change: evidence from the auto industry. *Journal of Political Economy,* 124(1), 1–51.

Aghion, P., Hepburn, C., Teytelboym, A. & Zenghelis, D. (2019). Path-dependence, innovation and the economics of climate change, in: Fouquet, R. (ed.). *Handbook on Green Growth.* Edward Elgar Publishing, Cheltenham, 67–83.

Aiginger, K. & Landesmann, M. (2007). Longer-term competitiveness of the Wider Europe, in: Eichengreen, B., Landesmann, M. & Stiefel, D. (eds.). *The European Economy in an American Mirror.* Routledge, London, 62–103.

Bradford, A. (2020). *The Brussels effect: How the European Union rules the world.* Oxford University Press, Oxford.

Bundesministerium für Wirtschaft und Energie/Ministère de l'Économie et des Finances (2019). A Franco-German manifesto for a European industrial policy fit for the 21st century. www.bmwk.de/Redaktion/DE/Downloads/F/

franco-german-manifesto-for-a-european-industrial-policy.pdf%3F__blob%3DpublicationFile%26v%3D2

Draghi, M. (2024). The future of European competitiveness – Report to the European Council. Brussels. https://commission.europa.eu/topics/eu-competitiveness/draghi-report_en

Engberg, K. (2025). Towards a European Total Defence Union? Swedish Institute for European Policy Studies (SIEPS), January. https://sieps.se/media/mqclelyg/2025_1epa.pdf

European Commission (2019). The European Green Deal. COM(2019) 640 final, Brussels. https://eur-lex.europa.eu/resource.html?uri=cellar:b828d165-1c22-11ea-8c1f-01aa75ed71a1.0002.02/DOC_1&format=PDF

European Commission (2020). A renewed trade policy for a stronger Europe: Consultation note. 16 June. https://circabc.europa.eu/rest/download/08516104-d6c6-4c75-8f26-59c5cd8bcc88

European Commission (2021). Updating the 2020 new industrial strategy: building a stronger single market for Europe's recovery. COM(2021) 350 final. https://eur-lex.europa.eu/legal-content/EN/TXT/?uri=CELEX%3A52021DC0350

European Commission (2022). A Chips Act for Europe. COM(2022) 45 final. https://eur-lex.europa.eu/legal-content/EN/TXT/?uri=CELEX%3A52022DC0045

European Commission (2023). A green deal industrial plan for the net-zero age. COM(2023) 62 final. https://eur-lex.europa.eu/legal-content/EN/TXT/PDF/?uri=CELEX:52023DC0062

European Commission (2024a). Trans-European Transport Network – TEN-T. https://transport.ec.europa.eu/transport-themes/infrastructure-and-investment/trans-european-transport-network-ten-t_en

European Commission (2024b). Trans-European Networks for Energy. https://energy.ec.europa.eu/infrastructure/trans-european-networks-energy_en

European Commission (2025). The Clean Industrial Deal: A joint roadmap for competitiveness and decarbonisation. COM(2025) 85 final. https://commission.europa.eu/document/download/9db1c5c8-9e82-467b-ab6a-905feeb4b6b0_en

European Political Strategy Centre (EPSC) (2019). EU industrial policy after Siemens-Alstom: finding a new balance between openness and protection. Brussels. https://ec.europa.eu/epsc/sites/epsc/files/epsc_industrial-policy.pdf

Foray, D. (2013). The economic fundamentals of smart specialisation. *Ekonomiaz*, 83(2), 54–78.

Foray, D., David, P. A. & Hall, B. (2009). Smart specialisation – the concept. Knowledge Economists Policy Brief No. 9, June.

Fuest, C., Gros, C., Mengel, P.-L., Presidente, G. & Tirole, J. (2024). EU Innovation Policy – How to escape the middle technology trap. Report by the European Policy Analysis Group, Bocconi and Toulouse Universities.

Grieveson, R. and Jovanovic, B., 2026. Growing challenges and ways forward in light of the war in Ukraine and regional tensions in the Western Balkans. In: Székely, I. P. and Halmai, P. (eds) The Future of European Integration, Palgrave-Macmillan, forthcoming.

Grossman, G. M. & Helpman, E. (2002). *Special Interest Politics.* MIT Press, Cambridge, MA.

Guriev, S., 2026. The recent rise of populism and European integration. In: Székely, I. P. and Halmai, P. (eds) *The Future of European Integration,* Palgrave-Macmillan, *forthcoming.*

Hicks, J. R. (1973). *Capital and time: A neo-Austrian theory.* Oxford University Press, Oxford.

IMF (2024a). The return of industrial policy in data. Prepared by: Evenett, S., Jakubik, A., Martin, F. & Ruta, M. International Monetary Fund, Working Paper, WP 24/1.

IMF (2024b). Industrial policy in Europe: A single market perspective. Prepared by: Hodge, A., Piazza, R., Hasanov, F., Li, X., Vaziri, M., Weller, A. & Wong, Y. C. International Monetary Fund, Working Paper, WP 24/249.

Juhasz, R., Lane, N. J., Oehlson, E. & Perez, V. C. (2023). The who, what, when and how of industrial policy: A text-based approach. STEG Working Paper, WP050, January. https://steg.cepr.org/sites/default/files/2023-01/WP050%20Juh%C3%A1szLaneOehlsenP%C3%A9rez%20TheWhoWhatWhenAndHowOfIndustrialPolicy.pdf

Landesmann, M. (2025). The European Union's Green Industrial Policy, in: Mathews, J. A. & Oqubay, A. (eds.). *The Oxford Handbook on the Greening of Economic Development*; Oxford University Press, Oxford.

Landesmann, M. & Stoellinger, R. (2019). Structural change, trade and global production networks: An 'appropriate industrial policy'. *Structural Change and Economic Dynamics*, 48, 7–23.

Landesmann, M. & Stoellinger, R. (2020a). The European Union's industrial policy: What are the main challenges? *Policy Notes and Reports* No. 36, The Vienna Institute for International Economic Studies (wiiw), Vienna.

Landesmann, M. & Stoellinger, R. (2020b). The European Union's industrial policy, in: Oqubay, A., Cramer, C., Chang, H.-J. & Kozul-Wright, R. (eds.). *The Oxford Handbook of Industrial Policy*, Oxford University Press, Oxford, 621–660.

Landesmann, M. & Szekely, I. (2021). *Does EU membership facilitate convergence? The experience of the EU's eastern enlargement.* Palgrave Macmillan.

Letta, E. (2024). Much more than a market – speed, security, solidarity: Empowering the single market to deliver a sustainable future and prosperity for all EU citizens. Report to the European Council. www.consilium.europa.eu/media/ny3j24sm/much-more-than-a-market-report-by-enrico-letta.pdf

Los, B. & Timmer, M. P. (2005). The 'appropriate technology' explanation of productivity growth differentials: An empirical approach. *Journal of Development Economics*, 77(2), 517–531.

Mazzucato, M. (2013). *The entrepreneurial state: debunking public vs. private myths*. Anthem Press, London.

McCann, P. & Ortega-Argiles, R. (2015). Smart specialization, regional growth and applications to European Union cohesion policy. *Regional Studies*, 49(8), 1291–1302.

Mihajlović M., Blockmans, S., Subotić, S. & Emerson, M. (2023). Template 2.0 for staged accession to the EU. Center for European Policy Studies (CEPS). https://cdn.ceps.eu/wp-content/uploads/2023/08/Template-2.0-for-Staged-Accession-to-the-EU.pdf

Rodriguez-Pose, A. (2018). The revenge of the places that don't matter (and what to do about it). *Cambridge Journal of Regions, Economy and Society*, Volume 11, Issue 1, March 2018, 189–209.

Stiglitz, J., Sen, A. & Fitoussi, J.-P. (2009). Report by the commission on the measurement of economic performance and social progress. Springer Publishing.

Tagliapietra, S. & Veugelers, R. (2021). Fostering the industrial component of the European Green Deal: key principles and policy options. *Intereconomics*, 56(6), 305–310. www.intereconomics.eu/contents/year/2021/number/6/article/fostering-the-industrial-component-of-the-european-green-deal-key-principles-and-policy-options.html

Tagliapietra, S., Trasi, C. & Veugelers, R. (2023a). Europe's green industrial policy, in: Tagliapietra, S. & Veugelers, R. (eds.). *Sparking Europe's New Industrial Revolution: A policy for net zero, growth and resilience*. Blueprint Series Volume XXXIII, Bruegel, 166–186.

Tagliapietra, S. & Veugelers, R. (eds.) (2023). *Sparking Europe's New Industrial Revolution: A policy for net zero, growth and resilience*. Blueprint Series Volume XXXIII, Bruegel. www.bruegel.org/book/sparking-europes-new-industrial-revolution-policy-net-zero-growth-and-resilience

Tagliapietra, S., Veugelers, R. & Zettelmeyer, J. (2023b). Rebooting the European Union's Net Zero Industry Act. Policy Brief, Bruegel. www.bruegel.org/policy-brief/rebooting-european-unions-net-zero-industry-act

Tordoir, S. & Setser, B. (2025). How German industry can survive the second China shock. Centre for European Reform (CER), London.

van Ark, B., O'Mahony, M. & Timmer, M. P. (2008). The productivity gap between Europe and the U.S.: Trends and causes. *Journal of Economic Perspectives*, 22(1), 25–44.

Veugelers, R. (2024). Memo to the commissioner responsible for research and innovation. Bruegel, Brussels.
Veugelers, R. & Cincera, M. (2010). Europe's missing yollies. Bruegel, Policy Brief 2010/06, Brussels.
Walther, U. (2024a). Strong risk capital markets: Vital for unlocking green & digital innovations. EU Monitor, Deutsche Bank Research, 29 January.
Walther, U. (2024b). European securitisation market – ready for a comeback? EU Monitor, Deutsche Bank Research, 19 August.
Weber, I. (2021). *How China escaped shock therapy: The market reform debate.* Routledge, London.

CHAPTER 11

The Role of Institutional Relatedness to Promote Regional Innovation in the EU

Ron Boschma

11.1 Introduction

A large body of literature has shed light on the importance of institutions for economic development (North 1990; Acemoglu et al. 2005). Institutions may facilitate (e.g., property rights, rule of law) or not (e.g., corruption, low trust) innovation and economic development. The Innovation System literature (Nelson 1993; Asheim and Coenen 2006) focuses on the nature of interactions between organisations that are coordinated by formal and informal institutions, which promote or not innovation. Institutions are also perceived to affect the nature of innovations because some institutional settings are considered to facilitate better radical innovations (Hollingsworth 2009; Acemoglu et al. 2014).

Many of these contributions treat institutions as if they act in isolation. This has been contradicted by scholars who have adopted a systemic approach to institutions instead. They advocate the idea that the

R. Boschma (✉)
Department of Human Geography and Planning, Utrecht University, Utrecht, The Netherlands

UiS Business School, University of Stavanger, Stavanger, Norway
e-mail: r.a.boschma@uu.nl

I. P. Székely, P. Halmai (eds.), *The Future of European Integration*, Studies in Economic Transition,
https://doi.org/10.1007/978-3-032-20186-7_11

institutional structure consists of elements that might be coherent or not (Streeck and Thelen 2005). Various literatures have described the nature of such institutional systems, such as the regulation theory (Boyer 1988), the business system perspective (Whitley 1999) and the Varieties of Capitalism framework (Hall and Soskice 2001). Institutional systems are presented as ideal types that show complementarities between institutions rather than tensions or inefficiencies inside institutional systems (Amable 2000; Hollingsworth 2000; Crouch 2005; Jessop 2011).

While the concept of institutional complementarities is appealing, it has remained rather underexplored. Most of the work follows a functional, pre-defined approach to institutional systems, such as the Varieties of Capitalism literature (Hall and Soskice 2001). What is more, systematic empirical research is lacking at the subnational scale. There is also little discussion on how to apply it to effective regional innovation policy in the EU.

The objective of this chapter is to propose a concept of institutional relatedness that aims to tackle these shortcomings. Section 11.2 reviews the Varieties of Capitalism literature as a prime example of a functional approach to institutional complementarities. Section 11.3 provides an alternative view, proposing a revealed relatedness approach to institutional complementarities based on the principle of relatedness (Boschma 2017; Hidalgo et al. 2018). Section 11.4 discusses how institutional relatedness can be applied in studies of economic geography and explains how this may be relevant for effective regional innovation policymaking in the European Union. Section 11.5 concludes.

11.2 Varieties of Capitalism

The concept of institutional complementarities suggests that, by definition, institutions within an institutional system are considered complementary. In such a conceptual setting, proximity between institutions is constructed, pre-defined and determined by theory. A prominent example of such a functional approach to institutional complementarities has been proposed by the Varieties of Capitalism literature (Hall and Soskice 2001; Amable 2003; Hall and Gingerich 2009; Hall and Thelen 2009).

A core claim of this body of literature is that countries have remained very different in the way they coordinate their actions despite the strong forces of globalisation. A key reason is that countries build a set of institutions over time that are tightly connected to each other and, therefore, hard to change. Such a systemic view on institutions argues that institutions may reinforce each other at the national scale, forming a system that includes industrial relations, education and research, finance, and the welfare state. It also implies it might be difficult to implement institutional change, as a change in one institution might be opposed because of its implications for or incompatibility with other institutions.[1]

According to Hall and Soskice (2001), this is embodied in the types of economic activities and innovations that countries specialise in. Other activities and types of innovations that do not fit the institutional system of countries are unlikely to prosper. Institutions in liberal market economies are perceived to promote science-driven industries in which radical innovations are more common. The institutional system of coordinated market economies would, instead, facilitate the development of sectors such as high-quality engineering in which incremental innovations prevail, as their key assets are specific and committed to such an extent that it is almost impossible to put them to alternative uses.

The institutional complementarity view of the Varieties of Capitalism literature has been criticised. Hall and Soskice (2001) proposed two ideal types of institutional systems (i.e., liberal and coordinated market economies) to which only a very limited number of countries, like the US, the UK, and Germany, could be assigned (Geffen and Kenyon 2006; Bathelt and Gertler 2009). However, many countries might represent very different institutional models, such as emerging economies (Schedelik et al. 2021). Institutional varieties have also been observed between countries in Europe, Asia and Latin America (Bizberg 2014; Hall 2018; Johnston and Regan 2018; Riedel and Anusik 2024).

Another critique was its prime focus on methodological nationalism, which overlooked regional varieties inside the same institutional system (Asheim and Coenen 2006; Peck and Theodore 2007; Gertler 2010). Moreover, there was a tendency to look for and identify institutional

[1] Another influential school of thinking on institutional complementarities has been initiated by Hofstede ([1980]2001) on cultural proximity. Hofstede identified groups of countries that share similar cultural work-related values on multiple dimensions. Individualism vs. collectivism refers to the degree to which societies are integrated into groups. Uncertainty avoidance concerns how societies are dealing with unknown situations and uncertainty. Long-term orientation refers to how society views its time horizon. Masculinity-femininity is associated with how society values traditional sex roles. Power distance indicates whether inequality, ranks, authority and power are tolerated. Kaasa et al. (2014) followed Hofstede to identify the cultural features of NUTS-2 regions.

functionalism and complementarities while downplaying the possibility of inefficiencies and tensions within institutional systems (Crouch 2005; Hancké et al. 2007; Peck and Theodore 2007; Jessop 2011). This also implied a focus on institutional stability and path dependency rather than institutional change and transformation (Deeg and Jackson 2007; Jackson and Deeg 2008; Schneider and Paunescu 2012; Amable and Palombarini 2009; Hay 2020).

Studies also found mixed support for some of the claims of the Varieties of Capitalism literature concerning the type of economic specialisations and innovations that would prevail in each institutional system (Taylor 2004; Allen et al. 2006; Kenworthy 2006; Akkermans et al. 2009; Meelen 2013). Boschma and Capone (2015) did not find a systematic pattern of economic specialisations in each of the institutional systems but showed instead that coordinated market economies stay closer to their own industrial structure when diversifying in new industries, in contrast to liberal market economies whose institutions give them more freedom to make jumps in their industrial evolution.

There is also an implicit implication in the Varieties of Capitalism literature that policies should reflect the institutional complementarities in a country, but this has remained understudied. This has been taken up by the policy mix literature (Howlett and Rayner 2007; Uyarra 2010; Howlett et al. 2017), which claims that policies are not developed in isolation but in the context of pre-existing policies. Most research done on policy mixes has adopted case study approaches, so there is little comparative work to date. There is also a tendency to follow a functional, normative approach, in which the 'right' set of policies is pre-defined, instead of following an approach in which revealed policy mixes made in practice are examined. Finally, the nexus between institutions and policies, in terms of complementarities between the two, remains rather underdeveloped.

11.3 Towards an Institutional Relatedness Approach to Institutions

One way to address these critiques on the Varieties of Capitalism literature is to adopt a data-driven approach to institutional complementarities that enables a comparison of all countries and regions in the world. This would mean that the research focus shifts to what territories do in practice rather than what we expect them to do based on theoretical assumptions. This approach enables us to address research questions, like which territories make similar combinations, do territories in the same institutional group perform in a similar way, and do territories that make rare combinations reflect tensions/inefficiencies in their institutional structures, and does that make them underperform economically.

We propose a data-driven approach to institutional complementarities that follows the methodology of the product space (Hidalgo et al. 2007). The product space concept has been developed to explain in which new export products countries specialise. The core claim is that countries specialise in new export products that build on their own capabilities, as represented by their existing set of export products. Countries cannot just specialise in any new product, but they are constrained by their existing set of capabilities. This requires a uniform method to determine which export products require similar capabilities. The product space concept makes use of co-occurrence analysis of export products in export portfolios of countries. It calculates how often countries have a comparative advantage (CA) in two export products simultaneously. A country has a CA when the share of a product in its exports is larger than the share of that product in world exports. If two export products co-occur frequently in the export portfolios of many countries, the two export products are assumed to demand similar capability requirements.

The calculation of relatedness between export products is done in a few steps. The first step is to calculate the probability of having a CA in product *i* by dividing the number of countries that have a CA in product *i* by the number of countries in the sample. The second step is to determine the joint probability of having a CA in product *i* and product *j*, dividing the number of countries that have a CA in product *i* and in product *j* by the number of countries in the sample. The third step is to calculate the probability of having a CA in product *i* conditional on having a CA in product *j*. Conditional probability is determined by dividing the joint probability of having a CA in export product *i* and export product *j* by the probability of having a CA in export product *j*. Doing the same steps, we also determined the probability of having a CA in export product *j* conditional on having a CA in export product *i*. Hence, for each pair of products (*i*, *j*), two conditional probabilities are measured: the probability of having a CA in product *i* conditional on having a CA in product *j*, and the probability of having a CA in product *j*, conditional on having a CA in product *i*. The relatedness is equal to the lowest value of the two conditional probabilities.

Formally, the relatedness (ϕ) of export products *i* and *j* at year *t* is defined as:

$$\phi_{ijt} = \min \left\{ P\left(x_{i,t} | x_{j,t}\right), P(x_{j,t} | x_{i,t}) \right\}$$

where $P(xi,t|xj,t)$ is the conditional probability of having a CA in product *i*, given that the country has a CA in product *j*, and $P(xj,t|xi,t)$ is the conditional probability of having a CA in product *j*, given that the country has a CA in product *i*.

This information is used to build a network of export products (product space) in which each node stands for an export product, and a link between two nodes represents their degree of relatedness based on their frequency of co-occurrence in the export portfolios of countries. In Hidalgo et al. (2007), the product space is used to predict in which new export products a country is more likely to diversify and build a comparative advantage.

To apply it to institutions and policies, we propose a co-occurrence analysis of country portfolios of institutions and policies. This will reveal which institutions and which policies are more often combined and will measure the relatedness between institutions and between policies based on the co-occurrence of institutions in the institutional profiles of countries and the co-occurrence of policies in the policy profiles of countries. Such a continuous variable of institutional and policy relatedness measures the degree of relatedness between any pair of institutions and between any pair of policies or policy instruments. Doing so, we can derive a network measure of institutional and policy relatedness that represents an 'institutional space' and a 'policy space', respectively, in which each node stands for an institution/policy, and each link between two nodes signals the degree of institutional and policy relatedness. The next step is to interpret the observed patterns of this data-driven approach: do the combined institutions make sense in the institutional space, do they represent a system that is interpretable or are they separate dimensions that just co-occur but to which no specific meaning can be attached?

Such a revealed institutional and policy relatedness indicator can systematically tackle a number of research questions: (1) which institutions and which policies are complementary to each other; (2) which territories make similar institutional and similar policy combinations; (3) what is the opportunity set of each territory in terms of institutional and policy changes. This framework is instrumental in determining for each territory the range of options a territory has to implement institutional change and policy change. We follow the principle of relatedness (Boschma 2017; Hidalgo et al. 2018) and argue that the more related an institution or policy is to the existing set of institutions or policy mix in a territory, the more likely this (new) institution or (new) policy is likely to emerge and become successful; (4) how coherent is the set of institutions and policy mixes that territories make in practice. This degree of coherence in a territory is based on how common these combinations are, as inspired by studies on the cohesion of technological portfolios inside firms or territories (Teece et al. 1994; Fleming 2001; Antonelli et al. 2010); (5) does a coherent set of institutions and policy mix in territories affect outcome indicators like economic performance, social well-being and environmental sustainability.

11.4 Fields of Application in Economic Geography

This section explores how the notion of institutional relatedness can be applied to three key topics in the field of economic geography. Section 11.4.1 discusses how regional diversification can be facilitated by institutional relatedness. Section 11.4.2 discusses how institutional change that is needed for structural change is facilitated or hindered by existing institutions in a region. Section 11.4.3 explores the role of policy mixes to enable structural change and to make regional innovation policy in the EU more effective.

11.4.1 Institutions and Regional Diversification

The literature on regional diversification has developed new insights into how territories diversify into new activities and develop new growth paths (Boschma 2017). A key claim is that territories are likely to develop new activities that require capabilities that are related to the capabilities of existing activities (Hidalgo et al. 2007, 2018; Neffke et al. 2011a). In other words, the local industrial structure makes the emergence of some but not all industries more feasible, depending on whether they are related to other local industries.

Many types of capabilities can affect the diversification process, such as specific knowledge, skills and institutions. Most often, studies refer to capabilities in technologies, industries and occupations in terms of knowledge and skills (Neffke et al. 2011a; Boschma et al. 2015). What is often missing is a full account of the role of institutions in regional diversification. In recent years, scholars (e.g., Boschma and Capone 2015; Cortinovis et al. 2017; Menzel and Kammer 2019) have taken the first step to address this issue. Boschma and Capone (2015) tested whether (formal) institutions matter for the type of diversification that prevails in countries. Inspired by Hall and Soskice (2001), they found institutions that regulate less tightly labour, capital and product markets give countries more freedom to diversify in less related activities. Cortinovis et al. (2017) found that bonding social capital and low quality of government turned out to have a negative impact on diversification in European regions.

However, what these studies did not investigate is whether different activities require similar institutions and, if so, whether this may explain diversification. While institutions may be sector-specific, in which each sector is embedded in a particular set of institutions (Malerba 2002), sectors might also have institutions in common with other sectors. This implies that a sector is more likely to be developed if it shares similar institutional requirements with other sectors that are already present in the region.

Carvalho and Vale (2018) were the first to work with the concept of institutional relatedness across sectors and apply it to the topic of regional diversification. They claimed that "the degree to which institutions associated with certain industries or activities can be transposed to provide resources and legitimacy to new industries may provide new avenues to understand path creation ..." (p. 291).[2] Following Boxenbaum and Battilana (2005), Padgett and McLean (2006) and Padgett and Powell (2012), Carvalho and Vale (2018) build on the concept of institutional transposition in which institutions new to a field are transposed from another field. In this way, institutional relatedness is proposed as an alternative explanation for regional diversification, besides technological or skill-relatedness. The study explains the development of a biotechnology path in the Portuguese region of Centro due to the local presence of institutional norms and practices that are associated with a local tradition of

[2] These papers build on the notion of institutional relatedness in management studies that examine diversification in firms (Peng et al. 2005; Dhandapani and Basant 2009). These works argue that besides product relatedness, institutional relatedness might be considered important. Institutional relatedness refers to the informal linkages an organisation has with institutions that confer resources and legitimacy (Peng et al. 2005), such as political ties and the international experience of CEOs (Sun et al. 2017).

commercialisation of academic research, knowledge transfer routines between universities and companies, and informal and relational arrangements.

Other studies applied a similar idea of institutional transposition. A study on institutional relatedness at the regional scale by Skog and Solvell (2020) looked at the transposition of trading institutions in Bordeaux in the eighteenth and nineteenth centuries. Skog and Solvell (2020) found that key trading institutions like business practices defining product quality, product classes and how prices were set were quite similar between slave trade and fine wine trade, which enabled a smooth transposition of institutions between the two fields in Bordeaux and a successful transition of trade from slaves into fine wine. Punt et al. (2022) also made use of the concept of institutional relatedness to explain the rise of renewable energy cooperatives as a new organisational form in German districts. This organisational innovation could emerge because it could build on the organisational knowledge and legitimacy spillovers from cooperatives in other industries in the region. This local institutional context, as embodied in the presence of cooperatives in other industries, provided less resistance and was perceived as perfectly legitimate. Mäkitie et al. (2019) studied different forms of relatedness between the oil and gas industry and offshore wind power technology. They found that low institutional relatedness challenged the resource redeployment for the Norwegian oil and gas industry to offshore wind power.

These studies on institutional relatedness have shed new light on the role of institutions in regional diversification. They focus on specific cases but do not adopt a systematic institutional view that accounts for the degree of institutional relatedness across all sectors and how that affects diversification in regions in general. They also do not examine the role of policies in terms of policy mixes. Moreover, they tend to employ a rather static perspective in which institutional change is not a key topic of concern.

11.4.2 Institutions and Institutional Change

It is well-known that new economic activities can only develop fully when new institutions are created or existing ones are transformed or abolished (Nelson 1994; Murmann 2003; Boschma and Frenken 2006). Institutions need to be constructed to enable their emergence, as existing institutions are unlikely to match their requirements and may even contest their development (MacKinnon et al. 2009; Dawley et al. 2015). This is well understood in the transition literature, showing that the institutional logic of an entrenched techno-economic system can block the green transition (Coenen et al. 2010; Smith and Stirling 2010).

Agents of change are considered to play a key role in breaking such path dependency and resistance. This role of agency, or what has been termed bricolage (Garud and Karnøe 2003; Boschma et al. 2017; Carvalho and Vale 2018), to create their own conditions of growth is associated with a mismatch between the needs of new activities and the prevailing cognitive and institutional environment in which new path creation unfolds (Storper and Walker 1989; Boschma 1997). The literature on institutional entrepreneurship (Garud et al. 2002; Maguire et al. 2004; Battilana et al. 2009) focuses attention on how institutional agents engage in collective action to mobilise resources and public opinion in order to build legitimacy and institutions that support new path creation (Strambach 2010; Sotarauta and Pulkkinen 2011; Sotarauta et al. 2012; Dawley et al. 2015).

However, if agency is deemed crucial to induce institutional change, is this more likely to happen in some regional institutional settings? The possibility of institutional adaptability may be higher in regions with a wide range of different activities. In such a context, it may be harder for activities or powerful players to monopolise and dominate the design of institutions (Neffke et al. 2011b). So, diversified regions may be in a better position to make institutional changes to support new path creation because there is redundant institutional capacity (Grabher 1993) and less opposition from vested players. This has a resemblance to what Hollingsworth (2009) calls a weak institutional environment, which allows for greater variation in organisations and the occurrence of radical innovations.

However, in diversified regions, there may be a lack of institutional cohesion with too many interests that may harm institutional focus, coordination and control. A fragmented institutional structure in a region may be more responsive to experimentation and newcomers, but creative actions might remain unnoticed and isolated, as new institutions have to be built from scratch, and local public support is hard to get when there are many competing local claims. Boschma (2015) proposed the notion of a loosely coherent institutional structure that comes close to the idea of institutional relatedness. It concerns an institutional constellation that supports multiple activities and facilitates institutional change to enable the development of new activities. In this institution-building process, the new institutions can build on and expand within the overarching institutional set-up with whom they share similar institutional requirements.

In other words, some activities have complementarities in institutional terms. That is, they have similar, though not identical, institutional requirements. Regions with such institutional overlap might be better equipped to make new combinations between activities. The overarching institutional framework is also not fundamentally challenged but can be exploited to accommodate the institutional demands of new activities. In other words, new institutions are not built from scratch but draw on existing institutions, and there is more likely to be little local resistance to such types of institutional change.

This implies that institutional change unfolds in a context alongside existing structures where history matters. Taxonomies of institutional change have been proposed that account for this, such as institutional layering and conversion (Thelen 2003; Streeck and Thelen 2005; Martin 2010). Although institutions may be replaced by new ones (Mahoney and Thelen 2010), new path creation does not necessarily mean that territories break with their institutional past. Ebbinghaus (2009) defines path departure as a partial renewal of current institutions in which its underlying core principles are not fundamentally challenged. Strambach (2010) proposed the notion of institutional plasticity to state that an institutional system has a range of options for new path creation within the dominant institutional framework. Agents can deviate from the established path by creating institutions but not breaking with the institutional system (Strambach and Klement 2012).

However, we still have little understanding of why some territories can make the required institutional change while other territories fail to do so. To account for institutional relatedness might contribute to a better understanding of why territories differ in their ability to induce institutional change and why they might be able to diversify in some activities while not in others. Existing institutional legacies may set sharp limits to the type and direction of institutional change. This makes the creation of some institutions more feasible, depending on whether they are coherent with the existing set of institutions (Amable 2000). We expect that regional branching is facilitated when new industries require institutions similar to those of other related industries in the region, so new institutions do not have to build from scratch, and this new institution-building will not be contested by (local) agents. Such a comprehensive approach to institutional relatedness assesses the effect of institutional change on new path creation, comparing many cases simultaneously. This would complement case study research on institutional change that has been predominant (e.g., Gertler 2005; Bathelt and Gluckler 2014; Fuenfschilling and Truffer 2014).

11.4.3 Institutions and Policy Mixes

Institutional change also requires policy interventions in a wide range of fields. Policies do not take place in a vacuum but unfold in institutional contexts. Existing institutions affect the ability of countries and regions to implement institutional change and adopt successful policies. Studies have shown that peripheral regions in Europe suffer from institutional weaknesses that limit the effectiveness of policy (Karo and Kattel 2015; McCann and Ortega-Argilés 2015; Rodríguez-Pose and Wilkie 2015; Morgan 2015; Boschma 2023), such as weak administrative capacity, poor collaboration culture, closed networks between vested players and low quality of government (Rodríguez-Pose and Di Cataldo 2015). This implies policies should adapt to the specific needs of territories and be aligned to the specific institutional context in which they are implemented.

But, it is not only about aligning policies to the institutional context. It is also about constructing a coherent set of policies or policy mixes that support each other (Crouch 2005; Flanagan et al. 2010; Jessop 2011). Uyarra (2010) underlined the importance of studying the dynamics of policies in such a policy context as follows: "interactions happen across policy domains, between instruments, across levels of governance and also across time ... These interactions are dynamic and path-dependent, for policies are not adopted on a tabula rasa, but in a context of pre-existing policy mixes and institutional frameworks which have been shaped through successive policy changes. Past policy decisions would constrain the range of options available for current decision-makers... Thus, while formulating policies, regions need not only take the knowledge and institutional base of the region as starting point, but also consider existing policy mixes and past policy history, for they will enable or constrain new policy goals" (p. 132).

So, the past conditions the range of options available to policymakers (Lambooy and Boschma 2001). There are constraints dictated by the institutional context and the mix of policies implemented in the past. As territories accumulate different sets of policies and institutions over time, there will be no room for a 'one-size-fits-all' policy. A change in policy can only become effective when it matches the institutional system and the current policy setting. There are limits to policy learning across countries that have little in common in terms of institutions and policy practices. Institutional learning across territories is more feasible and effective when they share institutional complementarities. Accordingly, 'one-size-fits-all' policies might make sense in territories that share similar institutional contexts but not in territories with little institutional proximity.

Current studies have drawn little attention to these challenges. Our framework on institutional relatedness proposed in Sect. 11.3 may be instrumental in taking up these challenges, as it has the potential to determine the degree of relatedness between institutions, between policies, and between institutions and policies. In other words, it has the potential to assess systematically whether there is a good or bad fit between policies and the institutional context in which they are implemented and which policies can be considered complementary and thus may effectively support each other. Applying this to the question of the effectiveness of regional innovation policy might give us a tool to develop a better understanding of how to improve the Smart Specialization policy in the EU.

11.5 Conclusions

This chapter aimed to outline the literature on institutional complementarities that looks at institutions and policies from a system perspective. We critically reviewed the Varieties of Capitalism literature that has been influential in the last decades. It has generated valuable insights but has also been criticised for its lack of comprehensiveness (limited coverage of countries), its methodological nationalism (how about regional varieties?), its prime focus on functionalism (what about internal tensions?), its predefined nature (what about revealed relatedness?), its focus on descriptive case studies (what about large-scale systematic comparative studies?), its preoccupation with stability (what about transformations?), its limited validity concerning economic outcomes and its little concern with policy mixes. To date, few studies exist that systematically assess the range of policy options territories have at their disposal, what policy combinations territories make in practice, how one can assess what are good or bad policy mixes, how one can assess whether a policy change might work and become effective in a unifying policy mix framework, and how different combinations or mixes of policies impact performance.

We critically discussed a number of applications in economic geography. We argued that institutional relatedness may provide an alternative explanation for regional diversification than other forms of relatedness (knowledge, skills). However, there are no systematic comparative studies yet that assess what the diversification opportunity sets of territories are, given their institutions. The literature on institutional change has strongly argued that structural change requires the creation of new institutions and the restructuring of existing ones. However, there is still little understanding of why some territories might be more successful in doing so. The institutional relatedness framework has the potential to shed new light on the question of what is possible and what is not. Institutional relatedness may be an enabling factor to implement institutional change, also because one expects little local resistance to institutional change in territories where such institutional overlap across local activities exists. The literature on policy mix literature has signalled the importance of coherent sets of policies across policy domains (Matti et al. 2017). However, there is little systematic knowledge of what is a good or bad fit of policy mixes, what are feasible policy options in specific territories given their existing sets of policies, and what are the limits to institutional learning across territories. We expect institutional learning across territories to be more successful when institutional complementarities exist.

These research avenues require a quantitative methodology that can assess the revealed relatedness between institutions and between policies and that can define the opportunity sets of territories to implement institutional change and policy change given their existing sets of institutions and policy mixes. We follow the logic of the product space concept (Hidalgo et al. 2007) and apply it to institutions and policies. Doing co-occurrence analysis of country portfolios of institutions and policies enables us to identify which institutions and policies share similar features, to measure relatedness between institutions and between policies based on the co-occurrence of institutions in the institutional profiles of countries ('institutional space') and the co-occurrence of policies in the policy profiles of countries ('policy space'), and to assess whether the existing set of institutions and policies (at the national and regional level) in each country ('the institutional-policy space') makes it feasible or not to create new institutions and to design new effective policies.

References

Acemoglu, D., Akcigit, U. and Celik, M.A. (2014) Young, restless and creative: openness to disruption and creative innovations. In: PIER Working Paper No. 14-004. The Penn Institute for Economic Research, Philadelphia.

Acemoglu, D., S. Johnson and J.A. Robinson (2005) Institutions as a fundamental cause of long-run growth, *Handbook of Economic Growth*, vol. 1, part A, 385–472.

Akkermans, D., Castaldi, C. and Los, B. (2009) Do liberal market economies really innovate more radically than coordinated market economies? Hall and Soskice reconsidered. *Research Policy* 38, 181–191.

Allen, M. L. Funk and H. Tüselman (2006) Can variation in public policies account for differences in comparative advantage? *Journal of Public Policy* 26, 1–19.t

Amable, B. (2000) Institutional complementarity and diversity of social systems of innovation and production. *Rev. Int. Political Econ.* 7, 645–687.

Amable B. (2003) *The Diversity of Modern Capitalism.* Oxford: Oxford University Press.

Amable B. and S. Palombarini (2009) A neorealist approach to institutional change and the diversity of capitalism, *Socio Economic Review* 7, 123–143.

Antonelli, C., Kraft, J. and Quatraro, F. (2010) Recombinant knowledge and growth: the case of ICTs. *Structural Change and Economic Dynamics* 21 (1), 50–69.

Asheim, B.T. and Coenen, L. (2006) Contextualising regional innovation systems in a globalising learning economy: On knowledge bases and institutional frameworks. *Journal of Technology Transfer* 31, 163–173.

Bathelt, H. and M. Gertler (2009) The German variety of capitalism. Forces and dynamics of evolutionary change, *Economic Geography* 81 (1), 1–9.

Bathelt, H. and J. Gluckler (2014) Institutional change in economic geography, *Progress in Human Geography*, 38 (3), 340–363.

Battilana, J, Leca, B and Boxenbaum, E (2009) How actors change institutions: Towards a theory of institutional entrepreneurship, *The Academy of Management Annals* 3, 65–107.

Bizberg, I. (2014) Types of capitalism in Latin America. *Revue Interventions économiques* 49, 1–31.

Boschma, R. (1997) New industries and windows of locational opportunity. A long-term analysis of Belgium. *Erdkunde* 51, 12–22.

Boschma, R. (2015) Towards an evolutionary perspective on regional resilience, *Regional Studies* 49 (5), 733–751.

Boschma, R. A. (2017) Relatedness as driver behind regional diversification: A research agenda, *Regional Studies* 51 (3), 351–364.

Boschma, R. (2023), Evolutionary Economic Geography and policy, in: Dopfer, K., R.R. Nelson, J. Potts and A. Pyka (eds.), Routledge Book of Evolutionary Economics, Routledge, Chapter 25, pp. 332–340.

Boschma, R. and G. Capone (2015) Institutions and diversification: related versus unrelated diversification in a varieties of capitalism framework, *Research Policy* 44, 1902–1914.

Boschma, R., P.A. Balland and D.F. Kogler (2015) Relatedness and technological change in cities: the rise and fall of technological knowledge in U.S. metropolitan areas from 1981 to 2010, *Industrial and Corporate Change* 24 (1), 223–250.

Boschma, R., L. Coenen, K. Frenken and B. Truffer (2017) Towards a theory of regional diversification: combining insights from evolutionary economic geography and transition studies, *Regional Studies* 51 (1), 31–45.

Boschma, R.A. and K. Frenken (2006) Why is economic geography not an evolutionary science? Towards an evolutionary economic geography, *Journal of Economic Geography* 6 (3), 273–302.

Boxenbaum, E., and Battilana, J. (2005) Importation as innovation: transposing managerial practices across fields. *Strategic Organization* 3, 355–383.

Boyer, R. (1988) Formalizing Growth Regimes. In Dosi G., Freeman C., Nelson R., Silverberg G. and Soete L. (eds.) *Technical change and economic theory*, London: Pinter, pp. 251–283.

Carvalho, L. and M. Vale (2018) Biotech by bricolage? Agency, institutional relatedness and new path development in peripheral regions, *Cambridge Journal of Regions, Economy and Society* 11 (2), 275–295.

Coenen, L., Raven, R. and Verbong, G. (2010) Local niche experimentation in energy transitions: A theoretical and empirical exploration of proximity advantages and disadvantages. *Technology in Society* 32, 295–302.

Cortinovis, N, Xiao, J, Boschma, R & van Oort, F, (2017), Quality of government and social capital as drivers of regional diversification in Europe, *Journal of Economic Geography*, 17(6), 1179–1208.

Crouch, C. (2005) *Capitalist diversity and change. Recombinant governance and institutional entrepreneurs*, Oxford: Oxford University Press.

Dawley, S., MacKinnon, D., Cumbers, A., and Pike, A. (2015) Policy activism and regional path creation: the promotion of offshore wind in North East England and Scotland, *Cambridge Journal of Regions, Economy and Society* 8, 257–272.

Deeg, R. and Jackson, G. (2007) Towards a more dynamic theory of capitalist diversity. *Socio-Economic Review* 5, 149–180.

Dhandapani, K. and R. Basant (2009) Measuring institutional relatedness, W.P. No. 2009-05-02, Ahmedabad: Indian Institute of Management.

Ebbinghaus B. (2009) Can path dependence explain institutional change? Two approaches applied to welfare state reform, in Magnusson, L. and Ottosson J. (Eds) *The Evolution of Path Dependence*, Cheltenham: Edward Elgar, pp. 191–218.

Flanagan, K., E. Uyarra and M. Laranja (2010), 'The Policy Mix' for Innovation: Re-thinking Innovation Policy in a Multi-level, Multi-actor Context, Manchester Institute of Innovation Research Working Paper Series, University of Manchester.

Fleming, L. (2001) Recombinant uncertainty in technological search. *Management Science* 47(1), 117–132.

Fuenfschilling, L. and Truffer, B. (2014) The structuration of socio-technical regimes – Conceptual foundations from institutional theory. *Research Policy* 43 (4), 772–791.

Garud, R., Jain, S. and Kumaraswamy, A (2002) Institutional entrepreneurship in the sponsorship of common technological standards: The case of Sun Microsystems and Java, *Academy of Management Journal* 45 (1), 196–214.

Garud, R., and Karnøe, P. (2003) Bricolage versus breakthrough: Distributed and embedded agency in technology entrepreneurship. *Research Policy* 32 (2), 277–300.

Geffen, D.A., and Kenyon, T., (2006) Heinz capitalism: how many varieties are there? An empirical reexamination of coordination mechanisms in advanced market economies. Available at SSRN: http://ssrn.com/abstract=1005407Gertler

Gertler, M.S. (2005) Economic and political determinants of regional investment and technical change in Canada, *Papers in Regional Science* 62 (1), 27–43.

Gertler, M. (2010) Rules of the game: the place of institutions in regional economic change, *Regional Studies* 44, 1–15.

Grabher G. (1993) The weakness of strong ties: the lock-in of regional development in the Ruhr area, in Grabher G. (Ed.) *The Embedded Firm*, London: Routledge, pp. 255–277.

Hall, P.A. (2018) Varieties of capitalism in light of the euro crisis, *Journal of European Public Policy* 25 (1), 7–30.

Hall, P.A. and D.W. Gingerich (2009) Varieties of capitalism and institutional complementarities in the political economy: an empirical analysis. *British Journal of Political Science* 39, 449–482.

Hall, P. and D. Soskice (2001) *Varieties of Capitalism: The Institutional Foundations of Comparative Advantage*. Oxford: Oxford University Press.

Hall, P.A. and K. Thelen (2009) Institutional change in varieties of capitalism, *Socio-Economic Review* 7, 7–34.

Hancké, B., Rhodes, M. and Thatcher, M. (2007) *Beyond Varieties of Capitalism: Conflict, Contradictions, and Complementarities in the European Economy*. Oxford: Oxford University Press.

Hay, C. (2020) Does capitalism (still) come in varieties? *Review of International Political Economy* 27 (2), 302–319.

Hidalgo, C., Balland, P.A., Boschma, R., Delgado, M., Feldman, M., Frenken, K., Glaeser, E., He, C., Kogler, D., Morrison, A., Neffke, F., Rigby, D., Stern, S.,

Zheng, S., and Zhu, S. (2018) *The principle of relatedness*, Springer Proceedings in Complexity, 451–457.
Hidalgo, C. A., Klinger, B., Barabasi, A. L. and Hausmann, R. (2007) The product space conditions the development of nations. *Science* 317, 482–487.
Hofstede, G. ([1980]2001) *Culture's consequences: Comparing values, behaviors, institutions, and organisations across nations*. Thousand Oaks, CA: Sage.
Hollingsworth, J.R. (2000) Doing institutional analysis: implications for the study of innovations, *Review of International Political Economy* 7, 595–644.
Hollingsworth, R. (2009) The role of institutions and organisations in shaping radical scientific innovations. In: Magnusson, L., Ottosson, J. (Eds.), *The Evolution of Path Dependence*. Edward Elgar, Cheltenham, pp. 139–165.
Howlett, M. and Rayner, J. (2007) Design principles for policy mixes: Cohesion and coherence in 'new governance arrangements'. *Policy and Society* 26 (4), 1–18.
Howlett, M., Vince, J. and Del Rio, P. (2017) Policy integration and multilevel governance: Dealing with the vertical dimension of policy mix designs. *Politics and Governance* 5 (2), 69–78.
Jackson, G. and Deeg, R. (2008) From comparing capitalisms to the politics of institutional change. *Review of International Political Economy* 15, 680–709.
Jessop, B. (2011) Rethinking the diversity and varieties of capitalism: on variegated capitalism, and the world market, in: G. Wood and C. Lane (eds.) *Capitalist diversity and diversity within capitalism*, London: Routledge, pp. 209–237.
Johnston, A. and A. Regan (2018) Introduction: Is the European Union Capable of Integrating Diverse Models of Capitalism? *New Political Economy* 23 (2), 145–159.
Kaasa, A., Vadi, M., Varblane, U. (2014) Regional Cultural Differences Within European Countries: Evidence from Multi-Country Surveys. *Management International Review*, 54(6): 825–852.
Karo, E. and Kattel, R. (2015) Economic development and evolving state capacities in Central and Eastern Europe: can 'smart specialisation' make a difference? *Journal of Economic Policy Reform* 18 (2), 172–187.
Kenworthy, L. (2006) Institutional Coherence and Macroeconomic Performance, *Socio-Economic Review* 4, 69–91.
Lambooy, J.G. and R.A. Boschma (2001) Evolutionary economics and regional policy, *Annals of Regional Science* 35 (1), 113–133.
MacKinnon, D., Cumbers, A., Pike, A., Birch, K., and McMaster, R. (2009) Evolution in economic geography: institutions, political economy, and adaptation, *Economic Geography* 85, 129–150.
Maguire, S., C. Hardy and T.B. Lawrence (2004) Institutional Entrepreneurship in Emerging Fields: HIV/AIDS Treatment Advocacy in Canada, *The Academy of Management Journal* 47 (5), 657–679.

Mahoney, J. and Thelen, K. (2010) A theory of gradual institutional change, in Mahoney, J. and Thelen, K. (eds.) *Explaining institutional change: Ambiguity, agency, and power.* Cambridge: Cambridge University Press. 1–37.

Mäkitie, T., A.D. Andersen and J. Hanson (2019) Multidimensional relatedness between innovation systems in sustainability transitions, Papers in Evolutionary Economic Geography, no. 19.26, Utrecht.

Malerba, F (2002) Sectoral systems of innovation and production. *Research Policy* 31, 247–264.

Martin R. (2010) Roepke Lecture in Economic Geography: Rethinking regional path dependence. Beyond lock-in to evolution, *Economic Geography* 86, 1–27.

Matti, C., Consoli, D. and Uyarra, E. (2017) Multi level policy mixes and industry emergence: The case of wind energy in Spain. *Environment and Planning C: Politics and Space* 35 (4), 661–683.

McCann, P. and Ortega-Argilés, R. (2015) Smart specialisation, regional growth and applications to European Union Cohesion Policy. *Regional Studies* 49 (8), 1291–1302.

Meelen, T., (2013) A Dynamic Analysis of the Comparative Advantage of Coordinated and Liberal Market Economies. Utrecht University, Utrecht. Research Policy

Menzel, M.P and J. Kammer (2019) Industry evolution in Varieties of Capitalism: a comparison of the Danish and US wind turbine industries, *Industrial and Corporate Change* 28 (6), 1381–1403.

Morgan, K. (2015) Smart specialisation: Opportunities and challenges for regional innovation policy. *Regional Studies* 49 (3), 480–482.

Murmann J. P. (2003) *Knowledge and Competitive Advantage. The Co-Evolution of Firms, Technology and National Institutions*, Cambridge: Cambridge University Press.

Neffke, F., Henning, M., and R. Boschma (2011a) How do regions diversify over time? Industry relatedness and the development of new growth paths in regions. *Economic Geography* 87 (3), 237–265.

Neffke, F., Henning M., Boschma R. A., Lundquist K. J. and Olander L. O. (2011b) The dynamics of agglomeration externalities along the life cycle of industries, *Regional Studies* 45, 49–65.

Nelson, R. R. (ed.) (1993) *National Innovation Systems – A Comparative Analysis.* Oxford: Oxford University Press.

Nelson R. R. (1994) The co-evolution of technology, industrial structure, and supporting institutions, *Industrial and Corporate Change* 3, 47–63.

North, D.C. (1990) *Institutions, institutional change, and economic performance*, New York: Cambridge University Press.

Padgett, J. F. and McLean, P. D. (2006) Organisational invention and elite transformation: the birth of partnership systems in Renaissance Florence. *American Journal of Sociology*, 111, 1463–1568.

Padgett, J. F. and Powell, W. W. (2012) The problem of emergence. In J. F. Padgett and W.W. Powell (eds). *The Emergence of Organizations and Markets*, Princeton: Princeton University Press, pp. 1–29.
Peck, J. and Theodore, N. (2007) Variegated capitalism. *Progress in Human Geography* 31, 731–772.
Peng, M.W., S.H. Lee and D. Y. L. Wang (2005) What determines the scope of the firm over time? A focus on institutional relatedness, *Academy of Management Review* 30, 3.
Punt, M.B., T. Bauwens, K. Frenken and L. Holstenkamp (2022) Institutional relatedness and the emergence of renewable energy cooperatives in German districts, *Regional Studies*, 56 (4), 548–562.
Riedel, R. and J. Anusik (2024) *Varieties of Capitalism and the Political Economy of Differentiated Integration in Europe*, New Horizons in European Politics series, Cheltenham: Edward Elgar.
Rodríguez-Pose, A. and Di Cataldo, M. (2015) Quality of government and innovative performance in the regions of Europe. *Journal of Economic Geography* 15 (4), 673–706.
Rodríguez-Pose, A. and Wilkie, C. (2015) Institutions and the entrepreneurial discovery process for smart specialisation (Papers in Evolutionary Economic Geography No. 15.23). Utrecht: Utrecht University.
Schedelik, A. Nölke, D. Mertens and C. May (2021) Comparative capitalism, growth models and emerging markets: The development of the field, *New Political Economy* 26 (4), 514–526.
Schneider, M. R. and Paunescu, M. (2012) Changing varieties of capitalism and revealed comparative advantages from 1990 to 2005: a test of the Hall and Soskice claims, *Socio-Economic Review* 10 (4), 731–753.
Skog, A. and O. Solvell (2020) The dark side of agglomeration, sustained wealth and transposition of trading institutions—the case of Bordeaux in the 18th and 19th centuries, *Journal of Economic Geography* 20, 67–91.
Smith, A., and A. Stirling (2010) The politics of social-ecological resilience and sustainable socio-technical transitions. *Ecology and Society* 15 (1), 11, http://www.ecologyandsociety.org/vol15/iss1/art11/
Sotarauta, M., L. Horlings and J. Liddle. (Eds) (2012) *Leadership and Change in Sustainable Regional Development*. Routledge, Abingdon.
Sotarauta, M. and Pulkkinen, R. (2011) Institutional entrepreneurship for knowledge regions: In search of a fresh set of questions for regional innovation studies, *Environment and Planning C* 29, 96–112.
Storper, M. and Walker, R. (1989) *The Capitalist Imperative: Territory, Technology and Industrial Growth*, New York: Basil Blackwell.
Strambach, S. (2010) Path dependence and path plasticity: the co-evolution of institutions and innovation–the German customised business software industry,

in Boschma, R. A. and Martin R. (eds.) *The Handbook of Evolutionary Economic Geography*. Cheltenham: Edward Elgar.
Strambach S. and Klement B. (2012) Cumulative and combinatorial micro-dynamics of knowledge. The role of space and place in knowledge integration, *European Planning Studies* 20, 1843–1866.
Streeck, W. and K. Thelen (eds.) (2005) *Beyond continuity: Institutional change in advanced political economies*, Oxford: Oxford University Press.
Sun, S.L., M. W. Peng and W. Tan (2017) Institutional relatedness behind product diversification and international diversification, *Asia Pacific Journal Management*, 34, 339–366.
Taylor, M.Z. (2004) Empirical Evidence Against Variety of Capitalism's Theory of Technological Innovation, *International Organization* 58, 601–31.
Teece, D.J., Rumelt, R., Dosi, G. and Winter, S. (1994) Understanding corporate coherence: theory and evidence. *Journal of Economic Behavior and Organisation* 23, 1–30.
Thelen K. (2003) How institutions evolve, in Mahoney, J. and Rueschemeyer, D. (Eds) *Comparative Historical Analysis in the Social Sciences*, Cambridge: Cambridge University Press, pp. 208–240.
Uyarra, E. (2010) What is evolutionary about 'regional systems of innovation'? Implications for regional policy, *Journal of Evolutionary Economics* 20, 115–137.
Whitley, R. (1999) *Divergent capitalisms*, Oxford: Oxford University Press.

CHAPTER 12

The Golden Age of Central and Eastern Europe: How to Keep It Going?

Marcin Piatkowski

12.1 Introduction

The eleven post-socialist new EU member states, hereafter referred to as the EU-11, have achieved a remarkable economic success over the past 30 years, during which, on average, they have more than doubled their income per capita. While there is quantitative and qualitative heterogeneity among the EU-11 in terms of their developmental outcomes, in general, the EU-11's levels of income, quality of life and happiness are now the highest on record, both in absolute terms and relative to Western Europe, the region's benchmark. EU members from Central and Eastern Europe have entered their economic Golden Age.

The findings, interpretations, and conclusions expressed in this chapter do not reflect the views of the World Bank, the Executive Directors of the World Bank, or the governments they represent.

M. Piatkowski (✉)
Kozminski University, Warsaw, Poland

World Bank, New Delhi, India
e-mail: mpiatkowski@kozminski.edu.pl

I. P. Székely, P. Halmai (eds.), *The Future of European Integration*, Studies in Economic Transition,
https://doi.org/10.1007/978-3-032-20186-7_12

Income convergence is projected to continue at least until the end of the decade, driven by, inter alia, a positive balance between the quality of human capital and costs of labor, macroeconomic stability, and the inflows of FDI due to the ongoing restructuring of the global value chains, which benefits most of the economies in the region. However, after 2030, the region's potential growth is likely to decline, driven by the accelerating negative impacts of population aging, decreasing space for technology absorption, and increasing competition from emerging markets. The European Commission (2024) projects that the region's average growth rate in the 2030s will decline to around 2 percent per year and income convergence will slow to a crawl. The region might come close to the EU income average but then never exceed it.

What should the EU-11 countries do to ensure that the fast pace of convergence continues until 2040 and that the whole region reaches and exceeds the EU-27 average income?

The first section of this chapter discusses the growth performance of the EU-11 so far; the second section discusses medium- and long-term growth projections relative to Western Europe; the third section examines the need for adjusting the region's growth model and offers policy recommendations. The final section provides concluding remarks and observations.

12.2 The Golden Age of Central and Eastern Europe

After centuries of economic decline and languishment on the European and global economic periphery (Piatkowski 2018) and following a bruising post-communist transition (Kolodko 2000), all EU-11 countries have entered their economic Golden Age, defined as the shortest distance to Western Europe in terms of the levels of income. Since 1820, the beginning of the Industrial Revolution (and the beginning of the available set of data), EU-11 have now achieved the highest levels of income relative to the West, proxied by the UK (Fig. 12.1). GDP per capita of Poland, for instance, which has stagnated at around one-third of the UK level of income PPP for most of the last 200 years, has skyrocketed to 85 percent in 2023.

The distance to Western Europe estimated by the actual individual consumption (AIC) which measures material welfare of households regardless

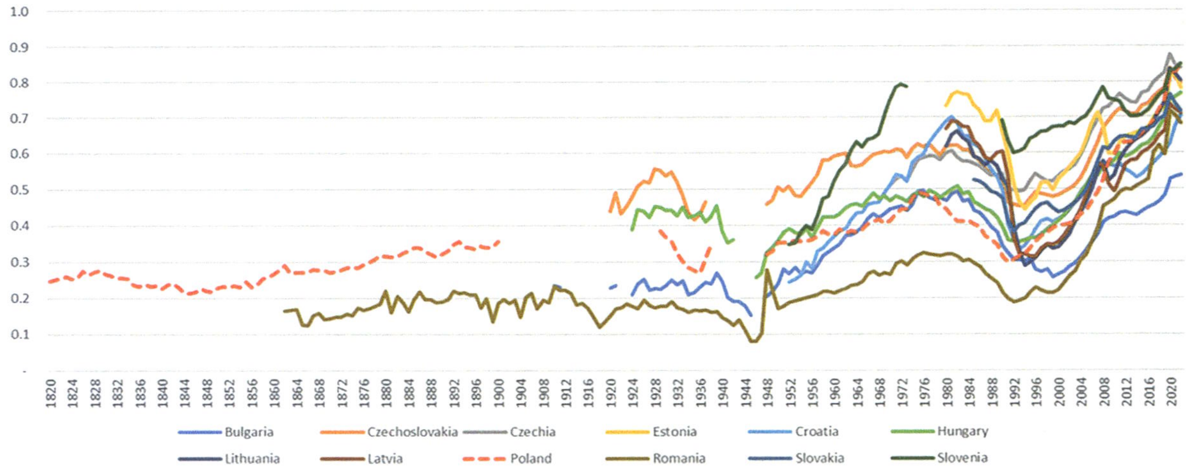

Fig. 12.1 GDP per capita of EU-11 countries vs. UK=1, 1820–2020, 2011 constant prices. Note: removed data for Slovenia for 1974–80, which showed levels of income higher than the UK, which is likely not credible. (Source: Author's own calculations based on Maddison Project 2023 database)

of whether their consumption was paid for by households directly, by government, or by nonprofit organizations, is even smaller.[1] Richer EU-11 countries such as Czechia, Slovenia, and Lithuania, have already overtaken Greece, Portugal, and Spain and will soon catch up with Italy.

In terms of the quality of life, EU-11 is even closer to Western Europe than in terms of income alone. Based on a well-justified assertion that "there is more to life than the cold numbers of GDP and economic statistics", the OECD has developed a Better Life Index, which compares quality of life across the OECD member countries based on 11 variables, including availability of housing, work-life balance, safety, and life satisfaction.[2] The OECD ranking shows that the quality of life among EU-11 countries that belong to the OECD—Estonia, Slovenia, Czechia, Poland, Slovakia, Lithuania, Latvia and Hungary—is higher than what would be suggested by their level of income.

Finally, EU-11 countries are the happiest ever, both in absolute and in relative terms.[3] According to the 2024 World Happiness Report, life satisfaction in Czechia, Slovenia, and Poland, was higher, than in, for instance, the UK and USA, while Romania, Estonia, Latvia, and Slovakia were not far behind. Only Bulgaria lagged its peers, mostly due to a lower level of income than elsewhere (Fig. 12.2).

What were the drivers on such an impressive convergence? As argued by Piatkowski (2018), the region's success was broadly driven by, inter alia, post-transition structural reforms, improvements in the quality of human capital—tertiary scholarization ratio in the region increased by more than three times since 1990—and generally prudent macroeconomic policy. Above all, however, the region's economic success would not have happened without the EU accession, which helped build institutions, opened the borders for investment, labor and trade, and supported growth through cohesion and structural funds. One study estimates that thanks to the EU, the GDP of eight EU member states from the region is on average almost one-third higher than in the non-EU accession scenario (Polish

[1] https://ec.europa.eu/eurostat/web/products-eurostat-news/w/ddn-20250618-1, accessed January 5, 2026.

[2] https://www.oecdbetterlifeindex.org/#/11111111111

[3] Although there are methodological limits to the happiness rankings, as they, for instance, do not measure the perceived increase in political polarization.

Fig. 12.2 Happiness: life evaluations in selected countries, 2023. Note: Countries are ranked according to their self-assessed life evaluations (answers to the Cantril ladder question in the Gallup World Poll). (Source: Author's own based on the World Happiness Report 2024)

Economic Institute 2024). In the case of Lithuania and Poland, GDP per capita is estimated to be even 60 percent and 40 percent higher than without the EU, respectively. Other studies are more conservative in terms of the size of the impact but corroborate the positive influence of the EU accession (Campos et al. 2019; Garoupa and Spruk 2023, Grassi 2024).

12.3 Mid-Term and Long-Term Growth Prospects

Prospects for further convergence of the EU-11 are solid, at least in the medium-term: the IMF (2024) projects that all EU-11 countries will grow faster than Western Europe at least until 2029. As a result, EU-11 levels of income relative to, for instance, Germany, will continue rising (Fig. 12.3). By 2029, Slovenia's level of GDP per capita PPP is projected to reach 85 percent of Germany; Lithuania should reach 83 percent and Poland 81 percent, the highest levels on record.

However, due to the increasingly negative effects of population aging, reduced space for technology absorption, and growing competition from emerging markets, the European Commission (2024) projects that GDP growth in the 2030s is projected to decline to below 2 percent for the region as a whole and to around and below 1.5 percent for Croatia, Czechia, Estonia, Latvia, and Lithuania (Fig. 12.4). GDP growth rates in the region are projected to decline further from 1.8 percent on average during the 2030s to only 1.5 percent during 2040s.[4]

12.4 The New Development Model for Central and Eastern Europe: Five Policy Directions

To continue to grow at a fast pace above 3 percent per year until at least 2040 and catch up with the level of income of the richest countries in the West for the first time in its history, EU-11 needs to adjust its development model and strengthen its growth fundamentals. While there are many drivers of growth, including macroeconomic stability, financial sector's development, and expanded trade, there are five priority policy areas in which the region lags Western Europe and whose improvement would support faster growth. These areas include institutions, investment, innovation, immigration, and inclusiveness (5i).

[4] Although the slowdown in convergence will likely be slower on a GDP per capita basis, as the demographic decline will result in a faster GDP per capita growth.

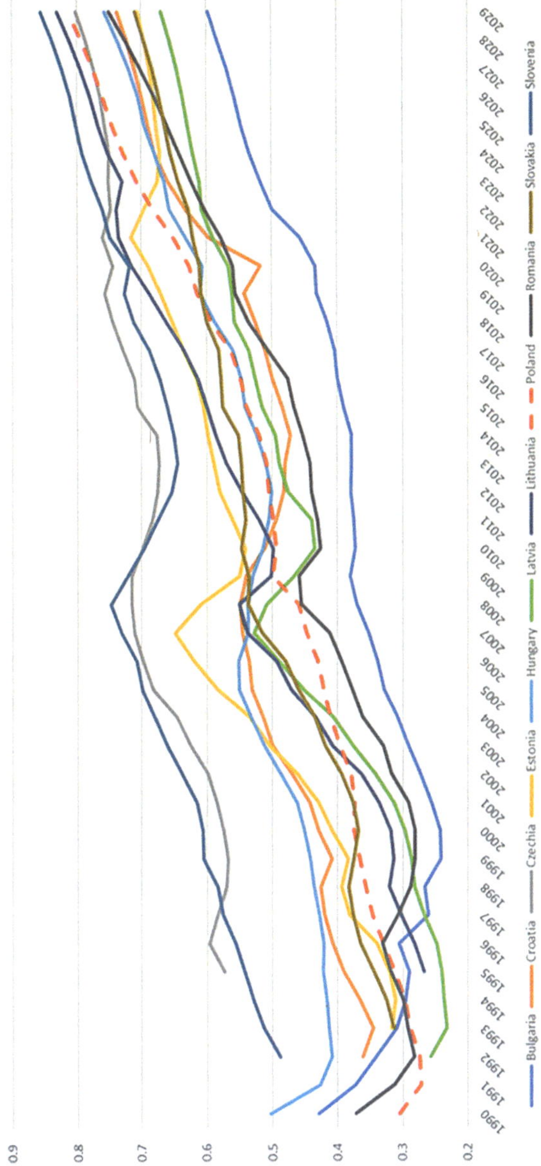

Fig. 12.3 Actual and projected GDP pc PPP relative to Germany=1, 1990–2029. Note: projections for 2024–2029. (Source: Author's own based on the IMF WEO April 2024 database)

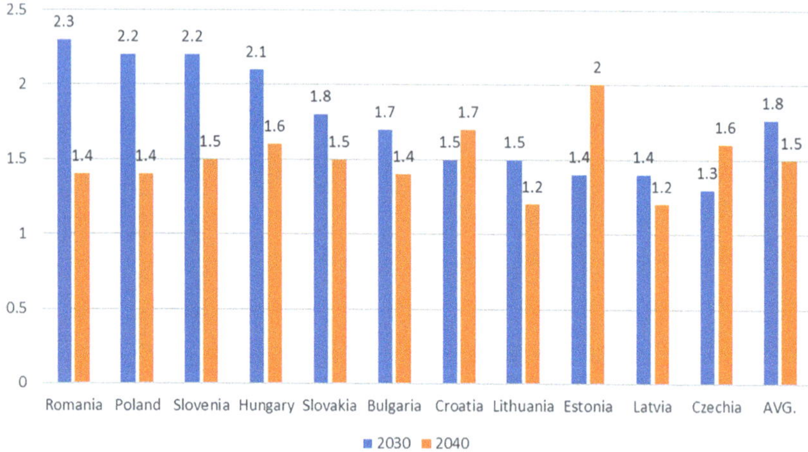

Fig. 12.4 Projected average GDP growth rates for EU-11 during 2030s and 2040s, in percent. (Source: European Commission (2024))

12.5 Institutions

Strong institutions are the foundation of economic development. Extensive evidence suggests that institutions such as secure property rights, open borders for trade, a high level of market competition, independent courts, meritocratic public administration, free media, and democracy are the key foundations of long-term development (North 1989, Piatkowski 2018). The importance of institutions is reflected, among others, in the fact that all as reflected in, for example, indicators of "government effectiveness", "regulatory quality" and "rule of law", is significantly lower than the average for OECD countries (Fig. 12.5). The same broadly applies to all other countries in the region, including special cases such as Hungary, which has developed a political and economic model that seems to be at a variance with the international benchmarks. This suggests that there is significant scope for improving institutions across the board to reach the OECD high-income average. Piatkowski (2019) and World Bank (2022) provide some of the ideas on how to improve such institutions, including by increasing wages of public servants—government ministers in Poland, for instance, make only about $55,000 per year on a gross basis, only a fraction of the equivalent salaries in the private sector—improving governance, and enhancing the use of e-government.

Fig. 12.5 Quality of institutions in Poland in relation to the average for high-income OECD countries, 2022. (Source: Worldwide Governance Indicators; https://www.worldbank.org/en/publication/worldwide-governance-indicators/interactive-data-access)

For CEE countries to continue growing, it is also important to strengthen the institutions at the European Union level. There is no shortage of ideas on how to do it, including by building a truly pan-European single market for capital, labor, trade, but also digital services and innovation (Letta 2024). Among many promising proposals, it would be useful, for instance, to introduce a European Code of Business Law, which would enable companies to operate throughout the European Union on the basis of uniform, supra-national laws, and regulations.

Further enlargement of the EU to Ukraine, Moldova, and the Balkans should provide additional opportunity to strengthen EU institutions, including by expanding the scope of decisions requiring only a majority rather than a unanimous vote, giving more authority to the European Commission, and finding a better balance of power among the EU member states.

12.6 Investment

EU-11 countries continue to be underinvested. Despite a spurt in public investment financed by the EU funds over the past 20 years, which has helped to improve EU-11 countries' infrastructure, the accumulated stock of public and private capital continues to be much lower than among the developed countries of Western Europe. In 2019, the average (unweighted) value of accumulated public and private capital stock per capita among the EU-11 countries amounted to about 57 percent of that in Germany and it ranged from 42 percent in Bulgaria to 85 percent in Czechia (Fig. 12.6).

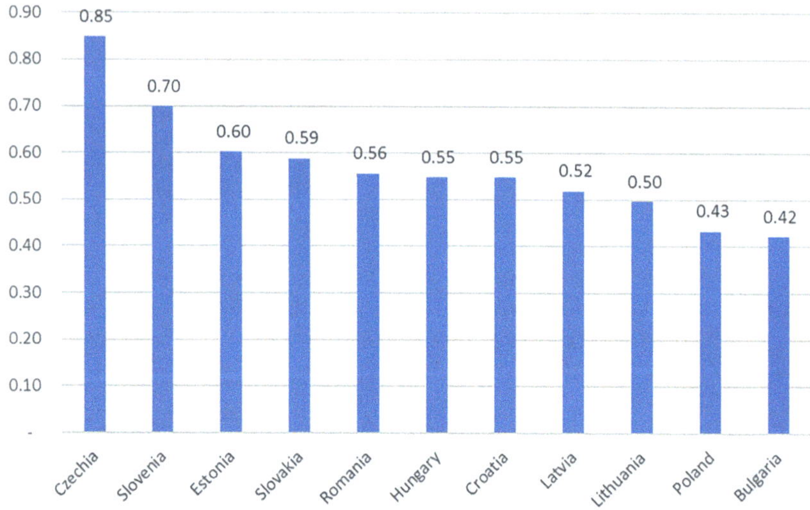

Fig. 12.6 Public and private capital stock per capita, 2019, Germany=1. Note: General government and private capital stock (constructed based on general government/private investment flows, in billions of constant 2017 international dollars, divided by population. (Source: Own calculations based on the IMF Investment and Capital Stock Dataset (ICSD) https://data.imf.org/?sk=1ce8a55f-cfa7-4bc0-bce2-256ee65ac0e4&sid=1390030341854; population from WDI)

Given the low level of capital stock and the resulting opportunities for high-return investment, all EU-11 countries should aim to significantly increase the level of public investment. In 2022, public investment in the region amounted to 4.3 percent of GDP on average (unweighted), ranging from 3.1 percent of GDP in Lithuania and 3.2 percent in Slovakia to 5.3 percent of GDP in Hungary and Slovenia (Fig. 12.7). EU-11 countries should aim to achieve the level of public investment of around 7 percent of GDP, about a double of the EU average but only about one-third of annual public investment in China. Higher public investment could focus on green energy transformation, digitalization, innovation, and infrastructure, including airports, highways, and high-speed trains. Higher public investment should go hand-in-hand with strengthening the institutional capacity of the relevant public institutions to ensure high efficiency of increased investment, transparent allocation of resources and reduction of opportunities for corruption and rent-seeking.

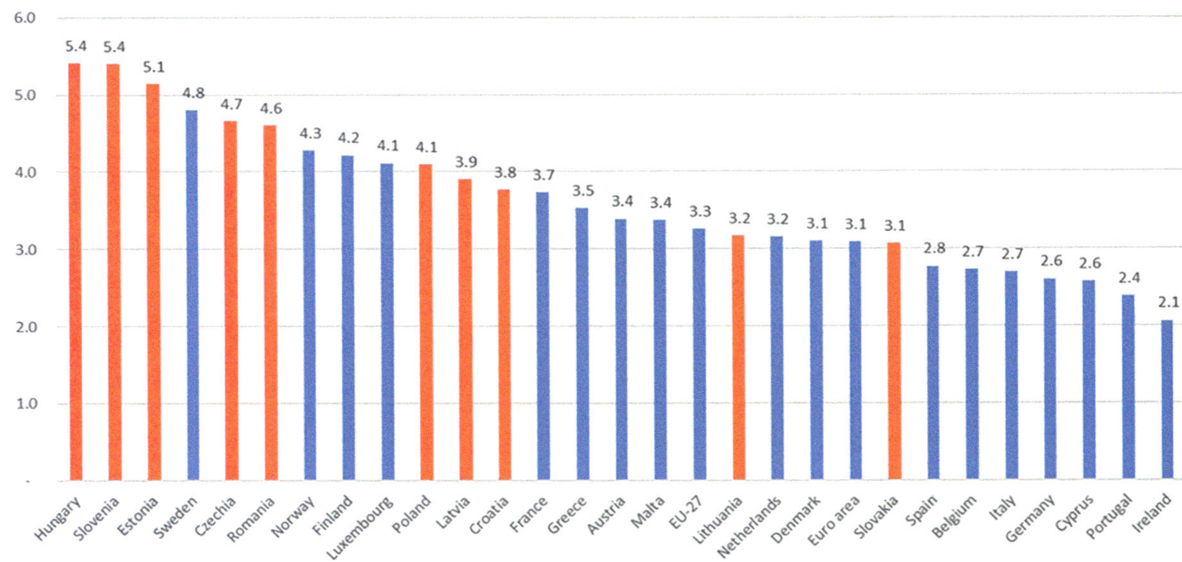

Fig. 12.7 Public investment in the European Union, in percent of GDP, 2022. (Source: Author's own based on Eurostat https://ec.europa.eu/eurostat/databrowser/view/sdg_08_11/default/table?lang=en)

Higher public investment would stimulate higher private investment to raise the overall investment rate from the 2022 (unweighted) EU-11 average of 22.8 percent of GDP, almost equal to the EU-27 average, to around 28 percent of GDP, the 2022 level of investment in Hungary (Fig. 12.8), closer to the total investment in South Korea (32 percent of GDP) and China (42 percent of GDP).[5] Assuming efficient and transparent allocation of additional resources, a 5 percentage point of GDP increase in total investment could likely accelerate GDP growth by up to 1 percentage point per year, significantly shortening the time needed for full convergence with the EU-27 average.

Higher public investment could be financed from additional budget revenues. General government revenues across all EU-11 countries are significantly lower than in Western Europe: in 2022, the average revenue to GDP in the region amounted to only 33.7 percent of GDP, an extraordinary 8.2 percent of GDP lower than the euro zone average (Fig. 12.9). If, for instance, Czechia (35.4 percent of GDP) could increase its government revenue to the level of Germany (42.1 percent of GDP), it would generate additional 6.7 percent of GDP of revenue.

If it proved to be politically impossible to significantly increase government revenue, higher public investment could also be financed with a temporary increase in public debt, although less so in the case of, for instance, Hungary, which has a public debt at around 73.5 percent of GDP. At the end of 2023, EU-11 public debt amounted on average to less than 40 percent of GDP, which was only half of the average debt-to-GDP ratio in the EU (81.5% of GDP) (Fig. 12.10).

Higher total investment could also be financed with additional investment by the private sector, which has a much lower financial leverage than in Western Europe (Fig. 12.11). If, for instance, Poland's private sector increased its financial leverage to the level of Germany, it would provide 70 percent of GDP of additional financing for investment.

Finally, higher investment could be financed by an increased inflow of foreign direct investment. EU-11 countries are the beneficiaries of the ongoing restructuring of the global value chains and a gradual withdrawal of Western capital from China. As a result, the FDI inflows into China have decreased, while they have increased in EU-11 countries (Fig. 12.12).

[5] https://data.worldbank.org/indicator/NE.GDI.FTOT.ZS?locations=CN-KR

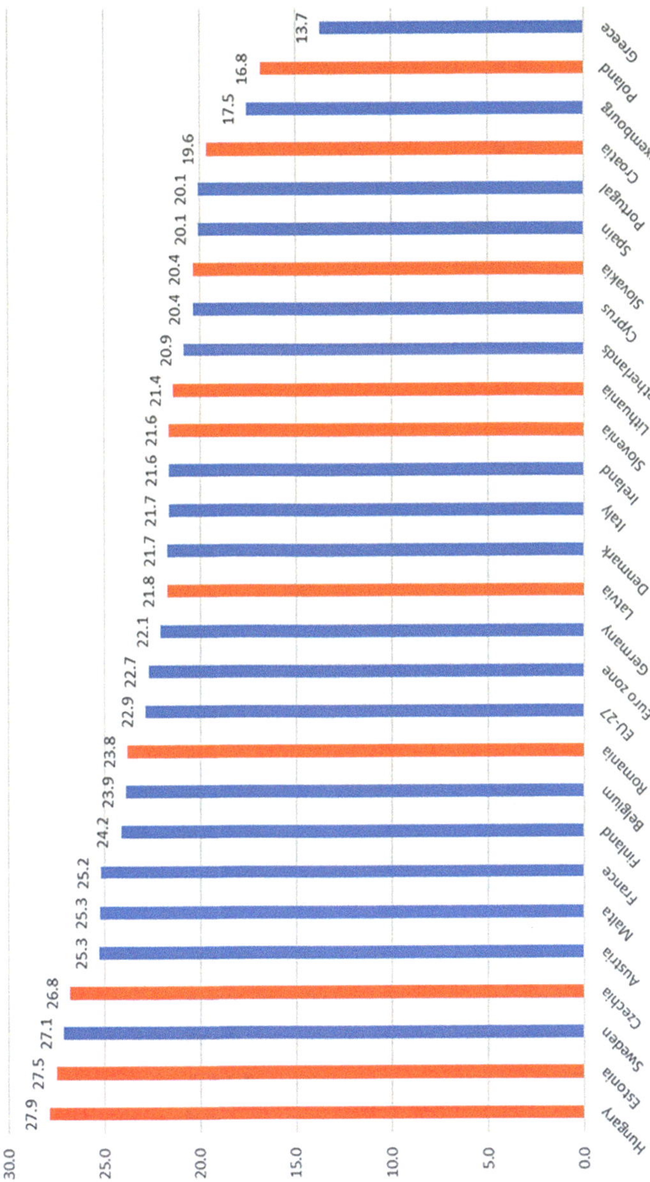

Fig. 12.8 Total investment in the European Union, in percent of GDP, 2022. (Source: Author's own based on Eurostat https://ec.europa.eu/eurostat/databrowser/view/sdg_08_11/default/table?lang=en)

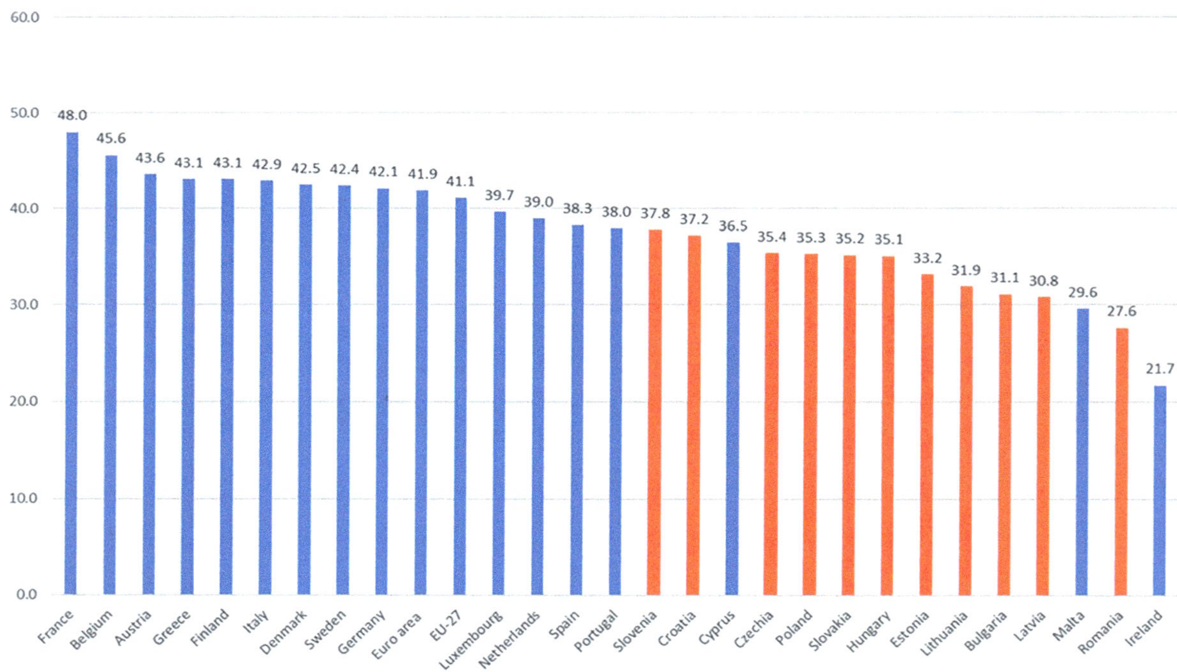

Fig. 12.9 General government revenues in the European Union, in percent of GDP, 2022. Note: Total receipts from taxes and social contributions (including imputed social contributions) after deduction of amounts assessed but unlikely to be collected. (Source: Author's own based on Eurostat https://ec.europa.eu/eurostat/databrowser/view/gov_10a_taxag/default/table?lang=en)

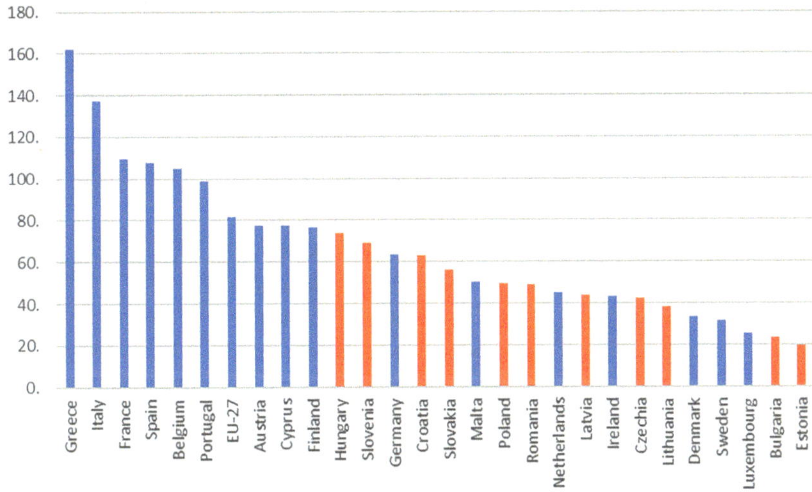

Fig. 12.10 Public debt in percent of GDP, 2023. (Source: Author's own calculations based on Eurostat (https://ec.europa.eu/eurostat/databrowser/view/gov_10q_ggdebt/default/table?lang=en))

There is also increased interest in investing in the region from China, including in electric vehicles and electric batteries, especially in Hungary.

12.7 Innovation

EU-11 might not be able to reach and exceed the EU-27 income average without further investment in innovation. Although the region as a whole has significantly increased its support to R&D over the past decade—Poland's investment in R&D, for instance, increased from 0.9 percent of GDP in 2012 to 1.5 percent of GDP in 2022—and boosted the number of innovative companies, it is clear that the region is nowhere close to become an innovation powerhouse.

The goal for the near future should be to gradually increase investment in R&D to 2.5 percent of GDP, slightly above the EU average of 2.3 percent of GDP. This will require, among others, further support for private venture capital, increased financing for basic research, and strengthened market competition (World Bank 2022). R&D investment of around 2.5 percent of GDP should be sufficient as there seem to be diminishing returns to higher R&D investment: during 2009–18, for instance, 1

Fig. 12.11 Private debt in percent of GDP, 2021–22. (Source: Author's own based on IMF WEO April 2024 database)

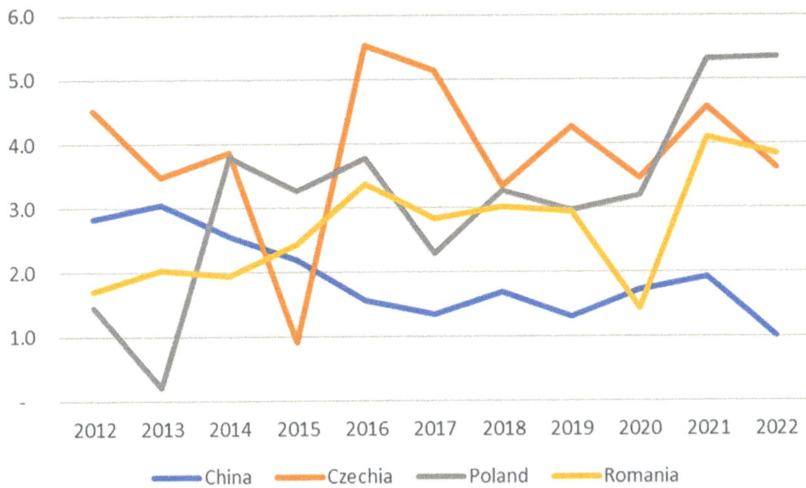

Fig. 12.12 FDI inflows into selected EU-11 countries and China, percent of GDP, 2010–2022. (Source: Author's own calculations based on the World Bank's WDI database)

percent of GDP that South Korea, one of the global leaders in R&D investment, spent on R&D translated into only a 0.1 percent growth in TFP. Similarly, high spending on R&D in Israel, the USA, Switzerland, and Sweden did not prevent the decline of TFP growth to around zero. In turn, the same 1 percent of GDP invested in R&D in Poland contributed to a much higher 1.4 percent growth in TFP (Fig. 12.13), suggesting high efficiency of R&D spending at low levels.

Additional measures to enhance innovation could include support for the emergence of large companies, which tend to be more innovative than smaller companies because they can afford additional expenses on R&D, technology absorption, and better managerial practices (Marć and Malec 2022). Although employment in large companies in Poland, Czechia, and Hungary is higher than in Spain or Italy, it is also significantly smaller than, for example, in Germany (Fig. 12.14).

EU-11 countries also lack global companies, which tend to be more innovative than large companies operating only domestically. For instance, the size of Polish listed companies is significantly smaller than in Western European economies (Fig. 12.15). The largest private companies are also much smaller than their global competitors. For example, the annual revenues of Nestle, a global giant in the food products market, are over 25

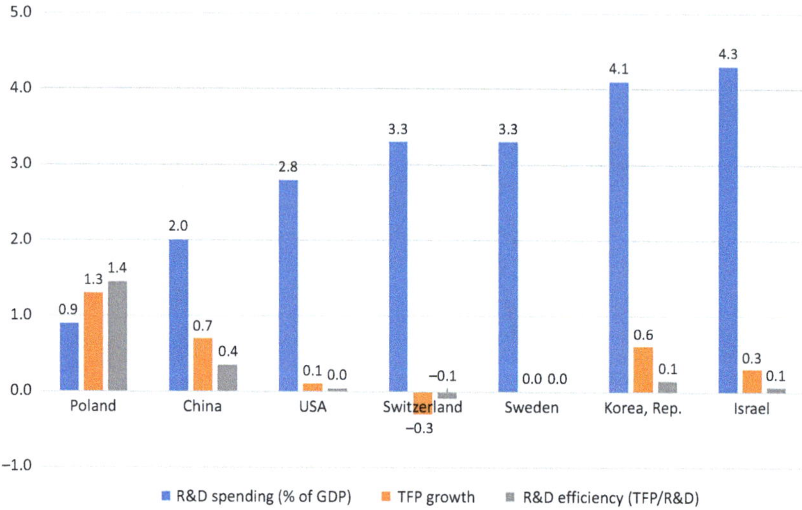

Fig. 12.13 R&D spending and TFP growth, selected countries, 2009–2018 average. Note: Countries sorted by average spending on R&D in percent of GDP. (Source: Author's own calculations based on WDI database (for R&D spending) and The Conference Board Total Economy Database (for TFP growth)

times higher than those of Maspex, a Polish peer.[6] The revenues of DHL, a logistics company, are 40 times higher than those of InPost, a leading Polish company specialized in delivery services.

The emergence of EU-11 global champions could be additionally supported with state-sponsored equity funding for foreign expansion (PFR, a Polish Development Fund, already operates such a fund, although only at a small scale), a special immigration path for high-class specialists to promote sales and investment abroad, and a coordinated economic diplomacy, including in the Global South.

[6] https://maspex.com/aktualnosci/maspex-wyda-na-inwestycje-w-tym-rokuokolo-650-mln-zl/#:~:text=W%202023%20roku%20zdrowie%20ze,Valenii%20de%20Munte%20w%20Romania; https://www.nestle.com/media/pressreleases/allpressreleases/full-yearresults-2023; https://logistyka.rp.pl/firmy/art40076851-rekordowe-przychody-i-zyskiinpost#:~:text=W%202023%20roku%20przychody%20firmy,przesy%C5%82ek%20wzros%C5%82a%20o%2020%20%; https://group.dhl.com/en/media-relations/pressreleases/2024/dhl-group-annual-earnings-2023.html#:~:text=global%20economic%20environment-,Resilient%20business% 20model%3A%20DHL%20Group%20achieves%20annual%20targets%20for%202023,a%20weak%20global%20economic%20environment&text=After%20a%20record%20year%20in,2022%3A%20EUR%208.4%20 billion

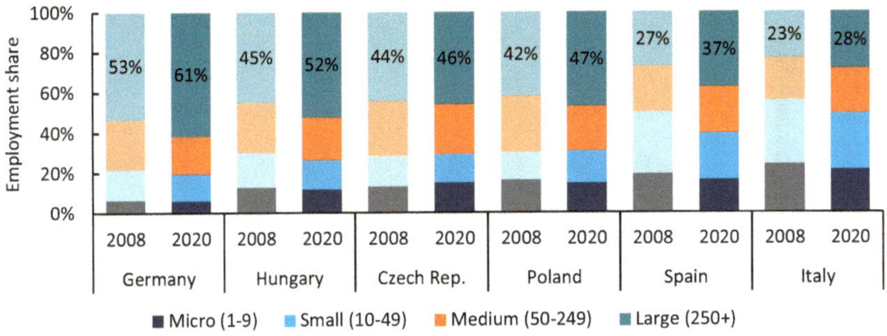

Fig. 12.14 Employment shares in industry depending on the size of the company, 2008 and 2020. (Source: Author's own based on Marć et al. (2024))

The region also needs to invest in high-quality science. There are hardly any EU-11 universities among the top universities in the world. According to the Academic Ranking of World Universities, the highest ranked university in the region, Charles University in Prague, is classified only in the 301–400 worldwide.[7] The highest ranked Polish universities, the Jagiellonian University and the University of Warsaw, are in 401–500 place worldwide. Universities in Bulgaria, Romania, Latvia, and Croatia do not even qualify among the world's top 1000 universities. This needs to change for the region to move from the current growth model based on imitation to a new growth model based on innovation.[8] To do so, it will be key to increase expenditure on publicly financed R&D from around below 0.4 percent of GDP in 2022 to the EU average of 0.7 percent of GDP[9], improve commercialization of the scientific outputs, and enhance support for university-based startups.

The region should also further increase the quality of the overall university education, albeit from an already relatively high level. It is important to note that the quality of scientific research, which is measured by various global rankings such as the Shanghai ranking, is not the same as the quality of teaching. The latter is quite high in the region, especially relative to the level of financing: in 2019, Poland, for instance, spent only USD 12,900 per student, on PPP basis, versus USD 19,600 in Germany.[10]

[7] https://www.shanghairanking.com/rankings/arwu/2023

[8] https://www.ft.com/content/0707ec55-f939-3f35-804a-c1ad2eb4b607

[9] https://ec.europa.eu/eurostat/databrowser/view/gba_nabsfin07__custom_11108716/default/table?lang=en

[10] https://www.oecd-ilibrary.org/docserver/b25ab7e2-en.pdf?expires=1725453553&id=id&accname=guest&checksum=1CFF91C15FF83C73E664C6C51D4D7CB1

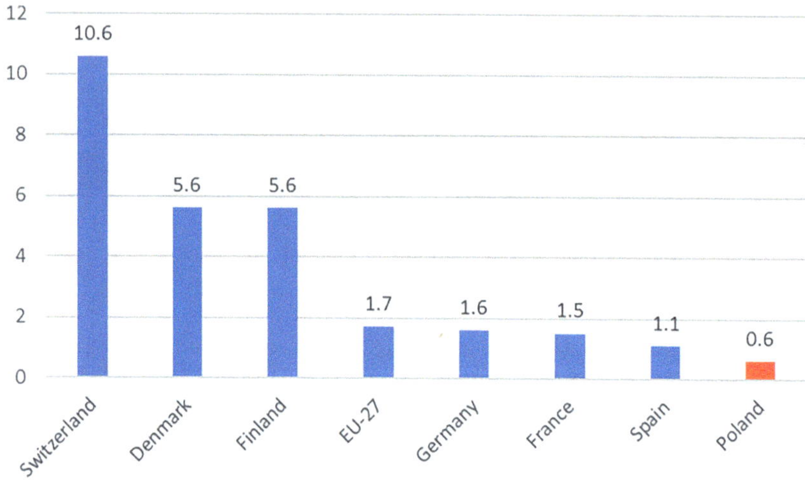

Fig. 12.15 Number of companies with stock market capitalization above USD 1 billion per million inhabitants, January 2023. (Source: Author's own based on McKinsey 2023)

Despite the lower spending, the average quality of German students is arguably not much different than in Poland. Relatively high level of the general quality of education should help the region to leverage new technologies, especially AI, where, according to the IMF AI Preparedness Index Dashboard, it currently lags the more developed countries.[11] The fact that countries such as Estonia are ahead of South Korea and on par with Switzerland and Sweden and that Czechia is on par with the average for developed countries suggests that it should be possible for other countries in the region to catch up too.

However, after the period of educational boom in the 1990s and the 2000s, the region's university enrollment ratios have stagnated. Since 2018, the percentage of the youth aged 30–34 with university education in the EU-11 countries began to stagnate and fall behind the EU-27 average (Fig. 12.16). It is lower than the scholarization ratio among the EU's leaders, such as Ireland, where almost two-thirds of young population

[11] https://www.imf.org/en/Blogs/Articles/2024/06/25/mapping-the-worlds-readiness-for-artificial-intelligence-shows-prospects-diverge#:~:text=Mapping%20the%20World's%20Readiness%20for%20Artificial%20Intelligence%20Shows%20Prospects%20Diverge&text=Artificial%20intelligence%20can%20increase%20productivity,of%20jobs%20and%20widen%20inequality

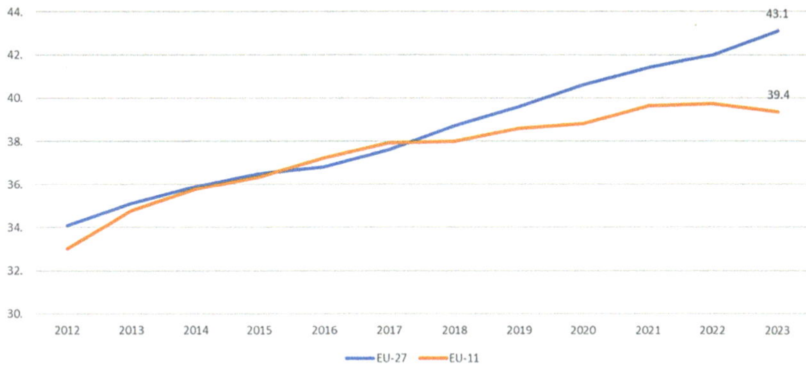

Fig. 12.16 Percentage of population aged 30–34 with university education in EU-11 and EU-27, 2012–2023. (Source: Own calculations based on Eurostat (https://ec.europa.eu/eurostat/databrowser/view/sdg_04_20/default/table?lang=en&category=t_educ.t_educ_outc))

have a university degree. The goal for the region should be to first exceed the EU average and then increase university level educational attainment to at least half of young population.

12.8 Immigration

Demographic decline and population aging is a key risk for the EU-11. According to the United Nations population forecasts, by 2050 the population of the region is expected to shrink by more than 10 percent and continue to decline until 2100. Estonia's population, for instance, is projected to shrink from 1.3 million now to 1.17 million in 2050. At the same time, the population pyramid will change substantially: older cohorts above the age of 50 will become dominant and the median age will rise.[12] In Poland, for instance, by 2050, the median age will increase from 43 years in 2023 to over 50 years in 2050, two to three years above the EU average.[13] The number of available workers will also begin to decline: by 2050, the size of the labor force in Poland is expected to decline by as much as 6 million workers or more than 20 percent of the total. As a result, the economic growth rate may decline by up to 1.5 percentage points percentage annually (Morawski et al. 2023).

[12] https://www.ined.fr/en/everything_about_population/population-games/tomorrow-population/

[13] *PKO BP*, "Makro Focus: 20 years of Poland in the European Union", April 24, 2024

Pro-family policies will likely not be sufficient to reverse the negative demographic trends. Despite increased outlays on pro-family policies, improved access to childcare, and better labor policies to incentivize women to stay in the labor force, the fertility rate in the EU-11, which at 1.3–1.6 is already way below the replacement rate of 2.1, may continue to fall, as has been in the case among all developed countries (in the EU-27 the average total fertility declined from 1.6 in 2010 to 1.5 in 2022).[14] While there is still scope to further improve pro-family policies, including by ensuring universal access to kindergartens and nurseries, upgrading family-friendly labor market policies, and promoting a greater role of men in raising children, it is difficult to expect that this will change the fertility trends.

Part of the growing gaps in the labor market due to population aging can be filled by further increasing the employment rate. Over the last ten years, the EU-11 has achieved great success in increasing the employment rate, from the EU average in 2014 to a higher rate than the EU in 2023 (Fig. 12.17). However, the employment rate can be further increased and catch up to the Western leaders such as the Netherlands (83%) or Iceland (85%). If, for instance, Poland had the same employment rate as the Netherlands, the number of working Poles could increase by as much as 3 million or about half of the projected gap in the labor market by 2050 (McKinsey 2023). An additional part of the gap in the labor market could be filled by new technologies, including AI.

However, to fully close the projected decline in the size of the labor force, EU-11 countries will need to attract additional immigrants. One way to bring such immigrants, which would simultaneously maximize economic benefits and minimize social costs, would be to attract foreign students to universities and encourage a portion of them to stay. An additional source of immigration could be the repatriation of a large diaspora. It is estimated that, for instance, in Poland alone there are up to 20 million people living abroad, who have a Polish background. Finally, it would be useful to open a special immigration path for high-value immigrants. A good example of such an approach would be for instance, a "Poland Business Harbour" program, which has attracted more than 74 thousand of IT specialists and their families, mainly from Belarus.[15]

[14] https://data.worldbank.org/indicator/SP.DYN.TFRT.IN?end=2022&locations=EU&start=2010

[15] https://www.rp.pl/rynek-pracy/art38408601-polska-znalazla-magnes-na-informatykow-ze-wschodu

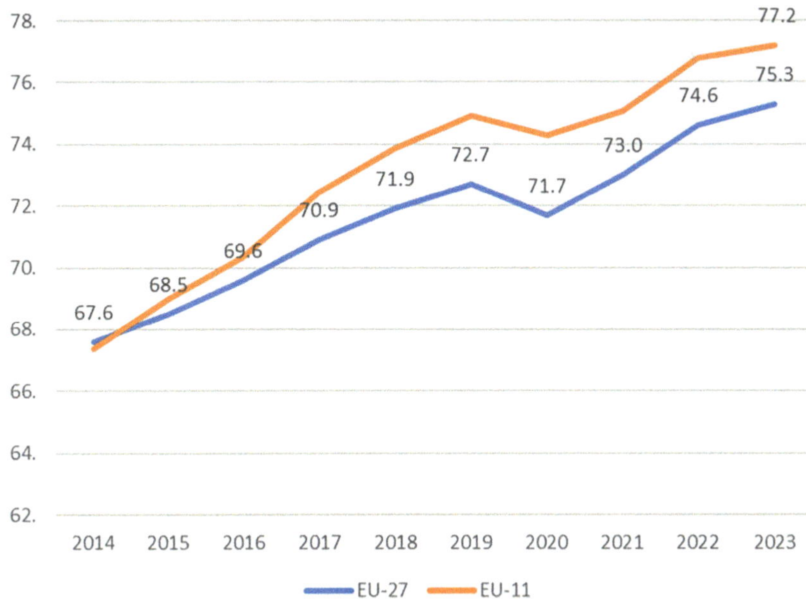

Fig. 12.17 Employment rate in EU-27 and EU-11, 2014–2023 (in % of employed population aged 20–64). (Source: Own calculations based on Eurostat (https://ec.europa.eu/eurostat/databrowser/view/LFSI_EMP_A/default/table))

12.9 Inclusiveness

Inclusiveness is not only a value in itself but also is key to maintaining high social mobility and rapid development. Even the International Monetary Fund admits that high inequality "weakens social cohesion, leads to political polarization and reduces economic growth".[16] Inclusiveness is also the foundation of maintaining democracy and reducing the appeal of populism (Wolf 2023).

Growing income inequalities and declining social mobility are a challenge for the region. Even though the official Gini coefficients across the region have fallen over the past decade and are now equal to the EU average (Fig. 12.18), new research, which measures inequality based on data

[16] https://www.imf.org/en/Topics/Inequality/introduction-to-inequality accessed: May 15, 2023

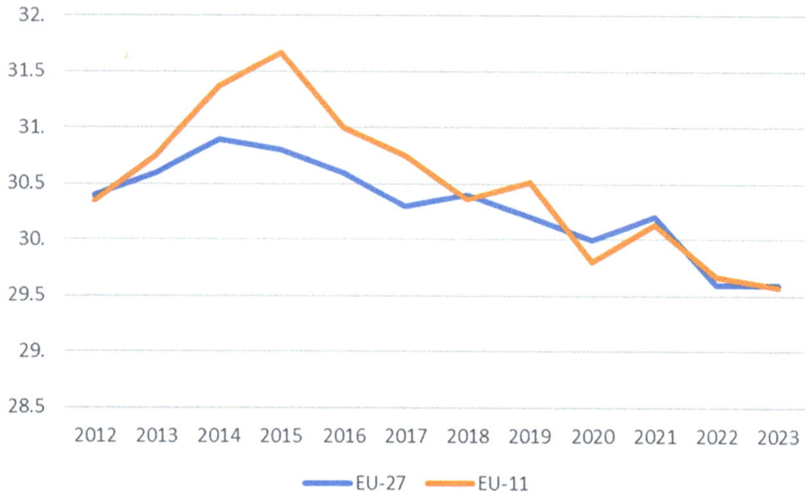

Fig. 12.18 Income inequality measured by the Gini coefficient in the EU-27 and EU-11, 2012–23. (Source: Author's own calculations based on Eurostat (https://ec.europa.eu/eurostat/databrowser/view/tessi190/default/table?lang=en))

from both survey and tax returns, shows that real income inequality is significantly higher than what is shown by the official statistics, mostly because the latter do not include the richest people, who refuse to participate in such surveys. The real Gini coefficients are much higher: the corrected Gini coefficient for, for instance, Poland equals almost 0.40 (Brzezinski et al. 2022), drastically higher than 0.27 published by Eurostat. Bukowski and Novokmet (2024) show similarly high measures of inequality for the rest of the region.

12.10 Conclusion

Central and Eastern Europe has never had it better before. It is now living through its Golden Age, defined as the shortest distance in income and quality of life relative to Western Europe in its history.

The good times are not likely to change soon: the region should continue to converge with the Western European levels of incomes for at least another decade. However, in the 2030s, the pace of convergence will gradually decline because of the combined effects of population aging, lower scope for technology absorption and competition from other parts of the world, especially China. By 2040 or so, the whole region may even stop converging and never reach the EU-27 level of income.

To continue fast growth and ensure full convergence with the richest countries in the EU, CEE countries should adjust its growth model, including by improving institutions, increasing investment, enhancing innovation, enlarging immigration, and sustaining high levels of inclusiveness and social mobility. This will be key to keeping the region's Golden Age going.

References

Brzezinski, Michal, Michal Myck, and Michal Najsztub. 2022. "Sharing the gains of transition: evaluating changes in income inequality and redistribution in Poland using combined survey and tax return data". *European Journal of Political Economy*, 73.

Bukowski, Pawel and Filip Novokmet. (2024). The evolution of income inequalities in Central Eastern Europe and its drivers. In: Oxford Handbook of Post-Socialist Economies, forthcoming.

Campos, N. F., Coricelli, F., & Moretti, L. (2019). Institutional integration and economic growth in Europe. Journal of Monetary Economics, 103, 88–104.

European Commission. 2024. "2024 Ageing Report Economic & Budgetary Projections for the EU Member States (2022–2070)", April.

Garoupa, Nuno, and Rok Spruk. 2023. "Does European Union Really Matter for Long-Run Growth and Development? In Search of the Missing Counterfactual", paper presented at the European Commission Annual Research Conference, 13–15 November, Brussels.

Grassi, B (2024), "The EU Miracle: When 75 million Reach High Income", IGIER Working paper, May.

IMF. 2024. World Economic Outlook. April

Kolodko, G. W. (2000). *From Shock to Therapy: The Political Economy of Postsocialist Transformation.* Oxford/New York: Oxford University Press.

Letta, Enrico. 2024. "Much more than a market—Speed, Security, Solidarity Empowering the Single Market to deliver a sustainable future and prosperity for all EU Citizens".

Marć, L., Malec, M. and M. Piatkowski. 2024. "World Bank's World Development Report Companion on Growth in Middle-Income Countries. A Case Study on Poland", background paper, unpublished.

Marć, L. and Malec, M. (2022). Drivers of Productivity Growth in Poland: A Firm Level Perspective on Technology Adoption and Firm Capabilities. Washington, D.C.: World Bank Group.

McKinsey. 2023. "Lifting Poland's ambition. On the cusp of a new era?", May.

Morawski, Ignacy, Joanna Tyrowicz and Krzysztof Makarski. 2023. "Koniec dywidendy demograficznej—stagnacja i inflacja, czy adaptacja technologiczna", raport specjalny, Impact CEE 2023

North, Douglass C. 1989. "Institutions and economic growth: An historical introduction". World Development, Volume 17, Issue 9, September, Pages 1319–1332

Polish Economic Institute. 2024. "The Big Bang Enlargement 20 Years of Central Europe's Membership in the EU". May.

Piatkowski, Marcin. 2018. *Europe's Growth Champion. Insights from the Economic Rise of Poland.* Oxford University Press.

Piatkowski, Marcin. 2019. "How the European Union Made Poland European Again", in: Michael Landesmann and István P. Székely (eds.) *Does EU Membership Facilitate Convergence? The Experience of the EU's Eastern Enlargement – Volume I. Overall Trends and Country Experiences.* Palgrave Macmillan, Pages 151–172.

Wolf, Martin. 2023. *The Crisis of Democratic Capitalism.* Penguin Books.

World Bank. 2022. "Poland Country Economic Memorandum: The Green Transformation in Poland—Opportunities and Challenges for Economic Growth". Washington, D.C.: World Bank Group.

INDEX[1]

[1] Note: Page numbers followed by 'n' refer to notes.

I. P. Székely, P. Halmai (eds.), *The Future of European Integration*, Studies in Economic Transition,
https://doi.org/10.1007/978-3-032-20186-7

FSC
www.fsc.org
MIX
Papier | Fördert
gute Waldnutzung
FSC® C083411

Zeitfracht Medien GmbH
Ferdinand-Jühlke-Straße 7
99095 Erfurt, Deutschland
produktsicherheit@kolibri360.de